THE NEW TERRORISM

THE NEW
TERRORISM

Fanaticism and the Arms of Mass Destruction

Walter Laqueur

NEW YORK   OXFORD
OXFORD UNIVERSITY PRESS
1999

Oxford University Press

Oxford   New York

Athens   Auckland   Bangkok   Bogotá   Buenos Aires   Calcutta
Cape Town   Chennai   Dar es Salaam   Delhi   Florence   Hong Kong   Istanbul
Karachi   Kuala Lumpur   Madrid   Melbourne   Mexico City   Mumbai
Nairobi   Paris   São Paulo   Singapore   Taipei   Tokyo   Toronto   Warsaw

and associated companies in

Berlin   Ibadan

Copyright © 1999 by Walter Laqueur

Published by Oxford University Press, Inc.,
198 Madison Avenue, New York, New York 10016

Oxford is a registered trademark of Oxford University Press, Inc.

Library of Congress Cataloging-in-Publication Data
Laqueur, Walter, 1921–
The new terrorism : fanaticism and the arms of mass destruction /
Walter Laqueur.
p. cm.
Includes bibliographical references.
ISBN 0–19–511816–2
1. Terrorism.   2. Terrorism—Forecasting.   3. Weapons of mass
destruction.   4. Radicalism.   5. Fanaticism.   I. Title.
HV6431.L35 1999
363.3'2—dc21   98-52012

Design by Adam B. Bohannon

Printing 1 3 5 7 9 8 6 4 2

Printed in the United States of America
on acid-free paper

Contents

Acknowledgments

In this endeavor I had the help and advice of a number of colleagues, including Bruce Hoffman, Jessica Stern, Seth Carus, Brad Roberts, Ehud Sprinzak, Zed Davis, Frank Ciluffo, Arnaud de Borchgrave, Dr. Martin Silverstein, and Josef Pilat. James K. Campbell, Rob Purvis, Frederique Sandretto, Tore Bjorgo, and Jeffrey Kaplan put unpublished material at my disposal. Larissa Dinsmore, Maureen Haggard, Will Young, and Benjamin Melenson, my research assistants, as well as Keri Anderson, CSIS librarian, helped me to get research material that was not easy to obtain and that I might have missed. Howard Sargent, Sherry Foehr, Jon Beckmann, and Thomas LeBien helped with editing the manuscript, and Steven Glick and Benjamin Graham guided my steps as far as computer work was concerned. Last but not least I would like to thank the Earhart Foundation for a generous research grant.

Washington, D.C.
October 1998

THE NEW TERRORISM

Introduction

Four hundred twelve men, women, and children were hacked to death by terrorists on the night of December 29, 1997, in three isolated villages in Algeria's Elizane region. Four hundred perished when a group of the Shah's opponents burned a cinema in Abadan during the last phase of the monarchy in Iran. There were 328 victims when an Air India aircraft was exploded by Sikh terrorists in 1985, and 278 were killed in the Lockerbie disaster in Scotland in 1988 which was commissioned by Libya's Colonel Khadafi and carried out by terrorists. Two hundred forty-one U.S. marines lost their lives when their barracks were attacked by suicide bombers in Beirut in 1983, 171 were killed when Libyan emissaries put a bomb on a French UTA plane in 1985. The largest toll in human life on American soil was paid when 169 men, women, and children died in the bombing of the Alfred P. Murrah building in Oklahoma City in 1995.

Terrorism has been with us for centuries, and it has always attracted inordinate attention because of its dramatic character and its sudden, often wholly unexpected, occurrence. It has been a tragedy for the victims, but seen in historical perspective it seldom has been more than a nuisance.

Even the bloodiest terrorist incidents in the past, such as those just re-counted, affected only a relatively few people. This is no longer true today, and may be even less so in the future. Yesterday's nuisance has become one of the gravest dangers facing mankind. For the first time in history, weapons of enormous destructive power are both readily acquired and harder to track. In this new age, even the cost of hundreds of lives may appear small in retrospect. Science and technology have made enormous progress, but human nature, alas, has not changed. There is as much fanaticism and madness as there ever was, and there are now very powerful weapons of mass destruction available to the terrorist. A hundred years ago a leading interpreter of international law, T. J. Lawrence, wrote that attempts made to "prevent the use of instruments that cause destruction on a large scale are doomed to failure. Man has always improved his weaponry, and always will as long as he has need for them." What Lawrence said then about warfare is *a fortiori* true with regard to terrorism.

In the near future it will be technologically possible to kill thousands, perhaps hundreds of thousands, not to mention the toll the panic that is likely to ensue may take. In brief, there has been a radical transformation, if not a revolution, in the character of terrorism, a fact we are still reluctant to accept. Even though Algerian terrorists never made a secret of their operations, there was disbelief in Europe that such atrocities as the Al-gerians committed were possible, and many thought some mysterious force was responsible for the mass slaughter.

There is public reluctance to accept the possibility that a few individ-uals could make use of the tremendous destructive power developed re-cently. It is the story of Prometheus and Epimetheus all over again: Pro-metheus tricked Zeus into giving him fire. But Zeus got his revenge; he sent to Epimetheus, Prometheus' less clever brother, Pandora's box, which he opened despite instructions not to do so under any circumstances. Out fluttered a host of calamities which have afflicted humankind ever since.

I do not suggest that most terrorist groups will use weapons of mass destruction in the near future; most of them probably will not. It is also quite possible that access to and the use of these weapons will not take a year or two but ten or fifteen. The technical difficulties standing in the way of effective use of the arms of mass destruction are still considerable. But the danger is so great, the consequences so incalculable, that even the occurrence of a few such attacks may have devastating consequences.

The traditional, "nuisance" terrorism will continue. But fanaticism in-spired by all kinds of religious-sectarian-nationalist convictions is now taking on a millenarian and apocalyptic tone. We are confronting the emergence of new kinds of terrorist violence, some based on ecological and quasireligious concerns, others basically criminal in character, and still others mixtures of these and other influences. We also are witnessing the rise of small sectarian groups that lack clear political or social agendas other than destroying civilization, and in some cases humankind. There was once a relatively clear dividing line between terrorists and guerrillas, between political terrorists and criminal gangs, and between genuine homegrown terrorism and state-sponsored terrorism. Today these lines have become blurred, and the situation is even more confused than it used to be.

While the traditional terrorist movements historically consisted of hundreds, sometimes even thousands of members, the new terrorist groups can be very small, consisting of a few people or sometimes even one individual. The smaller the group, the more radical it is likely to be, the more divorced from rational thought, and the more difficult to detect. A sizable terrorist movement can be infiltrated by informers, but it is nearly impossible to infiltrate a small, closely knit group, perhaps composed of members of the same family or clan, let alone a single human being.

Some believe it is unlikely that extremists or fanatics possess the technological know-how and the resources to make use of weapons of mass destruction. But the technological skill, as will be shown, is not that complex, and the resources needed, not that rare or expensive. It is also possible that rogue governments, which may themselves not use these weapons for fear of retaliation, can readily supply the raw materials or the finished product to terrorists either by political design or for commercial gain.

Some believe that the horrific consequences of using weapons of mass destruction will deter even fanatics from using them. But this underrates the element of blind aggression, of rage, of suicidal impulses, of sheer madness, which unfortunately has always been part of human nature. Emperor Caligula reportedly said that he wished the Roman people had but one neck, so that it could be easily cut. Caligula was not a unique case, merely the best known of a kind that will be examined in this book.

Can terrorism be defined? And is it not possible that in certain circumstances terrorism might be a legitimate form of resistance against tyranny? More than a hundred definitions have been offered (including a few of my own) for the phenomenon, and over the past three decades, a great deal of thought has been invested in the latter question. One of the better definitions of terrorism was provided by the U.S. Department of Defense, which in 1990 described terrorism as "the unlawful use of, or threatened use, of force or violence against individuals or property to coerce and intimidate governments or societies, often to achieve political, religious, or ideological objectives." But even this working definition has not found acceptance among those studying the subject. Perhaps the only characteristic generally agreed upon is that terrorism always involves violence or the threat of violence. Students of terrorism have received advice from philosophers and theologians, psychologists and even economists, on how to gain deeper insights into the subject. Some have suggested that we include every possible kind of violence and motivation in our analysis, from rape to income tax. Still others have insisted that unless Hitler, Stalin, and Pol Pot be considered terrorists, and feudalism, imperialism, repression, and slavery looked at as causes, our analysis of terrorism is bound to be shallow.

Why is it so difficult to find a generally accepted definition? Nietzsche provided part of the clue when he wrote that only things which have no history can be defined; terrorism, needless to say, has had a very long history. Furthermore, there has not been a single form of terrorism, but many, often with few traits in common. What was true of one variety was not necessarily true of another. Today there are more varieties than existed thirty years ago, and many are so different from those of the past and from each other that the term *terrorism* no longer fits some of them. In the future, new terms will probably be found for the new varieties of terrorism.

What of the legitimacy of terrorism in certain conditions? Terrorism seldom appeared in brutal dictatorships such as in Nazi Germany or Stalinist Russia, for the simple reason that repression in these regimes made it impossible for the terrorists to organize. Even in less effective dictatorships, such as Franco's Spain, there was little terrorism; it reared its head only after the regime was replaced by a democratic one. There have been some exceptions to this rule, but not many. But this, too, is no guide to the future: brutal, totalitarian dictatorships could prevent terrorism in Germany and Russia, but it is doubtful that even totalitarianism could cope with the chaos that might come to exist in some of the megacities of Asia, Africa, and Latin America in the twenty-first century.

But if one could justify or at least find mitigating circumstances for certain terrorist acts in the past, how could anyone defend the kind of genocidal and indiscriminate murder that has taken place, for instance, in Algeria and, above all, justify the use of weapons of mass destruction? Even if the terrorists' goal is not without merit, it is increasingly likely that the amount of suffering and the number of victims they cause will be wholly out of proportion. When they meet at a tavern, novelist Dostoevsky's character Ivan Karamazov tells his brother Alyosha that the happiness of all mankind is not worth the tears of a tortured child. But these days terrorists are willing to kill a great many children and their aim is by no means the happiness of mankind. Can there be any kind of "just terrorism" under these circumstances?

In an earlier work, I warned against overrating the danger of terrorism, which was neither a new phenomenon nor as politically effective as we are often led to believe. I argued that more often than not the political effect of terrorism was in inverse ratio to the publicity it received. This contrasts with the work of guerrillas, who in the twentieth century have been more successful. But guerrilla warfare has now become quite rare, and given the few current exceptions of Afghanistan and Chechnya, it has also become less effective. While I decried the idea that terrorism was steadily growing into a global threat, I also wrote that it could become one as the result of technological developments.

The ready availability of weapons of mass destruction has now come to pass, and much of what has been thought about terrorism, including some of our most basic assumptions, must be reconsidered. The character of terrorism is changing, any restraints that existed are disappearing, and, above all, the threat to human life has become infinitely greater than it was in the past.

TERRORISM
and History

Terrorism is violence, but not every form of violence is terrorism. It is vitally important to recognize that terrorism, although difficult to define precisely, as this brief history will show, is not a synonym for civil war, banditry, or guerrilla warfare.

The term *guerrilla* often has a positive connotation in our language, whereas *terrorism* almost always has a negative meaning. British and French news media will take a dim view of those engaging in terrorist operations in London and Paris, and will not hesitate to call the perpetrators "terrorists." But they are more reluctant to use such harsh terms with regard to those throwing bombs in distant countries, preferring more neutral terms such as "gunmen," "militants," Islamic or otherwise, or indeed "urban guerrilla." In fact, the term *urban guerrilla* is a contradiction in terms. The strategy of guerrilla warfare is to liberate territory, to establish counterinstitutions and eventually a regular army, and this is possible in jungles, mountains, or other sparsely inhabited zones. The classic case of guerrilla warfare is China in the 1930s and 1940s; others, such as Vietnam's defeat of the French colonials and Castro's struggle in Cuba, are roughly similar. It is virtually impossible to establish free zones in a city, and for this reason the inaccurate and misleading term *urban guerrilla* is usually politically motivated or based on a simple misunderstanding of the difference between the guerrilla and the terrorist. What makes the situation even more complicated is the fact that quite often guerrillas engage in terrorist acts both in the countryside and in urban centers. Algeria in the 1990s is a dramatic example.

There are other misunderstandings concerning the motives and the character of terrorism. For a long time there has been resistance in some circles to the use of the term to apply to small groups of people who engage in futile violence against the political establishment or certain sections of society. It was argued that the term should be reserved for states. It is perfectly true that tyrannies have caused infinitely more harm in history than terrorists, but it is hardly a relevant argument; with equal justice one could claim that it is not worthwhile to look for a cure for AIDS because this disease kills fewer people than cancer or heart disease, or that teaching French should be discontinued because there are twenty times as many Chinese as French people in the world.

During the 1960s and 1970s, when most terrorism was vaguely left wing in inspiration, arguments were made that terrorism was a response to injustice. Hence, if there were more political, social, and economic justice, terrorism would more or less automatically vanish. Seen in this light, terrorists were fanatical believers in justice driven to despair by intolerable conditions. But in the 1980s and '90s, when most terrorism in Europe and America came from the extreme right and the victims were foreigners, national minorities, or arbitrarily chosen, those who had previously shown understanding or even approval of terrorism no longer used these arguments. They could no longer possibly explain, let alone justify, murder with reference to political, social, or economic injustice.

At the other extreme, it has been proclaimed that all and every form of terrorism is morally wrong. But such a total condemnation of violence is hardly tenable in the light of history. Catholic theologians in the Middle Ages found arguments in favor of killing tyrants, and more recently, the attempted assassination of Hitler and the successful killing of Heydrich, Hitler's man in Prague, among many other examples, can hardly be considered morally reprehensible. Terrorism might be the only feasible means of overthrowing a cruel dictatorship, the last resort of free men and women facing intolerable persecution. In such conditions, terrorism could be a moral imperative rather than a crime—the killing of a Hitler or a Stalin earlier on in his career would have saved the lives of millions of people.

The trouble with terrorism is not that it has always been indefensible but that it has been chosen more often than not as the prima ratio of self-appointed saviors of freedom and justice, of fanatics and madmen, not as the ultima ratio of rebels against real tyranny.

ZEALOTS AND ASSASSINS

Political murder appears in the earliest annals of mankind, including the Bible. The stories of Judith and Holofernes, of Jael and Sisara the Old Testament heroes and villains, have provided inspiration to painters as well as to theologians and moral philosophers for ages. Seneca wrote that no sacrifice was as pleasing to the gods as the blood of a tyrant, and Cicero notes that tyrants always attracted a violent end. Harmodius and Aristogeiton, who killed the tyrant Hipparchus, were executed, but a statue was erected in their honor soon after. The civic virtues of Brutus were praised by his fellow Romans, but history—and Shakespeare—were of two minds about whether the murderer of Caesar was an honorable man.

The murder of oppressive rulers continued throughout history. It played an important role in the history of the Roman Empire. The emperors Caligula and Domitian were assassinated, as were Comodius and Elagabal, sometimes by their families, sometimes by their praetorian guards, and sometimes by their enemies (probably a few others were poisoned). Similar events can be found in the history of Byzantium.

The assassination of individuals has its origins in the prehistory of modern terrorism, but it is of course not quite the same. Historical terrorism almost always involves more than a single assassin and the carrying out of more than one operation. An exception might be the assassination of King Henri IV by a fanatic who believed that he had carried out a mission imposed on him by God; it might have been part of a conspiracy, but this we shall never know, because his interrogators were not very eager to find out. Another famous example from the same century was certainly part of an intrigue: the murder of Wallenstein, the famous seventeenth-century warlord. Historically, the favorite murder weapon has been the dagger, even though there were a few exceptions; William the Silent, Prince of Orange, was shot in Holland in 1584, when rifles and pistols were still new devices.

ORIGINS OF TERRORISM

There were also organized groups committed to systematic terrorism early in recorded human history. From Josephus Flavius's writings, a great deal is known about the *sicari*, an extreme Jewish faction, who were active after the Roman occupation of Palestine (they give us the word "zealot"). They were also involved in the siege of and the collective suicide at Masada. These patriots (or ultrapatriots, as they would be called in a later age) attacked their enemies, mainly other Jews, by daylight, very often during the celebrations of holidays, using a short dagger (*sica*) hidden under their coats. It was reported that they killed one high priest, burned the house of another, and torched the archives and the palace of the Herodian dynasts. There seems to have been a social element as well: their attacks were also directed against moneylenders. Whereas the zealots engaged in guerrilla warfare against the Romans outside the cities, they apparently concentrated their terrorist activities in Jerusalem. When the revolt of the year 66 took place, the *sicari* were actively involved; one of them was the commander of the fortress Masada. Josephus called them brigands of a new type, and he considered them mainly responsible for the national catastrophe of the year 70, when the second Temple was destroyed and the Jewish state ceased to exist.

Another early example of terrorists is the Order of the Assassins in the eleventh century, an offshoot of the Ismailis, a Muslim sect. Hassan I Sabah, the founder of the order, was born in Qom, the Shiite center in northern Persia. Sabah adopted an extreme form of Ismaili doctrine that called for the seizure of several mountain fortresses; the first such fortress, Alamut, was seized in 1090. Years later the Assassins decided to transfer their activities from remote mountain regions to the main urban centers. Their first urban victim was the chief minister of the Sultan of Baghdad, Nazim al Mulq, a Sunnite by religious persuasion and therefore an enemy. During the years that followed, Assassins were active in Persia, Syria, and Palestine, killing a great number of enemies, mainly Sunnis but also Christians, including Count Raymond II of Tripoli in Syria and Marquis Conrad of Montferrat, who ruled the kingdom of Jerusalem. There was a great deal of mystery about this movement and its master, owing to both the secrecy of its actions and the dissimulation used. Monferrat, for instance, was killed by a small group of emissaries who had disguised themselves as monks.

Seen in retrospect, the impact of the Assassins was small—they did not make many converts outside their mountain fortress, nor did they produce any significant changes in Muslim thought or practice. Alamut was occupied by Mongol invaders around 1270, but the Assassins had ceased to be a major force well before then. (Their main contribution was perhaps originating the strategy of the terrorist disguised—*taqfir*, or deception—as a devout emissary but in fact on a suicide mission, in exchange for which he was guaranteed the joys of paradise.)

Despite the considerable violence in Europe during the Middle Ages and, even worse, during the religious wars of the sixteenth and seventeenth centuries, in which monarchs as well as religious leaders were killed, there were no sustained terrorist campaigns during this time.

In cultures such as China and India secret societies have flourished from time immemorial. Many of these societies practiced violence and had their "enforcers." Their motivation was usually religious more than political, even though there was a pronounced element of xenophobia in both cases, such as the attacks against "foreign devils" culminating in the Boxer Rebellion of 1900. In India, the motivation of the *thuggee* (from which we get the word "thug"), who strangled their victims, was apparently to make an act of sacrifice to the goddess Kali.

The Chinese gangs of three or four hundred years ago had their own subculture, which practiced alternative medicine and meditation coupled with belief in all kinds of magic formulas. But they were not ascetic millenarians, as the Assassins are believed to have been, and they had more in common with the Mafia than with modern political terrorism.

MODERN TERRORISM

The nineteenth century, a time of great national tension and social ferment, witnessed the emergence of both modern—what I will call "traditional"—terrorism and guerrilla warfare. Guerrilla warfare appeared first in the framework of the Napoleonic Wars in Spain and Russia, then continued in various parts of Asia and Africa, and reached its high tide after the Second World War with the disintegration of the European empires. Terrorism as we know it grew out of the secret societies of Italian and Irish patriots, but it also manifested itself in most Balkan countries, in Turkey and Egypt, and of course among the extreme Anarchists, who believed in the strategy of propaganda by deed. Last but not least were the Russian terrorists, who prior to the First World War were by far the most active and successful. Terrorism was widely discussed among the European far left, not because the use of violence as a political statement was a monopoly of the left but because the right was the political establishment, and prior to World War I the left was the agent of change, trying to overthrow the party in power. However, most leaders of the left rejected terrorism for both philosophical and practical reasons. They favored collective action, such as strikes, demonstrations, perhaps even insurgency, but neither Marx nor the anti-Marxists of the left believed in the "philosophy of the bomb." They gave political support to the Irish patriots and the Russian revolutionaries without necessarily embracing their tactics.

THE PHILOSOPHERS OF MASS DESTRUCTION

The two main exceptions to this aversion to terrorism were Karl Heinzen and Johann Most, German radicals who pioneered the philosophy of using weapons of mass destruction and a more or less systematic doctrine of terrorism. Both believed that murder was a political necessity. Both left their native country and migrated to the United States, and both were theoreticians of terrorism—but, ironically, not practitioners of the activities they recommended in their writings.

Heinzen, a radical democrat, blamed the revolutionaries of 1848 for not having shown enough resolution and ruthlessness. The key to revolution, as he saw it, was in improved technology. He anticipated weapons of mass destruction such as rockets, poison gases, and land mines, that one day would destroy whole cities with 100,000 inhabitants, and he advocated prizes for research in fields such as the poisoning of food. Heinzen was firmly convinced that the cause of freedom, in which he fervently believed, would not prevail without the use of poison and explosives. But neither in Louisville, Kentucky, nor in Boston, where he later lived and is now buried, did he practice what he preached. The Sage of Roxbury (as he was called in radical circles in later years) became a staunch fighter for women's rights and one of the extreme spokesmen of abolitionism; he was a collaborator of William Lloyd Garrison, Horace Greeley, and Wendell Philips and a supporter of Abraham Lincoln. He attacked Marx, perhaps prophetically, since he believed communism would lead only to a new form of slavery. In a communist America, he wrote, he would not be permitted to travel from Boston to New York, to make a speech in favor of communism, without having official permission to do so. On his grave, in a cemetery in the Boston suburb of Forest Hill, there are two inscriptions, one in German to the effect that "freedom inspired my spirit, truth rejuvenated my heart," and one in English: "His life work—the elevation of mankind."

Johann Most belongs to a younger generation. Having been a radical social democrat in his native country, he came to America in the early 1880s. His New York–based newspaper, *Freiheit,* became the most influential Anarchist organ in the world. Most did not believe in patient organizational and propagandistic work; people were always ready for a revolution, he believed, and all that was needed was a small minority to show the lead. The present system was essentially barbaric and could be destroyed only by barbaric means.

For the masses to be free, as Most saw it, the rulers had to be killed. Dynamite and poison, fire and the sword, were much more telling than a thousand revolutionary speeches. Most did not rule out propaganda in principle, but it had to be propaganda by deed, sowing confusion among the rulers and mobilizing the masses.

Most fully appreciated the importance of the media, which he knew could publicize a terrorist action all over the globe. He pioneered the concept of the letter bomb, even though the technical difficulties in producing such bombs were still enormous at the time, and, although then a flight of fancy, he imagined aerial terrorist attacks. He predicted that it would be possible to throw bombs from the air on military parades attended by emperors and tsars. Like Heinzen, Most believed that science would give terrorists a great advantage over their enemies through the invention of new weapons. He also was one of the first to advocate indiscriminate bombing; the terrorist could not afford to be guided by considerations of chivalry against an oppressive and powerful enemy. Bombs had to be put wherever the enemy, defined as "the upper ten thousand," meaning the aristocracy and the very rich, congregated, be it a church or a dance hall.

In later years, beginning about 1890, Most mellowed inasmuch as he favored a dual strategy, putting somewhat greater emphasis on political action and propaganda. Killing enemy leaders was important, but obtaining large sums of money was even more essential; he who could somehow obtain $100 million to be used for agitation and propaganda could do mankind a greater service by doing so than by killing ten monarchs. Terrorist acts per se meant little unless they were carried out at the right time and the right place. He accepted that there had to be a division of labor between a political movement and its terrorist arm. Not every political revolutionary was born to be a terrorist; in fact, the less political leaders knew about terrorism, the better for everyone concerned.

In his younger years Most had worked for a while in an ammunition factory in Jersey City, and, based partly on his own experience with dynamite and partly on a book published by the Austrian General Staff, he wrote a little book on revolutionary warfare. This book became the inspiration for *The Anarchist Cookbook*, a book that was published by a faction of the American New Left in the 1960s and that remains a standard text in terrorist circles. (There have been similar texts issued by extremists in recent years, but all of them owe a debt of gratitude to Most.)

The New York atmosphere where Most lived in later years softened him. Gradually, his German group with its beer evenings, weekend excursions, and amateur theatricals came to resemble more a club, a Verein, than a terrorist action group. Most was not a practicing terrorist, and though he was a leading figure on the extreme left in the United States, the police did not regard him as a very dangerous man. They by and large left him alone and did not even ban his periodical and books.

The third great nineteenth-century theoretician of terrorism, and the best known by far, was Michael Bakunin. He was active in Russia as well as in Germany (during the revolution of 1848), and in France and Switzerland. In his *Principles of Revolution*, published in 1869, Bakunin wrote that he and his friends recognized no other action except destruction—through poison, knife, rope, etc. Their final aim was revolution: evil could be eradicated only by violence; Russian soil could be cleansed only by sword and fire.

Bakunin also published the *Revolutionary Catechism*, which presented the rules of conduct for terrorists. The terrorist, according to Bakunin, was a lost soul, without interests, belongings, or ties of family or friendship; he was nameless. (The idea of the anonymous terrorist was later taken up by other terrorist movements whose members were known by number rather than by name.) The terrorist had broken with society and its laws and conventions, and he was consumed by one passion: the revolution. Hard on himself, he had to be hard on others. Bakunin also provided tactical advice about infiltrating the old order by way of disguise and dissimulation, the Islamic *taqfir* in Russian style. The army, the bureaucracy, the world of business, and especially the church and the royal palace were all targets of infiltration.

He recommended that terrorists single out the most capable and intelligent enemies and kill them first, for such assassinations would inspire fear among society and the government. They should pretend to be friendly toward liberals and other well-wishers, even though these were dubious elements, only a few of whom would eventually become useful revolutionaries. A closing reference is made in this catechism to robbers and brigands, the only truly revolutionary element in society; if they would only unite and make common cause with the terrorists, they would become a terrible and invincible power. Seen in historical perspective Bakunin was, among many other things, also the ideological precursor of a tactical alliance between terrorists and crime syndicates, though it is doubtful he would have thought so highly of the revolutionary potential of the Mafia or the Cali drug syndicate.

The catechism stresses time and again the need for total destruction. Institutions, social structures, civilization, and morality are to be destroyed root and branch. Yet, in the last resort, Bakunin, like Heinzen and Most, lacked the stamina and the ruthlessness to carry out his own program.

This was left to small groups of Russian terrorists. The duo of Nechaev and Ishutin are an example, but the groups they purported to lead, with grandiloquent names such as "European Revolutionary Committee," were largely a figment of their imagination. Although they would occasionally kill one of their own members whom they suspected of treason, they did not cause physical harm to anyone else. Ishutin's largely imaginary terrorist group, called "Hell," was an interesting anticipation of the millennial sects of the next century.

Ironically, when the Russian terrorist movement of the late 1870s emerged, and culminated in the assassination of the tsar, its characteristics were very different from those described by Bakunin. Bakunin is remembered today mainly as one of the godfathers of modern anarchism, as a critic of Marx and Engels, and not as a terrorist.

WORDS INTO DEEDS

The two important terrorist exploits of the nineteenth century occurred in March 1881 and May 1882, respectively: the murder of Tsar Alexander II, and the assassination of Lord Cavendish and Thomas Henry Burke, the chief secretary of the British administration in Ireland and one of his principal aides. Neither event came out of the blue. As in Ireland, there had been a revolutionary tradition in Russia antedating the murder of the tsar by many years, but it was not necessarily terrorist in character. Even the Narodnaya Volya (People's Will), which was eventually to carry out the assassination of the tsar, began its political activities trying to propagate the idea of an uprising among the peasants, a venture that, not surprisingly, ended in total failure since the revolutionaries' aims were not those of the villagers. A split ensued among the revolutionaries, with the terrorists claiming that killing leading opponents was far more cost effective than the Marxists' preference for political action. A small number of people could cause a great deal of havoc if ten or fifteen pillars of the establishment were murdered at once; the government would panic and the masses would wake up. But the Russian ideologists of terrorism never made it quite clear whether they expected the government simply to collapse and disintegrate, or whether a popular uprising would have to take place. The early terrorists were convinced that this stage could be reached within two or three years. If, on the other hand, the government was ready to make far-reaching concessions, such as granting freedom of speech and and the right to organize, the terrorists might cease their campaign and reconsider the situation.

The tsar's assassination was prefaced in the year 1878 by the first major terrorist operation, the shooting of General Trepov, the governor of Moscow, by Vera Figner. The mood of public opinion was such that Figner was acquitted in the ensuing trial. True, at the time the majority of her comrades still thought that if there had to be armed struggle, it was to be "class against class," for the enemy was capitalism rather than the state, and they thought that the state might remain neutral in this battle. In the meantime, Nikolai Mezentsev, the head of the political police, had also been shot because of his role in the arrest and mistreatment of members of the People's Will group, and soon the organization was debating the fate of Mezentsev's successor, Drenteln. By that time the majority of the group had been won over to terrorism and the belief that a terrorist strategy would lead to quick successes. The revolutionary tribunals would pass their sentences; the militants would carry them out and then disappear without a trace.

The political views of the militants were at times very extreme, at others quite moderate, but they seemed not to have been very deeply held. Two of the most active terrorists, Tikhomirov and Romanenko, moved in later years to the extreme right, while another, Morozov, became a follower of the centrist Kadets. The terrorists proclaimed that they were fighting not only against naked tyranny, as in Russia, but also constitutional repression, as in Germany; they would not hesitate to assassinate a dictator like Bismarck, even though he was governing in a semidemocratic framework. On the other hand, two weeks after the assassination of Emperor Alexander II, the executive committee of Narodnaya Volya stated in an open letter to his successor that terrorism was an unfortunate necessity, and that all they wanted was a general amnesty and a constitution granting elementary freedoms. It was said in later years, not without justification, that the terrorists were not really extremists but "liberals with a bomb," that in the prevailing state of repression even mild and moderate people would join the terrorists because their conscience dictated such a course of action.

Seen in this light, terrorism was merely a manifestation of the general crisis in Russian society. Vera Figner, whose attack had started it all, wrote in later years that terror had been like a major storm in an enclosed space: "The waves were rising high but the unrest did not spread. It exhausted the moral force of the intelligentsia." After the murder of the tsar, most of the assailants were quickly apprehended and executed, and there was relative quiet on the Russian home front for twenty years. The number of conspirators had been small, and while they enjoyed considerable sympathies among the intelligentsia and the middle class in general, there were not enough replacements to continue the struggle. They were all very young and many of them were students, but there were also some young women and workers among them, the latter including Zhelyabov, who headed the operation against the tsar.

Seen in historical perspective, the terrorism of Narodnaya Volya was counterproductive. The reformer Tsar Alexander II was replaced by the more repressive regime of Alexander III. The assassination helped to shut the door to a political solution of the constant Russian crisis and led to the revolution in 1917. The tsarist regime bore principal responsibility for the events of 1917, but the activities of the terrorists, despite their political aims, had not helped to resolve the continuing political crisis.

The tradition of Narodnaya Volya, or People's Will, lingered on, but a second wave of organized, systematic terrorism began with the foundation of the Social Revolutionary Party in 1900. Unlike its predecessor, this party practiced political action in combination with industrial strikes and agrarian uprisings, and, in contrast to the Marxist Social Democrats, they supported terrorism. It established an armed wing, the BO (Boevaya Organisatsia—Fighting Organization), whose exploits shook the government to its foundations. There was greater support in society for terrorism than there had been twenty-five years earlier, and after the murder of Plehwe, the hated minister of the interior, even some leading Social Democrats considered supporting terrorism in certain circumstances. Among the more prominent victims of terror were the minister of education; two ministers of the interior; two police chiefs of Moscow; Stolypin, the prime minister; and Grand Duke Serge Aleksandrovich, governor general of Moscow.

An important difference between the second and the first wave of terrorism was the sheer magnitude of the terrorist campaign. Whereas the People's Will operations had been concentrated almost entirely in the two major cities, Social Revolutionary terrorism was active throughout the country. The governor generals of Finland and the Caucasus were killed, and there were many assassinations in other border areas, including Armenia and Poland, and in minor cities.

Following the general lawlessness and temporary loss of power of the government during the Russo-Japanese War (1904–5), kidnappings, bank robberies, and other "expropriations" took place. No leader in the established system felt himself secure, and a mood of defeatism spread through the country. The revolution of 1905 brought about certain concessions on the part of the government in the form of a constitution. This, in turn, caused a decline in terrorist activity, for if political action, strikes, and demonstrations could bring about results, it seemed pointless to engage in terrorism. But the tsarist regime recovered much of the lost ground as the revolutionary impetus ran out of steam, and while terrorist activities were resumed in 1906, including some spectacular acts of violence, the authorities succeeded in imposing their will.

The BO was successfully penetrated by police agents; the head of the organization, Azev, and many others turned out to be police spies. Azev's comrades refused to believe in his deception for a long time, but once this had been proven, the fighting spirit of the militants rapidly disintegrated in a general climate of mutual distrust. It is also true that whereas earlier the tsarist government had observed legal niceties, after 1906 it introduced a state of siege in many parts of Russia. Those apprehended were dealt with by court martial, and draconian measures were used without compunction. The number of death sentences rose from 144 in 1906 to 1,139 in 1907, and 825 were handed down in 1908. The total number of executions was in the thousands, and an even greater number of people were sentenced to hard labor. Taking into account that not all terrorists were apprehended, it is clear that the sheer scale of terrorism in Russia was unprecedented. And yet terrorism did not succeed in overthrowing the regime. The murder of Stolypin the prime minister in 1911 caused no political reverberations, and there were no major terrorist attacks during the years leading up to the revolution of 1917.

TERRORISM IN THE TWENTIETH CENTURY

Toward the end of the nineteenth century and up to the outbreak of the First World War, terrorist attacks took place in many places all over the globe. They were widespread in the Ottoman Empire, then in its last phase of disintegration. Armenian terrorism against the Turks began in the 1890s but ended in disaster with the mass murder of Armenians in World War I. This terrorist tradition among the Armenians continued outside Turkey after the massacres of the First World War and was directed against individual Turkish military leaders. There was a third wave of Armenian terrorism in the late 1970s and 1980s, when the Turkish ambassadors to Austria and France were killed.

Another terrorist group was IMRO, the Macedonian Revolutionary Organization, which for almost three decades engaged not only in terrorism but in political activity and in the preparation for a mass insurrection. The longevity of sustained Macedonian terrorism can be explained with reference to the support it received (in contrast to the Armenians) from governments protecting them, mainly the Bulgarians. The price the IMRO had to pay was high, because it became for all intents and purposes a tool of the Bulgarian government, and was used mainly against Yugoslavia as well as against domestic enemies. IMRO dependence on Sofia led eventually to internal splits and internecine warfare—more Macedonians were killed by IMRO than were enemies of Macedonian statehood. In the end Macedonia did not gain independence, except in part—and only very recently—after the disintegration of Yugoslavia.

Terrorism also occurred in India and Japan. Two prime ministers were killed in Tokyo toward the end of the last century, another in 1932, not to mention a variety of other government ministers. There was even an attempted assassination of the emperor. In India political murders became frequent during the decade prior to World War I, but a Viceroy, Lord Mayo, had been killed as far back as 1872.

The most striking terrorist movement prior to World War I was that of the anarchists, whose deeds all over Europe preoccupied public opinion, police chiefs, psychologists, and writers, including Henry James and Joseph Conrad, for many years. The French anarchists Ravachol, Auguste Vaillant, and Emile Henri created an enormous stir, giving the impression of a giant conspiracy, which, in fact, never existed. Ravachol was a bandit who would have robbed and killed even if anarchism had never existed; Vaillant was a bohemian; and Emile Henri was an excited and excitable young man. The three really did not have much in common. But as far as the general public was concerned, anarchists, socialists, and radicals were all birds of a feather. Governments and police chiefs probably knew better, although they saw no reason to correct this mistaken impression.

The panic was not entirely unjustified, inasmuch as there were a great many attempts on the life of leading statesmen between the 1880s and the first decade of the twentieth century. American presidents Garfield and McKinley were among those killed. There were several attempts to assassinate Bismarck and Emperor Wilhelm I of Germany. French president Carnot was killed in 1894; Antonio Canovas, the Spanish prime minister, in 1897; Empress Elizabeth (Zita) of Austria in 1898; and King Umberto of Italy in 1900. If one adds the sizable number of lesser figures and, of course, the Russian rulers and politicians, it should come as no surprise that a large public was fascinated and horrified by the mysterious character of these assassins and their motives. But closer examination of the phenomenon shows that although a few of the attackers were anarchists, they all acted on their own, without the knowledge and support of the groups to which they belonged. Terrorism was regarded as a wholly new phenomenon, and it was conveniently forgotten that political murder had a very long history. (In France, there had been countless attempts to murder Napoleon and Napoleon III in an age well before the rise of anarchism.) However psychologically interesting, this *ère des attentats,* as it was called, was of no great political consequence. By 1905, the wave of attacks and assassinations had abated, and though there were still a few isolated occurrences in Paris and London (for example the Bonnot gang and Peter the Painter), these were small criminal or semicriminal gangs. The era had come to an end.

During the years of World War I, few terrorist acts took place; one of the exceptions was the assassination of the Austrian chancellor Graf Stuergkh by a leading socialist, a dramatic form of protest against the war and against a not altogether appropriate target. By and large, individual terror seemed pointless at a time when millions of people were being killed on the battlefields. Under those circumstances the death of a politician, however prominent, would hardly attract much attention.

AFTER WORLD WAR I

Until the First World War, terrorism was thought to be mainly left wing in ideology. This assessment was dubious even at the time; it was certainly not true with regard to the postwar period and it was not true before 1914, given the highly individualistic character of the small terrorist groups. One could not possibly consider the Irish patriots, the Armenians, the Macedonians, or the Bengali partisans of the left.

One group, the Black Hundred, which appeared in Russia soon after the turn of the century, was certainly terrorist in character; however, its avowed aim was not to help the revolutionaries but to combat them. It engaged in anti-Jewish pogroms and killed some of the liberal leaders of the day. It was decidedly chauvinist, but it also adopted some populist demands. It certainly did not belong to the left, but it was not on the right, either. It represented a right-wing movement of a new type, something like a halfway house on the road toward fascism.

Generalizations with regard to terrorism are almost always misleading, but it can be said that terrorism in the 1920s and 1930s certainly stemmed more from the extreme right than the left. A typical example was the German Freikorps, small bands of ex-soldiers and students who had been too young to fight in the war. They wanted to defend the fatherland against foreign and domestic dangers; their most prominent victims were, in 1919, Rosa Luxemburg and Karl Liebknecht, the heroes and martyrs of the abortive German revolution, and the German foreign minister, Walther Rathenau, in 1922.

There were some terrorist operations in the early history of Italian fascism. Mussolini gave support to the extreme right-wing Croatian Ustasha. The Ustasha wanted independence for their country, and like many other terrorists, they welcomed help from any quarter. Their most striking operation was the dual murder of King Alexander of Yugoslavia and French prime minister Barthou as they met in Marseilles in April 1934.

The Rumanian Iron Guard (formerly the Legion of the Archangel Michael), a political party of the far right, engaged in terrorism, as did other similar movements in Eastern Europe, the Balkans, and the Middle East. The Irgun in Palestine, a country that was administered by Britain at the time, came into being in the late 1930s as the armed wing of the right-wing Revisionist Party. A few anarchists continued to be active in the 1920s where they had been traditionally strong (as in Spain), and the Communists also engaged on various occasions in terrorist operations (such as in Bulgaria in 1923 when they blew up the Sofia cathedral). But by and large, the interwar period witnessed little traditional terrorism, because this was the age of mass political parties on both right and left and of state terrorism.

While fascism and communism firmly subscribed to violence, they stood for collective rather than individual terrorism. In the case of communism, an ideological justification had been given by Lenin, who did not reject terrorism in principle but thought it in most cases harmful and counterproductive. Terrorism, Lenin wrote, was one form of the military struggle that might be usefully applied or even be essential during certain moments of battle. In October 1905, during the last phase of the Russian Revolution, he said that he regretted that his party only talked about making bombs but had never actually produced one. Some leading Marxists at the time rejected terrorism as a matter of principle, and others, such as Trotsky, were against it for pragmatic reasons. Even if successful, he wrote in 1911, terrorism would only cause confusion among the ruling classes for a short time. The capitalist system did not rest on a government minister and would not disappear with the eradication of one.

AFTER WORLD WAR II

With the end of the Second World War, the terrorist action shifted from Europe to the Middle East and Asia. There was no neo-Nazi or neo-fascist terrorism in the years after 1945, as many had feared; with the defeat of the Axis powers, the fanatical enthusiasm had vanished. In Eastern Europe and the Balkans, including those areas in which terrorism had been endemic, the presence of the Red Army and, later on, the heavy hand of the local secret police were sufficient to act as a deterrent. Even in Spain, one of the classic sites of terrorism, neither anarchists nor Basque separatists dared challenge the military dictatorship. Spanish anarchism was no longer a vital force, and the Basques had to wait for the relative freedom that followed Franco's death to resume their activities.

But in the colonies and other dependencies in North Africa and the Middle East, violent campaigns were launched by nationalist groups striving for independence. Terrorist acts had, of course, taken place before in the East, for example, prime ministers had been assassinated in Iraq and Egypt. But with the weakening of the colonial powers, violence gained a new, powerful momentum.

In predominantly agrarian societies, this usually took the form of guerrilla warfare, with China and Indochina as the classic examples, but the emergence of the terrorist Mau-Mau in Kenya and the activity of the Malayan insurgents (mainly Chinese) are others. In urban societies such as Palestine and Cyprus, the action, by necessity, took place mainly in the cities. In Algeria, the struggle against the French proceeded both in the cities and in the countryside, and elements of terrorism and guerrilla warfare appeared side by side.

Terrorism in Palestine, spearheaded by Irgun, had first appeared on the eve of the Second World War, but then Irgun called an armistice and some of its members joined the British forces. However, even before the war ended, the group renewed its attacks against the mandated power. A smaller, even more radical offshoot, the Stern Gang (Fighters for the Freedom of Israel), had attacked ceaselessly, and their leader was hunted down and shot by the British police in Tel Aviv in 1942. The politics of the Stern Gang were more than a little confused; in the early phase of the war they had looked for cooperation from the Italians and even the Germans, and later on they were attracted to Soviet communism. Their anti-imperialist manifestos often read as if they had been composed in Moscow. But their left-wing motivation was not deeply rooted. Both Irgun and the Stern Gang dissolved after the state of Israel came into being, and leading members of the Stern Gang were arrested following the murder of Count Bernadotte, the Swedish mediator, in 1948. The leader of Irgun, Menachem Begin, and one of the leaders of the Stern Gang, Yitzhak Shamir, in later years became prime ministers of Israel. These are just two examples of the many cases of guerrilla or terrorist leaders having a second, political career after their fighting days were over.

The Algerian war for independence began in 1954 in the mountainous regions of the country, was carried to the cities, and lasted for seven years. The terrorist part of the campaign was not too successful—the French smashed the rebel FLN cadres in the capital and the campaign did not go well in the countryside. But the rebels had the great advantage of having sanctuaries in the neighboring countries. Twenty thousand of their fighters were assembled outside the reach of the French, who gradually lost the stomach for making the effort needed to keep the renitent country under its control.

As in Israel, the terrorist campaigns were followed by decades of peace, but eventually radical elements again asserted themselves. This led to the second Algerian war in the 1990s and, in Israel, the murder of Prime Minister Rabin in 1995.

Generally speaking, Middle Eastern politics remained violent, marked by the assassination of a great many leaders—among them King Abdullah of Jordan in 1951 and Anwar Sadat of Egypt in 1981—and a variety of Syrian, Lebanese, and Iranian government ministers. After the emergence of radical Muslim elements, terrorism became even more rampant. Political assassinations, needless to say, occurred in many other parts of Asia and Africa. The murder of Gandhi in 1948, and in later years of Indira Gandhi and Rajiv, her son who succeeded her as prime minister, are particularly striking examples. But it was above all in the Muslim countries of North Africa and the Middle East that systematic and sustained terrorism prevailed in the 1950s, even before anti-Israeli terrorism became a major and well-publicized feature of world politics in the 1960s. Third World terrorism was, almost without exception, inspired by nationalism or political religion.

LATIN AMERICAN TERRORISM

In Latin America, there was a recurrence of terrorism in the late 1960s that was not nationalist-separatist in character but drew its inspiration from the extreme left. The Tupamaros of Uruguay were the prototype of this new terrorism. They emerged in a country that for years had been the most progressive in Latin America, and even in the 1960s was among the more liberal. The Tupamaros, who stood for radical political and social change, attracted some of the best and most idealistic from the younger generation, and they engaged in bank robberies and kidnappings but not in indiscriminate murder. Initially their activities were quite successful, proving that a civilian government could be easily disrupted. The Tupamaros attracted a great deal of attention in the world media, but in the final analysis the only result of their operations was the destruction of freedom in a country that almost alone in Latin America had an unbroken democratic tradition, however imperfect. The campaign of the Tupamaros caused the rise of a military dictatorship and destroyed the democratic system, and, at the same time, brought about the destruction of their own movement. By the 1970s, the remaining Tupamaros were in exile bemoaning the evil doings of an oppressive regime they themselves had helped to bring to power. The grave diggers of liberal Uruguay, as Regis Debray later wrote, had also dug their own graves. Facing defeat, the Tupamaros tried their hand at establishing a united front of the left together with nonterrorist parties, but they fared badly in popular elections.

Terrorism in Argentina began a few years after the outbreak in Uruguay. It was on a far more massive scale, and both the terrorist operations and the backlash were more indiscriminate and bloody. In contrast to their Uruguayan comrades, Argentinian terrorists consisted of two groups: the Montoneros (basically Peronist in orientation and social composition) and the smaller but better-equipped and organized ERP (more doctrinally left-wing in character, consisting mainly of students). The Montoneros, who had the whole Peronist left wing as a base of recruitment, began their campaign with the killing of ex-President Aramburu in May 1970. Initially, a considerable number of foreigners (or locals representing foreign economic interests) were among the victims, but gradually the terrorism turned against the army, the police, politicians, and moderate union leaders. There were also a great many unintended victims who died because they happened to be where bombs exploded.

Terrorism in Argentina reached its height in the period 1975–76. There were 646 political murders in 1976, and the terrorists attacked military installations in some provincial cities. Argentina is perhaps the only recorded example of urban guerrilla activity—that is, where terrorists came close to establishing liberated zones in urban areas. But the terrorists overreached precisely because they engaged in large-scale operations that made it easier for the army to combat them. Once the army received a free hand to retaliate, no mercy was shown. Four thousand members of the Montoneros and the ERP were detained, thousands more were arrested, and many were tortured or disappeared without a trace, including many innocent people. Thus, a terrible price was paid for the ill-conceived terrorist campaign. True, within a decade military dictatorship in Argentina, as in Uruguay, gave way to a civilian government that gradually became more democratic, but the experience of these countries did show that even weak and ineffective governments were capable of defending themselves when terrorists had no hope of gaining the support of significant sections of the population.

Latin America deserves mention here because of the strategy of its so-called urban guerrillas, despite the fact that guerrilla activities here were short-lived. Abraham Guillen, a refugee from Spain, advocated guerrilla cells consisting of no more than five or six members who would be constantly on the move. But in his writings Guillen also suggested stronger political action, and clandestine existence and constant mobility was not possible in combination with open political propaganda. And there were the writings of Brazilian Carlos Marighella, who had been a member of the Communist Party but left it because it had been too tame for his taste; he was probably more widely read among his European admirers than in his native country. His "mini-manual" was translated into many languages, but his advocacy of a scorched earth, sabotage of transport and oil pipelines, and destruction of food supplies was quite unrealistic. Marighella assumed that the masses would blame the authorities for these disasters, but the masses were less naive than he thought. Even among the extremists, not many accepted his strategy.

These terrorist theories can be lumped into an approach called the strategy of provocation, an approach that had failed everywhere else. The strategy was based on the assumption that violence would produce repression, which would generate more revolutionary violence, which in turn would provoke yet more draconian measures by the government, which would shatter its "liberal facade." Eventually society would be totally polarized, and in the confrontation between the left and the right, the extreme left was bound to win. The strategy was based on the tacit assumption that the intelligentsia, especially the students, represented the revolutionary vanguard, even though lip service was almost always paid to the crucial role of workers and peasants.

As Latin American terrorists later admitted, the strategy overestimated the strength of the terrorists and underestimated the forces of repression. If the terrorists succeeded in frightening off the police, usually weak and ill equipped, this merely resulted in their having to face the army, which was not hampered by state regulations and laws and could use repressive measures, including torture, as they saw fit. The Brazilian "urban guerrilla" campaign lasted three years, but it never reached the intensity seen in Uruguay and Argentina. It ended with Marighella being shot in a police ambush in São Paulo in November 1969, and the other terrorist commanders eliminated in similar circumstances.

The police in Latin American countries used systematic torture against terrorists, but it is also true that the terrorists had not shown an excess of humanity in their operations: agricultural workers were killed because they had stumbled on an arms cache or hideouts; motorists were murdered because the terrorists needed their cars; and boatmen were cut down after a getaway at gunpoint. These and similar deeds did not add to the popularity of the terrorists. It is useful to recall that Castro and the Cubans had foreseen some of these difficulties. Keeping in mind not only the obstacles of operating in cities but the temptation to excess, they called urban terrorism the "grave of the revolutionaries."

Most Latin American countries witnessed urban terror, and it would be tedious to survey all of them here. Venezuela was one of the first to confront urban terrorism, and in some respects the country seemed pre-destined for it, since two-thirds of the population lived in urban centers and a substantial part of the powerful Communist Party supported the terrorists. (This was a fairly rare exception, because relations between terrorists and Communists were usually not good; the Communists considered the terrorists dangerous adventurers far from the spirit of Marxism-Leninism, whereas the terrorists saw the Communists as no better than other conservative politicians who talked much and did little.) Terrorism in Venezuela failed not because of massive police repression—the measures taken by the democrat Betancourt were halfhearted—but because the terrorists caused more irritation and hardship for the general public than for the government, disrupted daily life, and brought about a public groundswell of revulsion against themselves.

Neither was terrorism very successful at the time in Colombia, even though this country had one of the most violent political traditions in Latin America. The terrorist movement M 19 appeared on the scene not when repression was most violent but, on the contrary, when a democratically elected government had taken over and when economic development was strong. In later years there was to be a resurgence of terrorism in Colombia, but this had more to do with the appearance of the drug cartels and their growing power than with revolutionary zeal.

LEFT-WING TERRORISM IN GERMANY AND ITALY

A new wave of terrorism of left-wing inspiration appeared in Europe in the late 1960s, partly in the wake of the student revolt of 1968. The German "Red Army" (the Baader Meinhof group) was active for about seven years, and it was succeeded by the movements "June 2nd" and the "Red Cells." According to Red Army ideology, this group was the vanguard of the exploited and oppressed Third World, terrorism being the only feasible strategy of weak revolutionary movements. But the Third World they invoked was a figment of their imagination, and if it had existed, it would not have wanted any part of these three dozen young men and women who called themselves an "army," and who lived in a world of infantile dreams.

The Baader Meinhof group was middle class by origin, which they regarded as a blemish. They tried to compensate for the absence of a proletarian background by the frequent use of four-letter words. There is reason to believe that some of its leading members were to some degree mentally unstable: Baader was heavily dependent on drugs, and Meinhof had suffered some brain damage earlier in her life. Their later suicides also tend to point in this direction. There were more women than men in the ranks of this group, and the women were often more fanatical.

Over the years the Red Army attacked several banks, burned a department store or two, and killed a number of bankers, industrialists, and judges. But none of the victims was very prominent, nor could they have been regarded as major enemies, of either Baader Meinhof, of the revolutionary movement, or of the Third World. Their names seem to have been picked out of a telephone directory. One victim, Dr. Drenkmann, the president of a Berlin court, was a Social Democrat who had never had any contact with the Red Army or its supporters.

Initially, the Red Army had hundreds of supporters, some of whom were willing to give active help. But gradually they lost sympathy, as it became obvious that the terrorists were living in a fantasy world and that their ill-conceived actions had no political impact whatsoever, except perhaps to tarnish the image of the left.

If Baader Meinhof had originally been deeply if unrealistically motivated by ideology, the second and third generation of German left-wing terrorists did not tend toward reflection. They engaged in terrorism because their predecessors had done so. If they had a specific political orientation, they were unwilling or unable to express it. A few terrorist acts took place during the 1980s and early 1990s, but by and large these groups had become irrelevant, and even the media, which originally had devoted inordinate attention to their activities, lost interest.

Italian left-wing terrorism was conducted on a considerably wider scale; it was spearheaded by the Brigate Rosse, which came into being in 1970. The inspiration in Italy came less from the New Left, which had never been very strong in that country, and more from radical groups within the Communist Youth League and, to some extent, from the student groups of the left wing of the Christian Democrats, which had undergone a rapid process of radicalization. As the Red Brigades saw it, Italy was not a democratic country but a bourgeois dictatorship; the language of arms was the only language understood by the ruling class. The Communist Party, these young radicals believed, was a reformist party that had lost its belief in revolution and radical fervor. The movement was also helped by a general feeling of discontent with the lack of progress on the domestic front; the social structures had been frozen since the end of the war, and one party had been in power throughout the period. As in Germany, the membership was predominantly middle class with a strong admixture of radical chic—such as the involvement of Giangiacomo Feltrinelli, a leading publisher, who blew himself up in circumstances that remain unclear to this day. There were working-class militants, but not many.

The Red Brigades engaged in some 14,000 terrorist attacks within their first ten years. While some parts of Italy were relatively free of terrorism, Rome and the industrial regions of the north were strongly affected. The legal system was almost paralyzed, since jurors were afraid to fulfill their duty; not all judges were prepared to be heroes, and the police were by and large unprepared to deal with this unprecedented challenge. Nevertheless, the Red Brigades alienated many of their erstwhile well-wishers as the result of their attacks on journalists and union officials, and above all their murder of Aldo Moro, who had been the most leftist of all the Christian Democrat prime ministers. Far from bringing about a weakening of the state apparatus, the abduction and murder of Aldo Moro caused a closing of ranks of all the democratic parties, including, for once, the Communists. The Italian terrorists had always believed that only one more push was needed to overthrow the Christian Democrats. Instead, through their violent, indiscriminate actions, they actually helped them survive politically for another decade.

The Italian Communists showed no sympathy for the terrorists who were indirectly causing harm to their political prospects; ironically, the Red Brigades had received, as emerged later on during their trials, logistical and other help from the Soviet Union through various East European countries. East Germany, too, gave shelter to the German and Italian terrorists and assisted them in other ways.

Gradually, the Italian police and the courts began showing greater sophistication in dealing with the terrorists. By 1982, some 1,400 leftist terrorists were in prison and more than a few of them, the so-called *pentiti,* had recanted. This led to splits in the ranks of the terrorists who had not been arrested. By 1984, only one member of the high command of the Brigades had not been apprehended, and the movement had ceased to exist.

AMERICA AND JAPAN

The upsurge in terrorism of the 1960s was not limited to Europe. It manifested itself in various ways in the United States and Japan. In America, it appeared on the radical fringe of the New Left in groups like the Weathermen. In a largely unconnected development, terrorism found adherents among black militants, above all the Black Panthers. The motives that induced young blacks to join the terrorist scene were quite different from those that made middle-class white students join the Weathermen. The students knew nothing about the problems of the ghetto and about unemployment. They were motivated by a crisis of identity, suburban boredom, and the desire for excitement and action. For them, more often than not terrorism was the cure for personal problems. All this was immersed in intellectual confusion that espoused the idea that almost anything was permitted and denounced the absence of values. But the things the white radicals were saying about the wickedness of American culture were *a fortiori* true of the radicals themselves.

Some of the blacks, like George Jackson, who had studied terrorist literature in prison, had reached the conclusion that the city-based industrial establishment had to be destroyed by creating conditions of "perfect disorder." Jackson was killed trying to escape from prison, and Eldridge Cleaver, who had also advocated "armed struggle," became disillusioned after being exposed to the realities of revolutionary society in Cuba and Algeria. Both men had accepted Mao's dictum that power grew out of the barrel of a gun, and they also thought, which Mao never did, that the lumpenproletariat could be the main revolutionary force in society. But all the black leaders did not quite live up to their own prescriptions; Stokely Carmichael, for instance, a leading figure of the movement, did not join the armed struggle of the lumpenproletariat but retreated to a comfortable existence in South Africa with his wife, a well-known singer, and eventually came to favor political rather than armed struggle.

Contemporary Japanese terrorism, which was limited principally to the Japanese Red Army, reflected native traditions as well as Western influences. Many of the ideological disputations of Japanese terrorists were imported from the West, but they also invoked the spirit of the samurai. Japanese terrorists hijacked a Japanese aircraft, committed murders, including several of their own comrades, and perpetrated a few acts of sabotage, most notably of a Shell refinery in Singapore and of the French embassy in the Hague. They were also instrumental in the massacre at Lod Airport in Israel, and they collaborated with Carlos, the famous multinational terrorist, as well as the Palestinians, and ultimately found asylum in Lebanon. This being the whole extent of their terrorist activities, the Japanese Red Army was much less dangerous than the Japanese sectarian terrorists of the 1990s, who had a true base inside Japan, which the Red Army never had.

TURKEY AND THE PALESTINIANS

Few countries outside the Communist world were as severely affected by terrorism as Turkey in the 1970s. Terrorist activities in that country had been initially sponsored by the extreme left, partly as the result of the resurgence of terrorism in Europe. But within a few years the extreme right joined the battle, and the situation was further complicated by the massive help provided to terrorists by outside countries. The left received support from Bulgaria and other Eastern bloc countries, the right from Syria and other Arab states. The left operated mainly out of the universities, which served as inviolate bases that the police could not enter, and the right used religious institutions for the same purpose. Since the police were in no position to cope with the situation, martial law was imposed in 1971, and by 1974 law and order was more or less restored and a general amnesty declared.

This turned out to be a costly mistake, because the amnesty enabled many militants to resume terrorist operations; in 1978–79, 2,400 political murders were committed in the country, and there was a danger that open warfare would break out in the streets. The army took over again in October 1980, and within a few days order was restored. More than 730,000 weapons were seized and 75,000 suspects arrested during the year following the army coup. Most of these suspects were soon released, but 24,000 were charged with terrorist offenses.

Most terrorist activity in Turkey took place in the big cities, but it was by no means confined to them. Some experts explained the roots of Turkish terrorism with reference to the rapid urbanization that had caused dislocation and internal tensions. The emergence of shantytowns in the vicinity of the big cities provided a great reservoir of uprooted and dissatisfied elements willing to join the terrorist movements. But closer examination shows that most terrorists of the left were not recruited in this milieu, and it is uncertain that they provided most of the rank and file of the right-wing terrorists. There was dissatisfaction with the gradual democratization that Ataturk had begun, and it was unclear whether Turkish society was ready for democracy. The democratic experiment in Turkey had been a partial success only, and while the country had made economic progress, not everyone had benefited in equal measure.

Turkish terrorism faded out in the late 1970s, but only a few years later a new form of violence appeared, sponsored by the Kurdish minority, mainly in nonurban areas. Terrorist acts were also committed by extreme Islamic groups trying to undo the secular Kemalist reforms that had taken place during the last seventy years of Turkish history.

Palestinian terrorism grew out of the Palestinian resistance movement against Israel. There had been attacks against Israeli settlements since the state came into being, mainly small raids across the border, but it was only after the war of 1967 and the occupation of the West Bank that a major terrorist campaign began. Among its main protagonists were initially two smaller, self-styled Marxist groups: the PFLP (Popular Front for the Liberation of Palestine), headed by Dr. Habash, and the Democratic Front for the Liberation of Palestine, led by Najib Hawatme. It should be stressed, however, that the Marxist-Leninist slogans that at one time appeared prominently in the publications of most nationalist terrorist movements, including the IRA and the Basque ETA, always had to be taken with a pinch of salt. They were a concession to the general zeitgeist. When communism became less fashionable, and eventually altogether unfashionable, the Marxist-Leninist slogans were dropped and the essentially nationalist character of these movements was given open expression.

Eventually the PLO, which was both a political organization and something akin to a guerrilla movement, also opted for terrorism through Black September and other ad hoc groups. The Palestinians engaged in a variety of horrific operations, such as the killing of Israeli athletes at the Munich Olympic Games in 1972 and the blowing up of several jumbo jets at Dawson Field in Jordan in September 1970. But these major operations usually backfired: for example, the Dawson Field incident threatened the existence of Jordan, whereupon Black September was suppressed by the Jordanian army. The Israelis retaliated with counterterror inside Israel and abroad, and the hijacking of planes, which at one time had been a main strategy, was given up.

Palestinian terrorism (which will be discussed in more detail later), although not a success per se, had a great advantage over most other terrorist movements—namely, the support extended by many Arab countries, which created considerable political difficulty for Israel. Eventually this pressure exerted by the Arab states through the major powers, combined with the Intifada (which was mass rather than individual violence), brought about concessions from Israel. Israel was also hurt by the enormous publicity given even to very minor terrorist events in Israel as compared with the much more destructive terrorism in Sri Lanka and Algeria, for example. The reason was obvious: the media were concentrated in Jerusalem rather than Sri Lanka or Algeria.

As the terrorism of the extreme left receded into the background or petered out altogether, the nationalist-separatist terrorism that had been mostly dormant since the Second World War experienced a major resurgence beginning in the 1970s.

TERRORISM OLD AND NEW: IRA AND ETA

A new age of terrorism is dawning, but the old terrorism is far from dead, even though it has declined markedly in Europe. An example is provided by the situation in Northern Ireland. Violence in Ireland goes back for centuries, and the memory of the battles of Kinsale (1601) and the Boyne (1690) between Protestants and Catholics is kept alive in Republican circles to this day. Terrorism in Ireland developed in 1968–69 following Catholic and Protestant demonstrations and has not ceased since. The last phase of the Troubles in Northern Ireland began in 1969. The early years of the Troubles (1972–76) were by far the bloodiest. Thereafter the annual number of victims declined to about a third of what it had been in the early years. There were spectacular exploits, such as the murder of Lord Mountbatten, the retired Viceroy of India; the killing of Airey Neave, a minister of the Crown; the placing of bombs in commercial centers of London and Manchester, causing much material damage; and the attempt to kill then Prime Minister Thatcher and the Conservative leadership at their party conference. There were also attacks against British forces in Europe, especially in Germany.

But the IRA could have conducted many more widescale and frequent attacks, given the financial support they received and the arms supply at their disposal. What kept their activities down to relatively low levels? The IRA leadership seems to have realized early on that their campaign against the British would be long, and that if it became too formidable a danger, especially on the British mainland, they would not only turn public opinion against themselves but also invite much sharper and more effective counterblows. Nor could they hope to substantially strengthen their position in their own community; in parliamentary elections they hardly ever scored more than 15 percent of the vote.

Their strategy from the late 1970s on seems to have been to wear out the British, perhaps to await a time when Britain would be in so weak a position that it would have to make concessions it had been reluctant to consider in the past. The aims of the Republicans were, after all, limited in scope compared with those of Palestinian groups such as Hamas. They wanted not the total destruction of their enemy but merely a united Ireland.

Hence the political negotiations that began in 1993. The ground had been prepared in talks between London and Dublin in which constitutional safeguards were laid out. On this basis the IRA declared an armistice in August 1994; the Protestant groups followed suit a month later. The truce lasted until February 1996, when the IRA resumed hostilities. The main bone of contention was the British demand that the IRA surrender its arsenal of arms. This was interpreted by Sinn Fein, the political wing of the IRA, as unilateral disarmament and hence unacceptable.

Multiparty talks went on, but Sinn Fein was excluded as long as the IRA attacks continued. Then, in 1997, Labor came to power in Britain, with the desire to make a new start. Sinn Fein, beset by internal divisions, did not at first respond. The Protestants, on the basis of their past experiences, were reluctant to participate as the new British government renewed negotiations with Sinn Fein in August 1997, with the decommissioning of arms still the main issue at stake. After many setbacks, these talks led to agreement in 1998.

There was the impression that while the old hostility and mutual suspicion continued unabated, a majority of IRA militants were in favor of trying to negotiate a settlement or at least opting for a long truce. But it was also clear that an extremist minority wanted to fight on. These diehards were largely motivated by temperament rather than ideological differences. There was a hard core of younger people (the Irish Continuity Army) who were professional terrorists, just as in an earlier age there had been professional revolutionaries all over Europe. This was their life and the only profession they had learned. What would they do once peace had been established? Hence the decision to kill a leading Protestant terrorist inside the Maze prison in Belfast, which led to a new round of terrorist actions.

Since it was unlikely that in a peaceful settlement all the demands of the extremists would be met, there was reason to assume that at least some terrorists would continue the struggle. This could well be a repeat performance of 1921, when the militants continued to fight after the agreement with London to establish an Irish Free State. They had been subdued only after a civil war, which had set Irish freedom fighters, that era's comrades in arms, against each other. This scenario is, of course, not limited to Ireland; it applies, in all probability, to every terrorist campaign. There always will be some ultras dissatisfied with a political settlement, eager to fight on. But the vote in Northern Ireland in the spring of 1998 showed clearly that the majority of Catholics wanted an end to the armed conflict and that a majority of Protestants, albeit not on the same scale, shared their feelings. And yet the peace agreement was followed by the bloodiest attack in the whole history of the conflict, carried out by a splinter group calling itself the "real IRA." Whether the peace will last cannot be predicted with certainty. But as of this writing in 1999, terrorism in Ireland has come to an end after long negotiations and the intervention of the American president, Bill Clinton, and the British prime minister, Tony Blair.

The parallels between the IRA and the Basque ETA are striking in many respects: both are motivated by enormous enthusiasm, even though the groups constitute only a minority within their own community. Basque opposition against what is perceived as oppression by the Madrid centralists goes back to the nineteenth century and possibly even further.

Basque nationalism was effectively suppressed under General Franco, and while the first acts of sabotage took place when Franco was still alive (the derailment of a railway in 1961), a major campaign started only after the dictator had died and most of the Basque militants had been released from prison. Admiral Carrero Blanco, Franco's successor, was assassinated, and in 1979 there were eighty-two political murders, eighty-eight the year after. Basque terrorism, despite setbacks, continued up to the fall of 1998, albeit on a smaller scale than before.

The ETA has achieved considerable political concessions, but this success has not been remotely sufficient to satisfy the nationalists. The aim of the extremists remains an independent Basque state. But given the demographic realities, especially the fact that the Basque are a minority in their own region, this can be achieved only by ethnic cleansing, the exodus of the non-Basques, or their voluntarily becoming Basques. This would mean transforming the war against the Spanish government into a war against the Spanish people and also eventually against the majority of Basques who do not subscribe to ETA ideology (semi-Trotskyite in the 1970s and early '80s, and ultranationalist in the 1990s). The political wing of ETA polled 12 percent of the votes in the Basque country in the general elections of 1996, in comparison to 14 percent in the previous elections. From a self-styled anti-colonialist, anti-capitalist, anti-imperialist revolutionary movement, ETA had turned into a purely nationalist movement, one that supported a social program that did not differ substantially from that of other Spanish parties.

The high tide of ETA terrorism came in 1978–80, certainly as far as the number of victims is concerned. After that, though the number of militants may have increased somewhat, the number of assassinations has decreased. Five occurred in 1996 and twelve in 1997, compared to the annual average in 1970–95 of more than twenty. (ETA differs from the IRA in its involvement in kidnapping and extortion, for which the IRA has little appetite.)

ETA's prospects seem dim. It has largely lost its bases in France following an agreement between the French and Spanish governments. There is no goodwill for its cause among Spaniards, and no attempt has been made to generate such goodwill. Nevertheless, ETA still has the support of a fanatical minority in their own region. Eventually, a political solution might be found; this will undoubtedly lead to a split, as in the case of the IRA, since the ultranationalists cannot possibly achieve all they want.

In the Basque region, as in Northern Ireland, a culture of violence has developed over the years that tends to perpetuate itself. It is, in all probability, a generational question. As one generation of professional terrorists ages and by necessity opts out of the armed struggle, a new one may or may not emerge. Or it may appear after an interruption of a few decades, as has happened in Irish history time and again.

A PROFILE OF TERRORISM

Who are the persons behind the masks of terrorist movements? Are there any distinguishing characteristics that can be observed about the individuals or the groups? Terrorist groups have frequently consisted of younger members of the educated middle classes, but there have also been instances of agrarian terrorism and terrorism by the uprooted and rejected in society. In a very few cases—for example, the Molly Maguires in the United States—there has been working-class terrorism, but it clearly has been the exception.

In nationalist-separatist groups, the middle-class element has usually been less influential than it has been in terrorist cells of the extreme left. Movements of national liberation and social revolution have turned to terrorism after political action failed. But terrorism has also been the first resort, chosen by militant groups impatient for quick results.

Assassinations of leading officials have been tried within modern totalitarian regimes, but the means of repression at the disposal of the totalitarian state have effectively ruled out any systematic terrorism. Terrorism has been infrequent in societies in which violence has not been part of the tradition and political culture, but few parts of the world have been altogether free of it.

National oppression and social inequities are frequently mentioned as the root causes of terrorism, and it is, of course, true that happy, contented groups of people seldom, if ever, throw bombs. But this does not explain why the struggle for political freedom, for national liberation, or for secession has only occasionally led to terrorism, and why certain national minorities have opted for terrorism and others have not—why, for instance, the Basque militants have engaged in a long terrorist campaign, whereas the Catalan have not. History shows it has little to do with the severity of the oppression measured by any acceptable standard; terrorism is largely a matter of perception, of historical, social, and cultural traditions, and of political calculus.

Generalizations about terrorism are difficult for yet another reason. Terrorist groups are usually small; some are very small indeed. While historians and sociologists can sometimes account for mass movements, the movement of small particles in politics, as in physics, often defies explanation. Some of the most striking assassinations in history, including that of U.S. president Kennedy, were carried out by lone individuals rather than groups; the investigation of their motives belongs to the realm of psychology rather than politics.

Having said this, some general statements can be made about the mainsprings of terrorism, its strategy, and its tactics. Seldom, if ever, have terrorists assumed that they would be able to seize power outright—most believe in the strategy of provocation. The Irish believed that their attacks would lead to counterterrorism, that, as a result, the fighting spirit of Ireland would reawaken, and, in the end, that Britain would have to make concessions. The Russian revolutionaries decided to kill the German ambassador to Moscow and the German governor in Kiev in 1918, assuming that this would lead to a resumption of hostilities between the young Soviet regime and Imperial Germany. In a similar way, the Armenian terrorists before 1914 and the Palestinian terrorists after 1967 aimed at bringing about foreign intervention.

The choice of victims is often arbitrary; while the Russian terrorists concentrated their attacks in the beginning against tsarist officials who had shown particular brutality, later terrorists, on the contrary, killed moderate political leaders who they thought were more dangerous political enemies. Two examples already mentioned are the murder of Walther Rathenau, the German foreign minister, in 1922, and the Italian politician Aldo Moro; a third is Grand Duke Franz Ferdinand of Austria, who was killed by Serbian terrorists precisely because he had the reputation of a liberal willing to make concessions.

On a few occasions, terrorists achieved their aims. Count Orsini was acting on his own when he carried out his spectacular bomb attack in Paris in 1857, but it pushed Napoleon III to decide to give the Italians military assistance against Austria. Orsini would not have succeeded unless Napoleon had favored such a policy in any case. When terrorism has been successful, it has usually been because the terrorist demands were limited and clearly defined. That the wages of American ironworkers more than doubled between 1905 and 1910 was at least in part connected with the fact that during this period about one hundred buildings and bridges were bombed. Alternatively, systematic terror has been successful when carried out within the framework of a wider strategy. Thus, the Vietcong killed some 10,000 village elders in the late 1950s and early 1960s, and the Algerian FLN systematically killed their political rivals, the followers of Messali Haj, as a prologue to a wider and more ambitious strategy.

Many terrorist groups have without hesitation attacked the police and, of course, civilians, but have shown reluctance to attack the military. They must have assumed that the military would be a harder target and that there would be massive retaliation.

A TERRORIST PERSONALITY?

Is there a terrorist personality? That is to say, do certain individuals have a predisposition toward engaging in terrorist operations? Even if the Russian terrorists of the last century shared certain distinct traits of character, they had little in common with the Irish, let alone latter-day terrorists such as the Palestinians. Much has always depended on the social and political conditions in which terrorism occurred. Most terrorists have been young, many of them very young; the three assassins of Prince Franz Ferdinand in 1914 were seventeen, eighteen, and twenty years of age. Calls to action fill younger people with greater enthusiasm than they do the middle-aged or the elderly. Furthermore, terrorism requires strength, stamina, and speed, physical qualities of youth. Carlos Marighella, mentioned earlier, became a terrorist in his fifties, but this is a rare exception. An even rarer one is Joseliani, the Georgian playwright and filmmaker who at the age of seventy-one was imprisoned for having engaged in terrorist activities, including a plot to assassinate Eduard Shevardnadze, the Georgian president, in 1997. Some of the masterminds of the pan-Islamic terrorist groups in Pakistan and Egypt were also men in their fifties and sixties, but they were mainly engaged in the training of terrorists rather than active participation in their exploits.

Nor is there a clear pattern with respect to family background and beliefs. Some German terrorists grew up in fatherless families, hated their fathers, or were children of divorced parents. But others lived in closely knit families. Some studies have found that terrorists on the extreme right suffered frequently from autodestructiveness, believed in superstition, and revealed traits of an "authoritarian personality." It has also been found that ideology has played a lesser role among terrorists of the extreme right. However, the reason could simply be that they came from a lower educational background and were less articulate.

Women constituted about a quarter of the Russian terrorists of the nineteenth century, and attention has been drawn to the high percentage of women among the German and American terrorists of the seventies. This was true of the white groups, but not the black, and it was certainly not true of the Irish or the Muslim terrorists, among whom bomb throwing was clearly considered a man's job. In fact, a pronounced anti-female streak could be detected among some of the most militant Islamic groups, such as the Taliban and the Algerians.

Subsequent investigations have shown that women terrorists are more fanatical and have a greater capacity for suffering. Their motivation is predominantly emotional and can not be shaken through intellectual argument. Among female terrorists there are few, if any, of working-class origin. This has been explained with reference to women's emancipation, by and large a middle-class phenomenon, or alternatively as a "break with rejected femininity."

Minorities used to be prominently represented among terrorists—for example, Jews in the Russian terrorist movement. At one stage, some of the central figures of the Palestinian terrorists, including Dr. Habash and Hawatme, were Christian, but in later years the leaders have become exclusively Muslim, just as the leaders of Irish activism until 1921 were almost all Protestant, and now, given the recent religious character of the movement, are almost all Catholic. In Irgun, there was a relatively high percentage of young Oriental Jews; perhaps they perceived grievances more acutely than did others or felt a psychological need to prove themselves.

Close foreign observers of the Russian terrorist scene in the nineteenth century stressed that most of the terrorists were young people of the highest ethical standards; Dostoevsky's villains in his novel *Demons* were mere caricatures. The Russian terrorists anxiously asked themselves whether they had the right to kill, and bombs were not thrown when the target was accompanied by his wife and children. These terrorists had little in common with later generations of terrorists who had no compunction about killing people indiscriminately. The preoccupation with ethical problems was confined to Europe and the nineteenth century. Outside Europe there was no hesitation to kill, and even in Europe after the First World War the belief that compassion is a bourgeois prejudice gained ground.

There is another interesting difference between nineteenth- and twentieth-century terrorists. The former expected as a matter of course that they would be executed or at the very least get long prison sentences. Contemporary terrorists, on the other hand, more often than not maintain that no one has the right to punish them, that while terrorists have the right to attack, the state and society have no right to defend themselves. They claim that killed or imprisoned terrorists are therefore martyrs. Many terrorist groups demand to be treated as prisoners of war, but they deny the state the right to take them to court as war criminals for the indiscriminate killing of civilians. Twentieth-century terrorists argue that they, and only they, know the truth, and therefore ordinary law does not apply to them.

A mystical element has been noted in nineteenth-century Russian terrorism, an element also present in Irish, Rumanian, Japanese, and Arab terrorists. These terrorists' belief in their cause has a religious quality; the idea of martyrs gaining eternal life appears in Irish terrorism from the very beginning, and it has been pronounced among the Shiite and other

Muslims. Masaryk, the historian who specialized in Russian intellectual history and who became the first president of the Czechoslovak republic, detected among Russian terrorists and the anarchists a "mystique of death," which could also be found among Fascist groups and some Arab terrorists. As Sheikh Hassan Nasralla, secretary general of Hizbullah, said in an interview, "we love death," referring to those he was sending out on suicide missions. Between the two world wars, the sentiment expressed by the slogan "long live death" was pronounced among Rumanian as well as Spanish Fascists.

The murkier the political purpose of terrorism, the greater its appeal to mentally unbalanced persons. The motives of people fighting a cruel tyranny are quite different from those of rebels against a democratically elected regime. Rather than idealism, a social conscience, or ardent patriotism, one finds among the latter free-floating aggression, boredom, and mental confusion.

TERRORIST STRATEGIES

Terrorism involves careful planning. The habits and movements of the targets have to be watched, weapons have to be procured, and transport as well as safe houses have to be provided. To make the most of their operations, terrorists need publicity, ideally even a public relations department. All major terrorist groups have a central command, sometimes a highly professional one. Decisions among the Russian terrorists were often made in committee meetings, but this was not a very effective approach. Sometimes the central command has been located outside the country, and this is now the case in the Middle East. This gives the leaders freedom of maneuver and freedom from fear of arrest. But the drawbacks of remoteness from the scene of terrorist action are serious.

The general tendency among terrorists has embraced centralization and the leadership principle. But this trend has its dangers, for terrorism always involves a great deal of improvisation, and even the best-laid plans may go wrong. If elaborate planning sacrifices the element of improvisation, this may rebound to the disadvantage of the terrorists.

Ideally, terrorist units should be small, because the bigger they are, the more open to infiltration they are. But very small units often have not had the resources and the know-how to carry out major operations. Many terrorist groups in the past were very small; they include the Japanese Red Army, Baader Meinhof, and the Symbionese Liberation Army, with its eight members. But others were large, including the Russian terrorists, Irgun, the IRA, and the Argentinian and Uruguayan groups.

To be effective, terrorists need the anonymity of a big city for their operations; in a small town people know each other, and new faces attract attention and suspicion. Separatist religious movements are sometimes based in refugee camps, in certain quarters of a big city (as in Belfast), or in small cities where it is known that police control is less than perfect.

Small groups of terrorists usually develop a certain mind-set, an esprit de corps, but they exhibit also a tendency to isolate themselves from the political movement of which they are frequently a part. In larger units, on the other hand, there are often clashes between personalities and a tendency toward splits. Internal dissent is most likely to be a reaction to setbacks. Dissent also occurs amid success when the struggle becomes more important than the attainment of the goal for some of the militants.

Modern terrorists need money to finance their operations, whereas nineteenth-century terrorism could be run on a shoestring. The money needed is obtained from wealthy well-wishers at home or abroad, through robbing banks, or from foreign governments that, for reasons of their own, support terrorist groups as surrogates in the struggle against a common enemy. Some terrorist groups forge money, others engage in kidnapping and other forms of blackmail, including protection money, and others, such as the IRA, run legitimate businesses. The sums obtained through ransom have been impressive; the Argentinian Montoneros received 60 million dollars for releasing Jorge and Juan Born, the sons of the owner of one of the country's largest corporations. Of late, some terrorist money has come from drug dealers and cartels. Obtaining significant funds has been necessary to the terrorists, but it has also made it possible for the recipients to live a lifestyle to which they were not accustomed. Ideally, terrorists should be lean, hungry, and unspoiled by the temptations of the high life; when the infamous Carlos the Jackal grew fat and spent much of his time in nightclubs, his terrorist days were over.

TOOLS OF THE TRADE

Originally the dagger and later the pistol were the favored weapons of terrorists. The bomb we associate with the activity was first used in the Napoleonic age, and extended damage well beyond the intended target. In Orsini's attempt on the life of Napoleon III in 1858, eight people were killed; in the Fenian attack on Clerkenwell Prison in 1867, there were twelve killed and 120 injured. But the quantities of explosive used were considerable—five hundred pounds of black powder in the case of Clerkenwell. The Russian terrorists of Narodnaya Volya, which included some accomplished scientists, were the first to use dynamite, which had recently been discovered. But even then, the quantities needed were substantial and the terrorist attempts frequently failed, including one at the tsar's winter palace, because the perpetrators did not have sufficient explosives. When Johann Most predicted that a ten-pound bomb could destroy a warship, he was right, but he was off by a hundred years. The Irish militants in America in the last century had many innovative ideas, including a type of Molotov cocktail, poison gas, and a submarine, but nothing came of these schemes at the time. The first letter bombs—parcel bombs, to be precise—were used on the eve of the First World War. At the same time, Russian and some of the French terrorists played with the idea of using motorcars, and the Russians invested money in the construction of an airplane. These schemes did not materialize, but they did presage the future.

Explosives were perfected during the First and Second World Wars, and these innovations soon reached the hands of terrorists. TNT was the explosive of choice after World War I, and plastic explosives such as Semtex became the favorite material after World War II. Automatic rifles and pistols replaced the old revolvers and guns, and RPGs (rocket-propelled grenades) were first used in Ireland, France, Germany, and Italy in the 1970s. Another favorite weapon was the car bomb, first used by Al Capone and his gang in Chicago. Limpet mines of various sorts were also used, sometimes exploded by remote control. While a small quantity of explosives sufficed to bring down an aircraft, much more substantial quantities were needed for attacks on land. It is estimated that one ton of explosives was needed for the bombing of the U.S. embassy in Beirut in April 1983, two tons for the bombing of the U.S. embassy in Kuwait, and up to six tons for blowing up the U.S. Marine headquarters in Beirut in October 1983. Preventive measures were taken to safeguard military installations, and few such attacks succeeded after 1983, but it was difficult to protect against attacks in civilian settings, such as the bombing of the World Trade Center in New York and the attack on Argentine Jewish institutions.

The old terrorist movements and many of the more recent ones have employed intelligence officers who penetrate "enemy" installations and provide maps and timetables. This was of great importance as long as the attacks were directed against specific individuals. Once terrorism became more indiscriminate, intelligence became less important, as a bomb could be put in any supermarket or bus.

Nineteenth-century terrorist groups, as well as the IRA and Irgun, invested much effort in liberating from prison comrades in arms who had been captured. More recently, such operations have become rare because they involve too many risks.

Kidnapping was frequently used in Latin America as well as in other parts of the world. In many cases, ransom was demanded; in others, the victim was killed after a few hours or days.

One of the most dramatic kinds of terrorist action is the hijacking of airplanes. The first known case occurred in Peru in the 1930s, and there were a few more in the years immediately after World War II. In the 1960s, a great many U.S. planes were forced to fly to Cuba, although not always by terrorists, and there were dozens of other such attempts all over the world—sixty-four in 1971. Toward the end of the decade, this figure declined and has remained relatively low ever since. Airplanes are still hijacked, but usually by criminals or lunatics or people trying to escape from dictatorial regimes. What deters terrorists is probably not so much the controls at airports, which are often lax and superficial, but the fact that fewer and fewer countries are willing to listen to any demands from terrorists.

Some terrorist groups have tried to cause economic damage to their enemies. ETA conducted a campaign directed against tourist sites; since Spain accommodated more tourists than any other European country, it was hoped that the damage caused would be substantial. Similar tactics were used at one time or another by Arab terrorists against Israel and by Muslim fundamentalists against Egypt.

To be effective, terrorist movements depend on popular support, or at least support by a certain segment of society. Nationalist-separatist groups usually have had a broad base of sympathizers; the extremists of the left and right much less so. Aware of the fact that they have some such support, terrorist leaders have often come to overrate the extent of their political influence. The moment they have decided to take part in parliamentary elections, they have hardly ever done well, as the results in Ireland and in the Basque region of Spain have shown. Nor did Irgun do well when it contested the elections after the establishment of the state of Israel; more than thirty years were to pass before they became a major force in Israeli politics. This pattern has repeated itself in Uruguay, Colombia, and other countries.

TERRORISM AND PUBLICITY

Classic terrorism is propaganda by deed, and propaganda is impossible without the use of the media. The alternative is the massive elimination of rivals or potential political rivals, such as the killing of the village elders in Vietnam and the Messalists in Algeria.

It has been said that journalists are terrorists' best friends, because they are willing to give terrorist operations maximum exposure. This is not to say that journalists as a group are sympathetic to terrorists, although it may appear so. It simply means that violence is news, whereas peace and harmony are not. The terrorists need the media, and the media find in terrorism all the ingredients of an exciting story. Their attitude toward terrorism has run the gamut from exaggerated respect to sycophancy (such as calling a terrorist a freedom fighter, an activist, a patriot, a militant, or a revolutionary). Media coverage has supplied constant grist to the terrorist mill; it has magnified the political importance of many terrorist acts out of all proportion. In some cases it has even been responsible for the murder of innocents and obstructed complicated rescue missions. The media cannot ignore terrorism, but society would certainly be better off if the media were not driven by sensationalism.

Terrorists have always recognized the importance of manipulating the media. The British War Office noted in 1922 that Sinn Fein's mastery of publicity was unrivaled. "Its publicity department was energetic, subtle and exceptionally skillful in mixing truth, falsehood and exaggeration." Irgun and the Stern Gang in Palestine had excellent relations with journalists, who helped magnify their strength and thus aided their cause. The shift in Latin America from guerrilla warfare to urban terrorism was motivated at least in part by the hope of gaining greater media attention. As one terrorist leader put it at the time: "If we put even a small bomb in a house in town, we could be certain of making the headlines in the press. But if the rural guerrilleros liquidated thirty soldiers in some village, there was just a small news item on the last page." Guerrilla warfare can exist without publicity, but urban terrorism cannot, and the smaller the group, the more it needs publicity. One of the reasons for the virtual absence of terrorism in totalitarian regimes and other effective dictatorships, besides the efficacy of the police forces, is the suppression of publicity. Unless the terrorists succeed in killing the dictator, which would be impossible to ignore, their deeds will pass unheralded.

It is also true that the media are mainly interested in some countries and not in others. Twelve people fell victim to terrorist attacks in Israel in 1985, two British soldiers were killed in Northern Ireland the same year, and the number of Americans killed by terrorists in 1982 was seven. There was great publicity in all these cases, whereas the tens of thousands killed in Iran and Iraq, in the Ugandan civil war, and in Cambodia (where hundreds of thousands were killed) went virtually unreported, because Western media either had no access or were not interested. This preoccupation of the media with some countries and with big cities rather than the countryside has on occasion induced terrorist groups to change their tactics in order to gain maximum exposure. Guerrillas, on the other hand, have no such interest in publicity, which would only harm them in their efforts to establish bases in the countryside without attracting the attention of the authorities. Mao's Long March and Tito's partisans were not covered by film crews, but in the end they were far more successful than any terrorist group. These are two examples of the difference between terrorism and guerrilla warfare.

Journalists can be a fickle ally from terrorists' point of view, however, since they need new angles and fresh excitement, and mere repetition of terrorist acts will not keep their attention. And since the repertory of the terrorists is limited, they cannot always depend on the same measure of exposure in the media each time they act.

COUNTERTERRORISM

Counterterrorism naturally goes hand in hand with terrorism, but over the ages it has become less successful for a variety of reasons. Modern technology in this area has made enormous progress; for example, it can trace the movements of even small units and single tanks over a wide area day and night. But it cannot keep track of the movements of single individuals in a town carrying miniaturized bombs. The only effective weapon against terrorism in the modern era has been the infiltration of their ranks and the use of informers. Police in the last century had a much freer hand against terrorism than today's police: they placed their agents in all major and most minor terrorist movements, and paid them from special funds to which only they had access. It is probably no exaggeration to state that most of the terrorist journals at the time were paid for by secret police funds. If a police informer in the course of his duty had to carry out a terrorist act, no questions would be asked, nor would he be put to trial or lose his pension rights.

Present-day police forces in democratic societies have little freedom of maneuver. Too many people are involved in decisions and operations, and bureaucratic formalities have to be observed. Payments to informers have to be signed and countersigned; the interception of communications between terrorist suspects has to be approved by the judiciary; and a skillful lawyer has a good chance to get his client, the terrorist, off the hook even if he was apprehended *in flagranti*. Because of these factors the successful infiltration of terrorist groups is almost impossible.

Counterterrorism's success in democratic societies is mainly the result of advanced computer technology and the cooperation of a population that provides important leads. On the other hand, cooperation in the international arena has been less than perfect. Governments have been afraid of extraditing terrorists for fear of retaliation and for other reasons, or they have released convicted foreign terrorists from prison after a token stay. Also, governments have invoked "higher interests of state"—France and Greece are examples—as reasons for not dealing with terrorists harshly. In a few cases, terrorists who have lost their usefulness or lacked influential protectors have been extradited. But by and large, counterefforts against terrorists by democractic states have been only partly effective in recent times.

TERRORISM'S LEGACY

As we have seen, terrorism has been defined in many different ways, and little can be said about it with certainty except that it is the use of violence by a group for political ends, usually directed against a government, but at times also against another ethnic group, class, race, religion, or political movement. Any attempt to be more specific is bound to fail, for the simple reason that there is not one but many different terrorisms.

Traditional terrorism appeared in various forms: in conjunction with a civil war or guerrilla warfare, in the framework of a political campaign, and also in "pure" form. It has been waged by religious and secular groups, by the left and the right, by nationalist and internationalist movements, and by governments who engage in state-sponsored terrorism. Terrorists have seldom, if ever, seized power, in contrast to guerrilla movements. But they have on occasion brought about political change, inasmuch as they have helped to bring down democratic governments that were replaced by military dictatorships. They have also on occasion helped to trigger war. The assassination in Sarajevo in 1914 that led to the outbreak of World War I is the most famous example. In a few cases, terrorism has had an effect on world history, but it has not always been the one the terrorists intended.

The impact of terrorism has been so erratic and diffuse that its impact on history has been slight. It can hardly be doubted that the murder of Napoleon, of Lenin, or of Hitler early in his career would have made a great difference in later events. But these are hypothetical exceptions. The number of prime ministers and heads of state murdered since the end of the Second World War is in excess of sixty, but it is difficult to think of a single case in which the policy of a country has been radically changed as the result of a terrorist campaign. Indira Gandhi was killed and her son, Rajiv Gandhi, continued her policy, and in the years after the assassination of her son there was no significant change in Indian policy. There was no change at all in American policy as the result of the murder of John Kennedy, or in Swedish policy following the killing of Olof Palme.

True, the killing in Sarajevo in 1914 triggered the First World War, but given the conflicts and tensions prevailing at the time, there is good reason to believe that war would have broken out anyway. If the Russian government temporarily adopted a more liberal line in 1905, it was the result of the nation's defeat in the war against Japan, not because of terrorist intimidation. Some argue that if Stolypin had not been assassinated in 1911, the agrarian reforms would have continued and the Bolsheviks might not have prevailed in 1917, but given the unyielding nature of the tsarist regime, it is doubtful that Stolypin would have remained in office and been able to push through his policy. King Abdullah of Jordan was killed by a Muslim fanatic, but Hussein, his grandson, continued his policies. Anwar Sadat was assassinated by a member of a fanatical sect, but Mubarak, broadly speaking, continued his policy with regard to Israel and in other respects.

The murder of Yitzhak Rabin in 1995 is one of the few exceptions, as is the bombing of Israeli buses by Arab terrorists instigated by Iran in early 1996. It seems likely that but for these bombings, the Israeli Labor Party would have won the next elections and would have continued the peace process. Still, this is not certain, for Rabin and Shimon Peres tackled the easier problems, whereas the more difficult ones, such as Jerusalem, were postponed. It is quite likely that given the widely divergent positions of Israelis and Palestinians, no agreement could have been reached between the two sides concerning the difficult issues and sooner or later the peace process would have run out of steam.

Ironically, when a terrorist campaign has had an effect, it has more often than not been the opposite from the one desired. We have seen the fatal consequences of the campaign of the Tupamaros in Uruguay and the Montoneros in Argentina. The Armenian terrorists in the era before 1914 helped to bring about the disaster that befell their people in the eastern parts of Turkey during World War I. The terrorists' actions were only one of several causes, but they certainly did have an effect.

Terrorist groups that have been more successful in achieving their goals can be divided, broadly speaking, into three categories: those who had narrow, clearly defined aims—for instance, in nineteenth-century industrial disputes; those with powerful outside protectors; and those facing an imperial power no longer able or willing to hold on, such as Britain in Cyprus or Palestine. But it is doubtful that in any of these countries terrorism was the most important single factor that brought about the exit of the imperial power. Political pressure, less dramatic and less widely publicized, has been more effective in the long run. The turnover of power in South Africa is a good example: terrorism played a minor role, while political pressure from the African National Congress was far more important. Terrorism has played a somewhat more important role in various Central American countries and probably also in Ireland.

By and large, as noted earlier, ethnic-separatist terrorism stands a better chance of success than does that of the extreme left or right. But national and religious minorities are dispersed in the modern world in such a way that resolving one grievance usually creates another one. Not every minority can have a state of its own, and if it did, it is not certain that such a state would be viable in the long run. Terrorism helped to bring about independence for the Greeks in Cyprus, but it also poisoned relations between Greeks and Turks, caused the division of the island, and made any permanent peaceful solution more difficult.

When terrorism has been effective in the past, it has usually been in the framework of a wider political strategy. In most cases, the political results of terrorism have been insignificant or even the opposite of what the terrorists intended, and its lasting impact has usually been in inverse proportion to the attention it got in the media. But these observations are true only with regard to the past; they do not offer a clue for the future. In the past, terrorists have not had access to means of mass destruction; technology has changed this state of affairs, and the consequences could be beyond our imagination.

Weapons of Mass Destruction

Weapons of mass destruction have long been a subject of the human imagination, in both the literary and literal sense. The use of biological and chemical weapons in war can be traced back for centuries; nuclear weapons, of course, appeared more recently, and have been used only twice, by one country. And there is even a new weapon, the potential of which is only now being understood: the computer. But as the twentieth century comes to a close, all these weapons, particularly biological/chemical, or so-called B/C weapons, are increasingly available to more states and, what is more frightening, to small groups, even individuals.

IMAGINING DOOMSDAY

The idea that life on earth will come to a violent end is ancient and has often been envisioned as the result of some giant conflagration, a flood, a collision with a comet, or some mysterious plague. The god or gods have been held responsible, either out of caprice or annoyance with what humankind had wrought. But the idea of human beings playing god is more recent, and for a long time was the preserve of science fiction writers, who, in the last century or so, have raised the specter of the mad scientist (or mere technician) capable of destroying whole cities, continents, perhaps even the planet.

Jules Verne and H. G. Wells are the best-known early practitioners of this type of fiction. Robur, the mad genius in Wells's *Invisible Man,* saw himself as the master of the world, and while many have read the book or watched one of the several film versions, very few remember that Robur's main purpose was to spread terror, as he himself put it. At about the same time—that is to say, the last decade of the nineteenth century and the first of the twentieth—stories with titles such as "The Last Days of Earth," "The Purple Cloud," "Crack of Doom," and "Lord of the World" were widely read. Critics interpreted their popularity as a symptom of the decline of religious faith, of the displacement of religion by science, or of general moral degeneracy.

This fiction, in which some scientifically inclined madman would deliberately bring about the end of life on earth, became a whole subgenre of literature, not well received critically but widely read and quite influential. No scientist in that age of great scientific achievement came forward to criticize these stories, and some of them, such as the French astronomer Flammarion, even made notable contributions to this literature.

Instead of summarizing a whole field, we will focus on two fairly typical examples. One is "The Enemy of All the World," a short story by Jack London. The hero, Emil Gluck, born in Syracuse, New York, in 1895, had a most unhappy childhood. He studied chemistry at the University of California but was thrown out for using the word *revolution* in a public speech. Even though he was persecuted, maligned, and misunderstood, this forlorn and lonely human being at first made no attempt at retaliation. But after being unlucky in love, failing in business, and being wrongfully arrested for murder, the patience of this almost saintly man snapped and he became a violent nihilist. Utilizing his scientific training, he came up with an invention that made it possible for him to dispose of all his enemies. Another of his inventions provided the money for carrying out his schemes. And so he became a mysterious terror, destroying property, taking countless lives, and causing frightful havoc. He caused a German-American war in which 800,000 people were killed, and from a little launch blew up seven warships. Then he destroyed the Atlantic seaboard from Maine to Florida, which was followed by the destruction of the northern shore of the Mediterranean from Gibraltar to Greece. "There was no defense against this unknown and all-powerful foe," London wrote, until Silas Bannerman, a U.S. secret service agent, arrested him. Gluck was executed on December 4, 1941. Earlier the French government had offered him a billion francs for his invention, which had something to do with powerful electrical discharges. But Gluck, a man of principle, indignantly rejected the offer: "Why sell you what would enable you to enslave and maltreat suffering humanity?"

The story of Emil Gluck, "one of the world's most unfortunate geniuses whose mighty powers were so twisted and warped that he became the most amazing of criminals," was first published in 1907 in a collection titled *Eccentricities of Crime.*

Fifteen years after London's story, a novel in installments appeared in Germany's leading illustrated weekly, *Berliner Illustrirte Zeitung.* Titled *Dr. Mabuse: The Gambler,* the novel proved to be the most popular ever published by this venerable periodical. It sold half a million copies in Germany alone (and there were many translations) and gave rise to a whole Mabuse industry. Millions who never read the book saw the silent film based on the book, produced by Fritz Lang. Seventy-five years later, the name Mabuse still crops up in Germany and to a lesser extent elsewhere in Europe, in rock music, as the title of an alternative-medicine journal, in advertisements for cars, and in books for young readers.

The author, Norbert Jacques, was born in Luxembourg and made a modest name for himself as the author of travelogues to exotic countries. Then he created the Mabuse character, a demonic criminal, a Nietzschean nihilist turned supergangster who believed that "there is no love, only desire, no happiness, only will to power." Mabuse wanted to show the world that he was a giant, a titan, and not bound by morality or religion. The Mabuse books would be of only limited interest to us except for the fact that, as Jacques went on producing sequels to the original work, he came to describe the Mabuse phenomenon more and more in terms of a terrorist group led by a fanatical madman out to dominate the world. Terrorists like Mabuse think of themselves as the vanguard of a regenerated mankind, but only if everyone else alive is destroyed. The salvation of mankind, by their logic, demands millions of corpses. In Jacques's books a chemist named Null, who is a scientific genius and an escapee from a lunatic asylum, discovers the power to realize their aim. The last Mabuse novel, titled *Chemiker Null,* deals with the terrorists out to decimate mankind. It was published in installments in a Swiss daily newspaper (*Neue Zuercher Zeitung*), but there was not sufficient interest at the time for publishing it as a book.

Jacques was never to repeat the success of the first Mabuse book. His character vanished from later novels, largely because the Mabuse phenomenon had been declared undesirable in Nazi Germany. Then Dr. Mabuse reappeared after the Second World War on the movie screen. No fewer than eight films with him as the chief villain were produced in the 1950s and 1960s; however, they were grade-B horror movies and did not deal with the theme of Nietzschean-scale terrorism.

Throughout history world destruction has usually been imagined as taking the form of, say, an all-consuming fire or global inundation. After the invention of dynamite by Alfred Nobel, these concerns were replaced by the concept of powerful explosives. With the progress in natural science around the last turn of the century, the search for such weapons proceeded in various directions and served as inspiration for doomsday writers. H. G. Wells was among the first to envisage nuclear war and biological warfare, in *War of the Worlds* (1898), a subject later taken up by Harold Nicolson (*Public Faces*, 1932) and others. Jules Verne's ultimate weapon was an unspecified combination of flying machines and powerful explosives. In one of his novels, *The Begum's Fortune*, a malevolent German scientist builds a shell filled with enough gas to kill the inhabitants of Franceville, a fictional French city with a population of 250,000. In the early works of Wells and some French novels of the period (notably Robida's *La Guerre aux Vingtième Siecle*), bacteriological and chemical warfare make an appearance; in Wells's case, interplanetary warfare is seen. Death rays (called Z rays, K rays, or other catchy names) also appeared before the First World War. They are imagined as bringing down the German zeppelins, at the time one of the most fearsome forms of modern warcraft. In the novels of Aleksei Tolstoi, such rays are used to destroy the moon, among other targets, not because the moon is thought to be of great strategic importance but because its destruction would occasion a great panic from which capitalist speculators would benefit.

Poison gas as a means of mass destruction had been described before 1914, but in World War I it was actually used. Then the effects of a coming gas war became a major topic in countless books and stories in many languages. At that time more rays—heat rays, disintegrator rays, cosmic rays, infrasound rays, and other deadly rays—emanated from the fertile imaginations of science fiction writers. Just before World War I, the character of Dr. Fu Manchu was created. The prototype of the evil scientist bent on world domination, he successfully experimented with deadly and exotic poisons rather than with the commonplace microbes, such as bubonic plague, introduced by earlier writers.

Planetary horror featuring alien invasion and interplanetary warfare were grist for the science fiction writer's mill even before the Second World War. Edmond Hamilton's "Crashing Suns" appeared in 1928, and Jack Williamson's *Space Patrol* novels about a doomsday device called

"AKKA" a few years later. In these books, whole galaxies disappear at the press of a button. (Hamilton was given the affectionate nickname "World Wrecker" and "World Destroyer" for his imagined catastrophes.) In H. G. Wells's *War of the Worlds*, Martians use a destructive ray of sorts. Alfred Noyes's 1940 novel *The Last Man* features the invention of a heart-stopping ray. Not surprisingly, when the the laser beam was invented in 1960, it inspired many new fictional death rays.

Biological terrorism has become quite commonplace in today's horror-science fiction. A few examples are Richard Preston's *Hot Zone* (1994) and *The Cobra Event* (1998). In the first novel, the villain is a mad scientist named Archimedes who uses the Ebola virus in attempts to destroy New York, London, Calcutta, and eventually the whole world. In *The Cobra Event*, the madman works for a small New Jersey biotech company and his methods are both more complicated and more nefarious.

Science fiction writers have been more creative with regard to technology than with the psychology of their heroes and villains. Quite frequently, weapons are used to aid a good cause, such as defending earth against the invasion of evil aliens from other planets. But the mad scientist is typically represented as a villain, simply because of his wish to dominate the world or because of his intrinsic evil. Interestingly, religious belief, the fanaticism of sects that believe in impending doom, seldom, if ever, plays a role. Sometimes, a quasiplausible justification for the desire to dominate the world is proposed, such as a plan to end further destructive world wars. Other times, horrific destruction is seen as a just punishment to a generation who has sinned, deteriorated morally, or succumbed to a blind belief in uncontrolled scientific progress. The question of whether or not life will continue after a general holocaust is occasionally raised. Some writers conjecture that even if life on the face of the earth ceased to exist, it might still continue in the oceans or elsewhere in the cosmos as the result of the migration of survivors to another galaxy.

In view of the great cost of producing weapons of mass destruction, one would think that science fiction writers would imagine these endeavors as being undertaken only by governments with unlimited resources at their disposal. But this has not been the case. In the fictions, the deadly inventions are always made by individuals or small groups of people rather than states. This probably has had more to do with the needs of the literary genre and the market for the stories. Whatever the reason, criminals and small terrorist groups figure far more often than geopolitics in this branch of prophetic literature.

FROM FICTION TO FACT

On March 20, 1995, life imitated art. That morning a Japanese cult called Aum Shinri Kyo (Supreme Truth) placed containers of sarin poison gas on five trains of the Tokyo underground network that converged in the Kasumigaseki station, where many government offices are situated. The attack resulted in 12 dead, 5,500 injured, and, of course, a great deal of chaos. The motives of this attack and the character of the perpetrators will be analyzed later on; in the present context the focus will be on the circumstances and the technical aspects of the incident. The attack took the Japanese police and both local and foreign observers by total surprise. Some in the media first put the blame on a left-wing group, the Japanese Red Army, although it had been defunct for a long time, while others blamed blackmailers and saw the incident as a prelude to extortion. Nor was there any immediate certainty with regard to the nature of the means of destruction; the Japanese police first thought that some binary weapon had been used. It took the police several weeks to narrow their search to the Aum sect, locate its leaders, and seize some of their arsenal, despite the fact that Aum was not a secret organization but one that paraded through the streets of Tokyo—albeit in masks that depicted the face of their guru and leader, Shoko Asahara.

The public had fewer doubts. The deputy leader of the sect, Hideyo Murai, was attacked and fatally knifed in a Tokyo street by an angry resident even before it was determined that the sect was responsible. Gradually a coherent picture emerged: The cult had been in existence for some time, and it had adherents not only in Japan but also in other countries, including Russia. Immediately after the attack and before it had fallen under suspicion, the cult had published an official announcement in which it denied involvement and accused the Japanese government and the United States of launching the attack.

Police searches, however, found tons of dangerous chemicals in warehouses near the Aum training center in the Mount Fuji area; these chemicals could be and had been used for the manufacture of sarin and other poison gases. Several similar and unexplained incidents were recalled that had occurred within the two years prior to the attack, especially one in June 1994 at Matsumoto, a resort west of Tokyo. In this case gas (apparently sarin) had seeped through the windows and doors of an apartment building, killing seven people and injuring 264. Suspicion then fell on a salesman who was thought to have manufactured herbicides in his home. The salesman was later cleared, and the event was thought to be an accident, although some experts continued to believe that the release of the gas had been a deliberate act. There had been other minor occurrences linked to Aum, all involving noxious vapors: aerosols had been found. Threats and anonymous letters referring to coming attacks had been received, even naming the Tokyo underground as the most likely target. But all these signals had been ignored.

The police cannot have been entirely unaware of the threat of a gas attack, for a massive training exercise for police officers in the use of gas masks had taken place a day prior to the Tokyo attack. Also, the day before, a raid had been carried out on the Osaka headquarters of Aum. And a book published earlier in March 1995 by Aum, *Disaster Approaches the Land of the Rising Sun,* mentioned sarin as the weapon of Armageddon. But it was not entirely clear whether the sect regarded itself as a victim of the coming attack or its perpetrator. During late March, April, and early May, police searches and raids continued, in the course of which a great deal of material was found that had been used in the preparation and dissemination of sarin. Several members of the sect made confessions, and on May 20 a warrant was issued for the arrest of the cult's leader, Asahara, and forty of his followers. All of them were subsequently charged with murder and attempted murder.

The investigations also showed that Aum specialists had experimented with a variety of chemical and biological agents. The underground attack left far fewer victims than could have been expected, partly because the chemical substance used, sarin, was not pure and because the means of distribution, polyethylene bags that had been punctured, were primitive and not very effective. Paradoxically, had the terrorists used old-fashioned gases of World War I vintage, the results would have been far more devastating. But it is also true that they would have needed much larger quantities, and they probably feared detection. The operation was a strange mixture of sophistication and primitiveness, of careful planning and rushed improvisation, which in many ways reflected the mind-set of the terrorists. After the arrests, the investigation and the trial went on for a long time; in April 1997, Asahara, in the course of a rambling and incoherent plea, argued that he had asked his followers to call off the attack two days before the event but that they had overruled him. Eventually nine former Aum members received sentences ranging from twenty-two months to seventeen years in prison, and one was acquitted. Though Aum continues to exist even after the trial and enlists new members, according to Japanese authorities it is powerless and no longer constitutes a danger to the country. Although hardly a doomsday event, Aum's attack gave the world a sense of the magnitude of destruction a few lunatics or terrorists can inflict on the public and the ease with which it can be caused.

A BRIEF HISTORY OF CHEMICAL WARFARE

Weapons technology during the twentieth century has caught up with the imaginations of earlier science fiction writers and in some respects exceeded them. The idea of using poison gas against one's enemies occurred first to the Fenians in the 1870s, who intended to spray it in the House of Commons in London. There seem to have been similar plans during the Boer War and the Japanese war with the Russians in 1905, but these did not go beyond an amateurish experimental stage.

Gas was first used on a massive scale in 1915 by the German High Command in the battle of Ypres. The substance used, chlorine gas, came as a total surprise to the Allies. The result was five thousand Allied dead, more injured, and a German breakthrough of four miles. There were two more German gas attacks within the next few days, but they led to no decisive victory. Although the concentration of gas was high and the clouds carried the poisonous substances miles away, only a small sector of the front line was affected, reducing the effectiveness of the gas. The German command, furthermore, failed to follow up the initial panic with a determined advance. Whether it would have been possible to advance into the territory that had been infected with poison gas is not known.

Seen in retrospect, this gas warfare was a failure at the time; the intention had been to put an end to the indecisiveness of trench warfare, and this was not achieved. The first poison-gas attack by the Allies came in Loos, Belgium, five months later. The immediate effects were horrible, as the Germans were as unprepared there as the Allies had been at Ypres. But again there was no decisive breakthrough. Gas subsequently played a considerable role in the battle of Fey-en-Haye, and gas artillery shells were fired in the battle for Verdun in 1916 and in the Battles of the Somme.

In the meantime, the use of phosgene and mixtures of phosgene and chlorine had been introduced into the war; mustard gas, which worked more slowly but produced equally deadly effects, was also used. The clouds of gas could penetrate up to twelve miles behind the front line. But while the psychological impact was enormous, poison gas had no decisive effect in any major battle, even though it is believed to have killed or injured hundreds of thousands of soldiers and civilians. The exact number of gas casualties is not known and will never be; estimates vary between 500,000 and 1.2 million, the lower figure being the more likely. The effects of poison gas were perhaps most devastating when it was used by the Germans against the Russians, east of Warsaw, in 1915. The Russians were unprepared and reportedly lost some 25,000 soldiers in the first attack. But the total number of Russian civilians killed and incapacitated is not known. Some deaths certainly occurred in the factories where gas was produced or where shells were filled with poison gas. Furthermore, civilians were killed and injured in villages and towns near the front line. The great shock of gas warfare is seen in many World War I memoirs. The painful, slow death of a poison-gas victim was never more starkly described than in Roger Martin du Gard's novel *Antoine Thibault.*

In the end, some twenty-five poison gases were used in the First World War. Some, like the chlorine and phosgene gases, were of use only against unprotected troops. The blistering gases, like mustard gas, were somewhat more effective, and had the war continued longer, the British would have used yet another family of gases consisting of arsenic compounds.

The idea that gases might be used in a coming war had occurred to politicians at the Hague peace conference of 1907, and the signatories of the protocols had agreed not to use projectiles diffusing asphyxiating and harmful gases, including tear gas. Poison gas was again banned in the Geneva protocols of 1925, which were signed mainly by the European powers; it was not specified in these documents what sanctions could be taken against the transgressors. The possibility that gas might be released from cylinders on the ground apparently had not occurred to them and was not banned. These protocols notwithstanding, the general public and many military writers took it for granted that poison gas would be used after all, and there was a huge literature describing its horrors. Such literature was not unwarranted. Poison gas was applied by the Italians in Ethiopia in the thirties; according to some estimates, almost one-third of the casualties of the Ethiopians following the Italian invasion were due to poison gas.

All powers prepared themselves for this eventuality to at least some degree. The Germans built gas-producing laboratories in the Soviet Union in accordance with a secret treaty with Moscow. Eventually, the Soviet Union made a great effort to have vaster quantities of poison gas at its disposal than any other power.

Why, then, were poison gases not used in the Second World War? It was certainly not a matter of humanitarian scruples. On a number of occasions the two sides seem to have been close to deploying these weapons. For the Germans, the use of gas would have been more a hindrance than an advantage in the early phase of the war, when their units were advancing rapidly. After 1942 the Allies had air superiority, and if the Germans had used gas they would have been more exposed to retaliation than their enemies. Another important consideration was the German army's use of horses, which could not be effectively protected in a gas attack. There were an insufficient number of horse gas masks, and a gas attack would have effectively immobilized the German artillery. What is more, the German civilian population was quite unprepared for gas attacks. A victim of a gas attack in World War I, Hitler himself had an aversion to the use of gas on the field of battle, though he did consider using gas when the tide of war turned against him. The temptation for the Germans was all the greater because they had gained an important advantage over the Allies in their manufacture of nerve gases, especially tabun and sarin, in the late 1930s. By 1944 the Germans had a huge arsenal of nerve-gas bombs. Several times after Stalingrad, when the Allied troops landed in Normandy, the use of the new gases was considered; Hitler's decision against it was based on the assumption that the Allies were bound to have these gases too, as his experts had told him. These substances had been known about for decades; only the extent of their lethal properties was not known. But the Allies did not have tabun and sarin. When they made their landings on the beaches of France they did not even carry gas masks.

The full extent of German superiority in chemical weaponry became known only after the war. The secret had been kept from the Allies for almost eight years; the Allies were aware of German experiments in nuclear science but were in the dark with regard to tabun and sarin. However, the use of the nerve gases would not have resulted in a German victory; it would probably have led to the use of nuclear bombs against Germany rather than Japan. But the war might have lasted a bit longer. In the end poison gases were used by the German leadership only against civilians, in the extermination camps of Eastern Europe—mainly against Jewish civilians—and also, to a lesser degree, against Soviet prisoners of war and others.

Since World War II, poison gas has been used mainly in the Middle East, specifically by Iraq against Iran. Mustard gas was employed in August 1983 at Haj Umran, and a year later, at Al Basra, when the Iraqis were on the defensive in a war they had provoked, they again used nerve gases. In 1985 and 1986, at Um Rashrash, Hawiza marsh, and elsewhere, thousands of Iranian soldiers were reportedly killed as the result of gas attacks. Saddam Hussein used poison gas against the Kurds at Panjwin and in March 1987 at Halabjah. In the 1980s, tabun was Saddam Hussein's weapon of choice. Gas was also reported to have been used by Nasser's Egypt during its military expedition in Yemen and possibly on a few other occasions.

The poisons originally used were chlorine and mustard gases, which affect the eyes, the upper and lower respiratory tract, and the skin. Although these gases are highly toxic, extremely painful, and often deadly, their effect was not immediate, whereas the substances discovered after World War I, such as sarin, GB, and VX, can cause instantaneous death. (The G family of gases enters the human organism by way of the respiratory tract; the V family penetrates through the skin.). The toxicity of the nerve gases manufactured during and after World War II was infinitely greater than that of their predecessors.

CHEMICAL WEAPONRY TODAY

In contrast to biological warfare, chemical warfare has already been waged on a massive scale. If there are in theory many thousands of biological agents that terrorists could use, there are probably even more poisonous chemical substances. Most chemical agents are not gases but liquids dispensed in droplets. They can be divided according to their chemical composition. Among the old, "classic" poisons, which appeared in the earliest detective novels, are Prussic acid, arsenic, and strychnine. Choking agents were used in World War I, including chlorine and phosgene, which cause pulmonary edema. The blistering agents used in that war were mustard gas, lewisite, and others that cause chemical burns and destroy lung tissue. Hydrogen cyanide and cyanogen chloride attack the respiratory system and result rapidly in coma and death. The nerve gases tabun, sarin, soman, and VX affect the neuromuscular system. They block the enzyme cholinesterase, causing paralysis of the neuromuscular system and thus death. Tabun and sarin are organophosphates, discovered in Germany as a byproduct of the search for new insecticides. Even more poisonous are the gases of the V (VX) series that penetrate the skin as well as the respiratory tract and bring about respiratory failure and death within a very short time. Also worth mentioning are LSD and other hallucinogenic agents, although they are not among the most likely agents to be used by terrorists at present.

Most of these chemical substances have a legitimate use. Arsenic and strychnine in small doses were once used for medical purposes. Eserin, one of the first of the nerve gases, was originally used as a drug against glaucoma. Some of the substances are insecticides, others are used in the pharmaceutical industry, and still others are compounds employed as cleaning agents, herbicides, or rodenticides. Therefore, many are available commercially. They can be stolen not only from military installations but from civilian laboratories; one writer has noted that truckloads of the insecticide parathion are on the roads every day. The quantities stored by both the armed forces and industry are so large that sizable amounts could easily go unaccounted for.

If terrorists want, they can manufacture potent chemical poisons from such substances as isopropyl alcohol, which is readily available, or from various pesticides and herbicides. Experts agree that the technical knowledge and experience needed to produce a chemical weapon is less than that required for manufacturing a biological weapon, probably on the level of a moderately conscientious graduate student. Some substances and compounds are, of course, more difficult to produce than others, but there is no reason to assume that a terrorist will choose the most complicated rather than the least sophisticated weapon. Experts also agree that virtually all the materials and equipment can be bought commercially, but there is no unanimity as to whether one chemist would be sufficient for an operation of this kind.

It is generally assumed that the real difficulty in waging chemical warfare is not the manufacture or acquisition of the poison but its dissemination. This refers to both volatile and nonvolatile agents. Vapors are affected by the direction of the wind as well as the temperature of the air. Nerve gases quickly hydrolize in water and are therefore not suitable for poisoning water reservoirs. Dispersal by means of an aerosol always involves a high loss of toxicity. While in laboratory conditions a few milligrams might be sufficient to kill several thousand human beings, experts believe that tons of poison would be needed in the open air or in water because there are always biological activities that diminish the toxicity of the agent. Thus, it was not an accident that the Japanese terrorists chose an enclosed space and preferred sarin, which is less volatile, to more toxic agents.

There are other ways of disseminating chemicals, such as by firing a mortar or artillery shell (an unlikely means to be chosen by a terrorist group) or crashing a van or a truck loaded with chemical substances against a building. But all of these involve many uncertainties, and though they might succeed in the case of a single building or enclosed space, it would become progressively more difficult to repeat the act in the future because of far greater police and public awareness.

Past threats or actual attempts to use chemical weapons have been made in several countries: by terrorists of the extreme right, by animal-liberation militants, by Tamil separatists on several occasions, by Palestinian terrorists, by the Alphabet bomber, by Minutemen, by Russian (or rather, ex-Soviet) extortionists, and by an ex–Stasi agent. Other incidents have been reported in Italy, the Philippines, Chile, Iraq, Tadzhikistan, Turkey, the United Kingdom, and at least a dozen other countries. A closer examination of these attempts reveals no evidence that the makers of the threats had, in fact, amounts of chemical agents sufficient to carry them out, and that most of the attempts themselves were amateurish. However, the fear of poison is great and the panic caused by an attack of this kind is bound to be enormous. It might cause more psychological than physical havoc. Even the authors of books on gas warfare in the 1930s warned that an enemy would launch such an attack mainly because of its devastating psychological impact.

A BRIEF HISTORY OF BIOLOGICAL WARFARE

The history of biological warfare goes back much further than the use of poison gases, but the biological agents that threaten us today are of recent invention. The great plague of the fourteenth century, which is said to have killed about one-third of the population of Europe, was allegedly spread by the Tartars besieging the fortress of Caffa in the Crimea. The Tartars catapulted plague-infected corpses into the fortress; according to reports, ships from Genoa carried the disease to northern Italy and the rest of Europe.

Another oft-cited example of early biological warfare occurred during the Indian wars in North America in the 1760s. It seems certain that local British commanders planned to give the Indians, as a peace offering, blankets from military hospitals that had been infected by smallpox. A smallpox epidemic did break out among the Indians of Pennsylvania, but it is not certain whether the blankets played any role in its spread.

During the First World War, Germans were charged with trying to spread cholera bacilli in Italy, the plague in St. Petersburg, and anthrax in Mesopotamia and Rumania, intending to kill cattle and horses. There were unconfirmed reports about all kinds of exotic biological agents being transmitted to other countries by such unlikely means as the ink containers of fountain pens. In Silver Spring, a Washington, D.C., suburb, a small German laboratory headed by one Dr. Anton Dilger produced a liter of anthrax and glanders (*Pseudomonas gladei*) intended to infect horses and mules that were to be shipped from Baltimore to the western front in Europe. The original seed culture had allegedly been supplied from Berlin. While these early attempts to engage in biological warfare were unsuccessful, research and stockpiling continued after the end of the First World War.

All major nations engaged in these preparations, but only the Japanese actually carried out biological warfare, dropping plague-infested fleas and grain over Chinese cities after the invasion of 1937. In the mid-1930s, a special biological-warfare unit called 731 was established under a General Ishi in Manchuria. Many biological agents were produced in the laboratories of this unit, including plague, smallpox, typhus, and gas gangrene. In tests on Chinese prisoners of war and civilians, about ten thousand people were killed. Toward the end of the war the production of these agents was stepped up; hundreds of millions of plague-infested fleas were bred and scheduled to be dropped over American airfields. In the end the order to use biological weapons against the Americans was not given, in part because an American submarine sunk the ship carrying key members of unit 731 in the Pacific. While the biological agents used by the Japanese were among the most toxic known, the means of spreading them were primitive; aerosols did not yet exist.

Whether and where biological agents were used after World War II is a matter of some dispute, but there is no doubt that all major powers and some smaller countries engaged in research and built up their stockpiles. Iraq under Saddam Hussein has been particularly active in this respect. The installations established in Iraq were far bigger and more advanced than outsiders had assumed. They had been built up within a short period, about five years, with the help of various European firms, and it proved easy to hide them. Even UNSCOM, the United Nations investigation committee that tried to locate them after Iraq's defeat in 1991, discovered only a small part. Had it not been for the defection in August 1995 of Husain Kamal, Saddam Hussein's son-in-law, who brought with him many documents, the number of laboratories found would have been only a tiny percentage of the total. If the Iraqi dictator eventually decided not to use these weapons, the reason seems to have been that retaliation would be swift and devastating.

Iraq, however, was not the only country in the Middle East to build up such weapons. Iran, Syria, and, above all, Libya were reported to have followed Baghdad's example. Altogether up to fifteeen countries in the Middle East and Asia developed these weapons, and the number of countries that had missiles with which to deliver them was even larger. Libya attracted the most attention, owing to the erratic behavior of Colonel Khadafi. With the help of German, Swiss, and other biological firms, large underground laboratories were built at Tarhuna and Rabta. These could be transformed within less than twenty-four hours from weapons factories into innocuous-looking pharmaceutical laboratories. Some foreign delegations were invited to inspect them, and a few even believed the official version put out by Tripoli. But parliamentary delegations do not normally include experts carrying detection equipment.

The Middle East countries are hardly alone in their production of these weapons. According to the U.S. State Department, "yellow rain," an agent difficult to classify but belonging to the general family of the mycotoxins, was applied in Laos, Kampuchea, and Afghanistan by Communist forces. Some five hundred instances of its use were documented and the number of fatalities was alleged to be in the thousands, but there have been doubts expressed at the time by some American scientists with regard to the use of this specific agent.

There was no doubt, however, about assassination attempts carried out by the KGB using biological agents. In the 1970s, sophisticated agents called ricin were employed against two Bulgarian émigrés, Georgi Markov in London and Vladimir Kostov in Paris. Markov was stabbed with the tip of an umbrella and killed. In Kostov's case, the pellet did not penetrate the skin and he lived to tell the story. During the *glasnost* period there was access to some KGB sources, and more details became known about its laboratories; the poisons that had been developed there had been employed not only against foreign enemies but also against Soviet citizens.

Accidents occurred in the germ-warfare installations, the most famous of which was the anthrax epidemic at Sverdlovsk, in the Urals, in April 1979. The details were kept secret by the Soviets, which was not difficult because Sverdlovsk was a city closed to foreigners. According to the assessment by American intelligence, a huge airborne (aerosol) release of anthrax spores used for bacteriological warfare resulted in many fatalities. But according to the initial Soviet version, some careless workers had thrown anthrax-infected meat on garbage heaps, causing the outbreak. The Soviet version seemed plausible, but because of the secrecy surrounding it—for five years the Russians had denied the accident altogether—the official version was not widely believed, even inside the Soviet Union. Under *glasnost* it became known that the initial Western suspicions were correct and that, furthermore, there had been several other minor such accidents that had not become known at all.

THE FUTURE OF GERM WARFARE

For decades interest in biological warfare has grown because it is thought to be the most cost-effective method to kill or incapacitate people. In war many shells and bullets are expended, often without killing or disabling a single human being. Even during World War I gas was far more efficient than bullets, and today the botulinum toxin is a thousand times more toxic than sarin, one of the most deadly of the early nerve gases. It is cheaper to produce, and little sophisticated knowledge is needed to manufacture it. Colin Powell, former U.S. Chief of Staff, said in 1993, "The one that frightens me to death, perhaps even more so than tactical nuclear weapons, and the one we have the least capability against, is biological weapons." Other political and military leaders have expressed similar fears in recent years.

Americans, British, Russians, and Japanese have been working since the late 1930s on biological arms, yet they remain one of the least predictable of all weapons. They could continue to be unpredictable or they could become one of the most deadly weapons of all. Epidemics throughout history in Europe, Asia, and the Americas have killed many more people than wars, and diseases of a new kind might become the weapon of choice of a new genus of terrorists.

Scientists and science fiction writers have presented a great many scenarios of biological warfare, all of them frightening. Consider these: According to a study published in 1972, an anthrax spore aerosol attack on New York could result in 600,000 deaths. According to a 1980 study, spreading one ounce of anthrax spores, which are far more deadly than the botulinum toxin, in a domed stadium could infect 60,000 to 80,000 people within an hour. Another scenario concerns threats to major water reservoirs. Research shows that only a pound or two of *Salmonella typhi* or botulinum toxin would be required to effect the same horrid result as ten tons of potassium cyanide. Anthrax is also frequently mentioned as a contaminant. Both anthrax and botulinum cause respiratory failure as well as external and internal bleeding within one to three days, and are usually fatal.

Other agents reportedly explored for military purposes are *Yersinia pestis*, which causes the bubonic plague, and tropical diseases such as Ebola, a highly contagious virus that leads within two or three days to bleeding, convulsions, and death. In principle, many agents of human and animal disease could be possible weapons. The list of potential agents is long, ranging from smallpox and psittacosis (parrot fever) to old diseases such as tuberculosis and pneumococci, which were once believed conquered but new strains of which have developed that are resistant to antibiotics and immunization. New diseases with possible appeal to terrorists have recently appeared, such as Lassa fever, which is spread by wild rodents in West Africa, Legionellosis (Legionnaire's disease), and fatal toxic septicemia (flesh-eating bacteria).

Nor can diseases affecting animals be excluded: Ebola fever appeared first as a disease affecting apes, and Creutzfeldt-Jakob disease, or mad cow disease, first appeared in cattle. The fact that a disease is seldom, if ever, fatal does not necessarily mean that terrorists in search of biological-warfare agents won't use it. Severe forms of conjunctivitis, to choose but one example, may effectively disable its victims. Whereas the military would hardly be interested in the application of a disease such as leprosy or AIDS because the incubation period is measured in years rather than months, this consideration may not be relevant to a small group of fanatics. Even diseases for which there are treatments might be used by those interested primarily in causing a panic rather than a pandemic.

Biological arms have a few well-known advantages over other weapons. They are easy to produce, and difficult to detect, once created. They are cheap and likely to cause not only human fatalities but economic damage by ruining crops. And they are as likely to cause as much panic as a gas attack. How easy is it to acquire a biological-weapons capability? On this issue expert opinions diverge. Some experts have maintained that biological agents can be produced in a garage, a toolroom, or a kitchen. The ease of making a biological weapon can be compared to that of brewing beer. According to one author, preparing the growth medium for bacteria is not more complicated than preparing Jell-O. Experts believe an amateur or a second-or third-year biology student could easily obtain the knowledge needed to create lethal weapons. Others, however, believe that those who want to engage in even the most primitive level of biological warfare must have the equivalent of a graduate science degree, and others believe even greater education is necessary. An individual would need knowledge and experience not only in microbiology and aerosol physics but three or four other fields as well, so it is more likely that a small group of experts would be needed. One expert believes that at least five specialists, including a pathologist and a pharmacologist, are needed. These experts also tend to dismiss the "kitchen table" argument and believe that access to a bacteriological laboratory is crucial. There are similar differences in estimates concerning the cost of such a venture, ranging from a few thousand to a few million dollars.

While a small crew working with primitive tools might produce bacteria of one form or another, dissemination of the weapon could present insurmountable obstacles. Unlike a scientist, the terrorist need not engage in experimental animal tests to check the toxicity of his agents. On the other hand, it is difficult to imagine from a practical point of view how best to utilize a weapon that has not been tested.

Which are the most likely biological agents to be used in the future? Various lists have been published over the years, including ones identifying agents combining the greatest toxicity with ease of production (or acquisition), cultivation, hardiness, immunity to detection and countermeasures, and rapidity of effect. According to estimates published in 1997 in the *Journal of the American Medical Association,* rift valley fever and tick-borne encephalitis, assuming a downwind reach of one kilometer, could cause between 400 and 9,500 fatalities and incapacitate approximately 35,000 people. Typhus and brucellosis, with a downwind reach of

5–10 kilometers, could kill up to to 19,000 people and affect 85,000 to 125,000 more. Most deadly are tularemia and anthrax, which, with a downwind reach of about 20 kilometers, might kill 30,000 to 95,000 and incapacitate 125,000.

Experts believe that bacterial rather than viral agents are more likely to be chosen because viruses are difficult to cultivate and more perishable. In a list by Berkowitz published in 1972, eight bacterial agents are most likely to appeal: anthrax, brucellosis, coccidioidomycosis, cryptococcosis, pneumonic plague, psittacosis, Rocky Mountain spotted fever, and tularemia. According to Berkowitz, plague and psittacosis can cause epidemics, and anthrax, plague, and Rocky Mountain spotted fever are highly lethal. Some of the bacilli are common, others less so, but all are highly infectious.

In a list compiled by Wayman Mullins published in 1992, *escherichia coli*, hemophilus influenzae, malaria, cholera, *Yersina pesti,* typhoid, bubonic plague, cobra venom, and shellfish toxin are also potential candidates for use in biological warfare. Coccidioidomycosis, Rocky Mountain spotted fever, and pneumonic plague were dropped from this list, possibly because these diseases are now treatable. Rocky Mountain spotted fever is seldom fatal and can be controlled by tetracycline. For the pneumonic plague, streptomycin or gentamycin are both quite effective if used early. Tetracycline and chloramphenicol are also effective against typhoid fever. There are cures for illness caused by most of the other epidemic agents if treatment is given early.

The U.S. Congress Office of Technology Assessment lists eight biological agents most likely to be used as weapons: anthrax, tularemia, *Yersina pestis, Shigella flexneri* (which causes a bacillary dysentery), another shigella, various salmonella species, botulinum, and staphylococcus enterotoxin B. This list seems to be based on the assumption that terrorists would decide to contaminate drinking water and food supplies. Other authors have mentioned ricin as a likely terrorist agent of choice. Ricin, which can be extracted from the castor bean, is highly toxic, but far less so than botulinal toxin, and probably more difficult to spread. It has, however, been successfully used in the assassination of individuals.

Even smallpox, a highly infectious and lethal disease that has been extinct for more than twenty years, might be used for offensive military or terrorist purposes, since considerable stockpiles of smallpox vaccine exist.

The most recent and authoritative list of possible biological agents is that published in the *Journal of the American Medical Association* in 1997. This list was based on biological agents that have already been made into weapons, not merely on theoretical considerations. Anthrax and botulinum figure prominently in this list; both were weaponized by Iraq and presumably by other countries. Brucellosis, plague, Q fever, tularemia, smallpox, viral encephalitis, viral hemorrhagic fever (which includes a whole group of tropical diseases, such as Lassa fever), and staphylococcal enterotoxin B are also on this list. Anthrax is the only agent that appears on every list; there are differences of opinion about the others.[1]

To prepare a biological weapon, one needs a seed culture that can be obtained from the natural environment. This is the most secure way, but also the one that demands the most skill. The agent, be it anthrax, botulism, or one of the others, has to be identified, isolated, and cultivated, processes that require considerable knowledge and experience. There are, however, other ways to obtain seed cultures. They can be stolen from laboratories, bought on the black market, gained under false pretenses, or even commissioned by mail order. Civilian laboratories are not well guarded, nor are military installations impregnable. Commercial firms offer specimen cultures for a few dollars, and they rarely check whether those placing an order are acquiring it for a legitimate use.[2] Lastly, those eager to engage in biological terrorism could obtain seed cultures from states supporting terrorist groups.

There has not yet been a single successful biological-weapons attack by terrorists. Most have been undertaken by blackmailers or people with a grudge rather than political terrorists or religious fanatics. However, there is evidence that terrorist groups of all stripes have shown interest in this new form of warfare. A Russian microbiologist, Viktor Pasechnik, who defected to the West at a scientific congress in London in 1989, reported that Russia, in contravention of the 1972 Biological Convention,

1 The literature on biological and chemical weapons of mass destruction is huge and highly technical. It is impossible to cover it all in this book. The most important studies are mentioned in the bibliography. I am particularly grateful to Jessica Stern for having shared with me the substance of her book *Risk and Dread: Preempting the New Terrorists* (Cambridge, Massachusetts, 1999) before publication. Her study deals with the technical aspects of the issues involved in far greater detail. An agency of the U.S. Department of Defense published in February 1998 the most authoritative collection of facts and figures so far available about Iraqi weapons of mass destruction, titled "Iraqi Weapons of Mass Destruction Programs." An exhaustive historical survey of the illicit use of biological agents in the twentieth century is provided by Seth Carus in "Bioterrorism and Biocrimes," National Defense University, August 1998.

2 The first such recorded use occurred before World War I. The details emerged in the trial in 1914 of Hans Hopf, who poisoned several family members in Frankfurt, Germany. He had ordered the cultures he needed from a laboratory in Vienna. W. Seth Carus, *Bioterrorism and Biocrimes: The Illicit Use of Biological Agents in the 20th Century* (National Defense University, 1998).

had continued to engage in such research, including work on a biologically engineered dry form of superplague. The Russians had also discussed providing terrorist groups with biological-warfare agents. According to official Soviet spokesmen, biological-warfare work continued up to 1992, but after the defection of Pasechnik and Ken Alibek, the latter a highly placed Russian official in the biological-weapons program, there were strong Western protests, which apparently led to a sizable reduction in the production of biological weapons, though probably not its cessation.

In the 1990s the Russians have developed new and very dangerous strains of biological agents (including a new form of anthrax and one of the Marburg virus). It has also become apparent that the United States, having stuck to the treaty banning these weapons, does not know how to cope with the agents. It is fairly certain that some of the scientists who participated in this Russian program and still eager to make use of their know-how have found their way to countries in the Middle East and Asia.

Threats to use biological-warfare agents have been reported from the Arab world, the Baader Meinhof gang in Germany, British Columbia, Queensland (Australia), Great Britain, and the United States, but in no case has it been proven that those threatening attacks had such agents in their possession. Media reports that terrorists were trying to obtain biological agents and were training specialists in this field have also come from the United States, Canada, Germany, the Arab world, and other countries. Several of these reports concerned a Rockville, Maryland, laboratory where telephone orders for botulinal toxin were received. Some of the reports were denied by the authorities; others were not.

In the 1980s, in a safe house of the Red Army faction in Paris, quantities of botulinal toxin were found, and in another safe house in Germany were found considerable quantities of organophosphorous compounds from which nerve gases are made. Mustard gas was stolen from a U.S. installation in Stuttgart, Germany, apparently by Baader Meinhof followers, and earlier there was an attempt by the Weather Underground to steal biological agents from a U.S. Army laboratory in Fort Derrick, Maryland.

In more than a few cases, lone individuals have posed a threat. In 1995, a man was arrested in Little Rock, Arkansas, charged with trying to bring 130 grams of ricin into Canada. He also carried $89,000 in cash, four guns, and 20,000 rounds of ammunition. According to his lawyer, the individual in question needed the ricin to kill coyotes threatening his chickens. The prosecutor commented that this was tantamount to claiming that a thermonuclear device was needed to protect one's home against burglary. There have been dozens of similar cases in which toxins were acquired and arrests made, and it stands to reason that there have been others which never came to light. The same is probably true of the purchase or theft of seed cultures. Among those who have been apprehended and arrested are extreme rightists who possessed ricin.

There was a successful small-scale attack in Oregon, where members of a religious cult (former members of Bhagwan Shree Rajneesh's group) contaminated salad bars with *Salmonella typhi*, poisoning some 750 people. Ma Anand Sheela, one of the principal aides of Rajneesh, was arrested on charges of attempted murder and assault.

The attractions of biological weapons are obvious: easy access, low cost, toxicity, and the panic they can cause. But there are drawbacks of various kinds that explain why almost no successful attacks have occurred. While explosive or nuclear devices or even chemical agents, however horrific, affect a definite space, biological agents are unpredictable: they can easily get out of control, backfire, or have no effect at all. They constitute a high risk to the attackers, although the same, of course, is true of chemical weapons. This consideration may not dissuade people willing to sacrifice their own lives, but the possibility that the attacker may kill himself before being able to launch an attack may make him hesitate to carry it out.

Biological agents, with some notable exceptions, are affected by changes in heat or cold, and, like chemical agents, by changes in the direction of the wind. They have a limited life span, and their means of delivery are usually complicated. The process of contaminating water reservoirs or foodstuffs involves serious technical problems. Even if an agent survives the various purification systems in water reservoirs, boiling the water would destroy most germs. Dispersing the agent as a vapor or via an aerosol system within a closed space—for instance, through the air-conditioning system of a big building or in a subway—would appear to offer better chances of success, but it is by no means foolproof.

There are well-known defenses against biological weapons, ranging from immunization, to gas masks and other protective clothing, to de-contamination processes. Antibiotics are effective against many bacteria if applied soon after infection; and there are also various antifungal medicines. Although not much progress has been made so far in the field of early detection, research in this area is under way. At the same time, researchers may be creating new strains of genetically engineered germs that are able to resist drug therapy. According to Dr. Joshua Lederberg, a Nobel prize–winning scientist, at the present time, there is no technical defense against biological weapons, only an ethical solution. But as Lederberg asked, Would an ethical solution deter a sociopath?

There are also political considerations that argue against the use of biological weapons. Weapons of mass destruction will not appeal to terrorists pursuing clear political aims, especially if friends might be among the victims. A biological weapon launched by terrorists in Northern Ireland would affect Catholics as well as Protestants; in India, it would affect Hindus as well as Muslims; in Israel, Arabs as well as Jews; in Spain, Basques as well as Spaniards. Ecoterrorists cannot be sure that a certain agent will wipe out only human beings, leaving animals and plants unaffected. But the most obvious political reason biological terrorism is risky is that it could produce an enormous backlash against those who perpetrated the attack. Another consideration is psychological in character: Most terrorists need the demonstration effect—that is, showy attacks producing a great deal of noise. A biological campaign would be silent.

Only the most extreme and least rational terrorist groups, or those motivated not by distinct political aims but by apocalyptic visions or by some pan-destructionist belief, are likely to employ weapons of this kind. This may reduce the risk that biological weapons will be used, but it does not rule it out.

THE NUCLEAR THREAT

The great fear of the post–Second World War years was of nuclear weapons. After the detonation of nuclear bombs over Hiroshima and Nagasaki, people were understandably anxious about what would happen if weapons somehow found their way into the hands of terrorists.

But the fear was not limited to the use of weapons like those employed at the end of World War II. A 1996 study called "Proliferation: Threat and Response," prepared by the Office of the American Secretary of Defense, said: "Mixed isotope plutonium (reactor-grade material) can be used in nuclear weapons; such a device would be less efficient and might have a less predictable yield. A weapon using non–weapon grade plutonium was successfully detonated in the 1960 test. Another alternative would be a radiological weapon that employed conventional explosives, or other means to scatter radioactive material. Such a weapon would not produce a nuclear yield; however, it could spread contamination. While such weapons would have less military significance than devices that result in nuclear detonations, radiological weapons have enormous potential for intimidation. Targeting a nuclear reactor in an antagonist's territory to produce an accident releasing nuclear material would be another option."

Fears were further fueled by accidents or near accidents at nuclear reactors, culminating with the meltdown at Chernobyl, and by the emergence of a black market in nuclear materials. There is good cause to fear because proliferation continues, and successful work is being done on nuclear devices in many states, some of which either openly or surreptitiously support terrorist groups.

After World War II, the fear of atomic war dominated the public consciousness in America and Western Europe, although it seemed less of a threat to Eastern Europeans and hardly bothered the Third World. As early as 1951, Hollywood produced a film titled *Fire* about life after an atomic holocaust. This was followed by works of fiction such as Nevil Shute's *On the Beach* (1957), Walter Miller's *Canticle for Leibowitz* (1959), Mordecai Roshwald's *Fail Safe* and *Level 7*, and, best remembered, Stanley Kubrick's 1964 film *Dr. Strangelove*.

After 1975, the number of movies and novels on this subject declined, partly because the public's interest had been satiated. But the idea that nuclear weapons could fall into the wrong hands, whether of rogue states or terrorists, continued to preoccupy the experts. The number of specialized papers on the subject and consideration of various nuclear scenarios grew from year to year in Washington and the military academies. Nuclear proliferation, the experts argued, was apparently unstoppable, particularly as popular magazines, and more recently the Internet, began to provide reliable information on how to produce nuclear devices cheaply in a nonlaboratory setting.

This information leads the reader step by step through the process of becoming an atom bomb designer. First, weapons-grade uranium must be acquired. Then one has to decide on the type of bomb to be made, preferably a small plutonium device, for which at least 2.5 kilos of plutonium is needed. Next the bomb's core has to be assembled, which entails putting a sphere of compacted plutonium oxide crystals in the center of a large cube of Semtex (one of the newer, more powerful explosives). The finished product will weigh about a ton and, in the absence of an aircraft or a missile powerful enough to deliver the bomb, will need a van or a truck to get to the target. All these steps, though intricate, do not in theory present insurmountable difficulties for determined amateurs with a little knowledge of nuclear physics and access to the literature available in many public libraries. The greatest challenge to making a bomb has always been the means to obtain uranium or plutonium.

At the same time that knowledge about how to make nuclear weapons has spread, however, the nuclear industry has grown. The number of reactors worldwide has increased, as have strategic and tactical nuclear weapons themselves, which are stored in a variety of places, with uranium and plutonium constantly in transit. Gradually a nuclear black market has come into being. What had initially been an American-Soviet issue has over the years became a global problem.

The issue of nuclear proliferation has been discussed ever since the first nuclear bomb was exploded. So far only governments have had the resources to produce nuclear devices and the planes and rockets to deliver them. However, nuclear terrorism has never been ruled out, and, indeed, acts of nuclear sabotage, by radical ecologists albeit on a minor scale, took place during the 1970s and '80s. One of the first occurred in 1973 when a commando from a left-wing Argentinian group, the ERP, entered the construction site of the Atucha atomic power station north of Buenos Aires. In 1976, bombs were thrown at an atomic power plant in Britanny, France, but the nuclear reactor was not damaged. During the following years, several attacks against the Lemoniz nuclear power station near Bilbao, Spain, were undertaken by the ETA, the Basque separatist organization. These attacks, and threats of further attacks, were also supported by Spanish radical ecologists who wanted the stations removed. Other attacks were directed against plants near San Sebastian, Pamplona, Tafalla, Beriz, and other sites in northern Spain. They included the murder of the head of the Lemoniz plant and the abduction of its chief engineer. In 1979, a nuclear instruments factory near Santander in northern Spain was attacked. Though there is no evidence that the attack was intended to bring about an explosion or massive contamination (the main victims of such an event would have been the Basques themselves), it is still possible that a major accident might have occurred as a result of mishap or the ignorance of the attackers.

In 1982, the terrorist wing of the African National Congress (ANC) sabotaged two South African nuclear plants, causing substantial damage. Both nuclear reactors were damaged, but since they were not operational at the time there was no emission of radiation. Most other such incidents have involved either individuals of uncertain motivation or have been directed against factories supplying machinery for nuclear installations, as has happened in Canada, Belgium, Holland, and Italy. In 1985, Philippine terrorists blew up the transmission cables of the country's first nuclear plant. It is impossible to speculate on the potential damage had any of these actions generated a major accident, but the accident at Chernobyl offers us clues.

What if a home-produced or stolen nuclear device did explode? A ten- to fifteen-kiloton device strategically placed in a major city would devastate several square miles and could cause 30,000 to 100,000 casualties. A thermonuclear device of greater size could devastate an area twenty times as large and the number of victims would be correspondingly larger. The bombing or sabotage of a civilian reactor might cause relatively little direct damage, provided it is located far from major cities; the ecological damage, on the other hand, would be great and lasting. But in view of the fact that so many reactors now exist around the globe, that many of them are located in or near major cities, and that radiological materials are also stored in laboratories and hospitals, even a small amount of radiological contamination could have major consequences.

For a long time public and specialist concern was focused on the danger of a nuclear device being used by a rogue state or terrorist group. Only more recently has attention been given to possibilities that do not involve fissionable radioactive materials, such as uranium and plutonium, but nonfissionable radioactive materials, such as cesium 137, strontium, and cobalt-60. Weapons using these materials could be exploded by conventional means, and though they would not cause as many fatalities as a nuclear device, they could lead to disruptions in the physical infrastructure of a locality—by contaminating water supplies and other essential facilities.

In a statement in March 1996, John M. Deutch, director of the CIA, mentioned that during the war in Chechnya, Chechen leaders threatened to turn Moscow into a desert by using radioactive waste. To make the threat more credible, the police were directed by anonymous callers to a container in a Moscow park in which cesium 137 was hidden. The quantities discovered were small and could not have done much harm, but it stands to reason that if the Chechen rebels had access to radioactive materials widely used for medical and industrial purposes, other terrorists could obtain greater quantities and use them if they so desired.

Though the danger of a nuclear attack by a hostile country or a terrorist group has figured prominently in the public consciousness and expert commentary, after more than fifty years of books, movies, and war games, the horrible event has not yet come to pass. It is not surprising, then, that there is now a belief among some experts that nuclear terrorism has been an overrated nightmare.

Belittlers of the threat argue as follows: In the past, threats of nuclear terrorism have almost always come from mentally disturbed people and the occasional criminal blackmailer who, it turned out, was bluffing. Real terrorists—that is to say, those pursuing political aims—are more interested in publicity than in a great number of victims. Furthermore, the use of the weapons of superviolence could likely lead to estrangement between the nuclear terrorists and their sympathizers, who might abhor mass murder.

Furthermore, it has been widely assumed that since the design of atomic bombs was more or less in the public domain, it was only a matter of time until the terrorists would build their own. But they have not. Critics point to the fact that even sovereign states with substantial resources at their disposal have failed to construct nuclear devices. After twenty years of trying and the outlay of more than a billion dollars, Iraq had not produced a single nuclear device by the time the Gulf War broke out. This may have been the result of the destruction by the Israelis of their main reactor, which set their progam back years. Also, critics doubt that even governments that sponsor terrorism would give nuclear devices to their surrogates, because these sorcerer's apprentices might get out of control and even turn against their patrons. Critics believe it is unlikely that terrorists could steal a nuclear weapon—from the former Soviet Union—for instance, and even if they succeeded, they might not be able to detonate it. These and other reasons have led skeptics to doubt that nuclear terrorism is a real threat at the present time.

During the Cold War, the threat of nuclear war was perhaps exaggerated in Europe, even more so than in America. Now that the Cold War has ended, the tendency to doubt a continuing threat is perfectly understandable. The fact that so many years have passed since Hiroshima and Nagasaki without any nuclear attacks also has influenced thinking on the matter. It seems likely that if there is a nuclear incident in the years to come, it will occur in the context of a regional war or as the result of a Chernobyl-like accident a rather than in the form of a terrorist attack. It is also true, as the critics argue, that sovereign states, however aggressive, will not easily give up control over their nuclear material or nuclear weapons.

But it is by no means certain that this reasoning is foolproof. There could always be an exception or two—for example, governments desperate and reckless enough to accept the risks. Furthermore, global nuclear proliferation has continued, and with the breakdown of the Soviet Union, the large of amounts of nuclear material that exist there could attract smugglers if the price is right. A large-scale sophisticated nuclear program is expensive, but countries who really wanted the nuclear bomb have acquired it, and others are sure to follow. Iraq in its war against Iran is a good example of a state that, had it possessed nuclear weapons, might well have used them. The situation in the Indian subcontinent is similar. Almost any country, forced to choose between defeat and the use of nuclear weapons, might just opt for the latter.

CYBERTERRORISM

The computer age has opened up possibilities for terrorists that did not exist before, even in the realm of dreams. Just as it has brought about a revolution in military planning and preparation, it has given birth to information terrorism, or cyberterrorism, which, although it doesn't resemble the other means of destruction we have been discussing in the sense of causing immediate and immense death and destruction, should be taken seriously.

If only because of the new ways to disseminate of information, the computer age has given new cause for concern. Manuals teaching computer intrusion are freely available on the Internet, and the same is true with respect to how-to manuals: everything from how to build an atomic bomb to how to make chlorine bombs, from how to generate electronic terror to how to construct letter bombs, from how to have fun with nitro to how to have fun with rockets, from how to build flamethrowers to the best ways to destroy entire telecommunication networks, and countless other ways to cause havoc. Anarchy toys and anti-modem weapons are included in these libraries of hacking and phreaking, to use the computer jargon. The Internet also carries a considerable amount of terrorist propaganda, more, perhaps, of the extreme right than of any other part of the political or religious spectrum. These descriptions and propaganda are not illegal, at least not in the United States, and they do not constitute, in principle, anything radically new, because similar material has always been available, though not as readily, in brochures and books. What makes cyberterrorism different is the ease with which an immense amount of damage can now be inflicted on the technological infrastructure of a political entity from a great distance and by a very few people at low personal risk.

Technological developments have given rise to much soul-searching about the digitized battlefield of the future, about smarter crime in the twenty-first century, and about the magnitude of data theft and destruction. The last has already occurred, and will continue to occur as hostile hackers attempt to wreck the electronic infrastructure. It has gradually dawned on the main users of the information systems that defense against hackers, whether of the terrorist variety or not, is difficult and in many cases even impossible. CIA Director John Deutch said in June 1996 that an "electronic Pearl Harbor" was a possibility and that hackers had offered their services to Iran, Iraq, and Libya with plans to break into American computers to gain information and to sabotage.

The main weapons in this new kind of warfare are computer viruses, programmed to damage software; logic bombs, set to detonate at a certain time and destroy or rewrite data; and HERF (high-energy radio frequency) guns that disable electronic targets through high-power radio signals. A suitcase-size device can generate high-powered electromagnetic impulses affecting all electronic components in the vicinity. Computer viruses can shut down entire computer systems through self-replication on available disc space. There are logic bombs (hostile programs clandestinely introduced into target computers), so-called trapdoors, Trojan horses, worms, and spy chips. And as technology develops, so does the number of possibilities to create havoc.

The number of potential targets is almost endless and is bound to grow along with the growth of information systems. Obvious targets are financial institutions, whose networks could be cracked and whose money could be stolen. Thinking more ambitiously, financial markets could be affected by the destruction of records and the introduction of phony information. Electrical transformers and power grids could be shut down. Air traffic control could be tampered with, causing collisions and eventually closing down civilian air transport. Interfering with the electronic avionic systems of planes in the air could also cause crashes. Similarly tanks and surveillance aircraft, as well as satellites, could be made to malfunction or even be destroyed by high-energy weapons, or, on a more primitive level, by interfering with their computer controls. Food and drugs could be poisoned by interfering with the production processes and formulas. Trains could be misrouted, and transport, especially urban, could be brought to a virtual standstill. Dozens of conferences attended by academic, military, and business experts have focused on these and other dangers in recent years, but no sure means has been found to prevent such attacks.

This does not mean that all the planes will suddenly fall out of the skies, or all trains will stop, or that all food will be poisoned. But some of the systems on which we rely have become very vulnerable. For example, a decade from now all radio navigation will depend entirely on one centralized system, the Global Positioning System (GPS). A few years ago, only several thousand people had the skills to launch a cyberattack; today it is estimated that there are 17 million people in the United States alone with such skills, and more than a million telecommunications systems are controlled by software specialists. It would be naive to assume that all of them are mentally stable, and that there are no fanatics or malcontents among them.

Cyberattacks have been carried out for years by hackers, amateur and mercenary—some mere children—by business rivals, by spies, by thieves, and by disgruntled employees. Some merely seek excitement or power, others gain. Estimates as to the amount of money stolen by electronic means vary; in the United States alone, estimates range between several hundreds of millions and ten billion dollars, and it is thought that only a small number of these thefts are reported.

Among the hackers there used to be a spirit of rebellion against big corporations and the telephone companies, which were thought to keep computing prices artificially high. Hence the emergence of the phenomenon of phone phreaks. The early hackers regarded themselves as the elite of a new electronic order, and while they exhibited a strong element of anarchism, their intention was not criminal in any meaningful way. However, gradually a digital underground developed. Some hackers resented the high prices of the components they needed, and there seemed to be no easier way of obtaining funds than by electronically tampering with the credit-card system. Only a minority of hackers were willing to go that far, but their activities were clearly criminal.

After the telephone companies, the main targets of the hackers were the Fortune 500 and government institutions such as NASA, NATO, the Department of Defense, and the police. The hackers' growing radicalization also expressed itself in the chosen names of their groups—"pirates," "bandits," "mafias," and so on. Greater amounts of information were circulated about napalm, bombs, and "revenge tactics," symbols for the war they thought they were waging against the establishment. Most of this was posturing. Hackers were trying to shock the authorities in the same way skinheads tried to shock the public by wearing swastikas and frequently invoking Auschwitz. However, what was originally thought to be a game and an intellectual challenge soon turned into something more dangerous. These were no mere pranks. There were reports of sixteen-year-old hackers shutting down telephone networks. It became impossible in such cases to call out emergency services, and people may have died for want of a fire truck or ambulance. There were reports of a young blackmailer in Germany trying to extort fifty million marks from airports, and of substantial sums of money stolen. One particularly dangerous hacker was allegedly kept in isolation for months for fear that he might set off World War III by gaining access to missile silos and activating nuclear weapons. His civil rights were clearly violated, but few protested. There were even reports of German hackers employed by the KGB to ferret out American scientific or military secrets.

The names of the leading hacker groups are suggestive. There was the American "Legion of Doom" and the German "Chaos Computer Club." The victims of the ingenious break-ins by teenage phreakers were not amused by the cartoon aspects of the situation, nor did they admire the persistence and the intellectual curiosity of the hackers. Neither were they impressed by attempts at self-policing on the part of the hacker underground. Related legislation was passed, security measures were introduced—including the use of scramblers and secured lines—and arrests were made. Still, the nature of the crime meant few perpetrators were caught; even if the terminal from which a crime had been committed was located, no arrest could be made unless the identity of the offender could be established.

Cyberattacks are expected to come not only from transnational organized crime and espionage agencies but also from terrorists. The motivation of terrorists could be twofold. One, cyberspace offers relatively simple and secure means to obtain substantial amounts of money to finance terrorism. Previous generations of terrorists were compelled to rob banks, which was difficult and risky. Cyberspace offers safer and more rewarding opportunities. But information terrorism also makes it possible to sabotage the vital interests of one's enemies and even to paralyze or destroy them. This terrorism through modern technology is not the big bang of previous generations of terrorists, but the final result, the weakening and possible defeat of the enemy, is now as likely to be achieved.

Admittedly, run-of-the-mill terrorists might not have the experience and know-how to employ hacking as a weapon. But, on the other hand, hacking does not involve gifts of genius. The Heaven's Gate sectarians, who believed that a spaceship hiding behind the Hale-Bopp comet was coming to pick them up, made their living providing computer services. Among the terrorists involved in the World Trade Center bombing in New York, there were several with technical degrees. Nor is it true that expensive or top-of-the-line equipment is needed to cause mayhem in cyberspace. In short, it is not far-fetched to believe that average terrorists will make increasing use of computers in the future.

This chapter has surveyed the four big weapons of mass destruction that the terrorist of the future might employ. Chemical agents, biological agents, nuclear devices, and cyberterrorism all have precedents in this century, if not before, and the technology needed to obtain and use each form of weapon has become increasingly available to the fanatic, the disgruntled, and the mentally unbalanced.

TERRORIST
Motives

Marx, Muhammad, and Armageddon

Traditionally, terrorists have had distinct motives and ideological orientations. There were the murderers of tyrants in ancient times and in the Middle Ages; the assassins of political and religious enemies; nationalists who felt or were oppressed and were not autonomous in their own state; and extremists of the left and right who felt the need for radical political and social change and who were convinced that such change could come only through what was called at one time the "propaganda of the deed." But a new kind of terrorist mentality has arisen, and the coincidence of this new fanaticism with the development of weapons of mass destruction creates a threat unprecedented in the history of mankind.

It is impossible to provide a psychogram or an Identikit (composite) picture of the typical terrorist, because there never was such a person. There has been no "terrorism" per se, only different terrorisms. At one time it was believed that an inclination toward terrorism could be traced to genetic factors, psychological difficulties in early childhood, a disturbed family life, or identification with the underclass. The search for a terrorist typology seemed reasonable, but at best it applied only to specific terrorist groups belonging to a particular generation in a particular country. It was not merely an accident that the great majority of German and Italian terrorists in the 1970s were students, young academics, or at least the hangers-on who frequented students' quarters, social and cultural meetings, bookshops, and coffeehouses. But what was true for the Baader Meinhof generation of German terrorists was only partially true for the generation that succeeded them, and it has not been at all true with regard to the German terrorists of the extreme right, let alone others, such as the IRA and Palestinian terrorists.

There were always obvious patterns, so obvious that they hardly need mentioning again. Most terrorists have been young, some very young. The great majority have been male. There have been more women among the terrorists of the left, but hardly any among the extreme right, except as fellow travelers. As far as social origin and educational level is concerned, the extreme left has traditionally been from a higher social class and been better educated than the extreme right. There have been exceptions; the Basque ETA originated among a group of middle-class students and became more "lower class" in character only when it grew in size.

As the twentieth century closes, changes are taking place on the terrorist scene. Although nationalist-separatist terrorism continues with undiminished fervor in various parts of the world, terrorism from the left has sharply declined and terrorism from the extreme right has increased. The decline of the leftist ideology has been also reflected in the absence of Marxist-Leninist-Maoist-Castroist slogans in most current nationalist-separatist terrorist doctrine. While the IRA, the ETA, and, of course, the extreme Palestinian groups, to name a few, had made wide use of leftist ideology, it vanished in the 1980s. (ETA still officially has a socialist ideology, but no one is quite clear what that means.)

The real innovation in the late twentieth century is the appearance of radical religious (or quasireligious) nationalist groups adopting terrorism as their main form of struggle, sometimes within the framework of established religion (mainly Islam, but also Christianity, Judaism, and Hinduism), and sometimes in the form of millenarian sects. Other forms of terrorism survive, such as state-sponsored terrorism, while new forms have appeared on the scene, such as ecoterrorism, narcoterrorism, and a few others that will be discussed later. Sectarian terrorism, however, has been by far the most virulent species in recent years, accounting for half or more of terrorist attacks worldwide. While official statistics about "international terrorism" list a few hundred victims a year around the world, the number of victims of the religious terror in a single country such as Algeria is counted in tens of thousands.

RELIGION AND MADNESS

Traditional terrorism, whether of the separatist or the ideological (left or right) variety, had political and social aims, such as gaining independence, getting rid of foreigners, or establishing a new social order. Such terrorist groups aimed at forcing concessions, sometimes far-reaching concessions, from their antagonists. The new terrorism is different in character, aiming not at clearly defined political demands but at the destruction of society and the elimination of large sections of the population. In its most extreme form, this new terrorism intends to liquidate all satanic forces, which may include the majority of a country or of mankind, as a precondition for the growth of another, better, and in any case different breed of human. In its maddest, most extreme form it may aim at the destruction of all life on earth, as the ultimate punishment for mankind's crimes.

Is it at all likely that traditional terrorist groups will make use of the weapons of mass destruction? The reasons militating against such a course of action are obvious, and some of them have already been mentioned. Why use relatively complicated weapons as long as explosives, such as Semtex, and automatic arms are available? The contemporary world does not consist of ghettoes, territorially separated, but of different social classes and ethnic groups who live close to each other: poor and rich, Protestant and Catholic, Arabs and Jews, Tamils and Sinhalese, Turks and Kurds. Arms of mass destruction are likely to injure friends as well as enemies. Both would drink water from the same contaminated reservoir and breathe the same poisoned air. Above all, weapons of mass destruction violate one of the basic principles of classic terrorism—namely, "propaganda by deed." No self-respecting terrorist group wants to appear to be openly advocating indiscriminate mass murder. And even if within one terrorist group extremist elements demand such action, arguing, for instance, that chemical substances will affect only one quarter of a city, other members of the same group may believe the risks too high and the benefits too uncertain.

But terrorist matters today are quite volatile and unpredictable. Traditional terrorists exist, yet not all terrorist groups are self-respecting. Their hate and fanaticism are in some cases so deeply ingrained that they are willing to use any weapon, however barbaric. For reasons given earlier, a group may be ready to accept any degree of destruction, even of itself, as justifiable. However, it still seems unlikely that in the near future political terrorists in Europe or America will use weapons of mass destruction.

This is less certain in North Africa—in fact, in Africa generally—the Middle East, Central Asia, Southeast Asia, and the Far East, where attitudes regarding the value of human life are different. Mao Tse-tung, who was, all things considered, a relatively sober politician, nevertheless speculated that a nuclear war resulting in hundreds of millions of victims might be worthwhile if it brought about the final demise of capitalism and the dominance of a communist world. Terrorist leaders not part of the Marxist tradition (as Mao was, up to a point) who are less cautious and restrained may find it easy to reach similar conclusions. In the final analysis, Mao was motivated by a political calculus, whereas members of a new generation of terrorism are driven by nationalist or religious hate, or a mixture of the two. This new generation includes the Islamic terrorists in Algeria, the Shiite rebels in Lebanon, various African militant groups, the Tamils in Sri Lanka, the Taliban in Afghanistan, and a variety of others. Their approach and logic is that of Pol Pot. Those who would murder a class of schoolchildren and their teachers, to whom they are ethnically and religiously related, would feel no compunction over killing hundreds of thousands if they had the means to do so. If terrorists are religious believers, they might regard the slaughter as a commandment to destroy the infidel enemy once and for all.

There are religious or quasireligious sects who believe that the end of the world is near and that it is their task to expedite it by eliminating their fellow human beings. And there have always been small groups of people who, driven either by a feeling of mission or by uncontrollable rage or revenge, want to inflict as much damage on society or the world as is humanly possible. In the past, such individuals could kill a single person or perhaps several, but in the years to come they will be able to murder many more. Two examples picked at random should suffice. At the University of Texas, Charles Whitman stabbed his wife and mother, then climbed the three-hundred-foot-high university tower and from there shot forty-four people, killing sixteen of them. Michael Ryan, in the small Scottish village of Rutherford, opened fire on female students in a schoolyard, killing sixteen of them. How many people will the Whitmans and Ryans of the future be able to kill if they put their minds to it? These two men were not, as far as can be established, driven by any specific ideological complaint. But if a few such people with a burning and uncontrollable rage got together under the leadership of a so-called charismatic leader—such as Charles Manson—they might well be able to enunciate a rationalization for their actions and greatly increase their impact.

With the discussion of violent sectarians and individuals, some may argue, we may have moved beyond the borders of terrorism. What have these men and women in common with the Russian terrorists of the last century, with the IRA or the ETA, with Baader Meinhof or the Red Brigades or contemporary terrorists of the extreme right? It is a legitimate

question, but whichever way it is answered, two facts seem beyond reasonable doubt. Terrorism has always been subject to change; the 1970s
European terrorists of the left and of the right did not have much in
common with the Russian terrorists or the anarchists of the century before. And as far as the victims are concerned it certainly does not make
much difference whether they are killed by a mass murderer suffering
from rage caused by an extra chromosome or a diminished serotonin level,
or by a terrorist filled by sectarian or ethnic rage. There is a great difference
between a mass murderer like Whitman and a terrorist engaged in a systematic campaign. But there are all kinds of varieties in between. Alongside
the old terrorism, new kinds of terrorism have appeared, and until a more
fitting term gains general currency, old labels will have to suffice.

Nineteenth-and twentieth-century political terrorism has to a large extent overshadowed the quasireligious historical sources of terrorism. In
the history of terrorism, the order of the Assassins, the *sicarii,* and the
Indian thugs played a central role, but with the rise of modern politics
this kind of terrorism seemed to vanish. But certain religious elements
continued to play a role, even in the traditional terrorist movements. The
Russian terrorists about to be hanged, the Irish terrorists starving themselves to death, and the Baader Meinhof suicides in Stammheim Prison
all thought themselves to be martyrs—a religious rather than a political
concept.

The full importance of these religious or quasireligious elements was
rediscovered only with the reemergence of Islamic radicalism among both
the Sunni and especially the Shiites, as well as the revival of Christian and
Jewish sectarianism. The cases of the People's Temple in Guyana (1978),
the Branch Davidians in Texas (1993), the Solar Temple in Switzerland
and Canada, and Heaven's Gate in California (1997) are only the most
publicized incidents that reflected a commitment to violence where it was
least expected. Whereas in these cases the violence was turned inward and
led mostly to mass suicide, it was clear that these groups could also commit violence against others. The Branch Davidians, for instance, were
stockpiling weapons for purposes other than suicide.

A variety of terms have been used to describe this new phenomenon:
the sects or cults have been called "millenarian," "apocalyptic," or "fundamentalist." None of these labels is entirely satisfactory, simply because
meaning varies from country to country and from religion to religion.
What is perhaps most remarkable about these sects is their number. While
there are only a few major world religions, the number of extreme religious sects is unlimited, especially among those of Christian persuasion.
The fundamentalist label is perhaps the most misleading, for many of

these radical groups have moved very far from the tenets of Christianity (Satanism, for instance). They cannot even be considered heretics. The impact of the occult or Gnostic tradition is more significant, and these sects are as much the offspring of the New Age movement as of traditional religions. The great majority of these sects and cults are not violent, or at least not more so than other political and religious groups. Neither are the majority millenarian—that is to say, living in the expectation of impending doom. What will be said about sectarianism as a factor in the spread of modern terrorism refers to the violent minority, not the majority.

The preoccupation with the Apocalypse, with eschatology, and with the coming of a Messiah or a Messiah-like figure can be found in many religions. It has been particularly strong in Christianity, its most famous biblical expressions in the Book of Revelation in the New Testament, the Book of Ezekiel, and the second chapter of the Book of Daniel. Revelation (19:11–24) contains the famous reference to the battle of Armageddon, the final struggle between God Almighty and the Antichrist, in which the usurper will be finally banished from the earth and the physical kingdom of God will be established. This will happen only after a very bloody battle in which the armies of the whole world will be destroyed.

The imagery of this early apocalyptic literature—the beast, the seventh seal, and even the more exotic symbols—can be found to this day in a variety of sects, even though they may have moved far from Christianity. There is even a Church of Armageddon. The believers in this apocalyptic perspective are convinced that there is no salvation outside their ranks and that those who do not believe will be destroyed and suffer eternal damnation, a belief that goes back, of course, to orthodox Christianity. But at this point there is a divergence: the optimistically inclined believers envisage a bright future following the defeat of the forces of evil, a vision not shared by the pessimists. Earth, as the pessimists understand it, is a sinful place that cannot be saved, and our punishment is to exist on earth, a concept related to original sin. And then there are the radical pessimists who believe that the human race is evil and doomed. The end is predestined, and all that remains is to hasten its coming.

The Christian idea of an apocalypse is not to be found in other major religions, but the concept of Messianism is fairly universal. It can be found in early Judaism, in Hinduism (Krishna, Kalki), in Buddhism (Maitreya), and in Islam (the Mahdi and, in the case of the Shiites, the fourth Imam). Such a tradition provides an opportunity for people with a feeling of mission (or impostors) to declare themselves messiahs. They can be found in every religion and sect, including Judaism (Rabbi Shneerson of the Lubavicher), among countless Indian gurus, who have been more successful in America than in their own country, and among a great many others.

There have been sects and cults throughout recorded history, their origins not that different from the origins of the major world religions. In its beginnings, Christianity was a Jewish sect, and Judaism, Islam, and Buddhism also began as local cults. The reasons for the recent upsurge of sects and cults are similar: they are rooted in the need for a level of security, faith, and spiritual uplift, which established religions seem no longer able to provide. The need often takes the form of revolt against reason; when the traditional religions (or science) cannot help the person in despair, shamans and faith healers take over.

Nor is millenarianism a recent phenomenon. The end of the world has been predicted repeatedly over the last two millennia, and, for all one knows, even before. The "great fear" that allegedly beset Europeans as the year 1000 approached is largely a romantic invention of nineteenth-century historians. It originated with a tract about the Antichrist ("De ortu et tempore Antichristi") written in the ninth century by a monk named Adso living in the monastery Montier-en-Der. The otherwise unknown author was consulted by the Queen Gerberga, the sister of Otto I, the German emperor, and the wife of Louis IV, king of France. Adso replied that there were greater experts concerning the Antichrist than he, but that in his opinion the time would not come as long as the Carolingian dynasty ruled. The tract was written in 953–54, and over the following four centuries it was copied and quoted many times. Adso left a great many questions unanswered, such as whether there would be one Antichrist or several (there is no clue in the Book of Revelation). Subsequent medieval writers were far more specific with regard to the origin of the Antichrist, his characteristics, and the date of his coming. The early Christians expected the second coming of Christ in their lifetime. Later interpreters referred to Revelation (Chapter 20:4), in which the figure 1000 refers to the reign of God. Others referred to Psalm 90, which says that "in the eyes of God a thousand years were like one day." St. John of Patmos, one of the earliest writers on the subject, also seems to have expected the Apocalypse in the very near future.

Later on, there were speculations as to whether the thousand years followed the birth of Christ, his death, or a period of time after the end of history. Since history was to last six thousand years, according to a view widely held at one time, the last choice seemed to be preferred. But since no one was quite certain when history had started, speculation continued. Augustine, who had himself been a millenarian in his younger years, later condemned the *chiliastai* and *millenarii* as heretics because he considered the thousand years a symbol, a figure of speech, rather than an exact date.

It simply meant "a very long time," and his view became Church dogma at the Council of Ephesus in 431. But dogma or no dogma, speculation continued for much more than a thousand years. And even though all the dates predicted passed without apocalyptic consequences, belief in the Apocalypse continued with undiminished vigor.

TV evangelist Pat Robertson predicted nuclear war in 1982, along with a world in flames and passing of the last judgment. Rabbi Shneerson, the spiritual head of a major orthodox Jewish sect, the Lubavicher Hasidim, thought the Messiah would come in 1991. The Children of God proclaimed that Christ would return in 1993, and the Church Universal and Triumphant has been building underground shelters for years at its headquarters in Montana in preparation for the coming holocaust, the details of which were described by its leader, Elizabeth Claire Prophet, in her book *Astrology of the Four Horsemen* (1991). These speculations and squabbles about the exact date of the end are not in the mainstream Christian tradition. It says in the New Testament that no one can know the day and the hour of the end of the world, and this has been the position of the Church since the Council of Ephesus. (An interesting twist was provided by William Partridge, an English preacher, who announced in 1697 that the world would come to an end imminently. This was followed by another tract in 1699, in which he sadly noted that the world had in fact come to an end but that no one had taken notice.)

Dire warnings were issued by the prophets of the Old Testament, but the millenarians created prophecy in a new idiom, as one theologian has put it, and it could well be that their inspiration is as much Persian (Zoroastrian, as Norman Cohn has shown in a recent book) as Jewish or Christian. The millenarians differ about the number of people likely to survive the final tribulations. Some sects have maintained that only a very few of the elected will live to witness the period of eternal bliss. But others have been somewhat more optimistic. Robert Logston, author of *The End Times Blood Bath,* states that only two-thirds of the five billion people on earth will die. There is dissent on other fine points: whether there will be only a second coming or a second and third coming of Christ, and whether the third world war will be the last or whether there will be also a fourth. Lastly, there is a controversy among the students of millenarianism as to whether it is legitimate to broaden the concept to include not only believers inspired by Christianity and Judaism but also secular proponents of end time, including, for instance, members of the Polynesian cargo cults.

The term *millenarian* has been used for a considerable time by a great many secular movements, including Nazism (whose leader frequently said the Reich would last a thousand years), communism, and countless other prophets and sects whose inspiration was neither Christian nor Jewish. Indeed, the religious millenarians do not have a monopoly on clairvoyance; hundreds of schools of occult "sciences," most significantly astrology, have engaged in future-gazing from time immemorial, and there have been individuals, such as Nostradamus, whose predictions continue to be printed. (Three of the planets—namely, Uranus, Neptune, and Pluto—were unknown in the time of Nostradamus and could not therefore appear in his astrological calculations, but this has not deterred latter-day believers in his predictions.) Numerology plays a role in at least one sect, the Nation of Islam.

Most identity movements profess millenarianism; so do various white-supremacy groups and the Ku Klux Klan. Such movements believe that white Protestants (or at least some of them) are the true Israelites and that America is the promised land that should be cleansed of all the forces of evil, mainly other races and religions. Some of these groups are survivalist and antigovernment, such as the Aryan Nation and the defunct Posse Comitatus; their relationship to Christianity is tenuous at best, despite their Bible-quoting. Some of them advocate violence; their activities will be discussed later on. The Rastafarians, a black identity movement, and its many ideological descendants also belong to this category. Whereas the white-supremacy movements claim that the Aryans were chosen by God and destined to rule the world, the Rastafarians moved in the opposite direction and were exclusionists, with Ras Tafari Makkonen (better known as Emperor Haile Selassie) replacing Jesus Christ and being viewed as the savior of blacks.

Not all millenarianism envisions doom or gloom or inspires violence. The New Age movement, for example, predicted the dawn of the new Aquarian Age that was to supersede the Age of Pisces (Christianity, with Jesus as the fisher of men). In the case of the New Agers, the outlook for the future is bright. This peaceful manifestation of religious millenarianism has led some of its adherents to a preoccupation with spiritual things, to quietism and resignation, to confession and repentance, in some cases even to something like a doctrine of nonviolence. But in most other cases it has led to violence and terrorism. The Anabaptists of Muenster, one of the best-known exponents of millenarianism in the sixteenth century, were originally a peace-loving sect, mainly interested in the realm of the religious and spiritual. In his youth, Ayatollah Khomeini was a believer in ascetic irfan (mysticism); Sheikh Fadlalla, the spiritual head of Hizbullah in Lebanon, wrote poetry in his younger years; and other militant Islamic groups drew their original inspiration from Sufism, a mystical, revivalist movement that did not preach violence. Shoko Asahara of the Aum Supreme Truth cult began his career in the underworld of Buddhist sects sprouting in Japan in the 1970s, and for inspiration went to the gurus of India and Tibet as well as to some Arab countries. He taught his followers various yoga practices, acupuncture, and palmistry. He sold patent medicines, recommended to his friends the inspirational book *Jonathan Livingstone Seagull,* and advocated daily masturbation without ejaculation. In short, he seemed hardly threatening.

In what circumstances and for what reasons do some sects give up the search for spiritual wisdom, religious perfection, and salvation, and turn to violence? Why did Asahara's attention turn from masturbation interruptus to bomb and nerve-gas production? This unfortunate conversion is crucial, and, as so often happens in our attempt to explain historical phenomena, there are no simple answers. In some Third World countries and in some black sects in the United States, millenarian cults became movements of national liberation. Elsewhere, the feeling of oppression, whatever the source, leads to violence. Extremists believe themselves under siege by a powerful enemy that has to be defeated at all cost. Leading students of violent sects have explained this trend by pointing to social change (and ensuing social resentment), to the growth of revolutionary expectations, and to the spread of millenarian fantasies. In some instances political and social elements have had a great impact; in others they were in no way decisive. In most sects the appearance of a prophet or a change in the visions and worldview of the prophet was the crucial factor. The official religion of the Roman Empire could have prevailed for several more centuries and the nomad tribes of Arabia would have stuck to their religious beliefs and practices for a long time if Jesus and Muhammad had not appeared. Social factors can help explain why one sect triumphed and gained millions of adherents, or, on the other hand, why another's influence remained limited to a faithful few. But even these explanations are helpful only up to a point.

Of greater significance is that just as some religions are more militant than others, some millenarian sects have from the very beginning put more emphasis on destruction than on creation and salvation. For the destructive sects, there has been an almost universal belief in the existence of a powerful enemy—a conspiracy, the Beast, the Antichrist, Satan, the unbelievers, the Pope, the Jews, American and Western imperialism. And since the perceived forces had no compunction about using violence, the community of the faithful had the obligation to defend itself. As Ulrike Meinhof wrote in her diary, the act of destruction was the act of liberation. This apothegm had been previously preached by terrorists of the extreme right and left—for example, by Ernst Juenger and the militants of the Freikorps after World War I, by the Rumanian fascists of the Legion of Archangel Michael, and by Frantz Fanon, who called the armed struggle in the colonial world an act of catharsis and self-purification. (There have also been exceptions: Martin Luther certainly thought of the Pope as the personification of the Antichrist, yet he did not declare war on him.)

The origins of millenarian sects have been explained by some against a background of despair and fear, and it is of course true that happy people, at peace with themselves and the world around them, are not likely candidates for conversion to such sects. But this explanation does not take us very far, because reasons for despair, spiritual and material, can be found in every period in history and in every society. But millenarians appear more often in certain societies than in others; even in contemporary America, the geographical distribution is by no means even. The frequency of their appearance in California, at a time when economic conditions were better there than in other parts of the United States, raises more questions. The state of affairs is less complicated in North Africa and the Middle East, where radical Islam has found most of its followers among the poor or, as in the case of the Muslim Brotherhood, among the lower middle class. It is yet another question to what extent movements of social protest were manipulated by members of the clergy. In many cases, but for the clergy's leadership these movements would have adopted other beliefs or ideologies, nationalist or socialist.

It is a hopeless endeavor to search for meaningful political patterns among contemporary millenarian sects. Jim Jones of the People's Temple expressed some vague pro-communist sentiments toward the end of his life, and David Koresh and the Branch Davidians became posthumous heroes of the extreme right—the Oklahoma City bombing was intentionally committed on the anniversary date of the Branch Davidians' death. But neither the left-wing orientation of the one sect or the right-wing of the other went very deep. They may have had minor ideological leanings for which there is no accounting, just as populist parties can turn left and right with equal ease, depending on the social and political context in which they are operating. In the case of the Islamic militants in Algeria and elsewhere, any attempt to define them by consulting the Western political dictionary is altogether hopeless.

Another group of sects should be mentioned. Satanism, in the form of the Church of Satan and a few dozen other groups in America and Europe, has always attracted a great deal of interest, but its influence and alleged misdeeds have been grotesquely exaggerated. While some Satanist splinter groups have engaged in human and animal sacrifices, the allegation that between fifty thousand and two million children are kidnapped and killed in Satanist sacrifices in the United States each year is ludicrous. The idea of a god (or goddess or fallen angel) as a rival of the good and all-powerful God can be found in various world religions. With respect to Christianity,

Satanism was an extreme reaction against an established religion that based itself partly on occult and pagan elements. Its modern prophet was Alisteir Crowley (1875–1947), who preached a hedonistic doctrine to the effect that anything was permitted as long as one liked it. The Seven Deadly Sins of Christianity were, in the view of another apostle of Satanism, La Vey, not to be condemned out of hand but indulged as long as no one was made to suffer and the laws of the land were observed. Satanism in its various manifestations (including most recently the various "chaos" groups, who draw their inspiration from postmodernism) has appeared as part of a rarefied intellectual scene, in the subcultures of the drug and heavy-metal rock scenes. Satanism has numbered among its members a general of the U.S. army as well as other respected and law-abiding citizens, who, at most, engaged in eccentric and outlandish rituals out of some psychological need. Two men who loosely fit into the Satanist camp might be mentioned as more violent examples of the mind-set: Jack Parsons, a member of the Church of Satan, a rocket scientist, and a comrade in arms of L. Ron Hubbard (the founder of Scientology), blew himself up in 1953 while experimenting with explosives. Of course Charles Manson, head of the famous "family" and mass murderer, drew his inspiration from the satanic tradition. He believed that the Apocalypse was near, and that its coming would be hastened if members of his family killed other whites and put the blame on blacks. Manson, an admirer of Hitler, was one of a group of itinerant prophets preaching extreme protest against society. He did not belong to mainstream Satanism and the sect cannot be made responsible for his political views or the mass murder. But it is precisely at the fringes of such sects that the "new" terrorism has appeared and is likely to appear again.

So where does Satanism fit into the ideological spectrum: was the devil on the left or the right? It is probably only a question of time until some earnest scholars address themselves to this fascinating question. But for now there is no intelligent answer, and the question itself is largely meaningless.

THE TERRORIST PERSONALITY

The accessibility of weapons of mass destruction makes it imperative to rethink the motivation of terrorists likely to employ them. Searches for a single "terrorist personality" have always failed owing to basic differences in character and motivation. In tsarist Russia, the terrorists were political militants who saw no other way to compel the authorities to make concessions toward greater freedom. Most of them were not even particularly radical, but they were willing to sacrifice their lives in what seemed to them a sacred struggle. Some, like in every such movement, joined because their friends did, but there was no doubt about the idealistic motivation of the leading figures.

In the case of nationalist-separatist movements, the state of affairs is more complicated simply because their struggle is not merely directed against the authorities but also against other national groups. The Irish terrorists, for instance, did not begin sectarian, and there were even Protestants among their leaders. However, as the struggle continued in Northern Ireland, the terrorists turned against their Protestant neighbors (and vice versa) as much as against the London government. As for terrorists active in democratic societies, there can be no doubt about the perverse idealism of members of Italy's Red Brigades or Germany's Red Army, inasmuch as they acted, or thought they were acting, on behalf of the downtrodden and oppressed all over the globe and particularly in the Third World. But there was also a strong element of feverish excitement and adventurism, the feeling that they could show off their power, and the desire or compulsion to solve their own psychological problems by way of assassination (they preferred to call it "armed struggle").

Terrorists in democratic societies tend to be elitists; they claim to know better than the masses what is good for them. While a few of the nineteenth-century terrorists claimed that no one in society was free of guilt and that innocent bystanders were bound to be killed, the great majority would target only leading political enemies. Indiscriminate murder is, by and large, a component of twentieth-century terrorism. The kind of person engaging in terrorism in 1880 would not understand the terrorist of the 1980s, who had no compunction about killing not only a businessman but his secretary and the members of his family as well. Furthermore, there is a basic difference between Europe and America and the parts of the globe where human lives count for little. The case of Nezar Hindawi is not atypical. Born in Jordan in 1954, he sent his pregnant fiancée with, unbeknownst to her, a parcel of Semtex hidden in a computer to board an Israeli plane from London to Tel Aviv. The planned explosion would have taken place over southern Europe, killing all 375 passengers, including his fiancée and unborn daughter. Owing to the vigilance of the airport guards, the plot was foiled. (Had Hindawi been a true martyr, he would have taken the suicide mission himself, but according to all the evidence he was not particularly religious, and he had been promised $250,000 for his part in the operation.) Western commentators denounced Hindawi as a particularly brutal criminal devoid of any shred of conscience, and during his trial he made it clear that he could not have cared less about the fate of his fiancée and unborn child. But it is also true that his behavior was not thought to be particularly loathsome in the part of the world where he came from, partly because his wife was not Muslim. But even if she had been Muslim, would the reaction have been different? Hindawi was not a psychopath, and there are many like him, mercenaries from Afghanistan to Algeria, who would kill with relish. The culture they live in, the combination of nationalism and religion, gives them the legitimation for acting out their cruelty.

The search for terrorist motivations has concentrated, not without justification, on real political and social conditions, which, it was believed, could drive people to extreme actions. Investigations focus on the interaction of ideology and the frustration-aggression link, believed for a long time to be the cardinal psychological mechanism of terrorism. The evidence for such an interaction is, however, not compelling at best. In actuality, those likely to use weapons of mass destruction are to be found on the fringes of religious-nationalist sects and among madmen; any ideological element is likely to be just rhetoric.

So, what kind of people are likely to join sects or small groups engaging in such acts of violence? Aggression and intense hate can manifest themselves in a variety of ways, in writing a manifesto or making a speech as well as in throwing a bomb. Psychologists, psychiatrists, criminologists, anthropologists, and neurologists have given much thought to the issue of whether or not there is a predisposition toward violence in human beings. Biological and clinical research has produced ambiguous answers. There have been cross-cultural studies in interpersonal violence, but their results have also been unstartling. The studies have shown that there are cultural patterns of violence but that they tend to change over time. For example, Switzerland and Sweden were at one time among the most bellicose countries in Europe, their armies greatly feared, but this has not been the case since the eighteenth century. Studies show that societies high in some types of violence are likely to be high in others. But they also show that most violence occurs inside families and that alcohol (and to a lesser extent other drugs) plays a significant role in homicide. Drugs have also played a role in Middle Eastern terrorism, a fact that is frequently ignored (this will be discussed later). The question of whether there is more violent crime in complex social systems than in primitive societies is unresolved, and it is uncertain whether there is less in egalitarian societies than in those with palpable economic and social polarization. Size could be a greater factor. If the murder rate is considerably lower in the Scandinavian countries, where there is also hardly any terrorism, than in other industrialized countries, this could be related to the fact that these are small countries, with more personal interaction than is seen in big, anonymous societies where the murder rate is much higher.

Genetic, biological, and neurophysiological research has produced certain indicators with regard to the propensity toward aggression and violence. But researchers, by necessity, have been more preoccupied with animal research than with human. Genetic factors do play a role, as the study of twins has shown, as does low intelligence and family and peer influence. Aggression has been explained with reference to innate human instincts as well as to neurochemical changes that affect aggressive tendencies—for example, the brain contains chemical substances, such as serotonin, that can influence aggression. While not denying the presence of these and other biological factors, psychoanalysts have asserted that there are also psychological structures that inhibit aggression, and that "learning" and "socialization," in the widest sense, play a role that is equally if not more important; in brief, it is not only the fear of punishment but the formation of a conscience that inhibits people from engaging in acts of violence.

In the last century Cesare Lombroso, founder of modern criminology, believed that criminals were born. Then, beginning with sociologist Émile Durkheim, it became the fashion to explain various forms of crime mainly as the result of social and economic factors. More recently, psychological and physiological explanations have come to the fore. All this theorizing reveals that there has been no comprehensive explanation of aggressive behavior and violence; each case has to be viewed in its specific context. This is not to endorse an indiscriminate multiculturalism that accepts cruelty and torture as normal behavior in some societies. On the contrary, the answer might be far simpler. Psychological, biological, and sociological attempts to explain violence and crime have almost extinguished the concept of evil and evil-doing that was familiar to earlier generations.

But what has terrorism to do with criminology and psychiatry? Could it not be shown that most terrorists of the past were perfectly normal men and women and that their opting for terrorism was a rational choice rather than a mental aberration? That terrorist violence, in other words, was a political phenomenon and thus essentially different from ordinary crime or psychopathology. The question might be legitimate with reference to the terrorism of the period between 1870 and 1970. It does not relate to recent changes. It is also true that in the history of terrorism there have been ideas and actions that could not be called rational, and that there have been a fair number of individual terrorists exhibiting mental disorders. Suicide, for example, is prevalent among terrorists. Many of the Russian terrorists at the beginning of this century had a history of attempted suicide. These tendencies became more pronounced in groups such as Baader Meinhof in West Germany. The slogan of the second generation of Baader Meinhof belonging to the self-proclaimed "patients collective" at the University of Heidelberg was "the system has made us kaput, we shall destroy the system." Even more recently, as terrorist activities emerge on the fringes of certain sects, issues of personality and personality disorders are bound to figure much more prominently. A phenomenon such as Shoko Asahara and his Aum cult, or the savage brutalities committed in Algeria and in other Middle Eastern countries, cannot be interpreted in traditional political and sociological terms or simply as economic deprivation and holy rage.

The question as to what kind of people are likely to join terrorist groups therefore remains largely unanswered. Terrorists' motives differed widely in the past—and they will differ even more so in the future. But there are discernible patterns that can be broadly applied.

The composition of the membership of extremist cults and violent sects varies from country to country according to social conditions, religious traditions, and historical factors. In the Muslim world terrorists are likely to be from two classes: the unemployed young from poor families, and numerous individuals who went to universities or seminaries and are also unemployed. In the United States, many terrorists hail from middle-class families. They include university dropouts, but also people with degrees in subjects such as psychology. Material deprivation does not play a significant role in Western societies; the German Red Army had no working-class members, and in the Italian Red Brigades only a few became terrorists by way of the Communist Youth League. In some of the separatist terrorists organizations, such as the IRA, the lower-class element is much larger.

What makes young people join sects and cults is spiritual emptiness rather than an empty stomach. There is boredom and the desire for excitement on the one hand, and on the other the thirst for some kind of religion or higher purpose. The stresses and strains of modern life frequently have been adduced as reasons why such people turn to violence. But are these stresses really so intolerable, or is there a tendency to magnify them? In the case of the German Red Army, it was probably more a matter of the unresolved psychological tensions of a young man and a young woman. Andreas Baader, who lived in a dreamworld and stole motorcycles, had a tendency toward sadomasochism. The young woman, Gudrun Ensslin, had a penchant for the occult. Loneliness was an important factor. Being part of a closely knit, exclusive community gave its members the self-confidence and certainties they lacked. These people had weak egos and were in need of a message and a leader. The role of the leader in terrorism is crucial, as it was in fascism and communism. Those who join are willing and expected to abdicate their critical faculties; they become mindless subordinates out of choice. Though these observations apply less to the small German and Italian groups, which consisted mainly of university students, where a culture of discussion existed, they are certainly true with regard to nationalist-separatist groups and religious sects.

The central role of the leader in sects that turn violent is a source of puzzlement to outsiders. Observers have been baffled by the fact that people of common sense and, in some cases, superior intelligence have accepted the authority of poorly educated and sometimes half-crazy leaders such as Asahara (the Aum), David Koresh (the Branch Davidians), and Jim Jones (Jonestown). Nor can it be argued that the leaders of the terrorist groups in North Africa or the Middle East are outstanding, brilliant figures. Most of them, in fact, did not even participate in the terrorist struggle; they were desk or pulpit terrorists, and led their groups by remote control.

To explain this puzzle, reference is usually made to "charisma," which in practice consists of almost unlimited self-confidence and ambition. A leader may have doubts, but he must never show them. A leader expects that even his most ludicrous explanations will be believed, even the most absurd orders obeyed. In reality, however, there is often dissent, and there may be rivals for leadership, or the charisma of one leader may not be strong enough to stifle opposition. It is difficult to think of a single cult or sect that has not split, and the conflicts that follow are usually very bitter. If outside the church there is no salvation, those leaving the sect or the cult are worse than infidels; they are traitors to be exterminated. These splits have been more frequent in the small European terrorist groups consisting mostly of people with a higher education who find it difficult to shed the last vestiges of critical thinking. In groups with less sophisticated members, who may be poorly educated and unfamiliar with critical thinking, the leadership has fewer problems in asserting and maintaining itself. But splits, purges, and excommunications still occur.

Once a cult or group is in a state of splitting, apostasy is likely to have bloody consequences. The Japanese Red Army killed a significant number of its own comrades, and there were similar assassinations in the ranks of terrorist groups in Sri Lanka as well as in Algeria and among Islamic terrorists elsewhere.

One typical feature of most, if not all, such groups is a strong paranoid streak and the belief in omnipresent conspiracies. This they have in common with fascism, communism, and other extreme movements. Other fairly typical features are delusions and self-deception. Delusions are often a manifestation of schizophrenia, and they can produce highly organized belief systems. The link with violence is obvious: voices can tell the deluded to kill or to engage in other violent behavior.

These delusions may take a great variety of forms and appear with varying intensity. Those joining such sects and cults are not likely to be suffering from extreme mental disorders, because they would have clashed with society before and more likely than not ended up in mental asylums. Odds are that they are borderline cases with a tendency toward delusion and paranoid schizophrenia, a tendency intensified by the dynamics of group behavior. The experience in the new community may release or strengthen latent tendencies. The basic principles of mass psychology and collective behavior have been known for a long time—people in a group may do things they would never do on their own. It could also be that the indoctrination (and sometimes drug use) inside a group might increase the delusions. The question arises of whether the leaders of extreme sectarian groups are what is popularly known as "mental cases," frauds, or true believers acting on convictions, or perhaps a mixture of all these things. The pronouncements of the leaders of the sects are sometimes so contradictory and absurd as to beg the question. Are they just senseless or have they been playing a huge and dangerous game with their adherents? But the fact that these leaders have often acted in a suicidal fashion and that their decisions have had deadly consequences, not just for their followers but for themselves, tends to indicate that their behavior is often genuine.

Probably the most frequent and most intense of the delusions found among extreme religious and political groups is the paranoid conspiracy delusion. In its modern, systematic form, it goes back to the French counterrevolutionary ideologists and the dramatic and seemingly inexplicable events that took place afterward in Paris and the rest of France in 1789. Abbe Barruel's book, which became a classic, *Memoires pour servir a l'histoire du Jacobinisme,* published in London in 1797–98, proved to his satisfaction that the Revolution had actually been a conspiracy against church and state by various forces who had all been part of the Enlightenment, including the Illuminati, the Freemasons, and others. Less than a century later, the Jews became a main factor in the thinking of conspiracy theorists. This new departure found its classic manifestation in the "Protocols of the Elders of Zion." The Russian Revolution of 1917 added fuel to conspiratorial fires. Ever since then, these theories have been part and parcel of the ideology of the extreme right, with many local variations.

For certain Protestant fundamentalists the Jesuits and the Pope were the chief agents of evil. In parts of Asia with sizable Chinese or Indian minorities, the local Chinese and Indians became the subject of hate and suspicion. In the Arab world "Zionism" became the personification of Satan, the demonic force out to ruin the self-esteem and way of life of the Arab peoples. But the conspiracy theories were by no means confined to the extreme right. Communist Russia, especially in its Stalinist phase, was an example of extreme delusion, with its attacks against Wall Street, the Trotskyites, the "Cosmopolitans," and the secret services of all countries who joined forces to destroy communism. Although these general examples of the tendency toward paranoia seem far afield from the subject of terrorism, they illustrate that this affliction often fills the practical function of providing the glue or cohesion for keeping groups of fervent believers together. But for the existence of a powerful and omnipresent enemy, there would be no need for militancy and vigilance, and, of course, violent action.

FANATICISM

Another typical feature of small terrorist groups is their fanaticism. The term has been used in the English language since the seventeenth century, and it originally meant excessive enthusiasm in religious practice. In Greek it referred to people who experienced a state of ecstasy in holy sites (*fanum* is a holy place, a site of prophecy). The term *fanaticus* was used by many Roman writers. The phenomenon of fanaticism did, of course, exist well before the term gained currency in the English language.

Fanaticism became a subject of paramount importance for the *philosophes* of the Enlightenment in the eighteenth century, and no one was more preoccupied with its study and the need to combat it than Voltaire. He dealt with it specifically in a philosophical play titled *Le fanatisme ou Mahomet le Prophete* (Amsterdam, 1743) as well as in his Philosophical Dictionary. It was no accident that Voltaire chose the prophet Muhammad as the villain of his treatise, for Islam had the reputation of being a particularly fanatical religion. But his target was fanatical religion in general, and it was also no accident that the play was dedicated to the Pope. In Voltaire's writings one finds a fairly accurate description of fanaticism in its various manifestations. Voltaire thought that charlatanism was an intrinsic component of the fanatic; Muhammad was, he wrote, Tartuffe with weapons in his hands. Voltaire believed fanaticism was a madness rooted in superstition. Of religious origins, it was supported by blind faith and imposture. It reigned among those whose hearts were true and minds were false. The hearts belonged to the followers; the false minds belonged to the leaders. While Voltaire devoted much of his life to the struggle against superstition, he was not optimistic that the fight would end in victory. In his article for the *Encyclopedie,* he compared fanaticism to gangrene of the brain, a disease that was nearly incurable. Nicolas Linguet, a contemporary of Voltaire, also called it the most incurable of all the diseases of the human spirit. If so, what was the point of heaping scorn and ridicule on the fanatics? Would it induce those afflicted to return to truth, reason, and tolerance? Voltaire quite obviously did not aim at the fanatics who were beyond redemption. On one occasion he defined them as persons of blind and passionate zeal, which had been born of superstitious opinions, and who engaged in unjust and cruel acts, feeling no shame or remorse but, rather, a sense of joy, relief, or consolation. Voltaire and his fellow *philosophes* aimed their barbs at the gurus of the fanatics and at their fellow travelers, those who were not quite fanatics themselves but associated with them for their own purposes. Voltaire clearly saw the connection between fanaticism and violence—against oneself and against others. He mentioned the self-destructive maniacs who lacerated their bodies with whips, and said that the entire species of fanatics was divided into two classes: those who wanted nothing but to pray and die, and those who wanted to reign and massacre. The observation is of considerable truth to this very day.

Every religion has had its fanatic proponents, especially during its early stages. Throughout history, a routinization of religion has taken place over the centuries, but in many places there have been attempts to return to the original pure and pristine message. If fundamentalism is interpreted not as a return to the words, to the holy texts of a religion, but as a return to the uncompromising spirit of its early days, it can be viewed as a regression to the spirit of fanaticism.

But the spirit of fanaticism has not been confined to the religious sphere. Fanaticism was one of Adolf Hitler's favorite terms, and it appeared again and again in his speeches. It has appeared in every religious and political creed, especially the radical ones, in one way or another. It is not quite the same as fundamentalism, because the fundamentalist is (or in any case, should be) bound by the holy texts, whereas the fanatic frequently feels free to provide his own interpretations. Fanaticism can turn inward and express itself in asceticism or self-flagellation, as it still does, for example, among the Shiites. But in our day and age it shows itself more frequently as hostility toward an outside enemy, an unwillingness to compromise, and an eagerness not just to defeat the enemy but to destroy him. The modern fanatic is more eager to castigate the flesh of others than his own.

It is easier to describe various aspects of fanaticism than to account for its mainsprings. Various psychodynamic and behaviorist schools of psychiatry have provided different theories, and biologists have added some hypotheses of their own. Fanaticism has been interpreted as a sadomasochist fixation, as a compulsion, as a paranoid delusion, and as the overstimulation of certain parts of the brain. While there can be no doubt that a strong and sometimes overwhelming pathological element exists in fanaticism, one need not conclude that fanaticism itself is pathological. If this were the case, every political mass murderer could be acquitted on grounds of diminished responsibility.

Is fanaticism merely the excessive pursuit of religiously inspired beliefs and goals to the neglect of all others, as the original definition implied? If so, at a certain point does this single-mindedness become a new psychological phenomenon? When one thinks of fanaticism in history, above all the fighters for religious purity come to mind: Savonarola and the Inquisition, Calvin, the Wahhabites of Arabia (who have had a recent revival in parts of the Caucasus), the so-called Whirling Dervishes, and the Mahdi, who claimed messiahship in the Sudan in the 1880s.

Religious fanaticism can also be interpreted as a defensive strategy to keep out foreign influences and so preserve the purity of the the believer's way of life. In our age, religious fanaticism frequently appears in a secular form, or as a mixture of religion and politics. But there can be no doubt about its origins. The Irish terrorists who starved themselves to death, and Holger Meins of Baader Meinhof, who did the same, saw themselves at least in part as following the traditions of religious martyrs. The Nazi elite, S.S., and the fanatical cadres of the Soviet Young Communist League in the 1920s and early '30s followed a different tradition; their allegiance was to a leader and to a country or a party, and they were willing to die for the cause. In some instances the belief in a cause, transcendental or secular, is decisive; in others it is the loyalty to the leader and the comrades that plays the predominant role in fanaticism. Generations of Praetorian Guards, Janissaries, and other such elite units fought to the bitter end without the incentive of a religious belief. Offensive and defensive fanatics, religious believers, and political soldiers all have in common an absolute certainty as to the justness of their cause, the legitimacy of their leader, the inability to recognize other moral values and considerations, and the abdication of critical judgment. These preconditions apply to members and candidates of violent sects despite their level of education. Their knowledge becomes compartmentalized; they do not forget their academic learning, but it is kept quite separate from the cause. Fanatics (and many paranoiacs, sufferers of hallucinations, and believers in conspiracy theories) can function, continue to do their jobs, and lead reasonable family lives. It is only when demands are made on them by the leader, on behalf of the cause in which they totally believe, that the inherent dangers in fanaticism come to the fore.

SUICIDE

Suicide—both of individuals and of groups en masse—has played an important role in a number of religious sects and terrorist groups. Needless to say, suicide, has many psychological causes, not all stemming from mental instability, and in some instances it may be the result of a rational decision.

It is widely accepted that there are psychocultural patterns in suicide. Here are a few examples. Suicide is considered to be a mortal sin in the Catholic Church, and some of the Catholic countries of southern Europe have considerably lower suicide rates than do Protestant societies to their north. Societies that are not primarily achievement-oriented, such as Malaya and large parts of the Middle East, have lower suicide rates than does the United States. Within most cultures, the more responsible the position in society, the higher the suicide rate. For example, more army officers commit suicide than soldiers.

A tradition of collective suicide in the history of religious sects begins, as far as we know, with the Circumcellion wing of the Donatists, a fourth-century Christian sect in North Africa, and continues to the present day. These sects, or at least their extreme wings, regard life on earth as a relatively unimportant prelude to life after death, to paradise. This mind-set can acquire additional impetus at a time when it is thought that the world is about to come to an end. The sects, religious or secular, consciously and physically distance themselves from society, deciding to settle in places like Georgetown, Guyana, or in Waco, Texas. The sects who commit collective suicide have typically withdrawn from reality in general. Anything and everything seems possible. The transition to paradise may be by way of a spaceship hiding behind a comet, as in the case of the Heaven's Gate sect. A Hamas terrorist who was captured after his failed suicide attempt told his Israelis captors the following story: He had viewed a trick-photography film prepared before his mission that showed him handing Allah his detached head as he entered paradise. Israeli interrogators explained to him that in the case of a major explosion his head was unlikely to be in one piece. He and other unsuccessful suicide candidates may aim to protest the Israeli occupation, hate America and the Jews, and intend to liberate all of Palestine, but they also see their suicides as joyful occasions: awaiting them in paradise are rivers of milk and honey, and beautiful young women. Those entering paradise are eventually reunited with their families and as martyrs stand in front of God as innocent as a new-born baby.

The indoctrination of the positive value of suicide has been especially intense in Sri Lanka where almost all the candidates among the Tamil

Tigers are in their teens. Carrying cyanide on their persons is considered to be an expression of their commitment to their cause: "We are married to our cyanide; it makes us clear-headed and purposeful." This commitment to self-destruction is combined with training in the commission of acts of the greatest cruelty. Some of the Palestinian candidates for suicide, on the other hand, display a more fatalistic attitude, and argue that since they are bound to die violently sooner or later, they might as well die for a good cause.

Some of the families of suicide bombers in the Middle East accept the fate of their dead heroes fatalistically. Others grieve deeply, complain about brainwashing, and ask why the spiritual leaders who prepared them for the mission had not sent their own children. Most of the suicide bombers are young, between eighteen and twenty-two years of age, but there are also some older ones, husbands and fathers, between twenty-five and thirty years old, who apparently are selected for want of younger candidates. According to their own words, their main motivation is religious, and only secondarily do they act as patriots and Arab nationalists. They have been misled, since Islam does not recommend suicide and the liberation of the homeland is not a religious duty, for Islam does not recognize homelands. But in the bombers' understanding (and in the minds of those who spiritually prepare them), religious and nationalist motives are confused to a large extent, and to distinguish between them may well be an impossible task.

TERRORISM, PSYCHOPATHOLOGY, AND LITERATURE

There is yet another category of potential terrorists that criminologists and psychiatrists have been notably reluctant to deal with, and which in the past has been considered outside the purview of students of terrorism. These are the psychopaths or sociopaths, whom an earlier generation of forensic experts described with a variety of terms, such as emotional and moral insanity, volitional insanity, epileptic insanity, temporary insanity, intellectual insanity, homicidal insanity, homicidal impulses, moral imbecility, and so on. Theologians and ordinary people of a bygone age used unscientific words such as villains and criminals. Specialists have been reluctant to deal with this category because, if such violence is indeed psychotic in nature and thus untreatable, it is irrelevant to their studies at both the theoretical and practical levels.

Psychopaths seem not to have developed the restraints that control the rest of humanity's behavior. Whether incited by greed, hate, the urge to dominate and impose their views on others, overpowering sexual instincts, or motives that cannot be fathomed, they are neither psychotic nor even neurotic in the textbook sense. Their personalities are constructed differently; some simply call them deviant or abnormal. Acts of violence committed by people of this kind are often done on the spur of the moment. But others may commit acts of terror on the grand scale—not on an impulse, but following long and detailed preparation. In the past such opportunities did not exist, and even today they are few and far between. But in the future, those eager to inflict maximum damage and harm on their fellow human beings will be in a much better position to do so.

This leads to the question of to what extent people in this psychopathic category can be driven by an ideology; does the ideology simply offer them a rationalization of their destructive instincts? It is unlikely that even the most extreme ideas will turn an otherwise peaceful human being into someone who runs amok. But even this cannot be stated with total certainty, for the laws governing collective behavior are not those of individual psychology. On the other hand, it seems likely that those with a predisposition for violence will usually find a cause, be it left wing or right wing in inspiration, religious or secular.

In any attempt to understand the psychology and the motives of people with such a predisposition, the literature of the last century is of more help than the textbooks of forensic medicine. The French realist writer Émile Zola was influenced by the then fashionable theories of degeneracy, and the murderers in his novels *La bete humaine, L'assomoir,* and *Therese Racquin* are driven by physiological and social factors: heredity, alcohol, greed, poverty. In the novels of Dostoevsky, the metaphysical dimension of murder is introduced. Both Smerdyakov and Ivan Karamazov in *The Brothers Karamazov* believe that there are no moral laws binding them, that "everything is permitted"—the old motive that has appeared from Hassan Sabah, the guru of the Assassins, to contemporary apostles of chaos. Smerdyakov is bored with life; he kills his father, the elder Karamazov, but suffers no guilt at all, and when he hangs himself in the end this has to do mainly, it would appear, with his epileptic attacks rather than moral considerations. In *Besy,* or *The Demons,* Dostoevsky's famous antiterrorist novel, we meet a character possessed by the idea of destruction who kills a fellow terrorist, not because he thinks that the victim is an informer as he pretends, but to give content to his otherwise empty life. Dostoevsky also introduces Satanists, as well as individuals who believe that a superior human being should rule over the rest.

Dostoevsky's novel was a caricature of the terrorists (the Nihilists), whose inner motivation was quite different from what he imagined. The story of the murder of the fellow conspirator was rooted in reality; it draws on the historic Bakunin and his theory of "pan-destructionism," on Nechaev, who tried to outflank Bakunin on the side of superviolence, and on the event of the mysterious killing of a student with the improbable name of Ivan Ivanovich Ivanov. Bakunin, incidentally, set high hopes on the involvement of religious sectarians in the revolutionary movement; in this as in some other respects, he was ahead of his times. Dostoevsky's fears as to what human beings were capable of doing once they set themselves up as the supreme judges and shed all moral restraints were not unwarranted. His characters and his message may have greater significance for the twenty-first century than they had for the nineteenth, when his writing was perceived as an apology for the tsarist status quo and a libel on the revolutionary movement.

Dostoevsky's villains, like Zola's, murdered and were driven by greed, boredom, and the wish to hurt society. These villains lived at a time when the means to create much greater havoc were not yet at their disposal. The idea that this would be possible in the future had occurred to Jules Verne (*Robur the Conqueror*), but it was spelled out in detail only by H. G. Wells, who had scientific training and lived at a time of great scientific breakthroughs. Two of his early and most important novels, *The Invisible Man* (1897) and *The Island of Dr. Moreau* (1896), deal with scientists willing and able to carry out experiments that would give them unprecedented power.

Perhaps the work of literature most prophetic with respect to terrorism is a novel first published in Berlin in 1897 by Stanislaw Przybyszewski, a Polish author then writing in German, titled *Satan's Kinder* (*Children of Satan*). It was exceedingly famous at the time but quickly forgotten. Przybyszewski was not concerned with the technology of terrorism but about its motives and aims. The heroes are all in deep despair. Gordon, the leader of the group, says that he wants to destroy for destruction's sake: "Destruction is my dogma, my creed, my religion." He belongs to a breed of aesthetes who murder a human in cold blood but would not let a canary starve to death. Factories, he suggests, should be burned down so that their workers will be unemployed and become children of Satan, pillaging and killing at random. The novel ends with the unnamed city they wanted to destroy going up in flames, as they experience a satanic feeling of happiness: "More, more, more . . . to destroy whole cities, provinces, an entire country, the whole world, this would be greatest happiness." Given the limited technical means available at the time, critics were justified in dismissing this horror story as a feverish fantasy or an example of the apocalyptic vision so fashionable at the turn of the last century. A hundred years later, however, there is more reluctance to dismiss such imaginings as fantasies.

After the Second World War, the theme of world destruction became very frequent indeed in movies and in novels. As this genre of fiction grew, so did the number of characters instrumental in bringing about such visions—radical terrorists enjoying destruction, mad scientists oblivious of the consequences of their inventions, and blackmailers—and now they had weapons of superviolence and mass destruction at their disposal. This literature dovetailed with the need to rethink earlier writings about the origins and motives of modern terrorism. Past investigations focused predominantly on social conditions and national aspirations, and on major terrorist movements with hundreds of members and thousands of sympathizers. In the age of the arms of mass destruction, research has to be extended beyond the search for objective conditions and rational aims to the possible motives of a handful of irrational terrorists, perhaps only one. And there is no known method of discovering exactly why such groups or individuals think and act as they do.

Maxwell Taylor and Ethel Quayle, coauthors of *Terrorist Lives*, have recently tried to refute the contention that a terrorist may be a psychopathic killer. They neatly debunk the caricatures of the terrorist drawn by nineteenth-century cartoonists and Dostoevsky at his worst: disheveled, sinister figures with big black beards and fierce facial expressions, like the classical pirate in children's books. If this were the case, the task of airport guards of identifying potential hijackers and terrorists would be easy indeed. But Taylor and Quayle continue: "The reality of the terrorist is that they are essentially unremarkable people, in psychological terms disturbingly similar to their victims." At this stage generalizations become problematic if not downright misleading. One recalls the unfortunate "banality of evil" thesis of Hannah Arendt, transferred to the field of terrorism. As Joseph Conrad once noted in the introduction to one of his novels, evil is seldom if ever banal. Terrorists, Taylor and Quayle argue, are not automatons or evil, heartless killers. But is this assertion borne out by the evidence, especially in more recent years, and especially outside the Americas and Western Europe? If the perpetrators were indeed similar in psychological terms to the victims, we would all be potential terrorists. This is clearly not the case, but it offers little comfort. For now that we have entered the age of the weapons of mass destruction, great havoc can be wrought by only a few psychopaths.

TERROR
and the Far Right

Nineteenth-century terrorism was either nationalist-separatist in inspiration or left wing, as in tsarist Russia. The terrorists of the 1920s more often than not belonged to the extreme right, while in the 1970s they were predominantly left wing. Today's terrorism is mainly right-wing extremist or religious-nationalist. The problematic character of the political terms "left" and "right" has been stressed more than once in this discussion. They used to apply more precisely than they do now, and are more helpful in describing the history of terrorism in Europe and the United States. Baader Meinhof in Germany and the Italian Red Brigades came out of the Marxist tradition and used Marxist-Leninist-Maoist slogans, whereas the neo-Nazis and the neo-Fascists derived their ideology, such as it was, from their historical predecessors. If displaying banners, the former would have opted for the red flag and hammer and sickle and the latter for the swastika; the former would have been singing the "Internationale" and the other the "Horst Wessel" song. But, as has been pointed out earlier in this study, traditional left-wing doctrine has favored terrorism only in rare cases, and the same is true with regard to the far right. This is not because they were humanitarians but because they feared that terrorism opened the door to all kinds of possibilities that might endanger their own cause. Of course, many of the notorious terrorist groups have taken on political coloring for their own purposes.

There were also some basic differences and commonalities between the terrorists of the extreme left and right. The left claimed to be internationalists, champions of the exploited and downtrodden everywhere, particularly in the Third World; the right put the interests and values of their own countries or race above all. But extreme left and right also shared values and ideas, including a distrust and even hate of parliamentary democracy and a populist orientation that could with almost equal ease turn left or right. Terrorists of both political extremes thought of themselves as revolutionaries.

Left-wing ideology was virtually all-pervasive in the 1970s, and this was reflected in the propaganda of nationalist groups such as the IRA, ETA, and the Palestinian terrorists—for example, in anti-imperialist slogans and calls for working-class solidarity, and so on. This kind of ideological mimicry misled many observers, who took the slogans at face value and misjudged the true orientation of these groups and overrated the depth of their doctrinal beliefs.

These misjudgments sometimes had amusing and embarrassing results. Some on the left, from Sartre to Fanon, from Marcuse to Chomsky, invoked a variety of arguments to explain and, in some cases, to justify this kind of violence. They took the revolutionary phraseology at face value and believed in the liberating and progressive mission of many, if not all, terrorists. Some of them argued that the publicity given terrorism was nothing but a smoke screen meant to divert attention from the true terrorism, that of the repressive imperialist state. At the very least it was argued that one man's terrorist was another person's freedom fighter, a dictum that was thought to be both witty and profound.

This kind of beatification continued as long as terrorism was predominantly left wing in inspiration (or was thought to be so). Times changed, however, and during the 1980s, left-wing terrorism petered out, a trend that coincided with the collapse of the Soviet bloc, though it was not caused by the collapse. Instead, the terrorist initiative in Western countries such as the United States, and also Germany and Turkey, moved to the extreme right. Yesterday's theories about the progressive character of terrorism ceased to make sense and became, in fact, embarrassing. The burning of a hostel housing foreign guest workers in Germany could hardly be described any longer as a liberating act. Neither could the bombing of the World Trade Center in New York or the bombing of a government building in Oklahoma City be interpreted as a prologue to a revolution that would help the masses. The old wisdom about one person's terrorist being another person's freedom fighter was no longer heard.

TERROR IN THE HEARTLAND

The swing from left- to right-wing terrorism manifested itself dramatically in the United States. Whereas in the 1970s the media and public attention focused on the Weathermen, and, to a lesser degree, on several black militant groups, attention in the 1990s concentrated on the violence of the extreme right. Similar extremist groups of the right had existed, of course, twenty years earlier, and, indeed, in one form or another throughout recent American history. But when they had been active, they had been ignored, and the lack of publicity had acted as a deterrent. For the aim of terrorism, more often than not, was propaganda by deed, and if their actions were not publicized—or if their actions were ascribed to their political foes—it must have seemed pointless or even counterproductive to engage in terrorist operations. Indeed, the public would have reached the conclusion that there was no real difference between the Weathermen and various other klans and patriotic posses, between white and black identity movements, and this was certainly not the impression militants wanted to create. There is no political law that says there is at any given time room for only the terrorists of one political persuasion. But by and large it seems to be true that only one species of terrorist can attract the limelight at a time, and in the case of America in the 1990s, as well as a number of European countries, this happened to be the extreme right.

The history of right-wing extremist movements advocating violence in the United States is long and well-documented. It is a field difficult to survey because it is so chaotic and internally divided. It has religious as well as political sources; at one time the stress was on the struggle against Catholics (during the big Irish immigration wave in the middle of the nineteenth century), at another it has been predominantly anti-black (in the South after the Civil War when the Ku Klux Klan allegedly numbered several million members). Following the integration of Jews in American society after the turn of the century, anti-Semitism became and remained a central theme. More recently, the fight against centralized government has become the central issue. Some of these groups have been anti-Christian and pagan in character (for example, Odinism, in which Nordic gods figure), especially the out-and-out neo-Nazi groups, but the majority have advocated a peculiar Christian Identity theology which claims that Aryan Americans are the true Israelites, whereas the Jews are the children of Satan. According to Identity theology, the tribe of Menasse, the chosen people, traveled from Palestine to Europe and eventually boarded the *Mayflower* bound for America. As for the other biblical tribes, Zebulun became France, Efraim took over Britain, Asher went to Sweden, Issachar to Finland, and so forth. They all made out reasonably well, with the exception of the tribe of Judah, which deteriorated in Babylonian captivity, became an evil force, and now constitutes world Jewry. The Identity movement accepts the Christian New Testament but rejects the (Jewish) Old Testament, following the "German Christians" in Germany during the Nazi era. Whereas the Klan was a nativist-American phenomenon reflecting southern farmers' fears of freed blacks, Anglo-Israelitism was a British importation that reached America by way of Canada. It was originally an intellectual fad, one among many at the time, and acquired its particularly aggressive and even violent character only recently in the United States.

However, in view of the countless splits within the Klan and the various Aryan resistance groups, only a very rough picture can be given of the extreme right. They all believe in the superiority of the white Aryan race, and want to destroy or at the very least reduce in influence all others. But they also hate liberals and Democrats, even if they are of pure Aryan stock, lesbians and homosexuals, policemen and-women, tax collectors, politicians, especially those located in Washington and New York, bankers, the media, and, generally speaking, everyone who disagrees with them. While few groups of this camp have rejected violence and terrorism in principle, still fewer have actually engaged in terrorist activities. The extreme right is not a highly organized and disciplined camp with a well-delineated party line, but more of a breeding ground from which individual terrorists and small terrorist groups have emerged and continue to develop. From time to time these groups have engaged in mutual help and shown solidarity, but there is no central command and little coordination.

Up to a point, the terrorism of the extreme right is a psychological phenomenon. But it is also true that in its less extreme form the doctrine of the extreme right appeals to the traditionally strong individualist streak found among farmers and small-town Americans, who tend to resent strong central government and taxation. Montana and Michigan are strongholds of this feeling. These men and women consider themselves, not always without reason, forgotten and neglected, politically, socially, economically, and culturally; the time and money of the central authorities is spent, as they see it, on welfare for people who should not be in America in the first place and on a great variety of causes that have nothing to do with traditional American interests and values. Washington is the enemy for many of these people, and the interference of any government official

above the local sheriff is considered an unwarranted and illegal intervention in local autonomy. To a considerable extent the origins of the extreme
right, especially in the Midwest, has been in tax-rebellion movements.
Ideologists of the extreme right have decried the lack of idealism among
contemporary white Americans, but there is much reason to believe that
if the tax issue were minimized, its appeal would be limited. The spread
of militias is a reaction against the progressive bureaucratization of so
many aspects of life in the United States since the 1960s. As a leader of
the group called the Patriots put it, America, having been once upon a
time the least bureaucratic of all countries, has become one of the most
annoyingly regulated. Americans must not just bow to the bureaucracy,
it must submit, register, file, take tests, get licenses, get stickers, and report.

The Patriots and their sympathizers do not accept that this is the inevitable price to be paid for population growth and the increasingly complex character of modern life. There is a growing feeling, not just among
the extremists, that much of this bureaucratic intervention has been
clumsy and unnecessary and demands a violent reaction. The Patriots have
been incensed by the flood of new immigrants, legal and illegal, who, as
they see it, exploit the welfare state. At the same time, the backlash has
been a cultural protest against blasphemous utterances and exhibitions,
against the burning of the flag, and against homosexuality. There have
been protests against the lunacies of the cultural establishment of the East
Coast and against the media and Hollywood, with their preoccupation
with everything likely to cause offense in small-town America. The success
of the far right can be understood only within this wider context. Only a
few individuals have joined the lunatic fringe of the right, but these small
groups have their roots in a far wider movement of protest.

The extreme right has also gained support among the arms lobby. The
traditional suspicions of foreigners, big business, and especially banks have
provided further impetus. Populist views, the opposition to capitalism as
well as socialism, let alone communism, have a long and powerful tradition in the United States, and so have the fears and the paranoia. If there
is an ideal society for members of these extremist groups, it is the small
communities of Paul Revere's Revolution-era New England, even though
a great many militants of the far right are by no means of Anglo-Saxon
stock. For others, the ideal society endorses the Hitlerite concept of a pure
Aryan race.

The Patriots, to use one example, are far more preoccupied with alleged
dangers and perceived enemies than with the positive parts of their program. They are hate and fear groups, and, as such, they could exist without
ideals but not without enemies. They genuinely believe that the American

government is constructing concentration camps in which the Patriots will be placed and destroyed, a belief that fuels their intense hatred of and attacks against various government agencies and their representatives.

America, as these people see it, is a country ruled by Illuminati, Jews, Wall Street, the United Nations, the Trilateral Commission, and a variety of other groups, all aiming to subjugate and Balkanize the nation. According to the broadcasts and written literature of these groups, foreign troops have actually entered the United States to disarm and ultimately to annihilate the white population. Among these foreign soldiers are Nepalese, Gurkhas, and Los Angeles street gangsters. They are the vanguard of the United Nations, which will equip them with tanks and troop carriers to establish the New World Order. (This New World Order is not to be confused with the Order, one of the most extreme and most violent groups within this camp.) As the extremists see it, there are conspiracies everywhere, with signs bearing secret meanings hidden on the highways as well as in the supermarkets. All these strange symbols have clandestine and sinister meanings. In this respect and others there is a striking resemblance between the white supremacists and some black groups, such as the Nation of Islam, which believes in numerology, in the idea that AIDS is a form of biological warfare against the black race, and, generally speaking, in the notion that all whites are the children of Satan.

Mention has been made of the many internal divisions within the extreme right, owing partly to personal animosities among its leaders and partly to regional differences, but also to genuine ideological divergences. Anti-Semitism, on the ideological level, plays a crucial role in some of these groups but not in others, and the same is true with regard to terrorist action. However, the far right movement has also encouraged "leaderless resistance" and "phantom" cells; this is based on the assumption that even if numbers of individuals are compromised or eliminated, the movement will still survive.

The concept of leaderless resistance has been promoted above all by Louis Beam, a former member of the Klan and one of the leaders of the militias. The basic principle of a division of labor between the political wing of a terrorist movement and the fighters carrying out assassinations and other terrorist operations is, of course, very old. It has been accepted by the Irish for at least a century, and more recently by the Basques and the Palestinians (the PLO has a military and a political wing, and so has Hamas). However, the American militias take "leaderless resistance" one step further inasmuch as the organizers leave the tactical initiative and the operations to individual members. They may provide weapons, logistics help, and safe houses, but they will not necessarily be told in advance what actions are prepared by their brothers in arms. This kind of approach may work as long as the militias engage in sporadic violence, but it is hardly practical with a sustained campaign of terror. Nor is it a new concept; it has been used with varying degrees of success by various illegal political and terrorist movements.

The militias are stronger in some states than in others. Montana and Michigan have been mentioned. Militias have not made much of an appearance, until recently, on the eastern seaboard. Other such groups and places are the Arizona Patriots; the Aryan Nation (a quasi-Nazi organization); the Covenant; the Sword and the Arm of the Lord (CSA), located on the Missouri-Arkansas border; Elohim City on the Oklahoma-Arkansas border; and the Order (an offshoot of the Aryan Brotherhood). The number of militias has declined somewhat in recent years, but those that survive have become more extreme and more activist. At the present time, they are most active in Texas, Florida, California, Ohio, Montana, and Michigan. They are active on the Internet; 179 Web sites of such groups have been counted. It was noted earlier that some of these groups have acquired large stretches of land, usually near the border between two states. This is partly to engage in military exercises undisturbed by on-lookers, and partly because border locations serve as effective hiding places and safe houses for members on the run, since those who have committed a crime in one state may not be automatically extradited to another.

The social composition of the more extremist militias tends to be working class or lower middle class. Members are predominantly male and, in contrast to terrorist groups in other parts of the world, not very young. Among their leaders are fundamentalist preachers (some of them self-appointed or self-styled), such as the founder of Aryan Nations, James Ellison; CSA's Kerry Noble; and Pastor Pete Peters, the leading figure in the Identity movement. The presence of several former army officers should be mentioned; examples are Colonel Jack Mohr of the Christian Patriots Defense League (CPDL) and Colonel James "Bo" Gritz, formerly of the Green Berets, a specialist in guerrilla warfare and presidential candidate of the Populist Party. However, some of the leaders of the smallest and most radical groups have neither a military nor a theological background but are drifters like the young Hitler or the young Mussolini, though without their charisma. Mark Koernke, for instance, was a janitor at the University of Michigan; William L. Pierce, author of *The Turner Diaries* (more on this later), is one of the rare exceptions—a university graduate with a Ph.D. in physics.

The groups called the militias came into being in 1993–94 partly as the result of the initiative of Colonel Gritz, who emphasized in his 1992 presidential campaign the existence of a new framework to combat the government. They based themselves on various Patriot and Identity organizations that have existed for at least three decades, and they received some fresh impetus from the Ruby Ridge incident in Idaho in 1992 and above all from the Waco, Texas, disaster. As federal agents at Ruby Ridge tried to arrest a white supremacist named Randy Weaver, against whom a warrant had been served for gun charges, they shot Weaver's wife and son. The bungled attempt to seize David Koresh in Waco, which resulted in the deaths of numerous Branch Davidians, only seemed to confirm the extremists' conviction that the government was about to move against them and kill all true patriots as well as their families.

In earlier years, particularly during the Cold War, the patriots of the extreme right were preoccupied with the danger of an imminent communist invasion, and also with the danger, nay certainty, of a communist takeover inside the United States, engineered by the Trilateral Commission, the Council of Foreign Relations, the Democrats, the anti-gun lobby, and so on. With the collapse of the Soviet Union this danger receded, but the militants of the extreme right found a new enemy in the New World Order, which President Bush proclaimed, on the eve of the Gulf War, when a coalition of countries made common cause to drive Iraq from Kuwait. The New World Order quickly became the symbol of Satan for the extreme right. But had President Bush not coined this phrase, providing grist for the patriots' mills, they would have found another target, however unreal and fantastic.

Within a short time over two hundred militias came into being: thirty in Michigan, twenty-two in California, twenty each in Alabama and Colorado, and others in Missouri, Texas, and Florida, the states where patriotic groups traditionally had footholds. By 1997 it was estimated that there were some six hundred of them, but this number included very tiny cells. These militias were not well organized, and their composition and number changed from month to month and sometimes from day to day. They all emphasized preparation for an apocalyptic showdown with a tyrannical government and a race war that would begin in the year 2000. Some were basically defensive in character, whereas others actively engaged in attacks on the federal government as well as on groups and individuals on their hit list.

The militias actively spread their message through a variety of channels: bulletins, periodicals, and above all radio broadcasts on middle and short waves. It is difficult to judge how many people were reached by these preachers of hate, but one person on whom they certainly had a considerable impact was Timothy McVeigh, who was convicted for the Oklahoma City bombing.

The internal divisions in the extreme-right groups and the considerable differences among them needs to be stressed again and again. Some of these groups advocate armed struggle, defensive and offensive. Others do not, even though they favor, in principle, the idea of a militia, which, they argue, is in the spirit of the Founding Fathers and the Constitution. Some of the extremists emphasize the need to study the Bible as well as the Constitution, whereas the most extreme do not think much of either; their bible is *Mein Kampf* and other Nazi inspirational writings. Some extremists see a tyrannical and corrupt government and a bureaucracy run wild as their main enemy, whereas others focus on homosexuals or racial and ethnic minorities. The most extreme activists are contemptuous of the law-abiding militias ("all talk and no action"), whereas the more responsible militias condemn the irresponsible "loose cannons" that have given the militia movement and the patriots in general "adverse publicity." Some of the violent groups collaborate with other terrorist or potentially terrorist factions, such as the confrontational wing of the anti-abortion movement, the "county movement" that demands state sovereignty, and small groups of Christian Patriots and Christian Reconstructionists. But other militias prefer to go their own way, avoiding groups sponsoring single-issue agendas that are not their own. Just as the Communist parties of Latin America were embarrassed by the activities of terrorists in their countries and distanced themselves from them, the nonviolent extreme right believes that even if the violent extremists' hearts are in the right place, their actions will cause more harm than good. The violent extremists, the majority argues, cannot possibly attract public sympathy, and consequently the "Resistance" finds itself extremely isolated.

The militias would have had far less impact had they based themselves only on the writings of Adolf Hitler admixed with apocalyptic fantasies about hidden satanic messages in supermarkets, UFOs, and the Mark of the Beast. Their appeal is due to real grievances and beliefs deeply anchored in the American tradition, such as the sovereign citizen and the sovereignty of the people. Unlike the pro-Nazis, they favor not a dictatorship but, on the contrary, something akin to a participatory democracy. They invoke not Hitler and Mussolini in their propaganda but Washington, Madison, Hamilton, and Jefferson. They claim that the elementary rights of free American citizens have been infringed by statutory laws imposed on them by politicians and bankers. They complain that free citizens are hamstrung by unending regulations and that their right to carry arms is being progressively denied. There is a substantial pool of angry Americans from which the militias have attracted followers, a reservoir for a protest movement but also for terrorist action.

THE TURNER DIARIES

The bible of the terrorists of the extreme right is *The Turner Diaries*, by Andrew Macdonald. Written in 1978, it has sold more than 200,000 copies without the benefit of bookstore distribution. It was the favorite book of Timothy McVeigh, who followed faithfully the content of the *Diaries* when he blew up the government building in Oklahoma City. Macdonald is a pen name of William Pierce, a longtime leader of the National Alliance, one of the most rabid pro-Nazi sects of the 1980s. The book is political science fiction; it begins in 1991 (year 8 before the New Era) and describes the Great Revolution that takes place in America and throughout the world through the eyes of a thirty-five-year-old rank-and-file member of the Organization, which is also called the Order. The pseudodiaries, written by the main character, Henry Turner, start as the armed struggle finally gets under way "after all these years of talking and nothing but talking." The revolutionary struggle as described in this book begins with the murder of Bermann, a Jewish deli owner: "Henry leaped on Bermann's back, seized him by the hair, and cut his throat from ear to ear in one, swift motion . . . altogether we got $1426 dollars." Though these and similar acts in the struggle for liberation are always successful, the pages of the book are strewn with the bodies of martyred so-called freedom fighters. Turner eventually concludes that the Order is failing because the great majority of white Americans are not reacting as they should. Initially, he had hoped there would be a positive response from "white" America to the Order's dramatic strikes against the System, such as the burning of a dozen synagogues. But though white Americans complained as blacks raped their women at will and saw welfare abused at will, they were not rebellious, not even potentially rebellious. Its call to arms being ignored, the Organization began to treat the American people "realistically, like a herd of cattle." Since they were no longer capable of responding to an idealistic appeal, "we began appealing to things they can understand, fear and hunger. We will take the food off their tables and empty their refrigerators . . . And when they begin getting hungry, we will make them fear us more than they fear the System."

The Order starts a scorched-earth campaign, destroying food supplies and factories, blowing up power plants, forging money, bombing places of public entertainment, and demolishing highways. One of their major operations is blowing up the FBI headquarters in Washington using forty-four one-hundred-pound bags of ammonium nitrate loaded in a van, the same substance used in the Oklahoma City bombing. Eventually a full-scale civil war breaks out in which three quarters of the American people are killed and most of the countryside is destroyed and radioactively poisoned. By 1994, only 50 million Americans survive, but most of them are Aryans and there is the hope of a new Aryan-American. Next the national revolution spreads abroad; first Toronto is nuked, then Israel is destroyed with nuclear bombs. China is also destroyed, "by a combination of chemical, biological and radiological means . . ." Europe and Russia are not spared; some 16 million square miles, including most of Asia, are "effectively sterilized, becoming the Great Eastern Waste." Thus ends the story of Henry Turner, "who gained immortality as he faithfully fulfilled his obligation to his race, to the Organization, and to the Holy Order which had accepted him into its ranks. And in so doing he helped greatly to assure that his race would survive and prosper, that the Organization would achieve its worldwide political and military goals, and that the Order would spread its wise and benevolent rule over the earth for all time to come."

Less widely read and quoted than *The Turner Diaries* is another work of fiction by the same author, titled *Hunter*, published in 1989 and dedicated to Joseph Paul Franklin, the "Lonely Hunter who saw his duty as a white man and did what a responsible man of his race must do, to the best of his ability and without regard of the personal consequences." What Franklin had done to the best of his ability was to kill an interracial couple in Madison, Wisconsin, to murder two black joggers in Salt Lake City, and to kill a man leaving a bar mitzvah service in St. Louis, Missouri. *Hunter* describes a truck bombing: once again, ammonium nitrate is used. In the novel, a little under 5,000 pounds is employed; the all-too-real bombing in Oklahoma City used a little over 4,300 pounds. In *The Turner Diaries*, a similar bomb kills seven hundred employees of the FBI; in Oklahoma City some 160 people perished. The author also relates in *Hunter* the murder of a senator, a TV talk-show host, several racially mixed couples, two bishops, a rabbi, a congressman, a cardinal, two governors, and several enemies of the patriots.

Most of the literature of the violent groups of the extreme right does not belong to the realm of fiction. It includes handbooks, field manuals, and guidebooks to prepare the "revolutionaries" for ambushes, teach them marksmanship, and instruct them on performing "battlefield executions" and bomb preparation (again mainly from readily available ammonium nitrate, freely found on farms). The need to kill all law-enforcement agents is stressed; also marked are sheriffs, county commissioners, journalists, homosexuals, nonwhites, and unassimilable white groups. (According to Louis Beam, his followers would set up their rule in Texas. Foreigners would have twenty-four hours to leave. But since most would not leave voluntarily, many would have to be exterminated so as to encourage the others.)

Some of these technical handbooks were originally composed for and by nineteenth-and twentieth-century anarchists; others belong to the literature of the far left of the 1970s and of the IRA. One of the earliest and most detailed such handbooks, originally published in 1973 but sold and circulated to this day, is "The Road Back" by Maccaba (a pseudonym), which gives precise practical information on how to prepare explosive devices, both primitive and sophisticated, and on how to blow up railroads and various other installations. It also gives information of use to small guerrilla bands with regard to communication networks, and while some of this is now outdated, much is still used by terrorist individuals and groups.

FROM WORDS TO ACTS

Ultraright terrorist groups have been enlisting members for a considerable time. "Join the Army and serve the UN or join the militia and serve America" is one of their slogans. They have been stockpiling weapons, partly through raiding armories and partly through legal purchases. There have been and still exist many combat courses in camps thought to belong to terrorist groups. Timothy McVeigh was arrested a few miles from such a compound, one of the many strange circumstances of his case.

There have been sporadic but numerous attacks. A natural-gas pipeline in Arkansas was dynamited. Gordon Kahl, a North Dakota farmer and one of the martyrs of the movement, killed two U.S. marshals in 1983 and wounded three others when they tried to arrest him for a violation of probation. He was chased to a farmhouse in Arkansas and killed in an exchange of fire in which a local sheriff was also killed. Between 1982 and 1984, the Order (also known as the Silent Brotherhood and Bruder Schweigen) killed a Denver talk-show host named Alan Berg, and attacked and robbed a Brinks armored car in California, stealing $3.5 million. Its leader, Robert Matthews, was shot and killed by police in Washington State in 1984. These are only two of their most spectacular operations. Other activities of these groups and individuals included firebombing, armed robberies, counterfeiting, the execution of at least one of their own members, as well as countless campaigns of threat and intimidation against local officials. In 1994, in Michigan, Missouri, and other states, significant numbers of machine guns and other weapons were found in the Order's possession. Sizable quantities of poison were also discovered. Around the same time, in Lancaster, Ohio, bubonic plague cultures were found in the possession of a militia sympathizer. In Missouri the same year, a state trooper was shot and dynamite seized during a raid of a compound held by a group calling itself Citizens for Christ. Among weapons found there that were stolen from army installations were Stinger missiles and rockets; about a ton of explosives stolen from commercial enterprises were also found.

In 1995, two members of the Patriotic Council were convicted in Minnesota for planning to use a biological toxin (ricin) against federal employees and police. Reports of stockpiled weapons of every kind were received in many states, as were threats against judges and other public officials. On more than one occasion, major attacks were prevented by law-enforcement officials who had received warnings from their agents. There seems to have been a plan to blow up the courthouse in Spokane, Washington, by a supporter of Randy Weaver, the militant whose family was killed in the Ruby Ridge standoff.

These activities were not without effect. The *New York Times* summarized the state of affairs in a June 14, 1997, editorial:

> Some counties in America can no longer enforce their land tax and weapons laws, unwilling to risk that an employee might be attacked by militia members. Firefighters say they cannot fly helicopters over land owned by certain militia members for fear they will be shot down. In at least 23 states militia members have filed phony liens against local officials. Government employees are so vilified in some communities that no one will sit with them in church.

Bureaucratic interference and high taxation can explain, up to a point, the popularity of the backlash against the government in parts of the United States. But in most developed countries the tax rates are even higher, and while there has been grumbling, complaints, and political reactions, citizens of these countries have not taken up arms.

In any case, objective conditions and subjective perceptions explain only in small part the hate mentality and the conspiracy theories that have sprouted in America. Although neither hate and aggression nor fear of conspiracies are unique features of the last quarter of the twentieth century, one might speculate that the persistence of various survivalist sects and the fear of dangers, real and imaginary, is a continuation of ancient instincts. It might be interpreted as a conditioned reflex that persists even after the reality of the danger has disappeared. Could it be that over the ages a need for enemies and the perception of danger has become ingrown, and that some people will not be able to function unless they can find objects of hate and fear?

In various countries, at various times, violence has not stopped even after civil wars ended; the activists simply turned to banditry, such as in the United States after the Civil War, in nineteenth-century southern Italy, and Angola in our time. In a similar way, the psychological need for a belief in an omnipotent and omnipresent "hidden hand" that is responsible for all the world's misfortunes may have become part of the human condition—at least for some humans. Such a fringe seems always to have existed and been tolerated by society. The real danger is when it spreads or finds itself armed with weapons of mass destruction.

By means of radio talk shows, the Internet, cassettes and videotapes, books and periodicals, the militias and other such groups produce and are subjected to a constant stream of hate and conspiracy propaganda. The time-honored forces of evil are Jews and Illuminati, but since the average citizen of Montana and Idaho is unlikely to come face-to-face with many Illuminati or even Jews in his or her daily life, the government becomes the main force and government offices and courthouses, rather than synagogues, the physical targets.

Mention has been made of the New World Order as the new bogey to be added to the traditional distrust of Europe and nonwhite people generally. "Feudal Europe" is said to be the center of all dangerous intrigues to deprive American citizens of their natural rights, with organizations such as the Bilderberg group, the Trilateral Commission, the Council of Foreign Relations, and the annual Davos meetings as the sites of the new witches' Sabbath. The Bible is quoted to prove that mixed marriages are an abomination and homosexuality an even greater sin. Ecologists are distrusted and hated, even as the extreme militants voice their own environmental concerns, and the government is held responsible for the contamination of water resources and other environmental disasters. The Holocaust is denied, and while the breakup of the Soviet Empire cannot possibly be ignored, it is announced that a second coming of communism is around the corner, and the fear of America's becoming socialist or communist has by no means disappeared.

There is a whole universe of conspiracy theories, which have hundreds of thousands of devotees and which, in the Middle East and some other parts of the world, have canonical status. Most Americans and Europeans are quite unaware of this world. Here are a few examples of this literature: John Daniel's three-volume *The Scarlet and the Beast: An Encyclopedia of Conspiracy History* and the "New World Order Intelligence Update." For those with a more religious bent, there are electronic prophecy reports on the Internet, lists of the secrets of the Talmud as well as White Nationalist phone lists, and hundreds of articles explaining who really is running America. In the world of conspiracy theorists there are no accidents. The death of Secretary of Commerce Ron Brown in a plane crash in the former Yugoslavia, of Princess Diana in a traffic accident, an earthquake in Japan, a civil war in Africa, all must have been caused by some hidden hand. For forty dollars, a patriot can order a book on the establishment of the North American concentration camps and their exact locations. There is also practical advice: for a small consideration patriots are instructed on how to invest their money in Switzerland and thus avoid the treasury of the Zionist Occupation Government of the United States.

For many readers this literature is the equivalent of a thriller. Entertaining, fascinating, perhaps even frightening, it is without real consequences for their own lives. But there is always a fringe element who, exposed to indoctrination of this kind, become believers. These may be people whose need for action is so great, they imagine that only violence on a massive scale can stem the otherwise inevitable coming disaster.

RIGHT-WING TERRORISM IN GERMANY

If America is one striking example of the terrorist pendulum swinging from extreme left to far right, Germany is another. The number of reported violent actions committed by individuals belonging to Germany's extreme right was relatively small in the 1980s. Offenses committed by left-wing extremists were far more numerous at the time. The number of right-wing actions rose dramatically, however, to a high of 2,600 in 1992, before falling to 1,489 in 1994 and 781 in 1996, levels still considerably above the average of the 1980s.

The decline in right-wing extremist terrorism between 1994 and 1996 was no doubt connected with the imposition of more draconian sentences and the dissolution of groups on the far right whose activities were found to be in violation of the constitution. It probably also had to do with measures taken to stop, or to limit severely, immigration to Germany from Africa, Asia, and the Middle East. At this point we face an apparent paradox: there is no simple correlation between the presence of foreign "guest workers" and the number of attacks against them. In Baden/Württemberg, for instance, which has a higher than average presence of foreigners and where the right-wing Republicans scored high in the elections, there were considerably fewer attacks than in Mecklenburg in the former East Germany, which has few foreigners. This paradox is not unique. In Weimar Germany, electoral results prove, anti-Semitism was by no means strongest where most Jews were concentrated but in regions of northern and eastern Germany with relatively few Jews.

There was another upswing of right-wing extremist activities in 1997–98, particularly in eastern Germany. How to account for this trend? The statistics unfortunately do not necessarily differentiate between a verbal altercation and an attack in which people were hurt or killed. But they are indicative of a trend. According to the annual report of the German Office for the Protection of the Constitution, all these acts of violence were committed by individuals, not organized terrorist groups acting in unison. Most of the violent acts committed by the extreme left in 1997–98 were protests against the disposal of nuclear waste, and more than half of the violent acts by the German extreme right were directed against foreigners. However, violence was by no means confined to the domestic German right; the number of attacks carried out by Islamists, left-wing Kurds, and right-wing Turks in Germany in 1996 (the last year for which detailed figures are available) constituted a substantial part of the total number of terrorist attacks carried out in Germany, and were certainly among the most spectacular. The Kurds attacked the Turks and vice versa, left-wing Turks attacked the right-wing Turks, and even extreme left-wing Turkish groups fought against one other.

If the great majority of perpetrators of right-wing terrorist acts who were caught did not belong to any identifiable political group, where did they come from? A small part, perhaps 15 percent, were "skinheads," but virtually all others were "unorganized." A second significant fact is that these perpetrators were very young; most were less than twenty years of age, and hardly anyone was over thirty, in stark contrast to the extreme right in the United States. Since individualism is not a trait of the extreme right youth in Germany, there is reason to believe that the terrorist actions were carried out on the spur of the moment by street gangs on the warpath. It is also widely believed that there was no countrywide terrorist network, although there is also some evidence to the contrary: the attacks carried out by German and British hooligans at the soccer World Cup in 1998 in France were clearly planned and logistically coordinated.

Attacks against foreign workers, including legal and illegal immigrants from Asia and Africa, reached their height in 1992–93 with the burning of the homes of asylum seekers in Hoyerswerda, Rostock-Lichtenhagen, Moelln, Brandenburg, and Solingen. These attacks were spontaneous and unorganized, and many of them occurred in the former GDR where relatively few foreigners were living at the time. They were, in all probability, triggered by disappointment with the results of reunification and by the fear that the authorities would direct the stream of asylum seekers to East Germany. The electoral successes of the extreme right in East Germany at that time are probably due to the same feelings.

These attacks had considerable support on the local level; masses of people applauded as the buildings burned. As so often happens in the annals of terrorist attacks, these kinds of actions escalated, lasted for a few months, and then died down. They did not entirely disappear, but the quick mobilization of the police in cases of a threatened pogrom or clash, the heavy sentences imposed on those apprehended, and the virtual cessation of immigration brought about a quick reversal of the trend. An analysis of the background of those involved in the attacks showed that at least 70 percent of those arrested were under twenty-one years of age, many had been drinking before the attacks were launched (beer drinking being an essential part of the German right-wing extremist scene), and none of them belonged to an organized group. As one official report put it at the time, there was a Red Army faction in Germany but no Brown Army. At most there existed some Wehrsportgruppen, or groups of people mostly in small and middle-size towns with a penchant for collecting arms and engaging in military exercises. Most of these groups are of right-wing extremist inspiration, and some of them were outlawed by the authorities. But in no cases could a connection between the Wehrsportgruppen and the terrorist actions be proven. While the military fans were intensely patriotic and their hatred of foreigners second to none, the lifestyle of the juvenile terrorists—the skinhead way of life, their music, the consumption of great quantities of beer—was not to their taste. The Wehrsportgruppen put discipline above everything else, and wanted a leader or at least a commander. In contrast, the skinheads stood for anything but discipline, would not recognize a leader, and were not interested in sustained effort.

A comparison of this chaotic right-wing German terrorist scene with its predecessors after World War I does not help to explain the phenomenon. While the early Nazi Party did not exactly frown on violence against political enemies, its leaders and many of its members were World War I veterans, and as such had been accustomed to discipline. Their strategic target, like that of the Italian Fascists, was "to conquer the street." Individual terror in both Germany and Italy was thought to be unimportant and a waste of time. As usual, there were a few exceptions, such as the murder of the Socialist leader Giacomo Mateotti, on instructions from Mussolini in 1925, and the Potempa case in 1932, when Nazis killed a Communist activist in a village in Upper Silesia. Hundreds of political opponents were killed or injured in street battles, particularly in 1931–32, by Nazis. But this was collective rather than individual violence. The Nazi strategy was to come to power legally, or at least semilegally; they had their private army but no terrorist groups in the established sense.

Neither is a comparison with the Freikorps, active in 1919–22, very relevant. The Freikorps consisted of veterans (with a high proportion of young officers) as well as of very young people who had not had a chance to fight in the war and wanted to redress Germany's defeat. These terrorists killed Walther Rathenau, the foreign minister of the Weimar Republic, as well as several other politicians, and tried to assassinate more. Why did they engage in terrorism? Precisely because they did not believe in parliamentary politics, and were so few and isolated, there seemed to be no hope whatsoever of achieving their aims in any way other than by eliminating some of the most influential people on the political stage. Human life was cheap after the carnage of World War I, and, like today's terrorists, the Freikorps had no scruples about killing.

These German terrorists of 1922 came predominantly from middle-class homes, with a sprinkling of aristocrats. Their justification was patriotism that sprang from the shame and humiliation that followed Germany's defeat in the Great War and their desire to defend Germany against enemies at home and abroad. Hatred of foreigners did not play a crucial role at the time. There was anti-Semitism, but it was not a central factor. In fact, some patriotic German Jews served in some of the Freikorps. In later years the Nazi leaders viewed the Freikorps with some suspicion, and few if any of them were incorporated in the top command of the Nazi Party.

A comparison of an earlier era of the left-wing terrorist and the now emerging right-wing terrorist is telling. Whereas the left-wing terrorists of the 1970s emerged from the clubs and cafeterias of the universities, those of the right have more in common with bars and street corners. While those of the left spent inordinate time in ideological discussions and used a language that was a mixture of Marxism-Leninism-Maoism and four-letter words, those on the right have not the slightest interest in doctrine, do not include even pseudo-intellectuals, and would have had no time for them were they to encounter them. True, the left-wing terrorist discourse proceeded on a level of higher lunacy, divorced from all reality, but they had at least absorbed in the universities or their clubs certain broad ideas concerning imperialism and capitalism. They believed that the Third World was exploited and needed their help, that the masses of Third World countries were good people, and that the political and social structures in their own country and the West in general were rotten. They believed that Germany and America were evil and that Albania and North Korea were on the road to progress and socialism. A small elite apart, those belonging to the extreme right in Europe have no interest in theory even on the most modest level. Their outlook is based instead on some simple beliefs: that the white race is better than all others, that the Germans are the best, that Germany should be strong, and that foreigners should be forced to leave. The traditional terrorists of left-wing persuasion made an effort, however weak, to go beyond Marx, Lenin, and Mao with infusions of novel ideologies (such as Third Worldism). The extreme right has simply copied Nazi ideas and symbols. The fact that American and Russian superpatriots, staunch enemies of internationalism, had to borrow ideas and slogans from a foreign country, namely Germany, is not just evidence of intellectual poverty. It demonstrates that ideas are simply not very important to them.

A comparison of German violence on the extreme right with the state of affairs in Italy reveals basic differences. There was a period in recent Italian history in which right-wing terrorism was a reality. The bomb placed in the waiting room of the Bologna railway station in August 1980 killed more people (eighty) than perished in any other terrorist attack in Europe except the Lockerbie disaster in Scotland. As in Germany, the terrorist scene in Italy was dominated by the extreme left during the 1970s, but there has always been a wing of the neo-Fascists favoring "revolutionary warfare." During certain periods this anti-parliamentarian wing, headed by Pino Rauti, Giorgio Freda, Giovanni Ventura, and some others, was the leading faction, and while the party as such did not engage in terrorist activities, it certainly tolerated and in some respects encouraged terrorism.

The Italian terrorists of the extreme right had a very specific doctrine and strategy, and unlike the German skinheads, they were quite able to express it orally and in writing. They were inspired by the obscurantist theories of Giulio Evola, an elitarian mystic who began his career as a Dadaist painter in pre-Fascist days, survived Mussolini, and became the idol and guru of a new generation of neo-Fascists. Evola and his disciples belonged to the lunatic fringe by any standards; they believed in a strategy of producing social tension and destabilization from which they thought they would benefit. But their following was no beer-drinking, lumpenproletarian football crowd; they thought of themselves as a new intellectual aristocracy, a spiritual avant-garde. In their eyes, the general lifestyle of the right-wing skinheads was American and thus decadent. Italian right-wing terrorism petered out after 1982, when the neo-Fascists made electoral advances and dissociated themselves altogether from their own extremists. But the enormous difference in social background and educational level between right-wing terrorism in Germany and Italy is still of considerable interest.

How is one to explain the specific "proletarian" and even subproletarian character of right-wing terrorism in Germany? Various interpretations have been presented. To begin with, there are historical differences between the former West and East Germany. Some close observers of the scene see the violence as a backlash against Communist rule in the East and, curiously, at the same time, against the left-wing and liberal predominance in the West German educational system and social order. Others see it as a nonpolitical phenomenon, part of the movement of youth protest that has always been present in one way or another. Social psychologists have argued that in 80 percent of individual cases observed, the perpetrators suffered from personal traumas or defects. They came from broken families, were borderline psychopaths, or were young people of lower than average intelligence who were poorly educated and either unemployed or in the most menial jobs.

Seen in this light, right-wing terrorism in Germany is part of the revolt of the losers, society's least successful. Some commentators blame the family and school for failing to integrate such people into society, but it remains unclear to what extent only outside influences can be blamed, or indeed whether these terrorists do represent a negative selection within German society—not all German right-wing extremists are sub-intelligent and hail from the lowest sections of society. Despite the exceptions, the sociological features commonly attributed to German right-wing terrorism seem to be beyond serious doubt. There is also a correlation between social and political trends: right-wing terrorism, youth unemployment, and the growing number of foreign asylum seekers made their appearance at the same time.

Although the number of terrorist acts has declined since 1994, the breeding ground in which right-wing terrorism developed continues to exist. There is a sizable political periphery of extreme right-wing and neo-Nazi sympathizers who, for strategic or tactical reasons, dissociate themselves from terrorist activities. They are usually older people without much sympathy for the outrageous manifestations of youth protest. But they still provide some of the basic political ideas for the young militants. Youth unemployment, which has grown over the years, will add to the tensions in the years to come. And not all those on the German far right and the terrorist scene hover on the brink of illiteracy and dire poverty; it has been precisely on the political periphery of these circles that modern means of communications have been widely used. "National Info Telephones" and other innovations of recent technologies make it much easier to mobilize members and sympathizers. Internet sites make it possible to engage in inexpensive propaganda and to maintain close contacts with distant friends. The young right-wing extremists claim to be very proud of their national cultural heritage, which they profess to defend against alien elements. When asked, they may not be able to recite more than a line or two of classic poetry, may have only the faintest idea of "Faust" and Beethoven, and may not be able to name more than one or two German painters. But they do know how to work the information pool on the World Wide Web and how to encode their secret communications. In brief, they or their successors might be perfectly capable of causing a great deal of havoc in the future.

Recent trends in extreme-right terrorism show common patterns from Russia to the United States, from France to Turkey. There has been an increase in right-wing action, while the terrorism of the extreme left has become relatively inactive. Theory, in the broadest sense, has been far less important for the extreme right than the extreme left, but this has traditionally been true for political movements of the right as well as for terrorist groups. It has been noted by some observers that there has been a considerably larger incidence of nonpolitical criminality among the extreme right than the extreme left, which is not to say that the recruits to left-wing terrorism are somehow morally superior or purer characters. It may simply mean that right-wing terrorism attracts more overtly violent people who are likely to have been in conflict with society before. One hesitates, however, to draw far-reaching conclusions in this area. There may have been latent aggression, not visible to the outside observer, that became manifest only when the psychology of group dynamics took over.

There still remain a great many unanswered questions. Much of right-wing terrorism is single-issue in character. Except for the immigration issue and the resulting fears and tensions, there almost certainly would have been much less violence in Europe. Much terrorism, as others have pointed out, is vigilante or reactive terrorism, terrorism not so much aiming at radical change as at preserving the status quo. Again, this is not to suggest that this "defensive" terrorism is in any way superior to other kinds, but it is a distinct feature that ought to be noted. It tends to disappear or change its character as soon as the perceived threat disappears. But for the stream of asylum seekers in Germany, and to a lesser extent in other European countries, there still would have been violence. However, it would probably have manifested itself on the football fields of Europe. The terrorism of the left or of the separatist groups, in contrast, has more ambitious aims.

It has also been noted that the terrorism of the extreme right is quite often a part-time occupation in contrast to the terrorism of the left and of the separatists. The part-time groups and the unorganized, spontaneous, and chaotic terrorisms come and go, whereas the more institutionalized or more committed are likely to have greater staying power, even if they are fewer in number.

The main unanswered question about the extreme right is a fundamental one: what is specifically right wing about these groups? This problem has plagued students of extreme political movements for a long time. While no one of sound mind is likely to define the American Identity Church or the German neo-Nazis as of the left, it is difficult to offer a more satisfying encompassing definition. These groups are radical and even revolutionary in a primitive way, rather than right wing, reactionary, or conservative. The fundamentalists and the millenarians of Christian persuasion may have something in common with pagan millenarians, but no common feature can be detected between the pro-life activists or the neo-Nazi terrorists or the skinheads with their "Bolshevik" or "anarchist" lifestyle. The terrorism of the skinheads is probably no more than yet another manifestation of youth protest and the working-class—or out-of-work class—counterculture. There is a strong and not unjustified temptation to use the term *populist* rather than right-wing terrorism. But, then, since there is no unanimity about the specific character of populism, this is merely transferring an unending debate from one name to another.

The terrorism of the extreme right, like that of the extreme left, has been shocking and outrageous, but in Europe and America it has not been very important politically, either in the distant or the recent past. Nowhere have governments been seriously endangered as the result of a few robberies, kidnappings, or killings. But, this offers little comfort as far as the future is concerned. The circumstances that have generated right-wing terrorism will certainly not disappear; in some respects they will become aggravated, as in the case of unemployment. There will be an accumulation of rage, anger, despair, and aggression that will find an outlet one way or another. At the same time, weapons more sophisticated and more murderous than Molotov cocktails will become far more accessible. This is the real danger.

Religion and TERRORISM

Twenty to thirty years ago, global terrorism was predominantly secular in inspiration and in orientation, right wing, left wing, or nationalist extremist. Since then there has been a worldwide resurgence of radical religious movements, and this development has had a significant effect on contemporary terrorism. This should not come as a surprise, because religion has always been a main feature of terrorism; the Sicari, the Assassins, and the Indian secret societies practicing thugee were religious sects, and have given us the words "zealot," "assassin," and "thug." But in the nineteenth and a large part of the twentieth century religion-inspired terrorism declined, displaced by politics. This will likely change again in the future.

ISLAMIC RADICALISM

The current resurgence of religious terrorism is largely identified with trends in the Muslim and the Arab world, much to the chagrin of the defenders of Islam and Islamists in the West and East. According to them, the revival of fundamentalist religion is a worldwide phenomenon, which is quite true, and most believers in fundamentalist Islam are not terrorists, which is also true. Furthermore, the West needed the image of an enemy after the end of the Cold War, and Islam, for a variety of reasons, has come to fill that role. They claim that Islam is a highly moral religion, espousing love rather than hate, and is pluralist and democratic in inspiration. Because of this energetic defense, it has become almost taboo to discuss terrorism in the Islamic context.

But those emphasizing the essentially peaceful character of radical Islam find it difficult to account for the fact that in the contemporary world most of the violent conflicts, internal and external, happened and continue to happen in Muslim countries or in those with active Muslim minorities. Such violence need not necessarily be terrorist in character; it also expresses itself in full-scale war (as between Iran and Iraq) or in civil war (as in Afghanistan and Algeria), as well as in terrorism. According to a survey by Freedom House, the leading American institute devoted to the study of human rights worldwide, forty-five of fifty-one states in the contemporary world defined as "unfree" are wholly or in part Muslim. This could be an accident, it may also have to do with social and cultural factors rather than religious, or with elements that are pre-Islamic. But it is difficult to ignore what is, at the very least, a compelling coincidence.

While Islam in modern history has not engaged in acts of mass violence on a Hitlerian or the Pol Pot scale, it is also true that the missionary, aggressive element in radical Islam is stronger than that in other religions, even though many Muslims, and particularly many Arabs, perceive of themselves as victims rather than aggressors. It is also true that a specifically anti-Western mood is more deeply rooted and pronounced in many Muslim countries than in any other part of the world. Such anti-Westernism could, of course, also have social and cultural, rather than religious, roots. For instance, it is quite likely that if the Arab world had not stagnated over the last two centuries, but made as much progress as have countries in the Far East and Southeast Asia, or if Arab countries were richer and more powerful today, there would be less resentment and a lesser sense of inferiority vis-à-vis America and the West. But lack of progress, combined with the breakdown of secular ideologies such as Marxism and purely secular nationalism on the Nasserist pattern, has generated something akin to a Holy Rage, which is, of course, not at all holy in character but can be found among a variety of peoples and groups. In 1945–47, Jewish terrorism in Palestine figured far more prominently than Arab or Persian terrorism, but since then the trend has been reversed, and it is not likely to change in the near future. The anti-Westernism of radical Islam is important, but it is certainly not its only specific feature. Most of the violence exercised by radical Islamists is directed against neither Westerners nor "Zionists," but against other Arabs or Muslims, as in the cases of Iraq, Afghanistan, and Algeria. The jihad has turned inward as the radicals have come to believe that the evil at home has to be eradicated before the infidels abroad can be destroyed.

Endorsements for nearly anything can be found in the holy writs of the major religions, and the Koran is no exception. In Sura 2, verse 256, it says that there should be no religious compulsion, but adherence to this rule is a rare exception in Islam. On the whole, violence is sanctified in Islam if it is carried out against infidels or heretics "in the path of Allah." On the philosophical-religious level, there is no room for nonbelievers in the Islamic system, even if minorities are temporarily tolerated. The faithful live, at least in theory, in a permanent state of war with the non-Islamic world, and this will change only if and when the nonbelievers have accepted the one true faith. Over the last thousand years, political realities have mitigated these absolutes, except for the fundamentalists, for whom the basic outlook of the faithful is the same as it always has been. But pacifism is still no virtue in Muslim eyes. In brief, the Islamic fundamentalist attitude toward violence is that the final aim justifies the means. There was a school of thought in the 1930s that drew parallels between Nazism and political Islam, particularly Islam's fanaticism, sense of mission, and use of violence against political enemies. In some respects these parallels were misleading, but in others they were striking. Radical Muslims exhibit hostility toward all those who are different, a free-floating rage, and a tradition of violence that favors the appearance of terrorism.

Popular Western perception equates radical Islam with terrorism. While many fundamentalists do not support terrorism, the perception is still more accurate than the apologist's claims that Western fears are "mythical" in character, based on unfounded apprehensions, prejudices, and insufficient knowledge about Islam. There is, of course, no Muslim or Arab monopoly in the field of religious fanaticism; it exists and leads to acts of violence in the United States, India, Israel, and many other countries. But the frequency of Muslim- and Arab-inspired terrorism is still striking. In twenty armed conflicts proceeding at present in the world, Islam is involved in sixteen, or 80 percent. Of the thirteen United Nations peace missions in action at the present time, nine concern Muslim countries or interests. The proportion of Muslim involvement in terrorism could well be of a similar magnitude. A discussion of religion-inspired terrorism cannot possibly confine itself to radical Islam, but it has to take into account the Muslim countries' preeminent position in this field. It has to devote more time and space to investigating Muslim and Islamic terrorism than other such movements simply because other such movements are less numerous, less effective, and politically less important.

Many interpreters of jihad in the Muslim world, and an equal number in the West, have explained that jihad has a double meaning: it stands for *jihad bi al saif* (holy war by means of the sword) and also for *jihad al nafs* (literally, the struggle for one's soul against one's own base instinct). Both interpretations are true, but Islamic militants have rejected the spiritual explanation as a dangerous heresy. They invoke time and again those sections in the Koran that say warfare is ordained for faithful Muslims; only cowards and the unfaithful will turn away from this sacred duty to fight those "in the path of Allah." They say the struggle should continue until there is no more sedition or competing religion in the world. As for those making war upon Allah and Muhammad, they should be killed, crucified, mutilated, or at the very least expelled from the land. The Taliban in Afghanistan and many militants are not impressed by the speeches and writings of more moderate exegetists about the "poverty of fanaticism" and the "spiritual mission of Islam," and this fact is what matters in the present discussion.

ALGERIA

In 1962, Algeria achieved independence from France after a protracted and bloody internal war, involving both guerrilla operations and urban terrorism and the heavy loss of life. During the twenty years that followed, the country was ruled by civilian and, later, military revolutionary leaders who at first gravitated to the left but later opted for something akin to a populist, integral nationalism. While it favored Islam, this leadership was secular and also showed massive ineptitude as far as economic and social development was concerned, despite the country's natural wealth, especially in oil and natural gas. And it did nothing to counteract the population explosion, so that by the early 1990s youth unemployment was close to 70 percent.

There was little religious fervor in Algeria in the 1960s; the mosques were not well attended and a foreign visitor would see few young people among the worshipers. In the late 1970s, however, there was an Islamic revival, part of a reaction against unfulfilled expectations and general malaise. The open conflict between the secular elements, especially the modern middle class, and the traditional, fundamentalist sections of the population began in 1982, and subsequently led to violence on an unprecedented level, claiming more than 60,000 victims by the end of 1997. This number compares with perhaps 1,200 victims of terror on both sides in the Arab-Israeli conflict over three decades.

Islam in Algeria developed manifestations that were quite distinct from the fundamentalism of other countries. The Islamists could not really claim that they were oppressed by the government. On the contrary, the heads of the government in the 1970s, Colonel Boumedien and his successors, favored the Islamic activists in order to keep the Communists and other left-wing elements at bay. Clerics were allowed to affect the educational system of the country and thus could educate a young generation in religious thinking. Whether the government gave such support out of conviction or for tactical reasons is beside the point: such support was not sufficient to stem the tide of misery and frustration in the country. The leadership had not succeeded in leading Algeria toward modernity, let alone prosperity. Secularization was rejected, and there was corruption in the ruling circles. Consequently, the conviction spread that socialism and, in fact, all modern Western ideas had failed in Algeria, and that a return to tradition and Islam was the only alternative.

Guerrilla and terrorist actions first occurred in the late 1980s. There was something akin to a popular uprising in October 1988, and in the elections of 1991 the Islamic Salvation Front (FIS) won an impressive victory. The government annulled the elections, declared a state of emergency, and banned the Islamic opposition. After having made far-reaching concessions to Islamism in earlier years, when there was no overwhelming reason to do so, the government, now faced with an emergency, showed no willingness to negotiate with the more moderate Islamic elements. The polarization continued, with an extreme Islamic terrorist group, the GIA, joining the fray. The core of the GIA consisted of a hundred or more Afghanistan veterans, young toughs from the proletarian quarters of Algiers, and a few survivors of a radical Islamic terrorist group of the 1980s led by Mustafa Boulyali, who had been killed in a shoot-out in 1987.

Algerian terrorism exhibits a number of specific features that differ from other terrorist movements in the contemporary world. The militant radicals operate in fairly large units, often as many as a hundred and on occasion even more, in the countryside. When a large group stormed a prison camp in Tazoult in the spring of 1994, it released almost a thousand sympathizers. They have occupied villages during the night, killing the inhabitants, but they have never tried to liberate territories and hold them against the superior fire-and airpower of the government units. On the other hand, there are certain regions, particularly in the Tell and Aures Mountains, that are considered to be guerrilla-dominated districts. Algerian terrorism has been particularly cruel, aiming like the Pol Pot regime at the elimination of whole groups of the population, especially teachers, journalists, intellectuals in general, and government workers. Cruelty rather than religious zeal has often been the distinguishing feature of these attacks; for example, the rape and abduction of girls and young women has been common.

Most Algerian intellectuals have no sympathy whatsoever for the un-democratic ruling junta, but they are even more afraid of the terrorists. Among the terrorists' victims were politicians such as Mohammed Bou-diaf, one of the central figures in the war against the French, and many other veterans of the war of liberation and their families. But the over-whelming majority of those assassinated were common people, gainfully employed, for example, as letter carriers, street sweepers, or drivers of commercial vehicles, and so easy targets. In the beginning the terrorists refrained from attacking the Berbers, the most numerous national mi-nority, but as their campaign continued, they extended their campaign to this group. In 1998, they killed Algeria's most famous singer, who was of Berber origin.

Support for the terrorists comes predominantly from the poorer sec-tions of Algiers, and while social resentment against the wealthy is fre-quently obvious (expressed, for instance, in the destruction of cars or new houses belonging to the more fortunate members of society), there is no "class angle" as far as the choice of victims of assassination is concerned. The terrorists have killed many more poor people than rich; they have intentionally killed many women and children; they have killed Muslim preachers who disagree with their views; and they have killed godless un-ionists and communists. Their favorite means of killing is by planting cars with explosives in public places where the number of victims is likely to be great. In the countryside, where such concentrations of the population are infrequent, the favorite means of killing is by cutting the throats of the victims, usually in the course of night attacks. It is unlikely that this method has been chosen because of lack of ammunition or other tactical considerations. Rather, the purpose is political-psychological, for cutting the throat of a person is not only effective but also bloody and likely to put even greater fear into the hearts of the rest of the population. The presence of a criminal element, and sadists in general, was probably more obvious in the case of Algerian terrorism than elsewhere. It was not that professional criminals joined the terrorists' bands but rather that the ter-rorists became criminalized. Probably a fair number of the militants would have engaged in banditry in any case, even if there had never been a "cause."

In 1993, a campaign against foreigners was launched, mainly by the GIA, the most extreme of the terrorist groups. The GIA demanded that all foreign nationals leave the country by January 1, 1994. Some did, but most refused to go. Among those killed were mainly "soft targets": twelve Croat technicians, a French bishop, several French monks and nuns, and even a number of French old-age pensioners. Altogether about one hundred foreign nationals were killed in 1994–95, fewer thereafter. To punish the French government and people for their support of the Algerian authorities, Islamic extremists also carried their attacks to metropolitan France in 1995, killing some eight civilians in the Paris metro, in markets, and in other public places. Also killed was Abdelbaki Sahraoui, a leader of the rival FIS, who was on a GIA hit list because of his moderation. The campaign in France did not last, partly because French police succeeded in arresting some of the perpetrators and seizing their arms depots, and partly because the strategy of hindering the French support for the Algerian government failed. Meanwhile, the Algerian government had limited success with its brutal antiterrorist campaign, in which many people merely suspected of involvement in terrorism were killed. The government, however, was more successful against the FIS than the smaller and therefore more elusive GIA.

Algerian militants do not agree on their political aims. The more moderate elements, at present the majority, favor a gradual transition to an Islamic society, less extreme in character than the Iranian system. The program of the FIS, for whatever it is worth, does mention free elections and freedom of the press, to give two examples. The more extreme elements, on the other hand, stand for an immediate and total break with the secular past, the elimination of all modern and foreign influences, and the establishment of a clerico-fascist regime.

The zealots have successfully warred against jeans and other Western influences, favored closing all places of public entertainment, and made the beard and the long white shirt, the *chamis*, the unofficial uniform of the militants. But religious fanaticism and the message of the Koran do not explain the widespread character of Algerian terrorism and its appalling violence. Decisive factors include a tradition and culture of violence, growing poverty, unemployment, and unfulfilled political and social promises. Since material progress in the kind of regime and society that the Islamists envisage is most unlikely, the educated members of society are voting with their feet and leaving the country, and if the population explosion continues, violence will not abate soon in Algeria.

ISRAEL AND THE PALESTINIANS

Before the Six Days' War in 1967, terrorism inside Israel consisted mainly of acts of murder and arson committed by infiltrators from across the border. There were not yet in Israel well-organized terrorist groups with massive budgets, sophisticated weapons, and their own intelligence services. This changed in 1967 when a substantial number of Arabs came under Israeli rule in Judaea and Samaria; it was part of the price Israel paid for holding on to the occupied territories.

The main group was Fatah, led by Yasser Arafat, and there were two lesser left-wing quasi-Marxist groups, the PFLP and the PDFLP (the Popular Front for the Liberation of Palestine and the Popular Democratic Front for the Liberation of Palestine, respectively). The former was headed by George Habash and the latter by Naif Hawatme. There also existed even smaller shadowy groups, such as Abu Nidal and PFLP General Command (a group directed by the Syrians), which, unlike the others, did not have a political ideology but simply engaged in terrorist operations, often apparently carrying out contracts issued by foreign governments.

The operations carried out by these groups were notorious: the hijacking of planes, the attack against Israeli participants in the Munich Olympic Games, and the occasional ambush of buses inside Israel. These groups had their outside supporters, Arab and non-Arab. The Palestine Liberation Organization, or PLO, of which Fatah was the military branch, in particular gained a considerable amount of international recognition. They did damage Israel, but the Jewish state was not decisively weakened; on the other hand, Fatah came under considerable pressure, first in Jordan, and later in Lebanon, where they had established a state within a state. After Lebanon's bloody civil war, Fatah transferred its headquarters to Tunis.

The 1980s witnessed the emergence of two new terrorist movements: Hizbullah in Lebanon and Hamas in Gaza and the occupied territories. Both of these groups were Muslim fundamentalist in inspiration, and they soon became more important than the smaller secular groups headed by leaders of Christian origin. These new groups caused far greater problems for Israel than either Fatah or the quasi-Marxist groups. Their emergence was, of course, not accidental; it was another part of the fundamentalist wave occurring in the Muslim world. Hizbullah was directly connected with the victory of Ayatollah Khomeini and his followers in Iran. Hamas was an offshoot of the Muslim Brotherhood that was founded in Egypt in the 1920s and had experienced a major revival in several Arab countries in the 1980s.

Hizbullah means the "party of god," a term that appears originally in the Koran. This movement was created during the Lebanese Civil War, which began in 1975, and grew ever more violent after interventions by the Syrians (in 1976) and the Israelis (in 1978 and in 1982). It is entirely Shiite in character. The Shiites were traditionally the poorer and politically less influential Muslim sect in Lebanon, the political structures of which were based on a complex consensus among its various ethnic and religious groups. There was a spirit of resentment and a feeling of discrimination among the Shiites, whose population had grown more rapidly than that of the Christians. In the past, the Lebanese Shiites had no outside backers, but with the victory of the fundamentalists in Iran a radical change occurred: the Shiites got not only fresh inspiration and a fresh impetus from Teheran but also weapons, money, instructors, and volunteers. It is not certain that the ire of the Lebanese Shiites would have turned primarily against Israel if not for the Israeli invasion of Lebanon in 1982. Before that, relations with Israel had not been bad, the Shiites being preoccupied with the Christians in Lebanon. Furthermore, considerable dissent existed inside the Shiite camp, with the more secular Amal militia confronting Hizbullah. If Israel had not become involved in the south Lebanon morass, Hizbullah might have concentrated its efforts against its internal enemies and, together with its Iranian allies, against the Great Satan, America, and the West in general. Hizbullah was not the only group to take Western hostages in Beirut, to attack foreign embassies, and to kill American and French soldiers, but they were certainly the most active. But once Hizbullah attacked Israel, Israel retaliated, invaded Lebanon, and abducted some of Hizbullah's leaders and killed others. Israel retreated in 1985 to the security zone north of its border, but the conflict spiraled and continued well after the civil war in Lebanon ended in 1989.

Sheikh Fadlalla, born in Iraq in 1935, has been the ideological leader of Hizbullah virtually since its beginning. A poet as a young man, he later turned toward a fundamentalist version of Shiite Islam and became something like the Khomeini of Lebanon, though less forbidding and more subtle than his counterpart in Teheran. He opposed any reconciliation with the West, the Israelis (and Jews in general), and the clerics in Iran. He was equally opposed to the Russians, the Chinese, non-Shiite Muslims, and the state of Lebanon. Elementary common sense dictated that he and his group could not tackle the whole world at once, and for this reason their attacks were concentrated against one or two enemies. Fadlalla saw no room for compromise with Israel, since the Jews were the enemies of God and Israel was guilty of having stolen the territory on which it had established its state. In Fadlalla's mind, Israel was therefore illegitimate and had to be destroyed. It was bound to be a long struggle, demanding fanaticism but also caution. While Fadlalla approved of suicide attacks against U.S. Marines, the French paratroopers, and the Israeli command post in Zidon, he stressed that these tactics should not become a habit, suicide being approved by Islam only in exceptional circumstances. He also pointed out to his more enthusiastic followers that hijacking should not become a practice, since it could be used against the hijackers. Similarly, he approved the taking of American hostages at the Teheran embassy, but he argued against doing so in Lebanon. Fadlalla understood that concessions had to be made. He did not, for instance, go as far as Khomeini in calling for the murder of Salman Rushdie, but neither did he publicly voice dissent. He was reluctant about his movement's participation in Lebanese general elections, but ultimately approved of them despite fundamentalist opposition to democratic practices. Hizbullah did not fare badly in the elections of 1992, getting eight out of 128 seats in the parliament and emerging as the single strongest faction. Fadlalla and his party bitterly opposed the Madrid conference and the Oslo accords that brought Arabs, Palestinians, and Israelis to the negotiating table. But this did not prevent them from reaching an unwritten agreement with the Israelis in 1995 to discontinue attacks against civilian targets from across the border. In principle, if not always in practice, he agreed that there can be no compromise. As Abbas Mussawi, the former leader of Hizbullah, put it, "We are not fighting so that the enemy recognizes us and offers us something. We are fighting to wipe out the enemy."

While Sheikh Fadlalla is the spiritual guru of Hizbullah, the political leader has been Hassan Nasralla, the secretary general since 1992. Originally he belonged to the Amal militia, which was, however, too tame and too secular for him. He succeeded Abbas Mussawi, the former secretary general, who was killed that year; Mussawi's chief aide, Abdul Karim Obeid, was abducted by an Israeli commando in 1989.

Hizbullah is heavily dependent on Iranian financial and military help and leadership. The main coordinator of Iranian support of Hizbullah was originally Ali Akhbar Mohtashemi, the Iranian ambassador in Damascus, who later became minister of the interior in Teheran. But Mohtashemi subsequently lost influence, and Hizbullah's operational contact with Teheran was maintained by the Iranian secret service and the organizations commissioned to promote the export of the Iranian revolution. While in most cases the Iranians were not engaged on the operational level, their financial support as well as the arms they supplied were of crucial importance. The operations undertaken by Hizbullah outside Lebanon would have been impossible without direct Iranian involvement. The Shiites' strength, the closely knit character of their societies in Lebanon, was also their weakness. Outside of their towns and villages they could not be effective without the guidance of more worldly and experienced foreign leaders.

The achievements of Hizbullah, especially during its early days, were impressive. They humbled America and France, bringing about the withdrawal of the multinational force from Lebanon following the bombing of the Beirut embassies and the Marine headquarters. They regarded the bombing of the Israeli command post at Tyre as yet another achievement, even though on that occasion more Arabs and Hizbullah sympathizers were killed than Israeli soldiers. Since then Hizbullah has engaged in a variety of operations, most prominently engaging in border warfare against Israel, attacking members of the SLA—the Israeli-sponsored Lebanese army in the Israeli security zone—and firing rockets into Israel. Though involving few victims, these actions made life uncomfortable for the Israelis in the north. Israel would retaliate from time to time, and its larger counterattacks often resulted in the temporary evacuation of Shiite villages in South Lebanon, where local leaders would welcome an armistice with the Israelis. This cross-border warfare was sui generis neither terrorist nor guerrilla warfare, possible only in a country such as Lebanon where a power vacuum existed and the central government was incapable of asserting its authority. The occupying power, the Syrians, had a vested interest in keeping up the pressure on the Israelis as long as they held on to the Golan Heights. On the other hand, Syria did not want to let the fighting get out of hand and lead to a Syrian military confrontation with Israel. Therefore, Hizbullah was given a free hand only within certain limits.

Like some other terrorist movements, Hizbullah provides social services to its followers, such as schools and medical services. It has engaged in a variety of business ventures, including supermarkets, bakeries, building, farming, bookshops, and clothing sales to true believers, partly to finance its terrorist activities. While some of its income has come from wealthy Shiites in Lebanon and abroad, the major part, including the military supplies, has come from Iran—perhaps $30 to $40 million out of a total budget in excess of $50 to $60 million. Providing social services reinforces the Hizbullah image as the champion of the poor and the oppressed. But its sectarian, religious character has limited its appeal; in the Lebanese elections of 1996, Hizbullah actually lost two of its seats. Though Hizbullah gives the Shiite minority new confidence and pride, it strengthens its own position as a player in Lebanese politics and is a real irritant to Israel; it is unlikely that it will progress much beyond what it has already achieved. The defeat of Israel becomes increasingly elusive, although an Israeli retreat from its security zone in Lebanon has become more and more likely. The initial impetus and enthusiasm of the 1980s has not altogether disappeared and the group's stalwarts, especially among the young, still thirst for action, but its leaders face the future with less optimism than they did fifteen years ago: Allah would not, of course, forsake them, but it seems equally clear that victory will not come in their time.

HAMAS

Hamas is the acronym of the Arab phrase for Islamic Resistance Movement. Founded in December 1987, when the Intifada first sprang up, it has its roots in other earlier forms of the movement in Gaza and elsewhere. It is a de facto branch of the Muslim Brotherhood, which engages primarily in religious indoctrination and various cultural and social activities in many Arab countries. In the 1980s, under the leadership of Sheikh Ahmed Yassin, the group underwent a process of radicalization. The reasons for the radicalization of Hamas, its growing popularity, and its rivalry with the PLO are related to the terrible social and economic conditions in Gaza, but there are also crucial ideological differences between Hamas and the PLO. The PLO wanted to establish a secular Palestinian state, in contrast to the deeply religious Hamas, and had few accomplishments to show over the years. Disappointed by Arafat and his henchmen, Palestinians, unwilling to compromise with Israel and insisting on the destruction of the Jewish state, tended to join this new and more radical force. Yassin was initially tolerated by the Israelis, who may even have wanted to play him against the PLO, but they soon regarded him as the greater danger. He was arrested in 1982 when it appeared that he had set up terrorist units within the framework of his movement. Some sixty rifles were found in his house, and though he was given a fifteen-year sentence, he was released from prison after only a few months. He was arrested again in 1989 after it was established that he had given orders to kill Israeli soldiers as well as fellow Arabs who collaborated with the Israelis. He was released in 1997 as part of an elaborate deal following the bungled Mossad attempt to kill a Hamas leader in Amman. From this date on, leadership of the organization passed to a strategically dispersed collective: a group of people located in Gaza, and others in Syria, Jordan, and even the United States. But Yassin remains an important and honored figure in Gaza. Arafat showered privileges on him, and even the Israeli authorities grant him free passage whenever he wants to travel.

Hamas was a driving force behind the Intifada, which consisted of violent demonstrations, stone throwing by young people, and the building of barricades on highroads. Up to 1995, Hamas' political victories were more striking than its terrorist operations. While the militants of Qassam, the Hamas terrorist units, managed to kill and injure some Israeli soldiers and civilians, many of their operations misfired, especially the early suicide attacks. Hamas terrorists were either captured or killed in shoot-outs with the Israelis.

Hamas stepped up its attacks in 1995 and 1996, partly because it wanted to show that it was the leading—indeed the only—militant force now that the PLO had abandoned terrorism for its new respectability. The peace process seemed to be in full swing, and Hamas tried to sabotage it through a series of massive attacks. Hamas became more sophisticated technically, mainly owing to the expertise of Yehya Ayash ("the engineer"), a resident of Gaza, who helped to miniaturize their bombs. Fewer attacks were carried out by Hamas in 1995 than in 1994, and fewer in 1996 than in 1995, but they were better planned and deadlier. A series of major suicide attacks began with the Bet Lid massacre, near Netanya, in which twenty-one persons, mainly soldiers, were killed by a group calling itself Islamic Jihad, in all probability a Hamas unit. Even earlier, in 1994, there were two minor attacks by suicide bombers near Afulah and Hadera in which twelve Israelis were killed.

"The engineer" was chased down by the Israelis and killed in January 1996 when his cellular telephone, containing a hidden explosive device, exploded in his hand. To avenge his death and the deaths of other Hamas military commanders, three major suicide missions were carried out: two on Jerusalem buses, on February 25 and March 3, killing respectively twenty-six and nineteen civilians, and one on March 4, in which twenty passersby were killed at Dizengof Center in northern Tel Aviv. In 1997–98 the attacks became less frequent; there were two more attacks near the Tel Aviv central bus station, but there were no fatalities.

These suicide bombings had a considerable political effect. While over a period of three years the number of deaths did not exceed one hundred, Israeli society felt particularly vulnerable. A hundred people might be killed in one single night in Algeria, but in Israel even smaller losses were unacceptable. The Rabin government was held responsible, and the bombings clearly contributed to the electoral victory of Likud in 1996. Whether this was the Hamas strategy all along is uncertain.

Israel was warned to be prepared for hundreds of attacks and to have thousands of coffins ready. But, in fact, the resources of Hamas were limited, and Israeli counterterrorism and the PLO, now installed in a position of authority, hampered its activities. Hamas was not in a position to fight a war on two fronts. In the summer of 1997, Hamas made it known that it was now ready to cooperate with Arafat. Neither its long-term aim, the destruction of Israel, nor its short-term strategy, armed resistance, had changed, but until further notice the group was going to stress political rather than terrorist activity. But if Israel was about to release further occupied Palestinian territories, it would not resist this development, and its cooperation with other Palestinian bodies would show its constructive spirit. Thus, for the time being, it has made the transition from revolutionary terrorism to political activism, which it had bitterly denounced in the past. However, this transition was neither irrevocable nor complete, for dissenting splinter groups prefer to continue the armed struggle, and the Netanyahu government has provided few incentives for more restrained behavior on the part of Islamic militants.

SUICIDE MISSIONS

An inordinate amount of fascination and horror has been generated by the suicide missions of Hizbullah and Hamas. If, according to the nineteenth-century creed, terrorism was propaganda by deed, a suicide terrorist mission was *a fortiori* such propaganda. The impression created by people willing to sacrifice themselves is that the cause must be both worthy and invincible. In fact, almost every aspect of the suicide missions has been exaggerated: their unique character, the number of the recruits, their motivation, and the consequences of the attacks.

Suicide missions have been carried out for as long as wars have been fought. The medieval Assassins, one of the earliest and best-known terrorist sects, specialized in suicide missions and were therefore particularly dreaded. There has been a mystique of death in Irish terrorism, which manifests itself in self-starvation in prison. Most of the nineteenth-century anarchist terrorist operations were suicide missions, because bombs had to be thrown from short distances and chances were high that the terrorists would blow themselves up. The suicide mission was part and parcel of the Russian Social Revolutionaries' terrorist tradition. Boris Savinkov, commander of the BO, the fighting branch of the party of the Social Revolutionaries in the early years of the century, recollected that the young people with whom he prepared the attacks competed for the honor to be permitted to die, whether by their own bombs or, if caught, from the certain death sentence. Chances for escape were nearly nil. In the 1908 novel *The Pale Horse,* the terrorist George says that there is no life and no love, only the overwhelming fascination of death. A similar preoccupation with death can be found in fascist movements of the 1920s and '30s, such as the Rumanian Legion of the Archangel Michael and the followers of Jose Primo de Rivera in Spain.

In the Japanese cultural tradition suicide plays an essential role, and it is well known that close to the end of the Second World War more than two thousand pilots volunteered for kamikaze missions. Police subinspector Beant Singh, the bodyguard of Indira Gandhi who killed the Indian prime minister, thought of himself as a martyr and said that God would reward him for what he did. Among contemporary terrorist groups, the Tamil Tigers make a specialty of suicide missions in which women apparently figure as often as men. One famous attack was carried out in 1989 by a "Captain Miller," who drove a truck of ammunition into a military camp in the Jaffna peninsula, killing thirty-nine soldiers. Subsequent victims of such suicide missions include Indian prime minister Rajiv Gandhi, killed by a female "tiger" in May 1991, and Sri Lankan prime president Ranasinghe Premadasa at a May Day rally in 1993. There were many other such missions in Sri Lanka. The Kurdish PKK made three suicide attacks in 1996, one at a military parade in Tunceli, in which nine soldiers were killed, and subsequently in Adana and Sivas.

In brief, it is difficult to think of terrorist movements that have not engaged in suicide missions. Virtually all attacks against leading public figures in countries that have capital punishment are suicide missions. The attacks have to be carried out at close range, the intended victims are usually well protected, and consequently, the chances for the assassin to make a getaway are small or nonexistent.

Public memories are notoriously short, so it should come as no surprise that when Hamas first launched suicide missions in Lebanon and then later in Israel, the media interpreted them as something wholly new and unprecedented. The facts concerning suicide missions of Hamas and Hizbullah are briefly as follows: Between 1982 and 1998, at most fifty such missions were carried out against Israel and in Lebanon, including those that failed—about three a year. Hizbullah never made a secret of its involvement, but Hamas did, and the responsibility was usually put on a mysterious organization called the Islamic Jihad, just as Fatah in its heyday used a group called Black September as a shield. This secrecy may have to do in part with certain theological qualms concerning these "martyrdom operations." The Koran does not permit suicide in principle; on the other hand, it is a religious duty to fight and die for Allah and Islam. In theory, the martyr is supposed to submit to the will of Allah, and it is to be his own personal decision to do so. In practice, the candidates for martyrdom are heavily indoctrinated, chosen by the leadership, and assured that after their death their families will be well taken care of. While it may sound frivolous, this is a sort of deluxe martyrdom: the Russian terrorists and the Japanese soldiers were not promised such elaborate rewards. Not only will the Islamic martyr live on in paradise, residing in golden palaces, eating exquisite food, and attended by beautiful young women, but their families will be paid a monthly stipend. In contrast, martyrs elsewhere committed suicide out of a feeling of duty without hope for any reward, spiritual or material.

The Islamic candidates selected for suicide missions are usually male, between sixteen and twenty-eight years old. There have been one or two cases of suicide missions performed by girls, but these have been the exception. It has been argued that candidates come from a wide cross section of society, poor and rich, married and single, educated and un-educated. But the known facts do not bear this out. While the evidence is not complete, it seems to be true that a suicide mission has never been committed by a child from a family with means or of a certain standing in society. In fact, there have been complaints that those indoctrinating the prospective martyrs never send their own children on such missions. Virtually all the suicide bombers come from poor families, and of those there is a preponderance of candidates who live in refugee camps in miserable conditions. While there have been a few married men with children among the suicide bombers, they have been the exceptions.

Ahmed Baydun, an Arab psychiatrist, has argued that suicide missions are intended to be manifestations of both religious faith and military strength. Undertaking such a mission provides a way of adding sense to a life otherwise devoid of it. But he also warned that such actions were isolating the martyrs from the realities of the world, and isolating Hizbullah within Arab society.

It seems clear that the Islamic martyrs are deeply religious but rather primitive, possessing at best an average intelligence and imagination. But there are a great many young people to whom these characteristics apply, and only a fraction of them are willing to be considered as suicide candidates. Is this fraction more religious or more dutiful, more idealistic or more willing to sacrifice themselves than the rest, or are these people who can easily be manipulated by their handlers? Is there perhaps an inclination to overrate the religious element, which did not play a role in Russia, Sri Lanka, or Japan? These questions have to be studied in far more detail, as there has been a tendency to take the official explanations given by the spiritual handlers of the martyrs at face value.

Suicide missions have also been criticized in the Arab camp. Perhaps they could be justified if the situation of the faithful were so hopeless that suicide was the only means of resistance against the infidels. But this is obviously not the case. If the Israelis have been willing to give up Gaza and subsequently other parts of the occupied territories, this had mainly to do with the Intifada, which was a mass uprising rather than the exercise of individual terrorism. This argument seems to have had some effect on the leaders of Hizbullah and Hamas. There never has been a formal decision to discontinue the suicide missions once and for all, but for long periods there have been no such attacks, and it is unlikely that the reason is an absence of candidates (though this may have played a role); it is much more probable that these leaders realized that the strategy of martyrdom was paying diminished returns, and that it had to be used sparingly and only in connection with other forms of violence.

Radical Islamic groups have engaged in terrorist operations throughout the Middle East and North Africa, and they have expanded their activities into Eastern Africa, Central Asia, and the Indian subcontinent. In some secular states with terrorist traditions of their own, such as Syria and Libya, religious fanatics engaging in terrorist activities have been unsuccessful, mainly no doubt because they faced a ruthless security apparatus that infiltrated their organizations and suppressed them. Elsewhere, as in Egypt, terrorism has been endemic for decades. Most of these groups are offshoots of the Muslim Brotherhood. During the last two decades Gama'at Islamiya has been the main group, its activities concentrated in Cairo and in two regions of Upper Egypt, Asyut and Minya. After a period of relative calm, a new wave of terrorist operations began in 1992, with attacks claiming 286 victims in 1994, 375 in 1995, and 202 in 1996. Radical Islamic terrorism's main targets were policemen and judges, their traditional enemies; inhabitants of Coptic villages, Christian by religion; and foreign tourists, such as those murdered in Luxor in 1997. Attacks against buses carrying foreign tourists and hotels catering to such visitors formed an integral part of this strategy; the intention was to undermine the prestige of the government and to cause economic destabilization in a country in which tourism plays a role of some importance.

These Egyptian terrorist groups tried to carry the terror abroad. An attempt was made to assassinate President Mubarak while he attended a conference in Ethiopia. A similar attempt was made on the life of the Egyptian minister of the interior, and the Egyptian embassy in Islamabad, Pakistan, was bombed in 1995 with a loss of sixteen lives. Arab terrorists, with Egyptian Sheikh Omar Abdul Rahman acting as their guide, were involved in the bombing of the World Trade Center in New York in 1994. In Egypt, the decision to engage in operations abroad, which were unlikely to have any domestic impact, was not a manifestation of strength but rather of weakness. It reflected the fact that the Egyptian police took a harsh line, arresting thousands and executing dozens. While this did not eliminate terrorism, it certainly made it less frequent. The radical Islamic groups were reduced to occasional attacks mainly in their traditional stronghold in Upper Egypt, where the colleges of Minya and Asyut have been fortresses of fundamentalism, and the Muslim Brotherhood, for a long time. Terrorist propaganda inciting the population toward sectarian violence falls on fertile ground in this part of Egypt, where Coptic Christians constitute about 20 percent of the population. The propaganda is directed against all secular elements and the rulers of Egypt, who are attacked as corrupt infidels. Even mild Islamic reformers have become their targets, including Naguib Mahfouz, a Nobel prize winner for literature, who survived the attack. Financial support for the Muslim Brotherhood and its violent offshoots was provided by the Saudi government up to the 1990s, and after that, when the Brotherhood's involvement in terrorism became obvious, by Iran.

In Sudan, internal violence has manifested itself more often in the form of a protracted civil war rather than of terrorism. Indeed, the military government that came to power as the result of a 1989 coup has provided training and help to terrorist groups from all over the world, but especially to those from Arab and Muslim countries. Religious fervor no doubt plays a role in Sudanese state terrorism; so does the prospect of receiving funds from wealthy sponsors for this poorest of all North African countries.

Saudi Arabia has experienced terrorist attacks in recent years, but these represent more a struggle for power than for Islamic orthodoxy. The religious law, the sharia, has always been the law of the land in Saudi Arabia, and on this count the dynasty can hardly be faulted by the Islamists. Their opponents did argue that the Saudi rulers were not sufficiently zealous in their enmity toward the foes of Islam such as America, and that they were rich and corrupt. But the chief antagonist of the Saudi regime, Usama Bin Ladin, who organized terrorists attacks from Khartoum and later out of Afghanistan, including the bombing of the U.S. embassies in Nairobi and Dar es Salam in 1998, is a billionaire who has benefited from the very corruption he decried. Therefore, it is hardly a case of a class struggle between impoverished populists and superrich feudal elites, but rather a fight for power between rival elites, with the Islamists fighting for their piece of the pie.

There were two major attacks on Saudi soil, one in November 1995 in the National Guard Headquarters in Ryadh, where seven persons died as the result of a car bomb; in a second attack in June 1996 at the Khubar Towers military base near Dhahran, nineteen U.S. soldiers died and five hundred were injured in the explosion of a fuel truck. Various previously unknown groups such as the Movement for Change and the Gulf Tigers claimed responsibility, but it has not been firmly established whether the attack of the military base was carried out by Sunni or Shiite Saudi nationals or whether Iranian agents and Afghan veterans were involved. Saudi official attitudes toward terrorism have been ambiguous. The Saudis have supported the Muslim Brotherhood throughout the Muslim world even when it engaged in violence, though perhaps this is simply a means of buying immunity from attack. On the other hand, the Saudis have clamped down harshly against violence from foreigners in their own country.

It is difficult to think of a single Middle Eastern country that has not experienced terrorism in recent times, except perhaps under the most severe dictatorships, such as Iran and Iraq, where the only kind of terrorism exercised is terrorism from above. During the early days of the Khomeini regime there was a great deal of terrorism, such as in June 1981, when in a single attack twelve government ministers and twenty-eight members of the parliament were killed. As the security forces became more effective, however, the oppositionist terrorist organizations were smashed, transferring their operations abroad, to Iraq, Western Europe, and North America. But with the coming disintegration of the two dictatorships, a recurrence of terrorism seems more likely than not in the years to come.

Elsewhere, in Afghanistan or Somalia, and to a lesser degree in Tadzhikistan, individual terror takes place but is relatively unimportant against the background of large-scale collective violence. In an indirect way, Afghanistan was of importance in the spread of terrorism, as many of the volunteers who trained there to fight the Russians subsequently applied their expertise in other parts of the world, including Pakistan and the Arab world, from whence many of the volunteers had originally come. They have played a crucial role in terrorism in the Muslim world in the 1990s, making themselves available to the highest bidder.

In the smaller states of the Persian Gulf, such as Bahrain, which has both ethnic and religious minorities as well as substantial foreign labor forces, terrorist operations have been directed against the government and, in some cases, against the "aliens." Given the wealth of these little countries, there has been frequent foreign involvement, especially on the part of Iran.

But not all this terrorism has been fundamentalist or radical Islamic in character. Terrorism existed in the Middle East well before fundamentalism, and in all probability it will continue after fundamentalism disappears. Turkey is a case in point. There is a strong fundamentalist movement in Turkey, but most of the terrorism has emanated from other quarters, above all from the Kurdish PKK, the Kurdistan Workers Party, and from Devrimci Sol, a Marxist-Leninist revolutionary group that saw its best days in the 1970s but still lingers on in the 1990s. The Turkish PKK began as a party of the extreme left headed by a small group of intellectuals at Turkish universities. It was not originally part of the Kurdish national movement, which, led by traditional chieftains, had been fighting for many decades for Kurdish statehood. Despite its substantial size, this movement's internal divisiveness has prevented it from making significant progress even at a time when its antagonists, such as Saddam Hussein, are greatly weakened. The PKK has not had a substantial presence among the Kurds of Iraq, except to try to protect them from raids by the Turkish armed forces. However, it has been very active in Turkey, especially since about 1990, when it realized that the appeal of Marxism-Leninism would never be sufficient to acquire a mass base. The group has transformed itself into a radical nationalist group that is not in any way religious in character.

The PKK has been very active against Turkish workers in Europe, and above all in Germany, where most of the violent street demonstrations in recent years have been instigated by its militants. Of the 500,000 Kurds living in Germany, fewer than 10,000 are members of the PKK, but they have been extraordinarily active, attacking travel agencies and other Turkish institutions in Europe. Attacks and extortion of Kurds on a massive scale led Germany in 1993 to ban the party as a menace to public order. According to a substantial body of evidence, the party also financed its activities through smuggling drugs. However, the activities of the PKK inside Turkey are our main concern. Their activities have been concentrated in southeast Turkey and have occurred on a massive scale, particularly after 1991. They reached a peak in 1994, when according to Turkish statistics more than four thousand militants were killed, as well as a thousand civilians and a thousand Turkish soldiers and policemen. Altogether the number of victims between 1985 and 1996 is estimated to be close to 20,000. According to Turkish spokesmen, Kurdish terrorism is unjustifiable because the Kurds could press for their demands through political rather than terrorist acts. In practice, political activism would meet with failure because those working for Kurdish autonomy have almost invariably been arrested as traitors and separatists, and been charged with endangering the territorial integrity of the Turkish state.

The fight has been bitter on both sides. The Kurdish militants, not unlike the Algerians, have engaged in indiscriminate slaughter (teachers have been one of their principal targets) and personal rivalries among their leadership has led to bloodshed within the ranks. It has been said that little of their initial Leninist fervor remains; the PKK's Marxist past has not prevented it from cooperating with the Islamic forces of the extreme Turkish right, which have pretended to be more willing to make concessions to the Kurds than to the secular center and left. For all its members' enthusiasm, the PKK would not have gone very far without massive outside help. This has come up to 1998 mainly from Syria, and to a lesser extent from Iraq and Iran, which, for their own reasons, were interested in weakening the Ankara government, or, as in the case of Syria and Iraq, in wringing greater concessions from Turkey concerning the supply of water controlled by the Turks. The PKK has been trained in the Beka Valley in Lebanon, and a considerable part of their weaponry and other help has also come from the Syrians. Such dependence on foreign powers is, of course, dangerous, as the Kurds know from their own bitter experience. There is always the danger that the patrons will drop them sooner or later as indeed happened, in the case of Syria, in 1998. The Kurdish struggle does show, in any case, that fundamentalism has no monopoly as far as terrorism in the Middle East is concerned.

ISRAELI TERRORISM

The extreme Israeli right would like to expand the borders of the country, or at least make the present borders permanent and expel as many Arabs as possible. The Israeli right was originally secular and, to a certain extent, still is. Genealogically, it is in the tradition of Vladimir Jabotinsky's Revisionist Party and that of Herut, the political party that succeeded it and, in turn, was succeeded by Likud. Jabotinsky was not a religious believer, and he did not wholly approve of the early terrorist operations of the Irgun. There was nothing messianic about his politics. He and his followers simply assumed that, in order to survive, the country had to be of a certain size, with borders that could be defended. They also believed that since the Arabs would respect only force, not much effort should be wasted on chasing the phantom of peace. This was, broadly speaking, the philosophy of Menachem Begin, Jabotinsky's faithful disciple, and of Begin's successors, who included secular leaders such as Ariel Sharon, a former defense minister, and Rafael Eitan, a former chief of staff. Indeed, Eitan was not only secular in outlook but deeply critical of organized religion in Israel.

The orthodox Jewish parties in Israel were originally dovish, and most of the ultraorthodox parties were traditionally anti-Zionist. They considered Zionism not just a secular movement but one deeply opposed to the fundamental tenets of the Jewish religion, and therefore a great menace if not a mortal sin. Some of them, the Neturei Karta, for instance, did not recognize the state of Israel, and at the time of the siege of Jerusalem in

1948, put out white flags of surrender. To this day, a high percentage of young orthodox men (and of course all orthodox women) refuse to serve in the Israeli army.

A radicalization of the attitudes of the national religious elements occurred following the Six-Day War of 1967 and deepened after the Yom Kippur war six years later. This coincided with a worldwide trend toward religious fundamentalism, but it also had specific Jewish and Israeli sources. One of the forerunners was Rabbi Meir Kahane, an American from Brooklyn, whose childhood and adolescence had been neither pious nor Zionist. Kahane underwent a conversion and persuaded himself that he was a prophet of a new extremist sect called the Jewish Defense League in America, and, later, in Israel, Kach. The JDL was messianic in character and firmly believed in violence, stressing that the redemption of the Jewish people in Israel was only a matter of years away, whereas those living in the diaspora would be hit by unspecified disasters.

Kahane's religious orthodoxy was not particularly extreme, but his nationalism certainly was. Based in Jerusalem, Kiryat Arba (one of the new settlements near Jerusalem), and a few other places, Kahane and his followers became more and more involved in terrorist activities; in America, the Jewish Defense League has been put on the FBI's list of terrorist organizations. Kahane was arrested by Israeli security forces for planning to blow up the Temple Mount, a sacred place for orthodox Jews and Muslims alike. The JDL tried to provoke Muslims praying in the Cave of the Patriarchs and elsewhere. They established an underground organization that attacked individual Arabs mainly in the occupied territories, killing some and injuring others. But Kahane's movement remained small and outside the pale; it was harassed by the government and ostracized by the other Israeli parties. Even the orthodox and the extreme nationalists abhorred it because of its racism, its leader principle, and other features considered un-Jewish. There was an element of madness in Kahane and some of his leading disciples. He was an outsider both in his origins and his opinions, and when he was gunned down by an American Arab in New York in November 1990, his movement was as marginal in Israel as it had been when it was founded twenty years earlier.

Far more important was the native Israeli movement of messianic, and often apocalyptic, Zionism, which was derived from an orthodox Zionist youth movement named Bne Akiba. Originally quite moderate, it was radicalized by the events of 1967. Many of its members later joined Gush Emunim, a political movement that established new settlements in the occupied territories. Some of its thinkers were educated at the famous religious seminary called Merkaz Harav, originally established by Rabbi Kook, chief Rabbi of Israel, and continued in an extreme nationalist spirit by his son. This seminary and a few like-minded others produced a series of rabbis who later came together in the movement called the Union for the Land and People of Israel, which promoted new settlements and a harsh line toward the Arabs. It also engaged in illegal broadcasting, and some of its members were involved in, or at least sanctioned, terrorist activities against individual Arabs, including the Arab mayors of nearby towns and villages. Some members, like Rabbi Levinger, who settled in Hebron early on, were clearly eccentrics in their lifestyle, their appearance, and their constant provocations. Others cultivated an aura of respectability and thought of themselves as mainstream religious Jews.

As the peace process progressed with the Oslo agreements, these ultraorthodox nationalists found themselves under growing pressure from various quarters. They feared that if the peace process continued, Israel would lose at least part of what it had conquered and the messianic dream, whose realization had seemed so close, would fade. At the same time, they could not count on the support of the anti-Zionist orthodox elements, who were more interested in consolidating their gains on the home front, such as acquiring funding to gradually transform Israel into a nondemocratic, theocratic state. Nor did they have full support among the orthodox of Oriental origin, the Sephardim, who, while not particularly dovish in outlook, by and large did not share the feeling of extreme urgency and apocalyptic despair of the settlers in Judaea and Samaria.

To kill or injure an Arab here or there, or to engage in minor acts of provocation, seemed of little help to what these nationalists viewed as a critical situation. Even Baruch Goldstein had managed to kill only a few dozen Arabs. Some antigovernment mass demonstrations were organized after three major suicide attacks by Arab terrorists in early 1996. But these demonstrations seemed an insufficient response to the danger perceived by the ultraorthodox nationalists. In these circumstances, they could think of three possible ways to bring the peace process to a halt and to bring the hated government down. But armed insurgency against the government seemed hopeless, and a major provocation, such as killing Arafat or blowing up the Dome of the Rock or another major Muslim shrine, seemed problematic.

The murder of Prime Minister Yitzhak Rabin must have appeared the most effective approach. This is not to suggest that the assassination of Rabin, a deed unprecedented in modern Jewish history, was planned by an assembly of religious sages and extremist political leaders. It was the act of an individual. This individual had, however, asked some leading rabbinical authorities whether killing a *rodef* or *moser* (the traditional terms for someone persecuting Jews or informing on them) was justifiable from a religious point of view. He was given equivocal answers prior to killing Rabin. The assassin, Yigal Amir, was a young man of Yemenite extraction and a law student at Bar Elan University, one of the strongholds of the national religious militants. He was as firmly convinced that he was carrying out the will of God as any martyr of Hizbullah or Hamas. Rabin, he believed, was a traitor and his government a threat to the survival of Israel and the Jewish people. Amir remained defiant throughout his trial. Though Amir was a loner, Rabin's murder was not committed in a vacuum. It was carried out in a general atmosphere in which the extreme right had incited their young militants to commit acts of violence, and in which such an act, while not perhaps inevitable, had become likely. Students of history were reminded of the murder in 1922 of Walther Rathenau, the Jewish foreign minister of the Weimar Republic, who was killed by a group of right-wing extremists in a similar climate of incitement to terrorist actions. It was no surprise that polls two years after Rabin's murder showed that a considerable portion of the young generation of the nationalist-religious persuasion did not denounce the assassination, and expressed understanding and support for the killer. This, in broad outline, was the background to the assassination that helped to bring down the Labor government and carried Likud to power.

INDIA, PAKISTAN, AND THE SIKHS

There has been a considerable amount of terrorism on the Indian subcontinent, certainly much more than between Israel and her neighbors—a fact that has not fully registered in the outside world. At least twenty thousand people have been killed in Kashmir alone since 1990. The lack of awareness may have to do with a general lack of interest in things Indian and Pakistani, an attitude that changes only at times of major international conflicts. There has perhaps also been the assumption that in a country populated by hundreds of millions, terrorism that claims a few thousand a year could not possibly be important. A thousand a year have been killed in Karachi alone, and national leaders and prime ministers murdered, but as far as the Western media were concerned it has had less of an impact than a few stones thrown in Bethlehem, for journalists and TV crews have been concentrated there. Also, it has not always been possible to differentiate between terrorism, on one hand, and banditry and ethnic clashes on the other, and this might have contributed to the outside world's lack of interest. Only after both India and Pakistan detonated nuclear devices in 1998 did world attention focus on the Kashmir conflict and other terrorist activites on the Indian subcontinent.

Terrorism has had a long tradition in India. Very broadly speaking, before 1939, it was more often than not Hindu in origin and directed against the British Raj, but after 1939, and particularly after 1945, it was quite often instigated by Muslims and Sikhs, as well as radical Hindu factions. There had always been tension between these groups, but after the division of the subcontinent in 1947, the secular forces in both countries weakened, and religious and national extremist parties grew stronger. Much of Indian terrorism has been concentrated in Kashmir and the Punjab, where ethnic and religious conflict dates back to the days of the division of India and even before. In regard to reconciling these factions, the Hindu Indian government has shown little political acumen. It might have been impossible to pacify the extremists among the Muslims in Kashmir and the Sikh in the Punjab, but this was a strategy the Indians did not even really try.

The Kashmiri Muslims were rather secular in outlook. Gandhi once called Kashmir an island of secularism on the Indian subcontinent. Its inhabitants were ethnic Hindus who had accepted Islam at one point in their history. But, instead of reaching a compromise with the moderate Muslims, the Indian authorities arrested Sheikh Abdullah, regarded as a leader by most Kashmiri Muslims, and the increased tensions led to a virtual civil war in which Pakistan played an important role. Today the situation is further complicated by the splits among the Kashmir rebels; some are nationalist-secular and want autonomy for their region, while some Muslim extremists want a merger with Pakistan. Pakistan has never denied that it gave political support to the Kashmiri radicals, the Jammu and Kashmir Islamic Front, but it does deny providing military help. In the meantime, another more radical group, the Harakat al Ansar, carried out bomb attacks in New Delhi and other parts of India; the Indians retaliated by supporting Pakistani separatists. What is beyond question, however, is that Pakistan helped to transform the conflict between the communities in Kashmir into a jihad, a holy war, complete with Islamists vying for martyrdom.

The general strategy of the Islamic radicals has been to attack and murder the local Hindus (called Kashmiri Pandits) and Sikhs and so force them to leave the region. Many houses have been burned, and to dramatize their struggle, Islamic radicals have kidnapped, and in some cases murdered, foreign tourists. According to Indian sources, there has been a systematic campaign since 1990 to exterminate the Hindu population of Kashmir or at least to force them to flee so that the region will become part of Pakistan.

The Pakistani strategy has been one of surrogate warfare. The country has been militarily weaker than India and therefore more vulnerable to full-scale attack. Following Pakistan's military defeat in 1965, warfare by proxy, guerrilla actions, and terrorism seemed not only the more rewarding strategy but the only possible one. The destabilization campaign against India was carried out by ISI, the Pakistani intelligence service, which trained native Kashmiri and Indian Muslims in camps in Pakistan with support of the Muslim world. Various Arab countries, including Saudi Arabia and Libya, gave money and instructors. This support was more quietly given than it would have been for anti-Israel groups, for the simple reason that Arab nations hesitated to openly provoke a major country such as India.

To complicate matters even further, there was even a small international Muslim brigade consisting of fighters returning from Afghanistan, and the Pakistanis made a systematic attempt to enlist Indian Muslims who felt particularly insecure after the widespread Ayodhya riots, in which thousands of them had been killed. On the other side, the radical Hindu BJP was instrumental in fanning the flames of ethnic conflict, and the extremists among them, such as Thackeray, the Bombay leader, intensified their anti-Muslim campaign after the electoral victory of the nationalist Hindu movement.

Pakistani sponsorship of terrorism inside India caused a great deal of irritation in India, not only in the bellicose nationalist circles. Since Pakistan is a country replete with ethnic and social conflicts, it is vulnerable to Indian counteraction. Internal Pakistani conflicts were aggravated by the arrival from India of millions of Mohajirs, Muslim refugees from India after 1948, who were not welcomed by the local population. The Mohajir Quawmi (MQM) soon established a terrorist movement of their own. In Sind, the soft underbelly of Pakistan, the Mohajirs fought the Pathan tribesmen, the Pathans fought the local Sindhis, and the Sindhis fought the Pakistan security services as well as the MQM. The situation was so bad in Karachi, Pakistan's largest city, that by 1994 it appeared to be a city out of control. One thousand eight hundred people were killed in a single year, and to complicate the situation further, Sunni terrorists attacked Shiites, who retaliated, while the MQM split into two factions that fought each other. In brief, the Indian security service has not been ineffective in their attempts to destabilize Pakistan.

Pakistan has returned the favor through its activity and has also been active in the Punjab conflict. Traditionally one of India's most prosperous regions, Punjab is the home of the Sikhs, who have pressed their demand for autonomy ever since India's independence. A relatively small ethnic group, but extremely active in economic and public life, the Sikhs have been outstanding soldiers in the Indian army, fighting loyally with the Indians against Pakistan. India did not discriminate against loyal Sikhs, one of whom became president of India, and another, commander in chief of the Indian army. But the Sikh separatists have demanded more than regional autonomy. They want a separate Punjabi-speaking state, and real-location of Punjab's water and hydroelectric power that supplies other Indian states. The separatists have become increasingly militant and have turned to terrorism, causing the Indian security forces to engage in a counteroffensive. In 1975, a state of emergency was declared in Punjab that lasted three years, but it did not significantly reduce the incidence of violence. Since 1984, another major anti-terrorist campaign was launched by the Indian government, which took the form of mass detentions and worse. It succeeded in bringing the "emergency" under control in the 1990s, but it is too early to say whether the flames of separatist terrorism have been extinguished forever. The radical Sikh terror was directed not only against the Indian authorities but equally against those in their own community who disagreed with their strategy. Many Sikh community figures were killed by the terrorists, some of them while praying in Sikh temples.

While most of Indian terrorism is concentrated in the north, in Kashmir and the Punjab, there has also been terrorist violence in the east, in particular in Assam, and some in the south, in Tamil Nadu. Terrorism all over India is preponderantly ethnic, or rather ethnic-religious, in motivation. However, other factors are frequently involved as well, as shown by the case of Assam. The ethnic composition of this state has changed as the result of the influx of Bengali Hindus. Like other states situated far away from New Delhi, the Assam radicals felt neglected by the capital; little patronage came their way, and they established yet another liberation front, the United Liberation Front of Assam (ULFA). The initiative came from radical elements at the universities, and ethnic and religious factors seem to have figured little in the movement, but it is very difficult to clearly distinguish between religious and nonreligious motivation among terrorists in Assam and in other parts of India.

Except in the case of Kashmir, political terrorism in India and Pakistan has declined somewhat in recent years. If hostility between India and Pakistan diminishes, it is likely that there will be a further decrease in terrorist activity. But a solution to the Kashmir problem is as remote as ever, and the danger of escalation into full-scale war is now greater than before. Furthermore, there has been increasing lawlessness and banditry, especially in the big cities, and it is never easy to differentiate between terrorism and crime, organized or unorganized.

The prospects for terrorism are even greater in Pakistan, where political stability is weaker than in India. Pakistan served as a training ground for volunteers in Afghanistan, and many among these fighters, Pakistani and foreigners, turned to terrorism when their services in Afghanistan were no longer needed. The Pakistani government seems to have at first believed that it could turn the presence of the warriors to their advantage, but it gradually realized that they constituted a real danger to Pakistan. Never fundamentalist itself, the Pakistani government has nevertheless tried to use the Islamic radicals for its own political purposes, a dangerous game that in the end has not been at all successful. Terrorism has continued in any case, especially in Sindh, Baluchistan, and the North West Frontier, all regions in which violence of one form or another has been endemic for a long time. On many occasions the Pakistani army and the "rangers" had to be called in because the police could no longer cope. Some of this terrorism is clearly political in inspiration, such as the Shaheed Bhutto group, a radical wing of Ben Azir Bhutto's Pakistan People's Party, some is separatist, as in the border areas of Sindh; and some is little more than banditry under a political label. Given the uncertainties of Pakistani political, social, and economic conditions, there is always the danger that the central government could be altogether destabilized, and that this would lead to general disintegration in a country that since its birth has never been far from chaos.

The global wave of religious fundamentalism—or radicalism, to be precise—will not, needless to say, last forever. It has already taken different forms in different countries. In Western developed countries, it has corresponded to a spiritual longing that official religions could not fulfill. Elsewhere, as in Israel and India, there has been an amalgam of religion and nationalism, whereas in the Muslim countries, radical Islam has appeared as the mouthpiece for the oppressed and despised and as the scourge of the materialist and decadent West. In the West, fundamentalism has been by and large a middle-class phenomenon, or in some manifestations lacking any specific class character. In the Muslim world its appeal has been mainly to the subproletariat, to recent arrivals from the countryside to the big cities, and to refugees and other victims of urbanization and modernization. There have been some intellectuals or quasi-intellectuals, but their numbers have not been very large, and they will be the first to leave once they realize that radical religion is going out of fashion. The rise of this religious radical wave has been as dramatic as the promises made, especially by the millenarians among the radicals. Their followers expect not only spiritual fulfillment, security, and a feeling of community, but also, especially in Asia and Africa, a society that is not only more moral but also more just and prosperous than the present corrupt order.

It goes without saying that this promise cannot be fulfilled, and the only question is how long it will take for disillusionment to set in. It is not sensible to predict what will replace it, whether a new nationalism, a new populism, or a mixture of the two. One would think that technological developments would tend to undermine radical religion, but that does not seem to be the case. The Koran is compatible to a large extent with the computer, just as Christian and Jewish sectarians (or, for that matter, believers in the prophecies of Nostradamus) make full use of the Internet.

The present fundamentalism has limited global appeal and has made progress in some countries but not in others. It has made its greatest advances in the most backward countries, such as Sudan and Afghanistan, among the Shiites, who always have tended to extremism, and in countries with the most acute social and economic problems. But in bigger Muslim countries, such as India, Indonesia, Turkey, and Bangladesh, as well as in the West, it may well have exhausted its potential. Fundamentalists' hopes for a better life are bound to be disappointed. The question then arises of what happens when current militant and radical movements change or decline. It is impossible to predict whether this process will take years or decades, but in any case it will be of limited relevance only with regard to the future of violence, especially terrorist violence. For even if the fundamentalist wave abates, even if there is a strong countermovement, even if radical religion becomes less enticing, there will still be small groups of true believers sticking to the old faith. And it is quite likely that the more isolated these radicals are, the greater will be the temptation to engage in terrorist action. This has been the case in the past and will be so in future. Religious violence, especially of the millenarian brand, will continue, whether supported by many millions or by mere thousands. And, no matter how small the numbers of fanatics become, the dawning era in which weapons of mass destruction will be widely accessible could make them more dangerous than a much larger number of terrorists using the traditional tools of their trade.

State TERRORISM

tate-sponsored terrorism, warfare by proxy, is as old as the history of military conflict. It was an established practice in ancient times in the Oriental empires, in Rome and Byzantium, in Asia and Europe. No empire, however powerful, could afford to live in a state of perpetual war with its neighbors. There was a cheaper and less risky alternative: to support dissenters, separatists, ambitious politicians, or simply malcontents inside a rival state. Sometimes this strategy was defensive, meant to forestall aggressive designs on the part of a potential enemy. At other times it was part of an offensive strategy, intended to weaken the neighbor and perhaps even to prepare the ground for invasion.

Since military technology was then primitive, such support for rebellious tribes manifested itself not in the supply of arms, as in modern times, but mainly by way of financial help and, of course, political promises. The Roman maxim *Divide et Impera* was applied not only to relations between other states but also to minorities and dissident tribes.

There are countless examples of state-sponsored terrorism in modern history. For instance, Britain used it against the French in the Indian wars in America, and vice versa. The rebellious Irish received help from Paris

156

during the age of the French Revolution, and the British helped forces opposed to Napoleon in Spain and elsewhere. This tactic was widely employed in Central Asia in the nineteenth century in the various Afghan wars. The Russians supported their fellow Slavs in the Balkans. In his novel *Greenmantle*, John Buchan described the attempt by the Central Powers in World War I to unleash a jihad, a Muslim holy war, from Turkey to India through a mixture of propaganda, political promises, and financial support. Though political science fiction, it is in many ways not that far from reality. Bulgaria used the Macedonian revolutionary terrorists against Yugoslavia after World War I, and the Croat extremists offered their services to Mussolini, who also employed the French Cagoule to liquidate political enemies in exile. The Western powers supported all kinds of nationalist and anti-Communist rebels, without much success, against the Soviet Union during the early years of its existence. And the Soviets made collaboration with national liberation fighters, mainly in Asia, its declared policy at the Baku congress in 1921. Warfare by substitutes has been common practice in the struggle for Kashmir between India and Pakistan. Terrorism was involved in one way or another in all these instances.

This kind of strategy has continued in one way or another to the present day in many parts of the world. The purpose is intimidation, to compel the enemy to waste resources and thereby to weaken him. On occasion it has been in the form of sustained terrorist campaigns, such as in the case of the Macedonian IMRO, but more frequently it shows itself in individual acts such as the assassination of hostile political leaders or émigrés deemed particularly dangerous. Such operations were more often than not carried out by substitutes, foreign nationals; only in a few cases was there a direct involvement. One of these exceptions was the kidnapping of Sun Yat-sen by Chinese imperial government officials in Portland Place, London, next door to the Chinese embassy in the early twentieth century. (The London police cordoned off the embassy and after a few days the Chinese émigré leader was released.)

A full-scale sustained terrorist campaign was frequently beyond the capacity of the tribe, the minority, or the political faction being supported from abroad, especially if the state under attack did not play by liberal rules but brutally combated terrorism. In other instances, the sponsors of state terrorism did not want to escalate their campaigns beyond a certain point, because this might have involved unacceptable political and military risks.

While the fascist and communist states were not opposed in principle to killing enemies on foreign territory, they did so infrequently in peacetime. The Nazis had a few political émigrés assassinated in Czechoslovakia and abducted a journalist in Switzerland. Mussolini was more active, and his agents were instrumental in killing King Alexander of Yugoslavia in Marseilles in 1934 and the Rosselli brothers, leading anti-Fascists, in Paris. The KGB murdered Trotsky in Mexico and several Russian and Ukrainian émigré leaders in the 1950s. In one of the most famous cases, mentioned earlier, the Bulgarians had an émigré broadcaster killed by means of a poisoned umbrella. But these incidents did not amount to systematic terrorism, and it is nearly impossible to establish precisely why these figures were singled out for liquidation. By and large, the totalitarian regimes seem to have believed that émigrés were not really dangerous, and that it might be sufficient to threaten or kill a few so as to discourage the others. It seems also likely that the decision not to engage in systematic terrorism was based on a simple reason: Nazis, Fascists, and Communists did not want to break established international norms, at least not up to the outbreak of war. Systematic terrorism would not have remained a secret for very long, and it would have diminished their international standing. The cost of these killings would have been greater than the possible benefits accruing from them. Fascism did not believe in exporting its political system, except by conquest. Communism wanted international converts, but the revolutionary situation in Europe was not ripe after 1920. Support was still given to national liberation movements on a small scale in Asia in the 1920s and on a larger scale in Asia and Africa in the 1960s and '70s, but terrorism was only one component in this struggle and usually a minor one.

State-sponsored terrorism on a massive scale reappeared on the international scene in the 1970s. Those involved were not major powers but minor actors, rogue states, who were little concerned with their international standing. They did not have the potential to engage in major military aggression except against other minor countries, but felt that they could engage in terrorism by right, divine or otherwise. The assassination of political émigrés was only one aspect of this upsurge of state-sponsored terrorism, but the numbers give an idea of its massive scale. The number of political émigrés killed by Nazis, Italian Fascists, and the KGB in the interwar period did not exceed twenty or thirty. In contrast, Iranian agents successfully assassinated sixty political enemies in Europe and Asia within a few years and attempted to murder at least an equal number.

THE SOVIET BLOC

The Soviet Union and, after World War II, the Soviet bloc as well as other Communist countries (China being a notable exception) were heavily involved in international terrorism. Such involvement was almost always denied, and the humanist traditions of communism and the denunciation in principle of individual terrorism by Marx and Lenin invoked. Principle or no principle, even Marx and Engels supported terrorism on occasion (for instance, the Irish and the Russian revolutionaries), and while terrorism on foreign soil had, for a variety of reasons, never been the major strategy of the Soviet Union and the world communist movement, it still had been used. The full extent of communist use of terrorism abroad became known only following the breakdown of the Soviet Empire, at which time the archives were opened and some of the witnesses told their stories.

The main communist argument was always that Marxism-Leninism favored revolutionary violence, demonstrations, perhaps the occasional civil war, not the physical elimination of individual enemies. Marx and Engels, Lenin, Trotsky, and other leaders argued on various occasions, that individual terrorism was not useful because individual leaders were expendable and easily replaced. Reference was frequently made to the "historical" opposition of the Bolsheviks to the Social Revolutionaries who had been strong supporters of revolutionary terrorism. However, in the real world of politics, the Soviet leaders, above all Stalin and his successors, rarely shied from violence and certainly treated their domestic enemies harshly. So why should Soviet leaders allow their enemies abroad to live if their elimination could be accomplished without major international complications?

During the period before the Second World War, the NKVD, the fore-runner of the KGB, did engage in international political murder. The most famous case was the assassination of Trotsky in Mexico, but there were other killings, including members of Trotsky's family and supporters in France and Spain, and of White Russian generals such as Miller and Ku-tepov. Defectors from the Russian secret police and other state organs were assassinated as well; the case of Ignaz Reiss in Switzerland in 1937 is probably the best known. In addition, several unsuccessful attempts were made to liquidate political opponents. Individual Communist parties, with or without the help of the Soviets, also engaged in terrorist actions on various occasions. Communists killed many of their political opponents on the left in Bulgaria and in Spain in 1936–38, as they did both before and during the years of political tension in Germany in 1922–23 and again in 1931–32. In sum, though the Communists believed in the primacy of political mass action, this did not prevent individual assassinations whenever they were thought advisable.

After the Second World War, the murder of political opponents continued, but the main targets were now the leaders of the NTS (a militant organization of post–World War II Soviet refugees) and other groups such as the Ukrainian militants. The assassinations were not numerous, but they showed that Soviet duplicity, claiming to follow one policy while carrying out another, had not changed.

Beginning in the late 1960s, new links between the Communist countries and a variety of "national liberation" movements, all engaging in terrorist action, became politically more important. These links included the support given not only to the PLO and other smaller, more radical Arab groups, but also that given to terrorists in Latin America, where the Cuban secret police, the DGI, acted as the main conduit, in Asia and Africa, and also to peripatetic individual terrorists such as the infamous Carlos and Abu Nidal. The Communist leadership did not support terrorists of the extreme right, but it did occasionally use them to provoke and embarrass Western countries—for instance, in the desecration of Jewish cemeteries in West Germany. To certain separatist terrorism groups, such as the IRA and the Basque ETA, the Soviet Union did extend help in various ways, directly or through its allies. Since many of the separatists had at the time a protective Marxist-Leninist, anti-imperialist coloring, such assistance could always be justified in ideological terms. These were, in Soviet eyes, progressive forces, and extending help to them was a duty quite apart from the political benefits accruing to the Soviet bloc from the terrorist activities.

Ties with the purely terrorist groups and individuals were kept secret. Maintained through intermediaries guided by the KGB, in the case of a leak it was always possible for the Soviet leadership to dissociate itself from the act. Officially, the Soviet Union and the other Communist countries had nothing to do with Carlos, Baader Meinhof, Mohammed Boudia, the Italian Red Brigades, and the ETA. On the other hand, Arafat, other Palestinian leaders, and the heads of the South African ANC were frequent official visitors in Moscow; the Soviet line was that these were leaders of political movements, statesmen recognized by many member states of the United Nations. If terrorism occurred in the statesman's home country, it was carried out by separate organizations (such as Black September), over which the political leaders had no control. It was argued in some cases that the alleged terrorist activities had not in fact taken place, were American or Zionist provocations, or, if they were too obvious to be denied, were explained as the acts of a few individuals driven to despair by imperialist outrages, and of no political importance. What is now evident is that while the KGB (and to a certain extent the International Department of the Central Committee of the Communist Party) would liaison with the terrorists, the Soviet Foreign Ministry would publish routine official declarations that "everyone was well aware of the principled position of the Soviet Union which has always denounced and is denouncing terrorism."

As a practical matter, the Soviet Union had no desire to monopolize the supervision of terrorist activities and therefore many of the activities were delegated both on the political and the military level. Training camps for terrorists were established not only in Russia but also in Czechoslovakia, Hungary, Bulgaria, and East Germany. While the Czechs took care of the Italian Red Brigades (providing money and asylum), the East Germans were in charge of dealing with the Baader Meinhof group as well as activities in some African countries. Cuba supervised Latin America, but the PLO was also involved to a smaller extent in that continent. How this collaboration proceeded in practice can now be reconstructed in considerable detail as far as East Germany is concerned, because the archives there have become much more accessible than in the ex–Soviet Union and other Communist countries.

Over time, the problematic character and the disadvantages of Communist collaboration with terrorism became more obvious. It is true that support for terrorism was financially cheap, being infinitely less expensive than massive arms shipments to Third World countries, which were never paid for and generated little if any lasting pro-Soviet feeling in these countries. Soviet policy had proceeded from the assumption that the global correlation of forces was gradually changing in favor of the Communist camp, that the influence of the imperialists would weaken, and that the countries of Asia and Africa would steadily move toward accepting the Soviet pattern. Events during the 1970s and '80s did not bear this assumption out. The Soviet influence sharply declined in Egypt, and the internal disputes between it and Arab and other Third World countries became more pronounced. Frequently the Soviet Union had to take sides in such disputes, invariably making enemies in the process. Guerrilla warfare and terrorism in Latin America died down; Africa, in view of its lack of economic progress, became more and more irrelevant to world politics. The Soviet invasion of Afghanistan had a major negative impact in the Third World.

Collaboration with the terrorists complicated relations with America and the West in general, while producing few tangible benefits for the Soviet Union in other parts of the world. This fact did not cause an immediate change in Soviet policy, partly because of inertia; like an overloyal gambler, the Soviets continued to bet on a horse with which they were familiar, even though that horse had won few races. But from around 1980 on, they did so with less and less conviction. At the same time critical voices were heard inside the Soviet Union, well before Gorbachev; there were also studies critical of some of the terrorist groups, especially those of the extreme left, which had received Soviet support in the past.

These Soviet studies, inspired no doubt by authorities in Moscow, argued that the "revolutionary" terrorists were doing more harm than good, and that their aspiration to be more radical than the Communists was both childish and dangerous. It was implied, and often opened stated, that these terrorist groups would be defeated sooner or later, and that this would result in the general weakening of the left, because the Communists, too, would be made responsible for terrorist outrages even though they had no control over the wild men and women who had committed the acts.

Directorate S, which handled illegal and special operations for the KGB, so-called wet deals, continued its activities, albeit on a reduced scale, as did Department 20, which dealt with developing countries. But the KGB leadership became increasingly concerned about a terrorist wave spilling over and into the Soviet Union, not necessarily fostered by anti-Soviet elements but by radicals, claiming that Moscow had not given them sufficient help. Such complaints were frequently voiced among European, Arab, and other extremists.

Even in the 1980s KGB officials seem to have passed on to their Western colleagues an occasional warning about possible terrorist acts, no doubt upon instructions from the Kremlin. Western commentators on terrorism (including this writer) were quoted in Soviet publications approvingly or at least without comment, something that would have been unthinkable even ten years earlier. Kryuchkov, head of the KGB First Directorate in the 1980s, anything but a liberal reformer, believed that there was a distinct danger of terrorist attacks inside the Soviet Union, that fifteen hundred people with terrorist designs had been identified, and that in the atomic age some degree of cooperation with Western intelligence was needed to defend the country against terrorist attack. For this purpose a new Directorate was set up in 1989, called the Defense of the Soviet Constitution.

The threat was probably exaggerated by the KGB chiefs, and there were in fact few, if any, terrorist acts inside the Soviet Union except for a bombing in the Moscow subway system in 1977. But it is quite true that there was a potential danger, mainly on the part of the separatists, that became only too clear when the Soviet Union disintegrated. It is to the professional credit of the KGB to have realized this internal weakness well before Gorbachev came to power.

Following *glasnost* and *perestroika,* the training camp for Arab and other terrorists at Balashikha near Moscow was closed and the cooperation with terrorists more or less ended. This was apparently one aspect of the new reform course that was welcomed by most of the KGB and Soviet foreign policy establishment, disappointed over the years with the results of the collaboration with Third World terrorists. Even most of the leaders of the national liberation movements were no longer trusted, since it had been realized that they had an agenda of their own, and that even their victory would be of little benefit to Moscow. In other cases, and Khadafi is the obvious example, it had become clear that they were loose cannons, unpredictable and dangerous for those in any way connected with them.

It is unlikely that students of terrorism will ever have full access to the records of the KGB departments in charge of liaison with terrorists in the 1970s and 1980s. These are matters of the highest security, and the files that were not destroyed when the departments were dissolved or reorganized will in all probability never be made public. But some records are known, and several intelligence operatives have come forward after the fall of the Soviet empire. Light has been shed on the preparation of the murder of Georgi Markov, the Bulgarian writer who defected to the West in 1969 and whose broadcasts over the BBC and Radio Free Europe revealed details about the entourage of Todor Zhivkov, the head of the Bulgarian party. Initially Markov had been sentenced in absentia in Bulgaria to a six-year prison term. But this seemed insufficient, and in order to punish Markov and deter others, Zhivkov had a new secret decree passed that legalized the murder of dangerous defectors. The Bulgarian minister of state security approached Yuri Andropov, at that time head of the KGB, with a request for help. According to the evidence that became available in 1991, Andropov was initially less than enthusiastic about the Bulgarian request and refused to get involved. Following continued Bulgarian pressure, he decided to send an instructor to Sofia and provide the technical equipment needed for the murder, but in such a way that Soviet involvement could not be proven.

Markov was killed in London in summer of 1978 by means of an umbrella, the tip of which had been dipped in ricin. It is unclear why the Bulgarians proposed and the Russians accepted such a complicated operation. It should have been obvious that the use of such an exotic weapon could not be kept secret and would attract much more attention than an ordinary assassination. The passing of a special decree in Sofia, on the other hand, conferred on the assassination the semblance of legality, which was quite typical Communist bloc practice in the post-Stalin period.

Some of the terrorist attacks sponsored by foreign governments, such as the attempted murder of the Pope by a Turkish terrorist, have not been cleared up to this day. But on others the opening of East German archives has shed some light. Thus, from the evidence at the Berlin trial in the 1990's dealing with the attack at the Mykonos restaurant in that town in which several Kurdish leaders were killed, it emerged that the decision to launch the attack had been made by a special government committee in Teheran headed by President Khameini and including the foreign minister and the chief of intelligence. It stands to reason that other such attacks, such as against Jewish institutions in Buenos Aires in 1992 and 1994, had been vetted by the same committee.

The cooperation between the terrorist Carlos, the so-called Jackal, and the secret services of East European countries has been documented by various files of East Germany's secret police, Stasi, including one dated February 10, 1981. According to this report, the Carlos unit consisted of a few members of the German Rote Zellen (a successor of Baader Meinhof) as well as Carlos's girlfriend, Magdalene Kopp, Johannes Weinrich, and Bruno Breguet, a Swiss citizen. Occasionally they collaborated with Italian terrorists, with members of the Basque ETA, and with Arab terrorists. They moved freely from one East European country to another and seem to have had special dispensation to carry arms while living or traveling in these countries.

According to this Stasi document the Carlos group had the blessing of the KGB but preferred (or were advised) not to stay for any length of time in the Soviet Union, most likely because the KGB wanted to keep them at a certain distance. The Czech and Hungarian secret services frequently complained because Carlos and his comrades blatantly disregarded all rules of conspiracy. There were also close contacts between Carlos and the security services of Yugoslavia and Rumania, and the group undertook certain "anti-imperialist operations" on behalf of Bucharest, usually attacks against political émigrés.

According to other East German documents, the Communist authorities eventually wanted Carlos to leave their territory but were afraid that he might defect to the enemy camp. This is difficult to believe, however, because these authorities could have easily arrested the members of the group and seized their arms and money. (Carlos, according to these reports, had millions of dollars at his disposal.) Eventually, Carlos moved on to Damascus, then to Yemen, and finally to the Sudan, where he was arrested and extradited to France, apparently as part of a financial transaction. His girlfriend returned to Germany and in her testimony to the authorities revealed details about the international nature of the gang's operations, detailing who had paid them and how passports and safe houses had been provided.

Of the records now available concerning Carlos and the Russians and East Europeans, those emanating from the East German archives are by far the most important. Even though they are not complete, a general picture emerges as to how terrorist affairs were managed in the Eastern bloc.

Following the murderous attack on Israeli athletes at the Munich Olympic Games in 1972, and fearful that similar occurrences might happen in East Germany in 1973, the ministry of State Security established Department XXII. A relatively small unit that consisted in the beginning of about a hundred officials headed by a major of state security, its assignment was to prevent terrorist attacks on the occasions of international gatherings in East Berlin.

During the years that followed there were virtually no terrorist attacks on the territory of the DDR or against East German institutions outside the country, but the department grew by leaps and bounds, much more quickly than the staff of the Ministry as a whole. By the time the East German regime collapsed, Department XXII had become a chief department with 997 permanent employees, not counting agents and informers. It was still named "Defense against Terrorism," but since there was no terrorism, the question arises as to what this unit, shrouded in the utmost secrecy even by the standards of state security, was doing all these years. Two of the subdepartments dealt with neo-Nazism and extreme right-wing groups, mainly in West Germany; it is of interest that East German state security was differentiating between these two in theory as well as in practice. The assignment of these subdepartments was to collect information on the activities of these groups, and to infiltrate them if possible. But West German neo-Nazi groups were weak and few and far between at the time; in any case, they had no intention to transfer their activities to the DDR. It seems to have been one of the tasks of these departments to magnify the potential of these right-wing groups both for domestic consumption and to create the impression in the West that neo-Nazism was a great and growing danger and that Bonn was ignoring this danger. In order to make this point more strongly, the department also engaged in active provocation, such as the publication of particularly outrageous leaflets allegedly produced by West German neo-Nazis. Some in West Germany suspected Communist provocateurs even before the Berlin Wall came down; later these suspicions became certainties.

More important, and of greater relevance to this discussion of terrorism, was subdepartment 3 (later subdepartment 8), which dealt with terrorist groups of the extreme left in Europe and the Middle East. One of its assignments was the collection of intelligence, which its agents seem to have done assiduously. There were no fewer than six full-time individuals at the Abu Nidal desk, at a time when the whole Abu Nidal group probably was not much larger. Five individuals dealt with Carlos, some fifteen to twenty with the various West German terrorist organizations (again the number of terrorist activists on the wanted list was about the same at the time), some thirty with the various Palestinian groups, two

with the ETA, one with the IRA, and three with the Japanese Red Army—
and this at a time when the JRA had gone out of business. Action Directe
of France and the Italian Brigades had one official each, even though both
groups had ceased their activities. There were other desks in charge of
terrorist organizations that were hardly known even to experts, such as
the groups Abu Muhammad and Abu Ibrahim. (These might have been
code names.) On the other hand, there were no desks dealing with the
chief actors in the field of international terrorism, Iran and its Hizbullah,
and Libya; these groups were probably covered by the regional (Middle
Eastern) units within the Ministry of State Security.

But operations were by no means limited to the more or less passive
collection of information; the departments also engaged in "active measures." Carlos provides an interesting example. Why should five desk officers deal with a man whose active terrorist career was restricted in the
1980s? The answer given by Markus Wolff, the East German spymaster,
was that Carlos was a star in the eyes of the Western media and that he
had chosen East Berlin, specifically the Palace Hotel, as his headquarters
because it had a better nightlife than any other East European or Middle
Eastern capital. According to Wolff, Carlos was a loudmouth, a spoiled
child from an upper-middle-class family who disregarded every rule of
conspiracy and caused many headaches to his East German sponsors.
Originally he had been grateful for the East German assistance, but as he
sensed that they were less than enthusiastic about his presence he turned
nasty. In *Man Without a Face*, Wolff wrote: "He began to make the same
threats against us that he carried out against enemy governments, warning
those who tried to dissuade him from a visit that he would seek out East
German targets abroad. When Carlos' West German wife, Magdalena, was
arrested in France he asked us to help spring her from jail in 1982. When
we refused, he threatened to storm our Paris embassy . . ." In the end,
East German state security had to increase security at their Paris embassy
to protect it against their terrorist ally. The story sounds incredible but it
is probably true. Carlos was not a representative of a sovereign country
who was in a position to threaten the DDR. But what could the DDR
"anti-terrorists" have done? Carlos might have met with an unfortunate
accident in East Berlin, but this would have become known sooner or later
and blemished East Berlin's historical record. Or they could have dropped
him without further ado, but in this case he might have made details
known about past collaboration between the East Germans and international terrorism, which would have been a major embarrassment. Under
these circumstances, the East Germans felt that while they could not give
in to all his demands, they had to continue to humor him, and to provide
at the very least shelter and some money.

Ten members of the Baader Meinhof gang, also known as RAF, were discovered and arrested in East Germany in 1990 after the fall of the Berlin wall. They included some of the leading surviving members of the group: Susanne Albrecht, Werner Lotze, Ekkehart von Seckendorf, Monika Helbing. The case of Susanne Albrecht in particular attracted much attention at the time. She had led a unit of the "Red Army Command" to the house of her godfather, Jürgen Ponto, chairman of the Dresdner Bank, and tried to kidnap him. They failed to do so and shot him. On the run, Susanne Albrecht settled in East Germany, where experts in counterterrorism gave her a new identity. The other members of the RAF moved to East Germany during the 1980s. The decision to give them asylum seems to have been made by Erich Mielke, the minister for state security, sometime between 1978 and 1980. There had been, in all probability, negotiations between a delegation of West German terrorists and East German officials during that period, but the protocols, if they ever existed, have been destroyed.

The motives for Mielke's decision are unclear and indeed contradictory to this day. Some have argued that it was simply an effort to preclude terrorist activities in the DDR, but a state that did not fear NATO would hardly have worried about the possible but most unlikely actions of a handful of terrorists. Markus Wolff and others contend that Mielke thought that in the case of a world war, these retired terrorists might be activated for operations in the rear of the Western enemy. But this, too, seems not quite convincing, because the terrorists were aging and had married and established families; this was not the ideal material for desperate suicide missions. On one hand, Western terrorists were given military training in the DDR even in the late 1970s and early '80s, especially in the use of explosives and anti-tank weapons, but on the other, they had to solemnly swear when given asylum that they would no longer engage in terrorist actions. In 1990, after the DDR had ceased to exist, five of the leading "anti-terrorism" officers of the DDR were arrested, not for providing asylum to West German terrorists but as accessories to attempted murder (the attempted assassination of U.S. General Kroesen in 1981 and similar operations). It seems quite likely that those responsible for aiding and abetting the West German terrorists could never quite make up their minds as to how far to take their collaboration. Ideological solidarity certainly did not play a role in these considerations, only the question of what conceivable use the RAF terrorists could be. In this respect East German officials seem to have found it difficult to come up with a clear answer. The idea that unless East Germany helped the terrorists, they would join "the camp of the enemy" seems far-fetched, to say the least. Or was it perhaps a case of a bureaucracy in search of a role? It ought to be mentioned that the DDR "anti-terrorists" seem to have been quite reluctant to share their information with other East bloc countries, even with the KGB. The DDR also seems to have opposed the establishment of an Eastern bloc centralized agency dealing with terrorism. One can only surmise what reasons lay behind these East German policies: probably the common conviction that their own services were superior to those of other Communist countries, and that by sharing confidences they might jeopardize valuable sources and contacts.

If there were hesitations with regard to the treatment of the ultrarevolutionary West Germans, there was no such vacillation with regard to operations carried out by other "progressive" terrorists. There were courses in the use of weapons and explosives several times annually for Third World terrorists, and DDR officials actively helped in two attacks carried out in West Berlin, one against the French consulate in 1983 carried out by the Libyans against La Belle Discotheque, previously mentioned. Again, there is no obvious rational explanation for the behavior of the DDR "anti-terrorists." They could not possibly have believed that Western countries would somehow be destabilized by isolated actions of this kind. It must have been obvious that the DDR connection with the terrorists would sooner or later be revealed and become a major embarrassment to the East German leadership. Perhaps there was a certain romanticism to the attitude of Honecker and Mielke, who had been Communist militants in their younger years, and for this reason felt a certain weakness for young people willing not only to make speeches but to take violent action. Before Hitler came to power, Mielke had been on the run in Germany after shooting two police officers in Berlin. In a similar way, Castro, for all his criticism of the futility of Che Guevara's campaigns, always had a soft spot for the rebel. Perhaps it is of some significance that one-third of the staff of the anti-terrorist personnel of Department XXII were very young, twenty-five and even younger. The revolutionary romanticism of an earlier period lingered on.

KHADAFI'S ADVENTURES

In the 1970s and 1980s, Libya was one of the foremost sponsors of international terrorism. Its involvement was almost as pervasive as that of Iran, a much larger and more populous country. Libya's sponsorship of terrorism predates that of Iran, dating back almost to the coup in 1969 that brought Colonel Khadafi to power. Khadafi's ambition was to spearhead an Arab-Islamic revolution in which he saw himself not only as the chief ideologist (by virtue of his little "Green Book") but also as chief strategist. Libya's income from the sale of oil provided the wherewithal to finance a variety of terrorist activities, but in subsequent years it became apparent that the country was too small and backward to sustain any major political and military initiatives. Furthermore, Khadafi's erratic behavior (to put the best possible gloss on it), his inordinate ambitions, and his rapidly changing alignments antagonized virtually everyone in the Arab world and isolated him from all but his most needy clients. Doubts were expressed concerning his mental state, not only in the West but also in the Arab and Third World capitals. Was he a madman in the clinical sense, or just highly emotional, unbalanced, and unpredictable? Khadafi even became an embarrassment to those closest to him in outlook.

Though Libya experienced strong economic growth in the early years of the Khadafi regime because of massive oil exports, its growth stalled after 1985 and eventually declined by 1995. Nevertheless, the Libyan regime was still able to spend considerable sums sponsoring terrorist activities abroad and on the construction of factories to produce poison gas and other chemical weapons. Support was given primarily to Arab terrorist groups, but also to a variety of Central and West African groups, and eventually to terrorists from Ireland to the Philippines. Among the recipients of Libyan help were the German RAF as well as the so-called Black September. According to unconfirmed reports, about eight thousand foreign terrorists, most of them Arabs, were trained each year in Libyan camps in the 1980s, and those select Palestinian groups favored by Khadafi received an annual subsidy of $100 million. Among the most famous terrorists on the Libyan payroll was Carlos the Jackal, who had been enlisted by the Popular Front for the Liberation of Palestine.

However, the list of recipients of Libyan money changed quickly, sometimes overnight. While relations with Fatah and Arafat had been close at one time, they deteriorated later, and the PLO (and many thousands of Palestinian guest workers) were expelled from Libya as Khadafi shifted his support to the most extreme Palestinian factions, such as the one headed by Abu Nidal. Even Carlos, who had been of so much use to the Libyans, was ultimately refused entry to Libya.

Libyan-sponsored terrorism manifested itself in a variety of other activities, including attacks against Libyan political émigrés. In 1984, some twenty-five such attacks were counted in Europe and the Middle East, and the assassinations continued in later years, albeit on a reduced scale. In one famous instance, Khadafi personally gave orders to his agents in London to open fire on the British police in front of the Libyan legation, an action that annoyed even the Soviets. Khadafi, they felt, was giving international terrorism a bad name. Attacks were carried out by Libyan agents against American and European targets but also against moderate Arab countries. To give a few examples, mines were laid in the Red Sea near the entrance to the Suez Canal after plots to kill President Mubarak of Egypt failed. The bombing of the Berlin nightclub La Belle Discotheque in April 1986 killed three American soldiers, wounded eighty, and claimed some two hundred German civilian victims. Six years later a German court established that while the attack had been carried out by a Palestinian, two officials of the Libyan legation in East Berlin had provided the explosives and logistic support and cover, and that East German espionage services had also been indirectly involved. In Africa, Libyan agents tried to destabilize and overthrow the then moderate government of Sudan, as well as those of the Central African countries of Chad, the Central African Republic, and Zaire.

By 1985, Khadafi's prestige was high among the terrorists, even though they were aware that the Libyan dictator tended to promise more than he delivered. But he certainly seemed more willing to accept the risks of provoking major powers than any other country. The more extreme the group, the more likely it was to find help and, if need be, a refuge in Tripoli. At the same time Khadafi's active and seemingly successful opposition to Islamic fundamentalism made some of Libya's unfriendly neighbors hesitate to take drastic action against Khadafi. Those who did not admire him seemed to fear him, at least in the Arab world. Khadafi's successes made him lose whatever remnants of a sense of reality he still possessed. He overstepped the limits of what was internationally acceptable, and invited a reaction that led to a drastic decline in his standing and a reduction of Libyan-sponsored terrorist operations.

Following Libyan terrorist attacks in Vienna and Rome airports, the Belle Discotheque bombing in West Berlin, and an attempt to bring down a TWA plane over Greece, the United States launched an air strike called El Dorado Canyon in April 1986 against selected targets in Libya. El Dorado Canyon was a one-time strike, not all targets were hit, and the damage caused was not very great. Nevertheless, to the surprise of most of America's European allies, the attack had an immediate effect. The Libyans showed much greater caution afterward, whereas earlier they had boasted of not being afraid to tackle a superpower.

America's European allies assumed that the American attack would have the opposite effect. France and Spain banned the F-111 aircraft engaged in the operation from flying over their territory. However, their fears were misplaced. During 1986–89, there was a decline in terrorist operations all over the Arab world, not just on the part of Libya. The fear that once America lost patience and felt that its vital interests were involved it might react violently and indiscriminately on a massive scale had been planted. While this might not have frightened small extremist groups, it certainly frightened their sponsors.

It was clear that the effect of a limited operation such as El Dorado Canyon would wear off, and after a number of years the bombing of Pan Am flight 103 over Lockerbie, Scotland, and the French airliner UTA flight 722 over Chad took place. (Khadafi apparently wanted to humiliate the French for having ousted the Libyan armed units from Chad, which Tripoli thought part of its sphere of influence.) In both cases, no one claimed credit for the operations, and traces of Libyan involvement were well hidden. Indeed, it seems likely that in the case of the Lockerbie disaster Iran and Syria might also have been involved. However, only Libyan involvement could eventually be proven with reasonable certainty. The matter was taken to the United Nations, where the Security Council unanimously adopted resolution 731, according to which the Libyan government was requested to hand over two of their agents who had been indicted in the United States and in Britain for their part in the Lockerbie disaster. The Security Council resolution also stipulated that Libya accept responsibility for the downing of the French airliner, disclose all evidence, and pay appropriate compensation. The Libyans refused to do so and brought upon themselves a series of sanctions, including an aviation embargo, limitations on the Libyan diplomatic presence in foreign capitals, drastic reductions in oil sales, and other measures that did considerable harm to the Libyan economy and to Libya's international standing. It was a humiliation for Khadafi, and for once he had no response.

The Libyan refusal to comply had no immediate dramatic consequences inasmuch as Khadafi remained in power. But it soon appeared that he had underrated the long-term consequences of being branded an outcast. While the Tripoli government continued to harass exiles from Libya (there were reports of the abduction of a human rights activist in Cairo and a murder in London), these occurred on a much smaller scale than before. Tripoli continued to give some help and shelter to the most extreme Arab terrorist groups, particularly those unwilling to contemplate peace with Israel under any conditions, but reduced its support of non-Arab terrorism. Libyan propaganda was almost as violent as before, but there was one considerable difference: hardly anyone in the outside world paid it any attention. Prior to 1985, Khadafi seemed to have almost gained the stature of a world leader. By the 1990s he was virtually ignored, not just by the outside world but even by his fellow Arabs. He had started his career with far-flung schemes to promote Arab unity, and terrorism had been one of the main means to that end. By the 1990s he had reached the conclusion that Libyan expansion to the south, toward Africa, was more promising and certainly less risky. The Khadafi saga demonstrates what should have been clear from the beginning: that an unscrupulous and relatively unimportant government could buy influence by investing heavily in international terrorism, but once it became more than a mere irritant, a backlash was inevitable and its power would wane.

IRANIAN FOREIGN TERRORISM

In the 1980s, Iran became the world's chief sponsor of international terrorism and maintained this dubious distinction throughout the subsequent decade. Terrorist operations had been launched by the Iranian government under the Shah. The ruthless Iranian secret police, Savak, had stalked exiled opponents of the regime and had given occasional support to separatist groups outside its borders, such as the Kurds in Iraq. However, while émigrés hostile to the Shah's regime had been harassed, they were not killed. Compared to the scale and deadliness of the activities of the clerico-fascist regime that succeeded the monarchy, Savak operations had been child's play. Furthermore, the Shah had conducted his operations in secret, whereas under Ayatollah Khomeini publicity was part of Teheran's terrorist campaign.

Iran was in a considerably stronger position than Libya to engage in state-sponsored terrorism. It is a much bigger country, and Persian nationals could be found in many parts of the world. Teheran could spend larger sums on its ventures, and it had a more inspiring message, that of radical Islam, which proved incomparably more powerful than Colonel Khadafi's "Green Book." While Khadafi's message was mainly nationalist and pan-Arab, the message sent by Teheran was not just anti-Western but pan-Islamic and populist. Iranian clerics appeared as the advocates of the downtrodden and oppressed. In contrast to Tripoli, Teheran hardly ever supported non-Islamic terrorists. On the other hand, the orthodox Shiite character of the regime did not preclude financial and military aid for radical Sunni groups in countries such as the Sudan, Egypt, Algeria, Israel, Lebanon, and elsewhere, despite their theological and ideological differences. Iran used terrorism for ideological reasons and to extend its influence in the Persian Gulf area, as well as to weaken Saudi Arabia and to undermine small states such as Kuwait and particularly Bahrain. It supported, as did other countries, certain factions in the civil war in Afghanistan, despite being on bad terms almost from the beginning with the most radical faction, the Taliban, and directly or indirectly assisted the Kurds in Iraq and Turkey. Iran had no direct interests in Israel, but the destruction of the Jewish state was identified by the Teheran clerics as a religious duty of the highest order, and Iran heavily supported Hizbullah, Hamas, and like groups. The Iranians also wanted to strengthen the Shiite element in the multi-ethnic, multi-religious, secular Lebanese state. Appearing as a leading sponsor of the anti-Israeli crusade and a bitter enemy of the peace process, Iran intended to score political points in the Arab world. No one knows to what extent deep religious conviction and true fanaticism were involved in Iran's policy vis-à-vis Israel or to what degree political calculation played a role, but it would be safe to say that both did. Furthermore, it must have appeared as an almost risk-free strategy, because Teheran was far from Tel Aviv and any Israeli retaliation was bound to affect its immediate neighbors.

Iran carried its terrorist war against its enemies, primarily émigrés, to virtually all parts of the globe, engaging in a systematic campaign of elimination of those considered most threatening. In one essential respect this campaign was unprecedented, because the Iranians claimed that their enemies were the enemies of God and divine right overruled the secular norms of the international right. The reward announced for the killing of Salman Rushdie, author of *The Satanic Verses* and an Indian by nationality, was almost unprecedented in the annals of international affairs. The *fatwa,* or religious injunction, issued by Khomeini was not withdrawn by his successors.

Shifts in the intensity of Teheran's terrorist campaign reflected the international situation as well as power struggles inside Iran, with some leaders taking a more aggressive line than others. But terrorism did not cease; it was considered by the Iranian rulers a legitimate—indeed, a vital—instrument of domestic and foreign policy.

Iranian terrorist operations in the Middle East were usually carried out by local Shiite militants such as Dawa in Iraq and Hizbullah in Lebanon, opponents to the regimes in the Gulf area, and Palestinian Sunni groups such as Hamas. Iranian nationals were only indirectly involved in these operations, mainly providing weapons and training, although some eight hundred Iranian "volunteers" were stationed for years in the Baqa Valley in Lebanon. In terrorist operations outside the Middle East, on the other hand, Iranians participated at every level. On the basis of a meticulous reconstruction of the assassination of activists of the Kurdish Democratic Party in a restaurant in West Berlin, a Berlin court issued a warrant in March 1996 for the arrest of Ali Fallahian, Iranian minister of security and information. It had been known for some time that assassinations were carried out by VEVAK, the Iranian secret police, with the help of Iranian military intelligence and other government agencies, but this was the first time that a Western court had documented the line of command. This decision by an independent German court caused no little embarrassment to the German Foreign Ministry, for Fallahian had once been the official guest of the German government and he had been active in negotiations for the release of German and other Western hostages kept in Lebanon and Iran. Fallahian was not, of course, the head of terrorist operations; the orders came from Khomeini and his successors, such as Ali Khameini. These spiritual and political leaders never made a secret of their great appreciation for their underlings who were "combating and uprooting" the enemies of Islam inside and outside Iran.

The enemies targeted by Iran were first and foremost political dissidents, including some very prominent figures, such as Shapour Bakhtiar, the last prime minister under the Shah, who was murdered in Paris in August 1991 at the age of seventy-six. This was not the first attempt on his life in Paris: in an earlier attempt a Frenchwoman and a police officer were killed. The terrorists were apprehended and given life sentences but released after a short time and returned to Teheran. European governments knew from bitter experience that the Iranian authorities would retaliate against the arrest of their agents, and the French had a tradition of caving in more quickly than other European governments. If Iranian diplomats involved in blatant terrorist activities were asked by the host government to leave, the Iranian would retaliate by expelling Western (or Turkish or Arab) diplomats. Occasionally, the Iranians would withdraw their diplomats before an official demand was made; this happened, for instance, in Buenos Aires, where Iranian terrorists had attacked Jewish schools and other organizations.

Among Iranian targets was the leadership of the left-wing Mojahedin, the main émigrés opposition group, but monarchists, Communists, and members of the Flag of Freedom group were also singled out for assassination, as well as Kurdish activists and some individuals who had no known political ties to Iran. In a variety of cases, Iranian agents attempted to abduct political émigrés in foreign countries even though such operations were always more complicated and the risk of failure or discovery greater. Altogether, Iranian terrorists assassinated more than sixty émigrés, although the number of attempted assassinations may have been closer to two hundred. These operations took place in Turkey, Iraq, and Pakistan, as well as in France, Germany, Switzerland, Austria, Italy, and other European countries, and even as far away as Venezuela.

While the risks involved from the Iranian point of view were not enormous, there was still the danger that, like Libya, Iran would be isolated as the result of blatant and frequent terrorist actions. Iran certainly suffered economically from retaliatory measures taken by the United States and other countries.

Why, then, did Iran continue to sponsor terrorism? It could be that the rulers in Teheran felt insecure even though open opposition had been suppressed inside Iran. It could also be that they were pessimistic about their long-term political future and thought that unless they crushed the émigré opposition their position inside Iran would weaken.

The Iranian leadership all agreed in principle on the use of terrorism outside the country, but there were differences of opinion as to how many abductions and assassinations could be safely carried out. The hard-line Montazeri faction seems to have advocated an aggressive policy in the early years of the regime, whereas president Ali Rafsanjani, who had recently prevailed in the struggle for power, advocated a more cautious approach. In any case terrorism, albeit on a somewhat reduced scale, has continued under his rule as before.

There was a decline in the number of political assassinations in foreign countries carried out by Iranian agents after 1992. That year there had been twenty such cases, whereas in the four years after there were only six, four, seven, and eight, respectively. The Iranians had to some extent achieved their aims, inasmuch as the French had expelled the Mojahedin from Paris, where they constituted a graver danger to the Iranian regime than in Baghdad, where they settled down next. Ironically, Khomeini, when exiled because of pressure from the Shah's government, had settled in France for many years. Thirty years later, the French no longer had the stomach for extending asylum to political refugees, as they were more afraid of the wrath of the clerics in Teheran than they had been of the displeasure of the Shah. However, the Iranian terrorist apparatus must have been given orders to slow down, because the continuing assassinations were causing more harm than good to the clerical regime; it made it more difficult, for instance, to acquire and develop weapons of mass destruction, which was an important long-term aim of Teheran.

By 1997, Iranian political ambitions had increased. They wanted to play host to a big Islamic conference in Teheran and to show that they were not only a militant but also a responsible power that abided by most of the norms of international relations. A new president, Khatemi, had been elected with a substantial moderate majority, and even though most of the key positions in the country were still in the hands of the diehards headed by Ali Khameini, the internal balance of power had changed somewhat. Terrorist operations directed against Western countries and the Arab Gulf states declined. Operations did not cease altogether, but they were camouflaged far better than in the past. When, for instance, terrorists attacked an American base in Saudi Arabia or Jewish institutions in Argentina, Iranian involvement seemed certain. There was insufficient legal proof, however, and other sponsors may have participated as well, so retaliation against Iran alone was difficult to justify. In various major terrorist attacks, a group that called itself Islamic Jihad took the credit.

But there was no independent organization named Islamic Jihad; it was part of the military wing of Hamas. To hide their tracks, the Iranians had used the surrogate of a surrogate.

The high tide of Iranian anti-Western terrorism occurred in the 1980s, and the main scene was Lebanon. These operations, carried out by surrogates, included the bombing of the U.S. embassy in Beirut and the American and French military barracks in 1983–84, which cost many lives; the bombing of a variety of embassies and Saudi travel agencies from Vienna to New Delhi; the taking of hostages, first in Teheran and later in Beirut; and the hijacking of planes. The hostage saga lasted for eight years (1984–92), and the Iranians played this game with consummate skill. They were instrumental in inspiring and guiding the kidnappers, and helping them to keep the hostages—altogether about one hundred over the years—in Lebanon and Iran. At the same time, they presented themselves as honest brokers eager to resolve the crisis between the kidnappers, with whom they pretended to have no connection, and the Western countries, which were trying to secure the release of their nationals. In this way they obtained from America all kinds of concessions, including economic help and even an official expression of thanks on the part of then President Bush.

But those who had hoped that moderation had prevailed in Teheran were disappointed when, in 1989, Ayatollah Khomeini, in the last months of his life, published his famous *fatwa* against Salman Rushdie. The Indian author's *Satanic Verses* was thought to be blasphemous, and every good Muslim was called upon to kill Rushdie as well as those instrumental in publishing it. To reinforce this appeal, an obscure foundation in Teheran announced an award of $2 million (plus expenses) for killing Rushdie. The Iranians dispatched a suicide bomber who accidentally blew himself up in a London hotel room. The book's Japanese translator was stabbed to death, and there were attempts on the lives of the Italian and Norwegian publishers. The *fatwa* was not withdrawn after Khomeini's death, despite strong diplomatic pressure and abject apologies by the author.

The Rushdie affair had many curious aspects. While the intention of the work was satirical, there have been many more outspoken attacks in Western literature against Islam and the prophet Muhammad, just as in Muslim countries there have been scurrilous attacks against Judaism and Christianity. The Teheran government could have demanded with greater justification, for instance, the ban and destruction of the works of Voltaire, who wrote in a truly outrageous manner about the prophet. Why single out Rushdie? And why promise a substantial monetary award for what was proclaimed to be no more than the holy duty of every Muslim believer? Did the Ayatollahs trust so little the religious fervor of their coreligionists as to bring in a demeaning material incentive? The affair attracted enormous attention, and it revealed an inconsistent component in the thinking of the Teheran rulers.

If there was a decline in Iranian-sponsored terrorist operations against the West and in the Gulf, there was an upsurge in such attacks against Israel and Jewish communities elsewhere, mainly in the form of arms support given to Hizbullah in Lebanon and also to Sunni anti-Israeli militants such as Hamas (groups named Hizbullah or Hamas also exist in other countries). Although, according to some reports, the annual subsidy to Hizbullah of about $150 million was subsequently halved, the supply of arms was not reduced. The monetary cuts might have been inevitable in light of Iran's strained economic circumstances and its need to fund other terrorists in the Middle East and Afghanistan.

What benefits did the Iranian rulers derive from their massive investment in international terrorism? The Ayatollahs may have believed during Iran's war against Iraq that, because they were not strong enough to achieve decisive victory, they had to turn to terrorism, which was infinitely cheaper. But Iran's involvement with terrorism did not begin with the war against Iraq, nor did it end with it. Up to a point the Iranian sponsorship of terrorist groups was successful: the fact that its substitutes had compelled the United States to flee Lebanon certainly added to Iran's image as the fearless champion of Arab extremism. But it did not enhance Iran's military and political standing in the long term. Though Iran was feared by its neighbors, such fear did not make them bow to Iranian demands, but rather induced closer collaboration against Teheran.

Investment in terrorism certainly did not help export the Iranian revolution. This would have been difficult in any case because of the traditional tension between Shiites and Sunni. Even Sunni fundamentalists of the Muslim Brotherhood variety, who accepted Iranian help, declared on every occasion that they were no admirers of the kind of government established in Iran, and that they aimed at a different kind of society.

Support for anti-Israeli terrorism was also problematic from an Iranian point of view. The intent was to be recognized as the staunchest and most radical champion of the Palestinian cause and as the opponent of any peace process. But since the now cautious Iranians seldom acknowledged openly their terrorist operations (they never claimed credit, for instance, for the two bombings in Buenos Aires in 1992 and 1994), their support must have appeared halfhearted to radical Palestinian militants, who always expected more assistance than they got. At the same time, the Iranian rulers exposed themselves to considerable risk. There was always the danger that if the terrorist threat became unacceptable, the Israelis, less inhibited than the Western countries, would strike back at Iran rather than the surrogates. Having never recovered from the war with Iraq, the Iranian military would be unable to effectively respond.

Seen from this perspective, massive Iranian involvement in terrorism was a double-edged sword. It undoubtedly reaped benefits for Iran at a relatively cheap price. On the other hand, it was a dangerous gamble, for even if Iranian leaders acted entirely rationally in weighing possible gains and risks, which they did not always do, there was the danger that their operations might get out of hand and backfire. The surrogates Teheran used had their own agenda and priorities, and it was impossible to control them fully.

SADDAM HUSSEIN ET AL.

As we have seen, during the 1970s and '80s many governments engaged in state-sponsored terrorism, but after that, these activities dwindled. Iraq had been so weakened by its ill-fated Kuwait venture that it could not afford to offend its neighbors, let alone countries farther afield. Cuba and North Korea, facing desperate economic and political difficulties, were fighting for their survival, and could not engage in major foreign political adventures. South Yemen had become part of the new state of Yemen, and its rulers no longer wished to support Arab terrorists and their nebulous radical causes. The Soviet Union and bloc dropped their terrorist clients as their political system collapsed.

All of these countries had actively supported the terrorists of their choice only a few years earlier. A small and poor country, South Yemen did not engage in any active measures of its own, and its political ambitions were limited even within the framework of the Arab world. But its remote geographical situation and the difficulties of access too it made it an ideal training ground and hiding place. In the camps of South Yemen, for which other countries paid, many terrorists received their training at one time or another, including those on the extreme left from Western European countries, such as the Baader Meinhof group. This began to change only in 1983–84 as the negotiations with North Yemen toward unification continued. Most of the camps were closed, the foreign terrorists were asked to leave, and only Arabs, mostly Palestinians, were permitted to stay on a temporary basis.

Like Iran, Iraq was at one time an active sponsor of international terrorism. The Iraqi secret service had concentrated its efforts against the political dissidents among its émigrés, many of whom were stalked by Iraqi agents abroad and some of whom were in fact assassinated. During the 1980s, as the war against Iran proceeded, Saddam Hussein had to limit his operations in the West so as not to endanger his sources of arms and other military support. In these years Iraq found itself at the receiving end of terrorist attacks, such as the bombing of the Iraqi embassy in Beirut by Iranian and Syrian terrorists in December 1981. The ambassador and sixty-two of his staff were killed on this occasion. Inside Iraq, the government had to defend itself against the attacks launched by Dawa'a, a Shiite terrorist group sponsored by Iran. During and after the Gulf War, the Iraqi regime again found itself on the defensive as far as terrorism was concerned. The Iraqi secret police had to concentrate on combating resistance at home and limit operations abroad.

But these developments by no means led to an end to all such activities. Baghdad played host to various small but very active Arab groups such as Abu Ibrahim, Abu Abbas, and Abu Nidal, as well as to the Kurdistan Workers Party, which it used for its own purposes. Attacks against Iraqi émigrés continued, and there were assassinations of Iraqi exiles in Beirut and Amman. In 1995, an Iraqi academic in the United States, Dr. Sargon Dadesho, brought a suit against the Iraqi government, and the court found that there had been an attempt to assassinate him; he was awarded $1.5 million by a Californian district court. Furthermore, there seems to have been an attempt to murder President Bush during his visit to Kuwait in 1993: three years later a local U.S. court pronounced death sentences against two Iraqi nationals for this attempt.

Syria has played host to many terrorist groups, both in Damascus and the Baqa Valley in Lebanon. Among them was one of the most notorious international terrorists of the 1970s and '80s: Abu Nidal, who, like the Fatah "General Command" directed by Ahmed Jibril, seems to have been largely dependent on Syria.

Syrian-sponsored terrorist activities were often directed against Israel, but also against Jordan in the early 1980s and against Iraq. Turkey was a permanent target of Syrian-sponsored terrorist operations, as were militant Armenians in the 1970s, and, later on, various Kurdish factions, hostile to both Turkey and Armenia, received training and weapons in the Syrian-occupied parts of Lebanon. In the 1980s Syria cooperated with Iran in helping Hizbullah, which developed and spread throughout Lebanon and operated against Western countries as well as Israel. Syria played second fiddle in this context, showing much more caution than Iran. The Syrian government seems to have feared that if terrorist organizations grew too strong, they might constitute a danger for Syria or at the very least might cause international complications beyond the control of Damascus. On the other hand, the Syrians had an interest in continuing attacks against Israel so as to make Israel more amenable to Syrian demands. Syria was also unwilling to offend Iran by refusing to cooperate.

As a result, Syria found itself on the U.S. list of governments sponsoring international terrorism.

If several Arab countries dropped out of this league or at least reduced their involvement, there was a very active newcomer, Sudan. In most ways Sudan began to play the role South Yemen had played twenty years earlier, as one of the most important training grounds and safe havens for terrorists, only on a much larger scale. All major and many minor Middle Eastern terrorist groups established a presence in the training camps of Sudan, most of which were in the vicinity of its capital, Khartoum. The camps became a home away from home for separatist and fundamentalist terrorists from Tunisia, Ethiopia, Kenya, Uganda, and Eritrea. The Sudanese government collaborated closely with Iran and Libya, assisting various terrorist initiatives all over the world, and it granted asylum to Carlos (though, as mentioned before, he was eventually sold to the French) and Usama Bin Ladin, a billionaire Saudi businessman, who was behind many terrorist attacks against his native country and other targets in the Middle East. (Bin Ladin later transferred his activities to Afghanistan.) In June 1995, a spectacular attempt was made to kill President Mubarak of Egypt in Addis Ababa, Ethiopia. The ambush on the road from the airport had been prepared in Sudan, and after it failed the perpetrators escaped back to Khartoum, one of them carrying an official Sudanese passport.

These and other activities brought about the inclusion in 1993 of Sudan on the list of state sponsors of international terrorism. The Sudanese motives for supporting terrorism are not entirely clear. While the ruling military junta in Sudan was, broadly speaking, fundamentalist in outlook, it was not fanatically so. It should have been clear that open sponsorship of terrorist activities would lead to the isolation of Sudan, not only in Western relations but also with Africa and Egypt. If there was deeper thought behind this strategy, an assumption by no means certain, it might be that the Sudanese rulers, in dire straits for years, simply wished to enhance their nuisance value. The country was desperately poor and faced a major insurgency in the south among the non-Muslim population. It is quite likely that Khartoum thought that involvement in terrorist activities would somehow enhance its position by threatening neighboring African countries who sided with the rebels in southern Sudan with support for secessionists in those eastern African countries. On the other hand, the fact that Carlos was extradited to France seems to indicate that Sudanese commitment to terrorism was by no means irreversible, and that a million dollars could override any loyalty it might have had to a terrorist.

As these lines are being written, Cuba and North Korea remain on America's list of state supporters of terrorism, even though their involvement has been minimal for a number of years. Gone are the days when these countries were among the foremost players in this field, though Cuba continues to offer a safe haven to former terrorists from Latin America who are on the wanted list. In its heyday, Castro's Cuba supported virtually all Latin American extremist movements irrespective of whether they engaged in guerrilla warfare or terrorism or a mixture of the two. Those were the days when the Latin American left looked up to Castro and his regime as the shining example, far more attractive than the Soviet Union and China. Today there is still nostalgia for the heroes of this romantic age, but this manifests itself in Che Guevara's reburial in Havana and unending publication of biographies of him, not in new revolutionary upsurges.

Revolutionary potential still exists in Latin America, but present-day fighters derive their inspiration from non-Cuban sources, and even in Havana there is not much enthusiasm about the Sendero Luminosos of this world or even the Colombian FARC. Once, Cuban fighters were involved in various African campaigns, but Cuban leaders realized a long time ago that these campaigns have mainly to do with tribal and ethnic conflict, not with any struggle for a better world or more social justice. The Cubans are mainly concerned with keeping their economy afloat and are far more interested in normal or better relations with the governments of Latin America, left, right, or center, than in wasting waning enthusiasm and resources on the extremists between Antofagasta and the Rio Grande. To the Latin American left, Castro is a relic from a distant past with little if any relevance for present-day concerns.

North Korea carried out a number of massive terrorist attacks in the 1980s, including one against a South Korean delegation in Rangoon in 1983 in which several government ministers were killed. Four years later, North Korean agents placed a bomb on Korean Airline flight 858; in the ensuing crash, 115 persons were killed. But since then the North Koreans have not engaged in international terrorism other than the usual espionage and diversion actions directed against South Korea. A North Korean government spokesman declared in 1993 that his government opposed all kinds of terrorism, including assistance to terrorist groups. This seems to have reflected a major tactical shift in North Korean strategy, a realization that investment in international terrorism was not productive, and possibly even counterproductive, while the production of weapons of mass destruction was far more promising and did indeed lead to certain American concessions. Furthermore, North Korea evidently realized it was unwise and impractical to pursue international terrorism and at the same time to engage in the building of long-range missiles and nuclear bombs.

The North Koreans still give safe haven to some members of the Japanese Red Army, but they do so halfheartedly, mainly for old times' sake. When one of these militants, Yoshimi Tanaka, was arrested in Cambodia in 1996 on counterfeiting charges, the North Koreans refused to take up his defense even though he carried a North Korean diplomatic passport.

In addition to the state agencies sponsoring terrorism, there have been and are individuals and small groups who do so—for example, the Landsknechte, named after the medieval swordsmen of fortune. They may have certain ideological convictions, but "actionism" seems to be the more important motive. They are guns for hire, as long they think it is for a good cause and the money is right. The Carlos and Abu Nidals of an earlier age have been replaced by the survivors of the terrorist groups of the 1980s, by Saudi businessmen, and above all by some 20,000 young Arabs and other Middle Easterners who volunteered to fight in Afghanistan. A fairly high percentage of these volunteers came from Yemen, and their operations were supported to a certain extent by the CIA stations in Cairo and Islamabad. Many of these volunteers were killed, but thousands survived, and they are now found among virtually all terrorist groups in the Middle East, from Algeria to Egypt, from Lebanon to the Far East. Originally they congregated in Pakistan, but the Pakistani government started to deport them at the request of the Egyptian and Algerian governments. Some of them took part in the Yemen civil war, while others launched the bloody attacks in Algeria and Egypt. Among the paymasters are reportedly Usama Bin Ladin and the Iranian secret service, and as a result the "Afghans" have become a major factor in international terrorism. This situation is unlikely to change until the current generation has passed from the scene.

In addition, there is a new phenomenon, the appearance of small groups, active especially in Western Europe, of Middle Eastern terrorists of no clear provenance, as the case of the World Trade Center bombing shows. These groups usually consist of young militants who act on their own initiative, and who have established links with one or more of the states sponsoring terrorism but are not under their full control. For example, they might include a radical Muslim preacher banned in his own country and a handful of former Afghan volunteers or Pakistanis with a grudge. This flotsam and jetsam of the terrorist underworld may be incapable of conducting a sustained campaign, but it can still engage in a major terrorist action or two, and, since the groups are so small and have no organizational structure, they are difficult for security forces to infiltrate.

Our survey of state-sponsored terrorism would not be complete without a mention of the fact that democratic countries have on occasion also engaged in terrorist operations, or at least contemplated such actions. To give two examples, the United States at one stage considered terrorist actions against Cuba and Castro in person, but these plans, usually half-baked, were seldom attempted. The Israelis systematically hunted down the perpetrators of the massacre in 1972 in the Munich Olympic village, and they have sometimes attacked leading members of Palestinian terrorist organizations; in a famous case in Lillehammer, Norway, they killed the wrong individual. In 1998, there was the grotesque attack against a leader of Hamas in Amman, Jordan; ill conceived and badly executed, it caused deep embarrassment to all involved.

Seen in a long-term perspective, state-sponsored terrorism has been on the decline, inasmuch as the number of actors has decreased. But it has by no means vanished, as the Iranian and Sudanese examples show. Those who have dropped out are countries vulnerable to international pressure. Those who remain are slightly bigger countries on which massive pressure has not been exerted so far, or are very remote and poor like Sudan, a nation whose situation is so precarious that it does not have much to lose. Iran succeeded in compelling the Americans and the French to leave Lebanon posthaste, but this was mainly because no core interest of the Western powers was involved in Lebanon. In similar circumstances, the Indians left Sri Lanka when it appeared that their presence would be too costly. What if the Iranians overstepped themselves and invaded a neighboring country or openly threatened other countries? There is little doubt that if this happened, a major destabilizing campaign would be launched against Iran or even military action taken. If little action has been taken against Sudan—the only one as of this writing has been a limited U.S. missile attack in August 1998, in response to embassy bombings in Kenya and Tanzania that destroyed a pharmaceutical installation suspected of producing chemical weapons—it has been because the Sudanese threat has been minimal even in the African context. If the Sudanese cross the line, severe measures are sure to be taken by those who feel threatened.

These are the dialectics of state-sponsored terrorism: Terrorism is effective as long as it does not constitute an overwhelming threat. In the cases of both Iran and Sudan, there is also the hope that the policies of these countries might change, and that those in power now might soon disappear. It is too early to say whether these speculations are justified, nor is it certain where exactly the line is beyond which state-sponsored terrorism becomes exceedingly dangerous to the sponsors. The sponsoring states have tried to find this out by trial and error, assuming that an error can always be corrected by a retreat from an exposed position. But it is not certain that this assumption will always be true, especially in the case of a country, such as Iran, that simultaneously engages in state terrorism and works to acquire an arsenal of weapons of mass destruction.

Exotic TERRORISM

The term *exotic* has more than one meaning in English. It pertains to faraway countries and civilizations, but it is also used to describe things that are foreign, non-native, that appear out of place in given circumstances. Seen from Lima, Colombo, or Kampala, the three terrorist movements covered in the first part of this chapter are altogether too familiar. But they are foreign importations, for Maoism is not a homegrown Peruvian ideology, and Christian fundamentalism did not develop originally in Uganda. At the same time, they are also nativist movements because in the process of importation they underwent curious changes that made them into a strange mixture of domestic and alien influences, ultimately exotic but with native alloys.

The terrorist group Sendero Luminoso, or Shining Path, is a clear case of social and ethnic protest combined with a primitive ideology—that is, Maoism of the age of the cultural revolution, which has been even more simplified for the remote Peruvian highlands. The Tamil Tigers, on the other hand, are purely nationalist in inspiration but have shown extreme fanaticism seldom found outside religious sects. The Ugandan Lord's Resistance Army, despite its seemingly Christian connection, can be understood only in the context of the complicated tribal structures and relations of East Africa. Ideology is completely confused in this movement in which the fundamentalist Islamic regime in Khartoum, Sudan, is the closest ally and protector of a self-styled Christian fundamentalist movement. What these groups have in common is their sectarian character, millenarian in some respects, the use of violence on a massive scale, and the application of both guerrilla and terrorist tactics. Later in this chapter, we will describe terrorists who are exotic in the sense that their politics are nonhuman. Their ideology is not inspired by religious or social movements or philosophies; they are neither of the right nor left, neither sectarian nor fundamentalist. They are foreign to the world of terrorism described in this book so far, except that they use violence to publicize their cause and to achieve their ends. They are the ecoterrorists, whose violence is aimed at those who would despoil the earth. In some cases, their rhetoric, like some millenarians', proposes the complete elimination of mankind. In addition, there are the so-called "animal liberationists," who fit into this category of terrorist exotica. Thus, no place, however uninhabitable, and no creature is beyond the purview of the determined terrorist.

PERU: THE SHINING PATH

When the Sendero Luminoso, or Shining Path, was founded in 1980, it was not a terrorist group but a political movement conducting a guerrilla war campaign. The Peruvian government was very weak at the time and not particularly tyrannical, and the Shining Path began not as a movement against acute political oppression but as a protest against widespread poverty, economic stagnation, and neglect of the Indians who constitute about half of Peruvian society. Semifeudal conditions prevailed in the countryside. If Christ stopped at Eboli, he certainly stopped well before Ayacucho, in the southern highlands of Peru, where Sendero was founded by a group of mestizo professors at the local university. Their ideology was strange even by the yardstick of half-educated intellectuals in an underdeveloped country: a mixture of Maoism, millenarianism, and traditional Indian tribal elements, something akin to voodoo socialism.

It was a movement against the rich, appealing to the local population's traditional suspicions and hatred of the central government, and thus a movement not dissimilar in character to the American militias but light-years from them in ideological inspiration. The guerrilla leaders, headed by Abimael Guzman, had both energy and idealism, and like the Russian

Narodovoltsy of the 1870s, they tried to become part of the people—
meaning the Indians—going native to the extent of even learning the
Indians' language.

To a certain degree their strategy was not without merits. They began
their operations far from Peru's urban centers, and the central government
paid little attention and, in any case, was too weak to do anything about
it. The Shining Path's strategy was a mixture of propaganda and ruthless
terror, and they began to dominate the local population by dictating loyal
supporters and killing those opposed to them. Even their strange and
primitive ideology had its attractions, because it fitted admirably those for
whom it was destined—namely, the poorest and most illiterate sections
of Peruvian rural society.

Eventually Guzman was to reject Maoism and its related subspecies
derived from the Vietcong, North Korean Juchne, and Enver Hodzha's
brand of Leninism. Guzman came to believe they were all ill-suited to the
cause. Also, as a practical matter, the Maoist strategy did not fit the country; though Peru was big, more than a million square kilometers, it was
not remotely as big as China, and modern military technology, such as
helicopters, gave advantages to the government that Chiang Kai-shek
never had. Guzman also seems to have forgotten that while the overwhelming majority of Chinese lived in the countryside at the time, three
quarters of the population of Peru was concentrated in cities. And above
all, unlike China, which was caught in a long and losing war with Japan,
the central government in Lima was not preoccupied with a foreign
enemy.

Under the circumstances, it is surprising that Sendero Luminoso and
another, smaller and less active terrorist movement, Tupac Amaru, were
comparatively successful and lasted as long as they did. The main reasons
were Peru's continuing poverty and the fact that only a small part of the
population benefited from the reforms introduced by Alberto Fujimori,
who was first elected in 1990 under the slogan "Work, Technology, Honesty." There was no doubt about Fujimori's personal honesty, and his
policy might have been the only practical one. It certainly attracted desperately needed foreign capital, but more than a third of the population
still lived below the starvation level. Neither Fujimori nor Sendero really
appealed to this bottom third of society. Fujimori was an autocrat, but
Sendero was no paragon of democracy. The rebels first made their name
by destroying ballot boxes and killing those daring to violate their ban
against participating in elections. During the fifteen years of the conflict,
Sendero killed at least 2,500 soldiers and policemen and an unspecified
but certainly much greater number of civilians, perhaps between 10,000
and 20,000. And they drove half a million people from the war zone to

the cities in the lowlands. The damage Sendero caused to the Peruvian economy through acts of sabotage was huge, perhaps fifteen to twenty billion dollars' worth.

The group's activities did not lose momentum over the years, and in some respects 1992 was its most violent year. But unlike the Maoists in wartime China, Sendero did not manage to establish a countersociety and a countereconomy, and so the people under their partial control suffered even more than before. This fact of life could not be counteracted by any amount of propaganda, and the inevitable happened: in September 1992, Guzman was captured, as were, soon after, most other members of the Sendero leadership. Since the movement very much rested on the cult of its leader and since they had foolishly prepared lists of their cells and militants that the police found, this was a blow from which Sendero never recovered.

Guzman was arrested in Lima because Sendero had realized in 1987 that its strategy had changed. The villages would never encircle the cities, as anticipated under the old Maoist strategy, and so the armed struggle had to be carried to the main cities. The new Shining Path strategy was at first modestly successful because the slums of Lima, a city of more than six million inhabitants, constituted the urban equivalent of an impassable and inaccessible jungle. The assassinations by the Sendero liquidation commandos continued, and even though all Peruvian political parties (including the Communists and the Trotskyites) condemned Sendero Luminoso, the movement continued to do considerable harm to the country's economy.

This began to change almost immediately after the arrest of Guzman and the other members of the central committee in 1992. While the Sendero commandos killed 516 of their enemies in 1993, this number fell to 150 the year after, and there was a further decline in 1995 and 1996. The movement split when some of the militants accepted the peace offers made by the government to their imprisoned leaders. At the same time, their financial lifeline was cut. A fungus damaged the Upper Huallaga Valley coca crop, which had been the principal source of income of Sendero for many years.

The other, much smaller Peruvian terrorist group was MRTA, the Tupac Amaru Revolutionary Movement, which came into being in the 1980s. Its leaders were middle class and the group was active mainly in Lima, and to a lesser extent in distant regions. Ideologically the MRTA differed from Sendero Luminoso, as the smaller movement was an offshoot of the most radical elements within APRA, the historical Peruvian left-wing party. Later on the MRTA adopted the theories of Che Guevara, even though this kind of adventurism had disastrously failed about everywhere in Latin America. The organization was a little less xenophobic than Sendero Luminoso, but in practice its operations were quite similar: robberies, murder, and cooperation with the coca growers. Most of the members of MRTA surrendered in 1993, but there was a spectacular last gasp in December 1996, when MRTA commandos invaded a party at the Japanese embassy and took the guests hostage. The prisoners included many leading officials, and the siege lasted up to April 22, 1997. It ended with an assault by government forces during which all the MRTA militants were killed. According to the Peruvian authorities, they had been shot during the fighting, but, according to other sources, they were killed after the fighting was over.

Just as Jean-Paul Sartre had extended moral support to the Baader Meinhof gang, Sendero and MRTA had backers and well-wishers both inside Peru and abroad. They complained about human rights abuses committed by the Peruvian government and the inhuman conditions in which the leaders of the two terrorist groups were kept. These accusations were probably true, but since terrorism had never adhered to humanist principles either, these complaints made little impact. A true revolutionary challenging the state must expect to be mistreated, for he has been claiming all along that the authorities were inhuman.

Thus ended, for the time being, the story of two of the most active Latin American terrorist groups of the 1980s. It may be too early to draw a line across the history of terrorism in Peru, however. Economic progress has been slow, up to 50 percent of the population is underemployed, and while hyperinflation has been brought to an end, the rich are still rich and the poor as poor as before, and the Indians have not made significant progress. The opposition against the government and the wealthier sections in society is likely to continue, and it might well again take violent forms at some future date. But the specific Peruvian contribution to the history of terrorism, Sendero Luminoso, failed and is unlikely to be revived.

COLOMBIA: DRUGS AND TERRORISM

Colombia has a tradition of violence that has dominated much of its history in the twentieth century. Its two major armed guerrilla forces, the FARC, originally an offshoot of the Colombian Communist Party, and the National Liberation Army (ELN), have been active for decades with many ups and downs in their history. In the 1990s, because the central government was weak and under international pressure to do more against the drug cartels, the fortunes of FARC improved, and whole regions in the south of the country passed out of the control of the central government. The rebels made prisoners of entire units of the Colombian army, only to release them again in a show of magnanimity. They negotiated with Bogotá, but there was no certainty that they really wanted an agreement. For many years they had received substantial financial support from the drug cartels who sought to counteract the power of the government. But not a few government officials also received money from the drug cartels, so that the overall situation became very muddled indeed.

The income of the drug cartels declined somewhat as certain government initiatives were successful against the coca growers. Furthermore, the drug cartels had no particular interest in replacing a weak central government by a stronger one headed by the guerrillas, so the financial help given to the guerrillas was reduced. To refresh their finances, the FARC engaged in a massive campaign of abductions involving hundreds of people, most of them not even very wealthy. But more often than not the families of those kidnapped paid up, and the financial situation of the FARC improved to a degree.

The terrorist situation in Colombia was further complicated by the prevalence of a good deal of criminal banditry that also engaged in similar activities, not to mention the activities of counterinsurgency gangs. The bandits did not bomb oil pipelines as did the FARC, but they too kidnapped civilians and took money from the drug cartels. In brief, the situation in Colombia had a great deal to do with the violence endemic to that country; there were elements of guerrilla warfare and also a little terrorism, but it belonged to an exotic and different species from what had once been known as revolutionary warfare. Mao and Guevara would spin in their graves if they learned of the exploits of their latter-day successors. "Coca and Liberty . . . Long Live the Revolutionary Struggle" was one slogan. While violence in its various forms continues in Colombia, the revolutionary terrorist phase seems to be long over and done with.

Following the general elections of 1998, the main guerrilla and terrorist groups entered peace talks with the victorious politicians. The negotiations took place in a monastery in southern Germany and the atmosphere was almost cordial. Some far-reaching understandings were agreed to, but it remains unknown whether these will lead to pacification. However, these negotiations tended to show that the conflict in Colombia was different from that in Peru. It was a conflict between rival elites, which could in certain circumstances agree on the division of the spoils.

At this stage some brief, general observations on the development of terrorism in Latin America are called for, even though they might be only indirectly connected with the subject of "exotic terrorism." Latin America was the scene of much terrorist activity in the 1970s. The Uruguayan militants, the Tupamaros, and later the Argentinian Montoneros had been idolized by enthusiasts of armed struggle all over the globe. Castro's rise to power was the model and Marighella's mini-manual for terrorists was translated and studied in many countries. But the Cuban example could not be copied in other countries, and Marighella's tactical wisdom was of little help even to its author, who was shot in a police ambush. The terrorists succeeded in overthrowing some inefficient democratic governments that were promptly replaced by more repressive authoritarian governments, as in Uruguay and Argentina. Elsewhere, as in Brazil, the terrorist threat was not formidable enough to cause any political changes at the top. In some places, such as Guatemala and in San Salvador, terrorists succeeded in triggering off civil wars that lasted for decades, but such civil wars were no novelty in the the continent's history. "Objective conditions" for discontent certainly existed, such as oppressive poverty in the big cities that had grown uncontrollably. By the mid-1990s, greater Mexico City and São Paulo had more than 16 million inhabitants each, and millions were living in the *favellas,* the poor suburbs which had mushroomed on the periphery of these conurbations. In the countryside, there were both poverty and semifeudal conditions, and the continued neglect of the Indian population. In Mexico, the armed struggles that were carried on in the 1990s by the EPR in Guerrero and by the Zapatistas (EZLN) in Chiapas were campaigns for long-overdue land reform as well as for the Indians' right of self-determination.

But these were not terrorist campaigns in any meaningful way. They were by and large manifestations of a political and social struggle in which, on occasion, terrorist tactics were used. Typical for this kind of internal warfare were the relations between the Mexican rebels and the government; periods of negotiations alternated with armed attacks when the talks stalled. The Guatemalan civil war claimed about 100,000 victims over its thirty-four-year duration. Peace negotiations began in 1991 and led to an accord five years later.

Despite appearances, Latin America was not ideal territory for classical guerrilla warfare. Those trying to hide in the mountains were exposed to observation, and if there were jungles, these were not really habitable for any length of time, nor could they serve as rallying grounds for paramilitary units of any size. In these circumstances, the rebels tried for a time a mixture of guerrilla warfare in the countryside and terrorism in the big cities, but this did not work well either. There were no charismatic personalities like Castro to unite the hopelessly split left-wing movement; in Peru alone there were about twenty rival groups on the extreme left. Nor was terrorism supported by the population it intended to help. If the terrorists bombed power plants or oil pipelines the poor suffered as much, if not more, than the rich. Yet it would be rash to write off Latin America as a battlefield of the terrorism of the future. The social, political, and economic tensions are such that there could well be a revival at some future date, which, in all probability, will take forms different from traditional Latin American terrorism. It will take place, no doubt, in the megacities of the continent rather than in the wilderness from which Che Guevara tried to launch the world revolution and so utterly failed. And it will have nothing to do with world revolution.

THE TAMIL TIGERS

Sri Lanka, an island just south of India formerly known as Ceylon, became independent of British rule in 1948. Its politics have been turbulent almost ever since. The Sinhalese majority faces a Tamil minority of less than 20 percent (about 3 million people), who are concentrated in the north of the country. However, the Tamils, some of whom were originally brought to the island from India as laborers, have the backing of a much larger Tamil population in South India, concentrated in the state of Tamil Nadu. The policy of the Sinhalese majority ruling the country has been less than enlightened toward the minority; this manifested itself in a illiberal language policy (Sinhalese only), the refusal to give all Tamils in Sri Lanka citizenship, and the attempt to repatriate some of them to India, even though they had been born in Sri Lanka. Sri Lankan politics, furthermore, has had a strong radical element; this was one of the very few countries in the world in which the Communist and Trotskyite parties had been strong simultaneously. At the same time, there was equal militancy on the right wing; when the then prime minister Bandaranaike was assassinated in 1959, the murderers were two Sinhalese monks for whom Bandaranaike was insufficiently nationalist.

The Tamil minority felt itself threatened once the British left, and various militant organizations developed in the 1950s and '60s. Originally the inspiration was revolutionary, and the writings of Castro and Guevara, of General Giap and Regis Debray, which reached them by way of India, had a powerful impact. But gradually the Marxist element faded, and what remained was militant separatism pure and simple. The tension was fueled by economic stagnation and a high unemployment rate, especially among the young. For an enterprising young Tamil, there seemed to be little to do but become a terrorist. But this explanation is not entirely satisfactory, as unemployment was equally high in Sinhalese and Muslim parts of the island. The fact that religious inspiration was not decisive among the

Tamil should be stressed, because religion has often been thought to be the decisive factor in suicide bombing. The Tamil Tigers had the highest rate of suicide missions in the world, with many hundreds of victims over the years. Their motives were not to be found in their religion or ideology but, like Colombia, in their cultural and social traditions—in brief, in their history.

Conflicts between Tamil and Sinhalese continued throughout the 1960s. At the same time, various Tamil groups were fighting each other in a struggle for leadership. The Tigers fighting for Eelam, a homeland, developed out of a revolutionary student's association in Britain, and in 1976 the LTTE (Liberation Tigers of Tamil Eelam) was founded. It became one of the most effective guerrilla/terrorist groups in the world within a year. Its ideological guru was a Marxist-Leninist turned extreme nationalist named Balasingham, but the undisputed political military leader was Prabhakaran. From the very beginning, he was less influenced by Marxism-Leninism than by various Hindu thinkers. One of these was Vivekananda, who taught him to concentrate on training and indoctrinating the very young; another was Gandhi (shorn of nonviolence but with an emphasis on sexual abstinence); and above all, Subhas Chandra Bose, a chameleonlike man who served as a left-wing Congress leader and strongly supported the Japanese and Nazis during World War II.

What is commonly referred to as the "Insurgency" began even earlier, in 1973, but during its first phase fighting was on a relatively minor scale. Growing Tamil militancy produced a Sinhalese backlash in 1981, resulting in riots and the murder of imprisoned Tamil leaders, which in turn led to a far bloodier Tamil campaign. This came to a halt only in July 1987, when Indian army units landed on the island in a peacekeeping effort. But the Indians faced Sinhalese resentment in addition to constant attack by the Tamil, who rejected the peace accord that had been worked out by Rajiv Gandhi, then Indian prime minister, and the Sri Lankan president. The Indians had little stomach for guerrilla fighting, and though some twelve thousand Tamils were killed, much of the Jaffna peninsula destroyed, and the Tamil Tigers forced to retreat to the jungle, the Indians decided to withdraw their troops from the island once they realized that peace between the two communities could not be achieved. Ever since then, civil war has continued on the island, with ambushes in the countryside as well as terrorist attacks in the towns, and while the Tigers have not achieved a significant victory, the Sri Lankan army has been unable to stamp out the insurrection.

The Tamil Tiger leadership committed two major political blunders: one, when they assassinated Rajiv Gandhi in 1991, and, two, when they rejected a generous autonomy offer by the Sri Lankan government in 1995. Despite the rebels' countless acts of indiscriminate violence, often against innocent civilians, the Tamil Tigers somehow preserved the reputation of an underdog, and thus attracted a certain amount of sympathy from the outside world. But much goodwill in India was lost following the assassination, and whatever sympathy was left disappeared when the Tigers showed extreme intransigence. It took six years for an Indian official inquiry committee to disentangle the circumstances of the assassination (its report was published only in December 1997); it appeared that not only had Tamil Nadu officials been involved, but that at an earlier stage in the insurgency the Tigers had been helped by the Indian secret services. The appeal of the Tamil Tigers was from then on restricted to the Tamil diaspora in foreign countries and their contributions, whether voluntary or forced, dwindled.

The Tamil Tigers, in their long fight against the ethnic majority, have shown inventiveness and extraordinary persistence. Mention has been made of the indoctrination of young Tigers in a spirit of national fanaticism, spiritualism, sexual ascesis, and a cult of suicide. The last usually involved cyanide, and is said to give the Tigers extra confidence in that they have an alternative to capture and imprisonment. They have been waging a guerrilla war based on the Chinese and Cuban pattern, and for a number of years they virtually ruled the Jaffna peninsula as a little state of their own, just as Mao had run Yenan. They had modern high-tech weapons, such as Soviet-made SA 7 ground-to-air missiles obtained from Cambodia, and dozens of tons of RDX, a powerful explosive, obtained from the Ukraine. They operated their own small navy, which plied between Sri Lanka and the Indian mainland, as well as Myanmar (Burma) and Thailand. They operated in large units of several thousand fighters, some of whom received their military training in Tamil Nadu and others in Lebanon in the camps of the PLO and the PFLP, and for years they maintained a military base in Myanmar. Like the IRA, they ran corporations and businesses, and have smuggled arms, drugs, and other commodities.

Despite the relative weakness of the Sinhalese army, and for all the Tigers' proficiency in guerrilla warfare, they have been unsuccessful in fighting in the open. They lost their main base in the Jaffna peninsula as the result of a government offensive in December 1995, and had to abandon their last urban base in Kilinochi in September 1996. In the latter operation alone, about a thousand Tamil Tigers were killed or taken prisoner. But as so often before, they still had enough strength to inflict major blows on the government. In July 1996, four thousand Tamil Tigers attacked and seized a government military base northeast of Colombo. All

1,200 military personnel at the base were killed, and it was the most severe military defeat the government suffered since the beginning of the war. In addition, there were frequent bomb attacks. In January 1996, almost a hundred civilians were killed and 1,400 injured in the Colombo banking district. On another occasion four Tiger frogmen blew up two gunboats at the naval base of Trinkomalee. On the other hand, a naval blockade imposed by India severely hampered Tamil Tiger arms supplies, which mainly came from across the sea. The small Tiger navy, consisting partly of speedboats, interferes with ships of other nations fairly regularly, committing acts of piracy against China, Malaya, and Indonesia, and this has not added to their popularity.

Tamil propaganda has been far more astute than government propaganda, and the Tigers have established a foreign service of their own with representations in thirty-eight countries, issuing daily news bulletins and running their own illegal radio station in Sri Lanka. Use is widely made of the Internet and video clips, which are distributed to leading media in foreign countries. Yet, with all this, the insurgency in Sri Lanka remains one of the most underreported in the world media. Estimates of the number of people killed vary between 50,000 and 100,000, but whenever guerrilla warfare and terrorism are discussed in Western capitals the emphasis is on events in the Middle East even though attacks there, except for Algeria, usually are on a much lesser scale.

The main bases of Tiger operations, such as the Jaffna peninsula, have been virtually destroyed; most of the peninsula's inhabitants have emigrated abroad. The war effort of the LTTE is mainly paid for by expatriate Tamil communities in Canada, the United States, Australia, South Africa, and several European countries. Some of the money has come in voluntarily, but the LTTE has also enlisted enforcers, extracting contributions from those reluctant to pay. This in turn has led to the arrest of the more aggressive collectors, and in some countries the Tamil Tigers have been banned altogether. The small Tamil community (some 25,000) in Switzerland allegedly contribute $8 million a year, a sizable sum considering that most of them recently were very poor asylum seekers. In 1996, the Tiger leadership in Switzerland was arrested and charged with extortion.

In the shadowy world of drug smuggling there is little hard evidence of official LTTE participation, but there is some circumstantial evidence that individual Tamils have played a considerable role in smuggling heroin from Asia to Europe. The Tiger leadership has certainly tolerated it and in all probability benefited from it, but has not advertised its active involvement. The Colombo government, however, has claimed that drug smuggling constitutes the single most important item in the war treasury of the LTTE, and ships that smuggle arms and other commodities are also used to carry drugs.

In the guerrilla and terrorist war against the government, at least ten thousand Tamil Tigers have been killed. There has been enormous material damage to the north of Sri Lanka and the creation of many refugees. Nevertheless, the Tigers claim that despite these losses and many major setbacks they will continue to fight until they have a fully independent state of their own. The most they are willing to concede is a loose economic union with the majority patterned on that of the European Community.

What makes them fight with such tenacity and fanaticism? Religious and ethnic differences do exist but are not crucial; the Sinhalese hail from northern India, the Tamil from the south. The Tamil originally had the Hindu caste system; the Sinhalese are predominantly Buddhist. The Tamil claim that they cannot possibly live with the Sinhalese in the framework of one state; they always had a state (a kingdom) of their own, and it was against their wishes that they were fused into one country under British rule. This state of affairs is obviously true for a great many nationalities and tribes all over the world, and it would be impossible to reconstitute all of these kingdoms, duchies, and principalities. The Tamil militants are not, however, impressed by considerations of this kind. Their leadership, originally Marxist-Leninist, has transformed itself into an intense nationalist group, preaching a fanaticism and a ruthlessness that in Europe could be found only in the fascist movements of the 1930s.

The extraordinary ruthlessness of the campaign waged by the Tamil Tigers has shown itself in the indiscriminate killing of Sinhalese and Muslim peasants in addition to the political murders committed against rivals within the Tamil camp. The Tigers were originally only one of several militant groups among the Tamil community, and their rise to power left a bloody trail of assassinations in their wake, including, for instance, the elected mayor of Jaffna, who was killed by the young Prabhakaran, who in later years became the undisputed commander of the Tigers. In 1998, yet another elected mayor of Jaffna, a Tamil woman, was killed by terrorists. By this time it was no longer clear whether the assassins were Tiger surrogates or a smaller group competing with them. Such internecine warfare has weakened the cause of the Tigers and other militant separatists.

Of all the terrorist movements that exist, the Tigers have used suicide missions most frequently, not only in attacks against prominent personalities such as India's Rajiv Gandhi and President Premdasa of Sri Lanka, but on countless other occasions. According to legend, the first known case of a young terrorist swallowing cyanide after he had failed in his mission to kill a police officer occurred early on in the history of the Tigers. Popular belief has it that every Tiger carries his cyanide pill with him, which is no doubt an exaggeration. But the number of suicides is estimated at five hundred and possibly more, and includes several Tigers who starved themselves to death.

The virulence of Tamil terrorism and its proclivity to suicide cannot be blamed on social and political circumstances. While it is true that their treatment by the Sinhalese majority has often been unjust, only a feverish imagination can refer to it as "genocide." Learning from bitter experience and its own mistakes, the Colombo government has made far-reaching concessions to the Tamils over the years, and Tamils have been represented in prominent positions in the government. (The Sri Lankan foreign minister, at the time of writing, is a Tamil by origin.) It is true that the rate of suicide in Sri Lanka is among the highest in Asia, and indeed in the world, and has been steadily rising, but this seems not to be true with regard to Tamil Nadu in India. Poor economic conditions (some 40 percent of the population live in absolute poverty) are largely the result, not the cause, of the civil war. The combination of a relatively well-educated young generation and youth unemployment can make for political radicalism and possibly even terrorism, but not necessarily for suicide. Hate is not directed against a foreign occupant or members of a religion distasteful to the Tamils, and the difference in language alone cannot explain the deep division, especially since the central government has made Tamil its second official language. Rather, there is a veritable "cult of the martyrs" among the Tamil. One day of the year is celebrated as Martyrs' Day, but this is recent; it is not part of Tamil history or Hindu religion. It seems more Christian or Muslim than Tamil.

It is certain that the Tigers would not have lasted so long and been able to inflict so many losses on their enemy if it were not for their fanaticism. Assistance from Tamil Nadu and the Tamil diaspora, from Norway to Botswana, has also played an important role. But this, again, does not fully explain the riddle, because while there is Tamil solidarity in Tamil Nadu, there is no intense fanaticism equal to that found in Sri Lanka, nor has there been a movement for separatism in Tamil Nadu. Therefore, in the final analysis, there is no satisfactory explanation for the Tamil Tigers and their fanaticism.

THE LORD'S RESISTANCE ARMY

The truly exotic Lord's Resistance Army (LRA) and the West Nile Bank Front (WNBF), both active in Uganda, lack any political agenda, unlike the Shining Path and Tamil Tigers. The LRA's very existence as well as the longevity of its struggle mystify those students of guerrilla and terrorist warfare who have traditionally looked for grievances, social or national, as the main motives. The hard core of the WNBF, which is considerably smaller and only slightly less mystifying, consists mainly of former soldiers of the Idi Amin and Milton Obote dictatorships who have turned to banditry.

The LRA came into being in the 1980s as the Holy Spirit Revolt, led by Alice Lakvena, a local cult leader. Lakvena promised her followers immunity from bullets if they applied holy water and certain ointments to their bodies. The revolt was suppressed by the Ugandan army and Alice fled to Kenya, where she was arrested and imprisoned in 1987. But the movement did not disappear altogether, and after 1990 Alice's place was taken by Josef Kony, a former Catholic choirboy and later faith healer who, like most prophets of this kind, claimed to talk directly to God.

Kony has declared himself a Christian fundamentalist who wants to topple Ugandan president Yoweri Museveni and establish a state based on the Ten Commandments. However, Kony's attachment to the Ten Commandments should not be taken too literally, since he has violated them as necessary, particularly the commandment "Thou shalt not kill." Elements of traditional witchcraft have been added to his theory and practice, and in subsequent years the growing influence of Islam has been manifest: Friday has been declared a second Sabbath and eating pork has been banned—in deference to Kony's sponsors, the Muslim fundamentalist regime in Khartoum. There are also elements in Kony's little army that are neither Christian nor Muslim nor witchcraft—it is forbidden to eat a white feathered chicken and anyone caught riding a bicycle is shot or maimed, usually by having his or her feet or nose cut off and bones broken with hammers. The LRA has established a reign of terror in northern Uganda, particularly in the Gulu and Kitgum regions, where villages have been destroyed and thousands of people killed, often with great cruelty, and hundreds of thousands made homeless refugees.

The LRA acquired notoriety because of its systematic abduction of children, mostly in their early teens. According to UNICEF figures, about ten thousand boys and girls have been kidnapped. The boys are drilled to become soldiers; according to various reports a fair number of them desert when they can, but at least an equal number became quite proficient killers, often attacking their own villages and tribes. The girls become camp followers, doing the domestic work and providing sexual comfort to the warriors. Protests by the United Nations, the pope, and other international bodies have been to no avail.

The staying power of the LRA has been explained by some as owing to a power shift in the Ugandan tribal structure. In the days of Idi Amin and Obote the key positions were held by people from the north. Under the rule of Museveni, the establishment has come from southern Uganda and the northern tribes have complained about discrimination. But this explanation is not altogether convincing, because Kony's attacks have been directed almost entirely against the northern Acholi tribe from which he himself hails.

How is one to explain the survival and the successes of the LRA in light of its lack of support in the local population? According to classic guerrilla theory established by Mao and others, the guerrilla had to befriend the people in order to move among them. The LRA have consisted of undisciplined gangs of murderers, thieves, and rapists, and yet by sheer terror they have succeeded in cowing a war-weary population into submission or making them flee.

The Ugandan army, lacking trained personnel and equipment, is not in a position to engage in serious military operations. The LRA, on the other hand, has a safe base in southern Sudan where it receives weapons and other supplies. At any given time, the majority of its fighters may be concentrated in the Sudan, engaging in hit-and-run actions across the border.

The interest of the Khartoum government in maintaining these gangs is obvious; it has been fighting a losing war against the southern black African forces in Sudan, where the SLA is resisting the domination of the Muslim north. The Sudanese leaders hope that by exerting pressure on the Ugandans they will be able to isolate the SLA rebels in southern Sudan, and ultimately destroy them with the acquiescence of the government in Kampala. The LRA cannot move too far away from their vital line of supply and retreat on the Sudanese border, but they do constitute a major irritation to the Ugandan government, and there has been pressure on Uganda's Museveni to negotiate a peaceful settlement with the LRA.

The case of the LRA is obviously an extreme one, given the killing, looting, and raping in a context of minimal political aims. It is banditry, but not even "social banditry," which since the 1990s has gone on in Central Africa. In theory, such a movement should not be able to survive for long; it ought to disappear, at the very latest, with the death of its leader. But since the LRA is a classic case of surrogate warfare, and it has a safe haven in another country from which it can stage raids whenever it is ready, its gangs can survive for a long time. Partly as the result of internal warfare, Uganda is the sixth-poorest country in the world. Conditions there are chaotic, and in the absence of a strong central power, mass killings like those in Rwanda and Burundi have been frequent. Thus, the persistence of banditry should not come as a surprise. Banditry was endemic in southern Europe in centuries past, and it has now become endemic in large parts of Africa. The Italian bandits of the eighteenth and nineteenth century operated in the pre-ideological age, and as such they did not need to invoke God, the Bible, the Koran, Satan, or Mao Tse-tung. The Lord's Resistance Army, on the other hand, operating in an age of mass politics, needs like all other self-respecting groups at least the appearance of a program if not a highly sophisticated theory. When Mussolini was asked by the Socialists before his March on Rome what his program was, he answered that his program was to break the heads of the Socialists. This laconic answer was found satisfactory, perhaps even witty, by many Italians at the time, and it might well be sufficient, at least for a while, in northern Uganda.

ECOTERRORISM

The term *ecology* (from the Greek *Oekologie*) was coined by Ernst Haeckel, the German natural scientist and philosopher, in a book published in 1866. The word *ecoterrorism* is of a much more recent date, and environmentalists, also called "greens" and other names, have frequently protested against the term as a gross distortion and calumny. Their complaints are as just as those of Christians, Muslims, Jews, Socialists, Anarchists, and indeed most other ideologies and religions of our time, who cannot possibly be made responsible for the actions of the extremists within their ranks. However, in all these value systems, there are beliefs that, if carried to an extreme, may provide inspiration for acts of violence. Fanatics find inspiration almost anywhere.

In the case of radical ecology, the borderline between environmentalism and terrorism is crossed once it is believed that the salvation of the planet depends on the destruction of civilization. If one accepts that our society is exterminist, the extermination of the exterminators can become a moral commandment. Some will hear such theories as rhetoric or a call for debate, but some militants see it as a call to action.

Radical, or "deep," ecologist belief rests on two assumptions: first, for thousands of years nature has been despoiled by man, and second, that once there was harmony in nature—a Golden Age during the Pleistocene Age. Man, however, has systematically ruined that Edenic state. Some blamed the spread of Christianity, which taught dominion over rather than respect for nature. Consequently, there has been a revival among some radical ecologists of pagan rituals and beliefs, under the assumption that early man and paganism showed greater respect to the forces of nature and indeed revered them. But can it really be taken for granted that prehistoric man was a lover of nature, a precursor of the Wandervogel and the environmentalists? Primitive man found constant danger in nature and had to fight for his survival. He also engaged in despoliation—for example, slash-and-burn agriculture and indiscriminate hunting. Other environmentalists see the fatal turning point in the Industrial Revolution of the eighteenth and nineteenth centuries and the rise of technology.

The cause of the friends of nature had its first upsurge in the late nineteenth century when the ravages wrought on the landscape by the Industrial Revolution—the "satanic mills"—became all too obvious, and the idea of conservation first appeared. The second major impetus was provided during the second half of the twentieth century when the extinction of whole species, water and air pollution, and the destruction of the forests became popular causes of alarm, and, above all, when it appeared that many finite natural resources had been abused and squandered. It was felt that a radically new environmental attitude was needed—not at some future date but immediately.

Haeckel was immensely popular at the time and read by the educated classes in every country. He had a major impact on the left as well as on the right, and his views inspired believers in materialism as well as neoromanticism. They had an impact on Nazism as well as social democracy, and even radical feminism. Traces of Haeckelian views can be found in D. H. Lawrence as well as Morris and Ruskin.

The origin of the modern environmental movement goes back to the early 1960s and was part of a cultural revolution that took place in many Western countries. This was the era of student revolts and holistic medicine, the rediscovery of Eastern wisdom in its various forms, the beginnings of radical feminism, and the Indian summer of Marxism, which would soon be replaced by the gurus of the New Age and postmodernism. As befitted any self-respecting ideology, environmentalism provided something akin to a scientific justification by invoking a kind of natural spirituality against mechanistic science. Some intrepid spirits even tried to find a synthesis between Marxism and ecology, truly a heroic endeavor given the views on industrial growth of Marx and Lenin, not to mention Stalin.

These aspects are of limited relevance in the context of ecoterrorism, and it is doubtful that those engaged in violent action are preoccupied with ideological debates about postclassical science, just as nineteenth-century bomb-throwing anarchists had probably never read Reclus or even Kropotkin. The political initiatives of the environmentalists are of interest mainly because they created a certain intellectual climate for the radicals. The Greens have been astonishingly successful. They became a major political force in Germany, where they are a coalition partner in the government, and in France, where one of them became a government minister in 1997. Green parties and pressure groups came into being in most European countries as well as in Australia and New Zealand, and they had considerable influence in the United States and Canada.

But politics is the art of the possible, and participating in politics involved concessions that the radicals were not willing to make, just as they did not want to work with and through the environmental establishment, such as the Sierra Club and the Audubon Society, or similar groups in other countries. The radical, or "deep," ecologists believed that the global ecological crisis was so profound that there was no time left for a policy of gradual improvement, and that in any case the scientific-technological-industrial establishment would never voluntarily take the revolutionary measures that had become necessary. It was no longer a matter of preserving nature so far unspoiled; civilization had to be rolled back or even destroyed. The workings of nature had to take precedence over anthropocentric needs, and since earth could not possibly sustain a rapidly growing number of people, the human population had to be reduced.

Just as the political ecologists split between left and right, between Realos (realists) and Fundis (fundamentalists), the "deep" ecologists were also deeply divided on a variety of issues. The ecofeminists went their own way, and so did the ecosocialists. The extreme right, as in France and Germany, had their own ecological concerns dating back in large part to the Nazi era. The ecoanarchists announced that time had come to stop glorifying the working class, and it declared all-out war on nationalism. For the few environmentalists in the Third World these were mostly non-issues. When the radical ecologists opted for violence, they again split between those willing to use terror only against things and those ready to kill people. One of the main sympathizers wrote early on that acts of sabotage would only further brutalize a brutal society, and that the environmental movement had to make up its mind whether it wanted to engage in reform or be an apocalyptic movement not bound by democratic or moral rules.

Resistance against pollution has existed for centuries, and the first laws that attempted to control it date back to Europe of the late Middle Ages. But laws and regulations have been disregarded or proven insufficient. Hence the widespread outrage in the United States, Britain, and other countries that led to nonviolent political action in the 1970s, and subsequently to the establishment of pressure groups and lobbies that had success in pursuing their aims. The environmentalists also employed passive resistance, direct action, and civil disobedience. Greenpeace, perhaps the best-known worldwide organization, began its activities when a dozen volunteers tried to block nuclear tests in the Aleutians. There were occasional violent operations, but Greenpeace aimed to destroy property, not to commit murder. When Greenpeace decided in 1977 to renounce the destruction of property, a Canadian-led, small, more radical group calling itself The Sea Shepherd split away to pursue its aims, mainly against ships engaged in whaling, sealing, and driftnet fishing.

Two of the most influential books for ecoterrorists were published in the 1970s: Robert Townsend's *Ecotage* (1972) and Edward Abbey's *The Monkey Wrench Gang* (1975). The latter describes how a small band of environmental idealists in the southwest United States commit ecosabotage, blowing up a mining train, pouring sugar into the crankcases of bulldozers, and so on. This fiction inspired action, such as antiherbicide protesters in California and elsewhere distributing free marijuana plants, and others pulling up survey stakes to protest suburban sprawl.

The history of radical ecoterrorism goes back to 1980 when a group of five militants belonging to mainstream organizations such as the Sierra Club and Friends of the Earth decided, at the end of a hike, that far more drastic action was needed in view of the imminent destruction of nature, or what remained of it. To them it seemed pointless to work within the system, and thus Earth First was born.

This turn to radicalism might have been connected with general political developments. The Carter administration initially was thought to sympathize with the aims of the ecologists, but these hopes proved false; on the contrary, more forests were put at the disposal of the timber industry. Environmentalists reacted in anger, which only increased as more deregulation occurred under President Reagan. The language of the radicals became more violent, as did the character of their actions. As one of the more radical thinkers maintained, the salvation of the earth required an end to civilization and to the vast majority of mankind. They saw human beings as no more important than any other member of the biological community, and with no more rights than animals—or, indeed, than inanimate objects such as forests, rivers, and mountains. Seen in this light, they felt it had been wrong for modern medicine to combat infectious diseases, for bacteria and viruses also had rights—as one of the ecological thinkers put it, eradicating smallpox had been immoral inasmuch as it had been an unwarranted interference with the balance of the ecosystem. As David Foreman, the best-known spokesman of the radical wing put it, it was not sufficient to preserve the 10 percent of the wilderness still remaining; civilization had to be rolled back and wilderness had to be restored. Exotic species such as cattle and sheep, which had been introduced by humans to the grasslands, had to be removed, whereas indigenous grizzly bears were to be given preferential treatment. It also meant dismantling or destroying dams, bridges, highways, power lines, and the other support systems of industrial society.

Therefore, it should not come as a surprise that bridges, transmission towers, and electrical power transformers have been dynamited and logging equipment destroyed, as was a helicopter engaged in spraying brush-control herbicides. The Glen Canyon Dam was not destroyed, but the militants made it clear in a demonstration that attracted much attention that they could do so if they wanted.

In 1984, a campaign of tree spiking ("monkey wrenching") began. Long metal spikes were driven into trees that were to be felled on public lands, which was certain to damage equipment such as chain saws and blades, and possibly injure the loggers. Practical instructions were given in David Foreman's 1985 book titled *Ecodefense: A Field Guide to Monkey Wrenching*. It would be tedious to enumerate even Earth First's most spectacular exploits in the United States throughout the 1980s; what had begun as little more than pranks had turned ugly. There were hundreds of incidents and also hundreds of arrests, people were injured, and the damage was estimated in the millions. Some of the activities were carried on outside the United States. A British militant and an American militant sabotaged and sank two whaling vessels in Reykjavík, Iceland, in 1986, and also destroyed a processing plant. They succeeded in escaping.

Attacks against a variety of targets continued throughout the 1980s, including a hydro station in British Columbia. Two leading members of Earth First were severely injured in California when a pipe bomb in their possession exploded. In 1989, David Foreman and several others were arrested and charged with plotting to blow up two nuclear plants, Arizona's Palo Verde and California's Diablo Canyon, as well as the Rocky Flats nuclear weapons plant in Colorado. Foreman was not convicted, and he and others left the movement in 1990 because it had become too radical for their taste, but ecoterrorism continued. Trees were spiked in Maine, Maryland, North Carolina, and other states. Machinery was smashed in a variety of places, and there was interference with construction projects. Dams were damaged, cattle were shot in Oregon and New Mexico, and death threats were made to individuals on the movement's blacklist. There was even a threat to poison courthouses. In one case in upstate New York there was interference with county health officials spraying insects because of reports that mosquitoes in the swamps were carrying deadly equine encephalitis.

There was a decline in the activities of Earth First and similar groups after 1990 for a variety of reasons. The main reason was no doubt internal dissent among the radical ecologists. With the breakup of the Soviet Union and the general decline in the fortunes of neo-Marxism, especially in the universities, many young people turned to environmentalism, which they tried to combine with leftwing ideology. But this went against the grain of the early militants who had no interest in socialist ideology or indeed in any traditional political agenda. The neo-Marxists, on the other hand, did not see eye to eye with the Green anarchists, who sponsored a return to agricultural communes and other ideas borrowed from the early utopian socialists. The ecofeminists put more emphasis on the feminist than on the eco in their conviction that women were essentially closer to nature than men, whereas the socialist ecofeminists were torn in three different directions. Environmentalism turned into a fad, enticing the trendy and the militant. Pagan ecomilitants introduced new rituals and songs, and at New Age fairs, all kinds of commodities were peddled with no relevance to the ecoterrorist's central aim—namely, saving nature by destroying industrial civilization.

THE ANIMAL LIBERATIONISTS

Ecomilitants have been critical of their colleagues in the Animal Liberation Front because their focus is so exclusive, but the ALF has certainly been active, so much so that it has been classified by the FBI as a terrorist group. This came after hundreds of physical attacks, acts of arson, fire-bombings, and threats against researchers in medical facilities. To give but one example, a brochure published in Britain ("To War for a Liberated Society," Camberley, 1997), its cover illustrated with a uniformed man with a submachine gun, called for the assassination of vivisectors and hunters.

The Animal Liberation Front has been most active in the United Kingdom. In the 1970s, militant animal liberationists formed the Band of Mercy, aiming to disrupt foxhunts by violent means. Britain has few trees to spike and not many dams to bomb, but it has a long and powerful tradition of protecting animals. However, the activities of the ALF have gone well beyond expressing love and care for abused animals. According to a leading member of the British ALF, it was conducting a war in which firebombs would be thrown, bombs put under cars, and researchers shot on their doorsteps. Such operations have in fact been carried out in Britain, and the number of ALF "prisoners of war"—terrorists apprehended and sentenced—considerably outstrips the number of those apprehended from other terrorist groups.

According to official statistics, violent incidents arising from ALF activity occurred at the rate of 80 per month in the United Kingdom in 1995, whereas a U.S. Department of Justice report listed a mere 313 such cases over several years. True, many of the incidents listed by the United Kingdom belong to the category of "twenty-five rabbits rescued in Sweden," "five cats freed in Oxfordshire," or "dog freed from poor conditions in Italy," to quote ALF chronicles. However, some operations have been far more massive, directed against furriers, butchers, restaurants, veterinary surgeons, zookeepers, abattoirs, and above all against medical research institutions. In the United States, Rodney Coronado was sentenced in 1995 to fifty-seven months in prison and ordered to pay more than $2.5 million in restitution for his role in firebombing research facilities at Michigan State, Oregon State, and Washington State Universities. Even greater damage was caused in attacks against Johns Hopkins Medical School in Baltimore and the veterinary diagnostic center at the University of California, Davis. In 1997, the Association of American Medical Colleges recorded more than 3,700 cases of harassment by animal rights activists. The campaign of intimidation waged by Coronado and others was not unsuccessful. As a result, certain research into Alzheimer's disease, cystic fibrosis, cancer, AIDS, and spinal cord regeneration has been delayed or shelved. Leading ALF activists argue that cures for these and other diseases found at the cost of animal suffering are unacceptable; they would prefer human to animal suffering.

The other case that ought to be mentioned in our discussion of ecoterrorism, however briefly, is that of Theodore J. Kaczinski, also known as the Unabomber. He is the gifted young mathematician who waged a one-man campaign against society beginning in 1978, mainly by means of letter and package bombs. He was arrested in April 1996, following one of the longest manhunts in American history. His targets were located all over the United States; some were scientists, others businessmen. Quite often the wrong people were wounded or killed, a matter, as the Unabomber later conceded, that was of no great concern to him. There had been serial murderers before with a grudge against certain segments of society, or society in general, but the case of the Unabomber was unique inasmuch as his bombs were accompanied or followed by letters explaining his motives and eventually by a long document that became known as the Unabomber Manifesto.

The central points of his manifesto, which was published in the *New York Times* and other papers in 1995, are made in its introduction. The

Industrial Revolution and its consequences have been a disaster for the human race. They have destabilized society and inflicted severe damage on the natural world. There is no way of reforming or modifying a system that deprives people of dignity and autonomy. The bigger the system grows, the more disastrous the consequences: "We therefore advocate a revolution against the industrial system." It is not a political revolution; the aim is the overthrow of the economic and technological basis of the present society. In the remainder of the manifesto, the Unabomber comments on a variety of topics, such as the power process in society, oversocialization, the motives of scientists, autonomy, the nature of freedom, and why the "bad" parts of technology cannot be separated from the "good." Revolution, he argues, is easier than reform. At the same time, he attacks the psychology of modern leftism and its ideological tenets. Some of his comments are plausible, others are not. Few, if any, are original. The real riddle is to establish the connection between the views of the Unabomber and his actions. Did he really think that sending out letter bombs would bring about the end of industrial civilization or at least act as a clarion call for action by others? To what extent were psychological disturbances involved, such as schizophrenia or paranoia?

The ecoterrorist movement and the Animal Liberation Front were and still are elitist; their members are of predominantly middle-class background. They did not intend to become mass movements. Earth First members, in particular, were uncomfortable when, in the 1980s, its numbers grew beyond what it had ever expected. They came into being as a deliberate contrast to the mainstream ecological and animal protection groups, which, as they saw it, had not achieved a radical change for the better and were not likely to do so in the foreseeable future. Neither ecoterrorists nor the AFL ruled out the use of violence, and, particularly in the case of the ALF, they engaged in such acts more or less systematically. They did not believe that it would be possible to reeducate humankind as quickly as the earth needed, and they also understood that their aims collided not just with big corporations but with a large part of the population that disagreed with their view that nature was good, *tout court,* and humans bad. Therefore, they needed to work outside the democratic system, to engage in acts of violence, and break the law. In the beginning there had been pacifists and Quakers among the radical ecologists, but they were either converted to the use of violence, pushed aside, or left of their own volition. Believing disaster was imminent, the radical ecologists, especially the biocentrists among them, had no patience for a gradualist or pacificist approach.

As David Foreman wrote in 1985, "the ice may come soon to wipe our nasty little acne off the broad smile of Ma Gaia." In short, some believe nature will strike back on her own. In 1987, leading radical ecologists discussed the question of whether AIDS was the answer to the deep ecologists' prayers, seeing it as nature's response to the pressures of overpopulation, pollution, and the extinction of other species. In a similar vein, an article in *Earth First* in 1994 rambled on to the effect that a sign had been received from the Goddess Mother (Earth) that she did not wish humans to pass the year 2000 and that she wanted her followers to monkey-wrench the millennium.

Millenarian and apocalyptic motives have persisted among many radical ecologists, though less so among the left-wingers, with their stress on social justice, or the ALF, with their preoccupation with whales and minks. The misanthropes among these groups do not regard an apocalyptic ending for humankind as a great disaster, but the majority want the human species to survive, albeit on a reduced scale and with a very much reduced place in the natural scheme of things.

The scale of violence, in particular deadly violence, carried out by the ecologists and the ALF has been tiny in comparison with the actions of political terrorist movements, and violence has been used predominantly against things, only infrequently against humans. This is less true with regard to the ALF, with its systematic campaign to bring about an end to medical research that depends on animal tests. The ALF has been more like one of the classic terrorist movements. But there has been a decline in the use of violence, perhaps only temporarily, on the part of the radical ecologists. This may be connected in part with the fact that not all their early fears have materialized. Ecological lobbying and political pressure have had a certain effect; rivers have been cleaned up and measures taken to preserve species in danger of extinction. It could be said with a certain justice that we are all ecologists now, and as a result the radical movement has lost some momentum.

But the case of the Unabomber is indicative of the dangers ahead. The Unabomber was not a registered member of the neo-Luddites, and while some of them may secretly sympathize with his views, if not with his indiscriminate actions, he was in no way representative of the radical ecologists. But even if the ecologists were not responsible for Kaczinski, he came from the same stable, just as the West European terrorists of the 1970s came from the Leninist-Maoist-Castroist camp, even if they had been excommunicated seven times over, and just as the Oklahoma City bomber received his inspiration from the extreme "patriots."

What if weapons of mass destruction had been at the disposal of the Unabomber, a person with considerable scientific knowledge? Would he have hesitated to use them? Is it not likely that sooner or later another person or small group of persons with similar but perhaps more radical views and fewer scruples will acquire such weapons?

It seems only a matter of time until an individual, or a small group on the fringes of the ecomilitants, reaches the conclusion that the crimes of human beings against the spotted owl and the red fox, against the water and the air, are such that mankind does not deserve to survive. The scientifically inclined among them, having read a little Jacques Ellul, a bit of Kirkpatrick Sale, and a few pages of Lewis Mumford, may turn to radical Luddism, reacting against the horrors of science and technology. As they see it, the scientific-technological complex has become so omnipotent, the danger of overpopulation and natural disasters so certain, that it is their duty, as the few who still deeply care, to destroy the system that aims to destroy the earth. Unlike the poor Luddites, however, they may have the means to cause significant damage to the system. It is not difficult to now imagine what the manifestos of the second and third generation of Unabombers will contain or to speculate about the arms they may use. Ecoterrorists will not lack for real and imaginary dangers, from the destruction of the ozone layer to desertification, the decline of water resources, the loss of hundreds of millions of acres of tree cover, to global warming and the despoliation of the oceans. A total ecological breakdown may not be just around the corner, as some of them thought in the 1970s, but few doubt that the final disaster is more than thirty or forty years away. Ironically, the fear of impending disaster, plus the increased availability of weapons of mass destruction, may precipitate a terrorist-orchestrated disaster.

The ecofeminists and the social justice ecologists are probably less likely to turn to terrorism precisely because their earth enthusiasm—or their pessimism—has been diluted by the intrusion of other causes in which they fervently believe. But they still share with the hard-core, radical ecologists their views about growth, science, and technology.

Despite all attempts to export radical ecology to the Second and Third Worlds, it still is very much a concern of only the most developed countries in the First World. The only exception was the Soviet Union during the last few years of its existence, when the extreme right adopted a "green" agenda at a time when open political opposition to the regime was as yet impossible. The Taliban in Afghanistan have been shooting people for using paper bags, because the paper, having been recycled, might have once been used for copies of the Koran, while European environmentalists take a very dim view of plastic bags. European Greens love bicycles and hate automobiles, but the Lord's Resurrection Army in northern Uganda, for reasons not entirely clear, maims cyclists. The Peruvian Sendero Luminoso began its career with mass killing of dogs, using curare or slitting their throats, oblivious of the fact that the British Animal Liberation Front would have severely punished them had they been in a position to do so. The differences go, of course, much deeper than such cultural peculiarities. There still is enormous population growth, particularly in Africa and India, and at a time when Northern Hemisphere radical ecologists complain that the world population is far too large anyway, the South wants still more people. Thus, as with all the forms of political and religious terrorism, the only common denominator in the forms of exotic terrorism is the violence.

TERRORISM and Organized Crime

Twenty years ago, organized crime had no place in studies of terrorism. It was, of course, well-known that historically many terrorist groups had improved their finances by criminal activities: the Russian terrorists of the early 1900s robbed banks, and so did the anarchist terrorists, the Macedonian IMRO, and the Irgun in Palestine. The Montoneros in Argentina collected millions of dollars from kidnapping and extortion, and the Irish terrorists of the nineteenth century considered and sometimes practiced a variety of criminal activities, including forging banknotes. Many terrorist groups ran a variety of protection rackets or engaged in smuggling. As a rule, terrorists were poor and needed money to pursue their activities.

But in all these instances the terrorists were not out to make money, individually or as a group; their aim was not to get rich and lead comfortable lives. They needed money to survive, to acquire weapons and safe houses, to obtain false documents, to bribe informers, and to travel. The acquisition of money was always a means toward an end, and the end was considered sacred. It was not always political; recall the "social banditry" of the Pancho Villas, horse thieves with a political agenda, who did not mind making a little money on the side. Robin Hood may have robbed the rich to help the poor, but since his accountants did not leave written records, the extent of his social conscience and munificence cannot be established with any degree of certainty. It is also true that early ideologists of terrorism such as Bakunin, the Narodnaya Volya, and some of the militant anarchists thought that criminals were the one truly revolutionary element in society and as such should be enlisted in the struggle against the existing order. Some of them went out of their way to mobilize robbers and thieves, but they came to realize sooner or later that these social outcasts had an agenda different from their own. If the criminals had political interests at all, they were conservative rather than revolutionary. A hundred years ago, even fifty, there was, all things considered, a clear dividing line between terrorism and crime. More recently, this line has become blurred, and in some cases a symbiosis between terrorism and organized crime has occurred that did not exist before. This chapter briefly recounts a few of those instances in which terrorism and organized crime have merged or at least collaborated.

As has been pointed out, organized crime has existed for centuries, and we are all familiar with the various mafias and gangsters, whether of the Prohibition era or, more contemporaneously, the slums of big cities. But its impact on the world scene has been nil until very recently. The drug trade and the breakdown of the Soviet empire appears to have opened up new opportunities to terrorist groups as well as to states sponsoring terrorism, not so much in Europe but in other parts of the world such as Latin America and the Middle and Far East.

NARCOTERRORISM

The age of "narcoterrorism" dawned in the 1970s, although the term has been rejected as illegitimate by some experts in the United States and Western Europe. These experts do not deny the existence of the drug cartels and the drug trade, but they believe that the two entities, the terrorists and the drug cartels, still have widely diverging interests and that the use of the term tends to obfuscate the situation rather than shed light on it. Others claim that the use of the term was an attempt by reactionary Western diplomats and journalists to cast aspersions on the purity of the revolutionary terrorists and guerrillas.

Originally, the terrorists and the guerrillas were mortal enemies of the drug producers and traders. On an ideological level, the revolutionaries opposed the use of drugs and punished those in their ranks who violated this rule. But, over time, the production and smuggling of drugs has been practiced by guerrilla and terrorist groups of the left as well as the right, and by others who are neither left nor right but nationalist-separatist in inspiration. I know of no terrorist group in modern times that has advocated the consumption of drugs, but the distance between ideology and economic reality is shrinking. The Sunni Taliban in Afghanistan and the extreme Shiite groups in Lebanon have long maintained that although the consumption of opium and similar drugs is forbidden by their religion, the production and trade of drugs is not. Those smoking opium are severely punished, but the growers of opium are encouraged. Thus Afghanistan under Taliban rule has become one of the main centers of opium production.

COLOMBIA

Mention was made in a previous chapter of the persistence of guerrilla warfare and terrorism in Colombia at a time when these are in retreat elsewhere in Latin America and in other parts of the world. FARC originally came into being as the armed wing of the local Colombian Communist Party and the Popular Liberation Army (ELP). FARC has doubled in strength over the last decade and its activities now extend over more than half of Colombia. In fact, it has expanded into Venezuela.

Historically, Colombia has been the most violent country in Latin America. It is a poor country and has not been blessed with governments capable of solving or at least attenuating its social problems. The rich are very rich, the poor extremely poor, and the middle class is still relatively weak. The pervasive corruption following the massive amounts of big money generated by the Cali and Medellín drug cartels have further discredited and weakened the government and made the pacification of the country very difficult. However, the peace negotiations of 1998 opened a window of opportunity.

Social and economic conditions help us to understand the situation in Colombia, yet they are not sufficient to explain the spread of the guerrillas. At one time, Cuba supported the guerrillas and helped to instill ideological fervor. But Cuba ceased providing arms and money a long time ago, and to explain the achievements of the FARC with reference to Marx and Lenin is far-fetched, to put it mildly. The single most important factor involved is the one least talked and written about—the fact that the guerrillas have grown rich. According to detailed estimates by the Colombian government, the income of FARC and ELN in 1994 was 620,000 million pesos, and it may well have doubled since. Of this, about two-thirds came from narcotrafficking, robberies, and extortion. According to other estimates, the present income of the two main groups is between a half billion and one and a half billion dollars. Such amounts of money go a long way in Latin America, and indeed anywhere else, considering that the total manpower of FARC and ELN is not more than 20,000 militants. Even twenty years ago the guerrillas could not even dream about making this kind of money, and it has created opportunities that no other terrorist group ever had.

How did the FARC acquire these riches? Originally, its bands were concentrated in the poor south of the country, but during the coca boom of the early 1980s, some of the areas under its control became the main centers of production of coca paste, and laboratories were established to process the paste. Control over the drug trade was still in the hands of the big drug traders, Restrepo, Escobar, Lehder, and others. Would the FARC and ELN cooperate with the cartels or fight them as they were fighting the government? It is not clear whether the leadership of the Communist Party at its Seventh National Congress in 1982 officially advocated cooperation, or whether it simply gave the FARC the green light to collaborate whenever expedient.

Seen from the Communist point of view, the militants had no alternative but to get involved in narcobusiness. The peasants were poor, and their income from growing coca was five or ten times more than if they had grown other crops. The Communists would have lost their base of mass support unless they went along. To save face and to justify their behavior in traditional Marxist terms, they argued that they were stubbornly fighting for farm wages higher than those the drug cartels were offering. In general, they maintained in their propaganda that they were the best friends of the poor, defending their interests against the government and other exploiters. But the difference between left-wing populism of this kind and the right-wing populism of the cartels and the anti-guerrilla gangs was not always visible to the naked eye; Escobar, for example, also argued that he supported schools and clinics in the areas under his control, and if the women of Cali could have a free annual checkup in mobile mammography units, it was entirely due to his sense of social responsibility. The guerrillas also claimed that they were patiently explaining to the peasants that ultimately they would have to grow crops other than coca, but they left open what "ultimately" meant in this context.

It is generally believed that the cost of carrying out a guerrilla campaign in Colombia involves less than 10 percent of the annual income of the FARC and the ELN. If so, what happens to the rest of the money? According to the information available, some of the income is invested in land, some in transport companies, some in the stock market. In brief, the guerrillas have become capitalists, collectively and, in some cases, individually. Quite often they can achieve their goals without even fighting; they can afford to buy friend and foe alike.

But not all guerrilla relations with the drug cartels have been smooth. In the areas where the FARC has been strong, such as Putumayo, Caqueta, and Guaviare, they have been involved in the drug business and the cartels have paid them taxes and protection money. In the areas where the cartels are more powerful, the guerrillas have not bothered them. Where both are active, such as in North Magdalena, Medio, and northern Valle, however, there has been a struggle for dominance. The FARC has kidnapped and killed members of the leading drug families, and the hit men of the cartels have assassinated leading members of the guerrillas. This fighting took place mainly in the 1980s and has abated somewhat during the past decade, when incidents of collaboration were more frequent than of confrontation. It would be quite misleading to interpret these conflicts as evidence of the incompatibility of the drug trade and terrorism. The guerrillas seem to have realized that it was not in their best interest to focus attacks against the army, and the cartels, which were under considerable pressure by the Bogotá government, which in turn, under pressure from Washington, wanted peace on the home front. Therefore, whatever their long-term differences, guerrillas and cartels had common, if short-term, interests. And so the FARC continued its political campaign, systematically killing local politicians, and the narcotraficantes continued to engage in their profitable business while the country descended into a state of near anarchy. One of the reasons for the inefficiency of government efforts at counterterrorism was the fact that the great drug-related wealth of the FARC enabled the guerrillas to be better equipped than the government troops.

ELSEWHERE IN LATIN AMERICA

The case of Colombia is not unique, even though it is the most important of the drug-producing countries in Latin America and has the strongest guerrilla-terrorist force. But the situation in Peru was not essentially different insofar as the cooperation between Sendero Luminoso and the drug cartels is concerned. The main coca-growing region in the Huallaga Valley was in the hands of Sendero; they taxed the local peasants and offered protection. The sums that changed hands in Peru were lower than those in Colombia, because the Peruvian cartels, in contrast to Colombia, were weaker, the government stronger, and the revolutionaries more sectarian.

The debate surrounding narcoterrorism continues, particularly with regard to individual cases of cooperation among guerrillas, Communists, and drug barons, as well as the concept as a whole. Four high-ranking members of the Cuban government, including two members of the Central Committee of the Communist Party, were indicted by the United States in 1982 for conspiracy to smuggle drugs into the United States. There seems to be little doubt that they were in touch with Guillot-Lara, a leading Colombian drug dealer with political ambitions, who also had links with M 19, which was at the time the leading force among the guerrillas.

M 19 was also instrumental in carrying out the single most bloody attack in Latin American terrorism, the storming of the Colombian Supreme Court in 1984, in the course of which 115 civilians were killed, including nine Supreme Court justices. In this case, the link with the narcotrafficantes was Carlos Lehder, a well-known person in the world of drug trafficking who also entered politics at a certain stage of his career. The action was in retaliation for the Colombian government's apparent willingness to extradite leading traffickers to the United States for trial.

In the shadowy world of Latin American politics and the manipulations of the drug cartels, it is impossible to know whether Guillot-Lara and Carlos Lehder acted on their own or on behalf of a united front among the cartels. It is quite possible that such a united front never existed, just as the Cuban government probably did not make smuggling drugs the cornerstone of its foreign-trade policy.

Not too much should be read into such isolated cases, but on the other hand there is no doubt that FARC and Sendero Luminoso and other, smaller movements did collaborate with the drug producers and dealers, and that they became part of the drug scene. The fact that there was also a considerable amount of fighting between them and the cartels is no refutation; the whole history of organized crime—the Mafia, for example—is a history of internecine warfare between rival families and clans, and there is no reason why Colombia should be seen as an exception.

The issue, finally, is not whether the concept of narcoterrorism is a valid one. The drug cartels are not guerrillas and terrorists and vice versa; there is no giant conspiracy linking together every act of guerrilla warfare and the drug trade. But the involvement of guerrillas and terrorists in the drug trade has decisively contributed to the survival and, indeed, the strengthening of some Latin American guerrilla movements, and it has equally decisively affected their character. A new species of terrorist has come into being, different in character, outlook, motivation, and prospects from guerrilla and terrorist groups in the past.

Many of those who doubt the extent of guerrilla and terrorist groups' involvement in the drug business tacitly assume that they are revolutionary in inspiration and pure in motivation. They ignore the fact that terrorists other than left-wingers have been involved in narcobusiness, which is worldwide and covers many countries. Until Noriega's fall, the center of the drug trade was Panama; Noriega, too, had his defenders, but it can hardly be argued that he was a pillar of Marxism-Leninism. The various contras have been equally involved in smuggling drugs and protecting growers. If absolution is given to left-wing guerrillas involved in the drug business, it would be unfair to make an exception of those on the right. In actual fact, political ideology has not been a matter of paramount importance concerning the involvement of guerrillas and terrorists in the drug business, whether it is plied in the Far East (including the "golden triangle"), in Afghanistan, in Lebanon and Syria, or in other parts of the world. Those who had the opportunity have done it despite Marx, the prophet Muhammad, or patriotic fervor.

TERRORISM AND GANGSTERISM

Among the Russian terrorists of the 1880s and the early twentieth century there were more than a few characters whose idealism was beyond question. No one would call them gangsters. But this has not been true for every such group in history, and it is now less true than ever before. Present-day terrorists are no innocents. The Algerian rebels, the Taliban, the Ugandan Lord's Resistance Army, and other such groups have shown extreme brutality even by the standards of their violent societies or in comparison with the practices of gang warfare.

There is a world of difference between the moral standards and the motives of some of the nineteenth-century terrorists and their present-day counterparts. For this reason, if for no other, it is unrealistic to assume that those who have become involved in narcobusiness or other forms of organized crime will decide that all they need is a few hundred million dollars, and that once it is acquired they will opt out of the dirty business and pursue their idealistic struggle for national and/or social justice. It is always easy to think of reasons why more money will be good for the cause, and there are always temptations of a less idealistic character. Guerrillas and terrorists age like other human beings, and if in their youth they are willing to undergo material deprivations, they will need and want greater comfort in later life. It is interesting to speculate what would have become of Mao and his faithful if early during the Long March they had come across a gold mine—and the same applies to the other classic guerrilla movements. A few ascetes would have remained "pure" and rejected the Golden Calf. But would most of the faithful have followed them?

It is unlikely that today's guerrilla and terrorist leaders will turn into drug barons or other pillars of Mafia-like organized crime, although there have been a few such cases in the past, especially in Southeast Asia. But the character of their movements is bound to change. The old revolutionary slogans will still be invoked by the leaders, just as Brezhnev and Ceauçescu invoked them, but what may happen below the surface is another story altogether.

While producing and smuggling drugs have made up the most rewarding branch of organized criminal activity in which terrorist groups of every political persuasion have taken part, there have been many other crimes in which terrorists have been involved, ranging from smuggling arms and nuclear materials to cars.

Through their illegal structure, their logistic skills, and their international connections, terrorists are in a good position to engage in such activities. Organizations that smuggle illegal pamphlets from place to place or from country to country can also smuggle other commodities. Ethnic-separatist groups with members and branches in a variety of countries, such as, for instance, the Tamil Tigers or the Kurdish militants, are in a favorable position to do so, for the ethnic diaspora provides the water in which the terrorist fish can move without hindrance.

To repeat: originally terrorism and organized crime had no basic, long-term common interests, only common enemies—the authorities and the state. Any collaboration between them was, or seemed, purely tactical, never strategic in character. But as terrorist groups have become involved in criminal activities, of which the drug trade is only one, organized crime, which originally had no aim other than the enrichment of the group and its members, has become more and more political in character. Historically, terrorist groups have come into being because of their desire to effect political change—social and political revolution, the elimination of individual enemies and whole groups in society, and the establishment of states of their own. The reasons for terrorist involvement in illegal activities have been discussed, and the causes of the politicization of organized crime are equally obvious. In order to make their position safe in the long run, gangsters need to acquire political influence, if not respectability. This need has manifested itself in the emergence of political structures from Tammany Hall to Sicilian municipal governments on which organized crime could depend. But while in the past it was enough to have such political structures on the local level, the globalization of the economy makes it necessary to have more than well-wishers installed in office in Kansas City or Palermo or Moscow. Just as many terrorist groups have political wings (and vice versa), organized crime may need political parties or at least lobbies and pressure groups to defend their interests.

But every self-respecting political movement needs an ideology or at least a program, and what political program beyond naked financial self-interest could the representatives of organized crime present to their followers and the country at large? They could present a vaguely populist program and they might also invoke patriotism. Quite often, drug money is acquired abroad and at least part of it brought back to the home country, helping to boost the economy. Smuggling and other such activities can be represented as new forms of the redistribution of global wealth, since the victims will be the most developed and richest countries. We may perhaps witness a new version of the original Leninist (and also fascist) theory of the struggle of the have-nots against the haves, of the "proletarian" nations against the capitalists—anti-imperialism in new attire.

All this will be anathema to the traditional left. But closing one's eyes to the changes that are taking place will not make them disappear. Throughout history terrorism has had many mainsprings; it has been value-insensitive and not limited to fighters for freedom and justice. It has accompanied the class struggle through many ages and in many countries. It is certainly not impossible that in the future, terrorism's partnership with organized crime may be interpreted as part of a new-style class struggle of the disadvantaged and unemployed, with new elites eager to replace old ones.

CHECHNYA

It is not always easy to draw the dividing lines between patriotism, wars of liberation, and organized crime. Recent events in Chechnya offer a good demonstration.

Chechnya declared itself a sovereign country in 1991 under General Dudaev, a senior official in the Soviet air force. This decision was supported initially only by part of the Chechen public, but the aggressive handling of the crisis by a bellicose faction in the Moscow leadership led to a bloody and protracted conflict, which began in November 1994 and ended only two years later with the massive withdrawal of Russian troops. In their wake arose a state of lawlessness and banditry inside a Chechnya that was close to civil war–like conditions. In the course of this war enormous destruction was caused to Chechnya, but the damage caused to Russia was equally great. The Russian armed forces showed themselves unprepared for a conflict they thought they could end in a matter of weeks if not days; many thousands of ill-trained soldiers were killed and Russia's loss of international prestige was enormous.

It took the Russians more than twenty years to occupy and "pacify" the region in the nineteenth century. The Russian military leadership seems to have believed that the guerrilla tactics used with considerable success by Shamil, the Chechens' legendary commander, were no longer feasible under modern conditions, and this proved to be a costly mistake. Much of the fighting on the part of the Chechens was in fact guerrilla warfare in the classic style, and, ironically, it was planned and led by Chechen fighters who had graduated from the KGB and GRU training schools for saboteurs near Ryazan and in other parts of the former Soviet Union. It was at these schools that some well-known international terrorists had also received their training in earlier years. These Chechen fighters were involved in two of the best-known guerrilla raids: the raid on Budennovsk in June 1995, and the one on Kizlyar (in the neighboring region of Dagestan) in January 1996. In both instances thousands were taken hostage and hundreds were killed.

To the outside world, the war between Russia and Chechnya was widely seen as a confrontation between David and Goliath, a small but brave people defending its religion, Islam, its way of life, and its cultural values against a brutal, imperialist oppressor. But the real situation in Chechnya did not fit into this simplistic picture. The influence of Islam in Chechnya was not very deep. Many mosques had been built there with Saudi money, but these were not well attended, and the Chechen leaders did not obey the injunctions of Islam. At the peace negotiations, the Chechen leaders partook of vodka and pork with the same gusto as their Russian counterparts. It was only after the war against the Russians that militant Islam-inspired terrorist groups emerged in Chechnya and the neighboring regions such as Dagestan. They were often called Wahhabites, a reference to the radical sect that had emerged in the Arab peninsula in the eighteenth century.

There is no denying the fanaticism of the Chechen fighters, but its roots seem to have been cultural rather than religious, and the struggle for power and money also figured highly on the Chechen agenda. The oil pipelines were at least as important a factor as the Shari'a, and the Chechen Mafia, which greatly helped to finance the war effort, was also of crucial importance.

With the breakdown of the Soviet order, major criminal gangs developed in Russia and the "Near Abroad." When the Chechen war broke out, some 150 such gangs were at work in Moscow, out of which six belonged to the major league by any standards. Of these six, three were

Chechen: the Tsentralnaya, one based in Ostankino (where Russian TV headquarters are located), and the Avtomobilnaya (named after the car factory). The number of members in these three gangs was estimated at over two thousand, and they were feared both for their cruelty and their sophistication. They had intelligence as well as legal departments, they bribed officials on a massive scale, and they maintained international connections with many countries, including several in Eastern and Western Europe and the Middle East. The Chechen gangs concentrated their foreign activities in London, which they seem to have preferred to Switzerland as a financial center.

There was a certain division of labor among these gangs along both functional and geographical lines. The Ostankino gang concentrated on road haulage and drug and arms smuggling, while the Tsentralnaya focused on kidnapping and extortion as well as counterfeiting, smuggling of food, and providing protection to hotels and restaurants. Avtomobilnaya specialized in the car trade, legal and illegal, stealing and reselling cars, and extortion of money from car importers and dealers, local and foreign.

While the Chechen gangs coordinated their activities to a large extent, they found themselves under constant pressure from the major Russian gangs in the capital, above all the Solntsevskaya. Dozens of gangsters on both sides were killed in gang warfare, and eventually the Chechens found themselves on the defensive. The struggle was not primarily about political and religious issues but rather a fight for turf. However, "ethnic" elements did play a role in the criminal subculture of the late Soviet Union. The Russian criminals resented the invasion of the "Caucasians" that began in the 1980s, as Georgians and other "persons of Caucasian appearance" were described in the media. Above all they resented the Chechens, who established a strong presence in Moscow, running protection markets and trying to monopolize the black market.

The causes of the Russian-Chechen war do not concern us here, but the interplay between organized crime, politics, and terrorism does. The Chechen members of the Moscow gangs, or at least most of them, were patriots, and hundreds of them returned to their native country to defend it against the Russians. They used their infrastructure to obtain weapons and ammunition, including sophisticated war materials, from inside Russia and abroad. There is reason to believe that they were bribing Russian military personnel in order to obtain intelligence, and, while they continued to invest a considerable amount of their gains abroad, they also seem to have bankrolled the Chechen war effort. At the same time, they refrained, by and large, from launching major terrorist attacks in the Russian capital, which should have been easy for them from a technical point of view. They must have realized that this would have resulted in a backlash that might have destroyed the main base from which they were transacting their business. (For similar reasons Russian gangs have been reluctant to expand their violent activities to Switzerland, their main laundering center, which they do not want to endanger.)

All this shows how difficult it is to define the relationship between "criminal" and "terrorist" activities in individual cases. If one knew how much money the Chechen Moscow gangs allocated to financing the war and how much they continued to take abroad, one could perhaps engage in a quantification of patriotism and gangsterism. But these figures will never be known.

Following the breakdown of the Communist system, Russia became the most widely discussed and the most important center of organized crime in the world. Organized crime has existed throughout Russian history; indeed, it is difficult to think of another people in the memory of which rebels and "social bandits" such as Stenka Razin and Pugachev played such a central role. But under tsarism such crime was not always widely reported, and during the Soviet period its ability to maneuver was limited. All this changed with the breakdown of the Communist system and the ensuing free-for-all race for the assets of the Soviet economy. The KGB took part in this race; officially it had been abolished, but in fact, as one wit said, no other organization in history had grown as rich at its own funeral as the dreaded secret police. Another important competitor in the race were the "new Russians," capitalists who had suddenly come to the fore owing to their special aptitude, good luck and connections, and the local crime chieftains who emerged during the Brezhnev period.

The extent of Russian organized crime is sometimes exaggerated, insofar as all successful business activities are popularly believed to be carried out by the "mafia," a term used quite indiscriminately. But even shorn of such exaggerations, the ramifications of Russian organized crime have been enormous, and the spoils mindboggling. The operations have included all the usual activities carried out by gangsters, such as protection rackets, robberies, kidnapping and extortion, prostitution, smuggling, contract killing, drug trafficking, and so on. Within a very short time these activities were expanded to many foreign countries and contacts were established with organized-crime cartels abroad. Among those assassinated were not only businessmen, bankers, and government officials, but also journalists, Soviet sportsmen, war veterans, and many others. The perpetrators of these murders were rarely apprehended, and never in the more important cases.

The extent of Russian army and police corruption is virtually unprecedented in history. Such organized crime has become a matter of increasing concern to many countries, since it has been a threat not only to the stability of Russia but to the security of other countries. One example is the smuggling of nuclear material and sophisticated weapons. While there does not exist, in all probability, a nuclear mafia in Russia, there have been several major and well-known cases of nuclear black market activity. In the Munich affair, and the Yatsevich, Smirnov, and Vasin cases, nuclear material, though mostly not of weapons-grade quality and of no conceivable interest to anyone but terrorists, was seized. On the other hand, it has been convincingly argued by Russian officials that, rather than smuggling radioactive material in relatively small quantities, it would be far more effective and safer were purchasers to simply order it through a firm belonging to the Russian Ministry of Atomic Energy. Under these conditions, weapons-grade material could be exported, and plutonium substituted for cesium 137. Most of the Russian border stations are not equipped with monitors and radiometers, and export licenses are not difficult to obtain in the circumstances now prevailing in Russia.

There is the danger that in addition to significant sectors of the Russian economy, state organs could be taken over by organized crime, and as a reaction against the criminalization of society, a harsh dictatorship might be established. In the past, the heads of organized crime have not shown political ambitions; they have usually preferred to act in the shadows rather than the light. Gangsters with political ambitions have usually failed. Given the parasitic character of their business, they typically support weak governments from the shadows and don't run for office. But it is no longer impossible, given the depth of the corruption and the absence of a developed civil society, to imagine the political structures of Russia collapsing, just as the Communist system imploded in the recent past. In such circumstances, the leading crime syndicates might transform themselves into legitimate business organizations and become the new pillars of society.

Interestingly, there has been little traditional terrorism in Russia proper since the downfall of the Soviet Union. There were a few explosions on trains and in public places for which no one claimed credit, and scattered threats by an organization called "The Revolutionary Military Council of the RSFSR" and a group calling itself "Soviet Khmer." True, there were also several political assassinations, such as the murder of Galina Starovoitova in November 1998.

Could it be that the massive extent of organized crime in Russia has inhibited, to a certain extent, traditional terrorism? The answer may be yes, because the gangsters, drug traders, and their private armies appeared on the scene earlier than the terrorists—in contrast to the situation in Colombia. A famous sociologist, Werner Sombart, asked around one hundred years ago: Why is there no socialism in America? The same question could be asked with regard to terrorism in Russia after the fall of communism. But it refers only to traditional, old-style terrorism, and only applies to the Russian heartland, not the outlying regions. And it could be a temporary phenomenon.

Those who are puzzled by the absence of traditional terrorism in today's Russia may be asking the wrong question. Politically motivated assassinations are taking place, and new variations of terrorism have appeared in accordance with new conditions. The enemy is no longer tsarism and its entourage, as it was in the last century, but rival groups representing competing interests. Some of these interests represent genuine political issues—for instance, national against international gangsterism, or ethnic gangsterism pitting criminals of one national minority against another, or diverging regional interests. If these criminal groups transform themselves into political movements, it would not be difficult to find ideological causes to justify their existence. They all appear as friends of the people; Russian cartels have been buying up newspapers and television stations to extend their influence, and the establishment of political parties or movements would be the next logical step. Changing times call for new forms of organized crime, terrorism, and politics, a process that in Russia may only be beginning. Organized crime and terrorism may still be different species of lawlessness, but providing precise definitions of each species has become incomparably more difficult.

Mention has been made of the Chechen example, which combined guerrilla-terrorist activities and organized crime. The case of Chechnya is not an exception; similar mergers have occurred in other parts of the Caucasus and Central Asia. According to 1995 Moscow crime statistics, thirty-two Azerbaijani criminal gangs had been identified in the Russian capital, twenty from Dagestan, the same number from Chechnya, seventeen from Armenia, six from North Ossetia, and five from Ingushetia. Large parts of the Caucasus are poor; Daghestan and Ingushetia, for instance, would collapse without Russian financial help. In addition, there are countless ethnic armed conflicts—between Chechnya and Russia, between Armenia and Azerbaijan, and between Georgia and Abkhasia—and there are tensions between the Ossets and the Ingush, and between Daghestan and its neighbors. What has been noted with regard to the absence of terrorism in Russia is certainly not true concerning the Caucasus. There have been several attempts to assassinate the presidents of Georgia, Dagestan, and Chechnya. Kidnappings and major acts of sabotage have become daily occurrences in Chechnya, Daghestan, and elsewhere.

In fact, it is difficult to think of peaceful relations among any of the numerous nationalities in the Caucasus; borders were drawn arbitrarily and there were frequent deportations and expulsions. Poverty by itself does not necessarily breed terrorism, but the mixture of poverty, national tensions, and opportunities to make money through organized crime will lead sooner or later to various forms of armed conflict, including terrorism. Small nations cannot afford to keep sizable standing armies, navies, and air forces, and such conflicts will manifest themselves in guerrilla warfare and terrorism.

The situation in Central Asia is different. These republics are richer in natural resources and lack the experience needed for successful organized crime. But, as in Tadzhikistan, there is conflict between regional clans and new elites, each of which wants to have a share in power and the spoils. Outside intervention or support could fan the conflict and provoke partisan warfare on an even larger scale than exists now.

Lastly, I should mention the militant Russian groups on the extreme right who still provide a breeding ground for terrorism. They are small— but contemporary terrorism does not need a mass basis—and they have contacts with like-minded elements in the armed forces. There was a tendency in the West in recent years to underestimate the destructive and terrorist potential of the extreme right in Russia following the breakdown of the Soviet Union. It is true that only a few trained militants belong to these groups, but in a time of growing social tensions and a deepening economic crisis, even a small, well-organized group can have a considerable impact on society. On a local basis, these armed units of the extreme right have been mobilized by the authorities to help the police maintain law and order. They also have served as bodyguards for major black-market figures or engaged in the blackmail of minor black-marketeers. The then chief of Russian counterintelligence, Mikhail Barzukov, only stated the obvious in an interview in Vek 30 in March 1996 when he spoke about the criminalization of the economic sphere and the simultaneous politicization of the criminal sphere occurring throughout society.

Neither nature nor politics can endure chaos indefinitely. There are too many strong interests involved that need a minimum of law and order; business as much as the black market and smuggling needs a minimum of stability. If chaos should rule, organized crime may be among those calling for the restoration of order. One can only guess at what kind of order this might be; it might lead to the takeover by organized crime, not just of part of the economy but of the state apparatus as a whole.

Organized crime has become increasingly politicized, and not only in Russia. This reflects not only an interest in material gain but also an interest in power. This trend may involve something greater than the personal ambitions of the leaders of these cartels and syndicates; acquiring political power may be inevitable, as pointed out earlier, in order for these groups to secure their holdings and areas of influence. At the same time, terrorist groups in some countries have increasingly engaged in activities that in the past were the domain of organized crime, and, of course, the opportunities to make money, for terrorist or gangster, have never been greater. Organized crime and terrorism have moved closer to each other and in a number of cases have interacted. The deep, irreconcilable differences that once existed between them have become fainter, and there is no telling what the future will hold. But as weapons of mass destruction have become more accessible, a future in which terrorists act as much from greed as ideology may hold danger of an unprecedented magnitude.

TERRORISM Today and Tomorrow

Terrorism has taken some odd turns in the last couple of decades, and the future will see it assume even an odder and more pathological complexion. Political and ideological motivations in the traditional sense, however far-fetched, will recede, as fanaticism, whether sectarian, ethnic, or just personal, moves into the foreground.

LEFT AND RIGHT AT THE CROSSROADS

The recent history of left-wing terrorism in Italy ended in 1983 when most leading figures of the Red Brigades had either been arrested or were in exile. The Italian terrorists' unfortunate habit of putting on paper names, addresses, and activities had made it easy for the security forces to destroy a whole branch of activists following the arrest of a single member. Many of those in prison dissociated themselves openly from the armed struggle that the Red Brigades had carried on for a number of years. They had come to realize that far from bringing about revolutionary changes in Italian society and politics, they had, in fact, delayed such change. The reforms they had fought for did come in the 1990s, but as the result of the initiative of a handful of magistrates who destroyed the old parties that had ruled Italy since the end of the war. These magistrates also brought about the downfall of many of the politicians of the old era, from Andreotti to Craxi. The gurus of the Italian terrorists had been convinced that only brute force and murder would bring about a change; how ironic for them to realize that the legal code proved more powerful.

In Germany, a second and third generation of terrorists succeeded the members of the original RAF (the so-called Red Army group), who had been arrested or committed suicide in Stammheim prison. Most of the successors subsequently abjured the armed struggle. There were sporadic killings, including the murders of a few government officials and bankers, and of a private in the U.S. army, carried out by the second and third generation. But if the first generation had an ideology, however primitive and divorced from reality, the latter-day terrorists were "actionists," believers in deeds rather than discussions. The only innovation they conceived of was a "West European action front," which meant, in practical terms, a certain coordination with Action Directe, a small French ultraleft group active between 1979 and 1987. But even the "action front" did not act very much, with the exception of the destruction by explosives of a partially built prison near Darmstadt.

The successors of the RAF were clearly on the defensive, and at times it was not even clear whether they remained active. There were demonstrations in Bonn for the release from prison of the terrorists of the first and second generation, but the number of protesters decreased every year. In 1998, the remaining members of the left-wing group informed the authorities that they had gone out of business.

According to estimates by the German Office for the Protection of the Constitution, there were in 1998 some six thousand believers in violence on the extreme left. Most belong to various "autonomous" groups that are not really organized, and for all one knows may never commit acts of violence in excess of what certain British and German football fans would consider usual behavior. The German Office estimates there are also about 6,000 such people on the extreme right. But the number of members of extremist Islamic groups (Turkish, Kurdish, Arab, and others) that, according to these sources, endanger the peace was estimated at 57,000. These figures show to what extent the situation has changed within two decades. The state of affairs in France was similar, inasmuch as most of the terrorist actions carried out there in the 1990s were by foreign groups such as the Algerians (GAL), the Basque ETA, or the Tamil Tigers, either to threaten the French or to settle accounts among themselves.

In Greece, terrorist activities continued throughout the 1980s and '90s, albeit on a relatively small scale. The principal group was called the Revolutionary Organization of November 17. Since this group, mainly anarchist in inspiration, was based in one quarter of Athens (Exarcheia, the old city) that includes the Technical University and the Faculty of Law of the University, it is surprising that the Greek authorities failed to gain control of the situation. Most of the attacks were directed against foreigners, especially Americans. Despite the danger that the terrorists could threaten its own citizens, the conclusion drawn by most observers was that the Greek government simply did not give terrorism much priority.

One cause of the persistence of Greek terrorism was widespread youth unemployment, and this factor is likely to play a crucial role in the future of European terrorism in general. But it seems unlikely that any of the existing European terrorist organizations will use weapons of mass destruction in the near future. They have a political agenda they want to achieve. The separatist groups cannot employ such weapons in Ulster, nor can the ETA in the Basque country, for the simple reason, discussed earlier, that such weapons are likely to kill as many followers and well-wishers as enemies. Those fighting for a left-wing revolution cannot use them because they would hurt the exploited masses on behalf of which they claim to act.

Given current social and demographic trends, it seems quite likely that in the years to come Europe will contain many discontented young people who may turn to mindless violence. There has been no decline in unemployment, which amounts to 20 percent in Spain, and 10 to 12 percent in France, Germany, Italy, Belgium, and Finland. Youth unemployment is about twice as high and will probably increase even further. The gap between rich and poor is likely to increase, and in these circumstances prophets of violence may find fertile soil for their messages. The violence might manifest itself in mass political action, as it did under fascism, but it could also be released as terrorism. The second and third generation of "guest workers"—North Africans in France, Turks in Germany, West Indians and Africans in Britain—could be particularly susceptible to the appeal of terrorism, because they feel themselves doubly oppressed, ethnically and economically. Furthermore, the technology of the weapons of mass destruction will be more readily available in Europe than in any other part of the world except North America. Nevertheless, the "objective conditions" of life in Europe offer reason for believing that Europe may be spared the application of the murderous advanced technologies of the new terrorism. But objectivity does not mean probability when very small groups of people are able to cause havoc. Fanatics can appear on the fringe of any political or social movement, or even in isolation, and Western Europe will be no exception.

Right-wing terrorist groups have been more active than those of the left in Europe and North America since the 1980s, and this trend may well continue in the future. Some of the old and new groups belonging to the extreme right have been mentioned already; and there are others, such as the extreme militant wing of the anti-abortion movement in the United States, which has gone so far as to kill doctors and nurses. Altogether, some 2,000 acts of violence were committed by these groups in the last two decades, including bombings, arson, kidnappings, and assault, not to mention 16,000 acts of disruption at abortion clinics. The American Coalition of Life Activists (ACLA) has conducted a campaign to prevent access to abortion clinics and has collected evidence to be used in future "crime against humanity" trials not only against medical providers but also against police officers, judges, and politicians. A manual published in the early 1990s titled "When Life Hurts, We Can Help" detailed ninety-nine covert ways to stop the performance of abortions, which included the manufacture of improvised explosives and the production of detonators from small-arms cartridge caps.

This campaign has not been without success. The number of physicians and nurses who found the risk of performing abortions too high has increased, and at the present time 84 percent of U.S. counties have no abortion providers. Among the extremist leaders of this movement are Protestant clergymen, Catholic priests, and laymen and women belonging to Operation Rescue and other organizations. Anti-choice leaders have argued that abortion is a capital crime for which the just punishment is death. Assassination in defense of human life according to this argument is "justifiable homicide." An extreme anti-abortionist group calling itself the "Army of God," which published the manual mentioned above, has developed a systematic strategy to close down abortion clinics by dismantling alarm systems and placing bombs on the premises. At the same time, this and other organizations have advocated legal action aimed at forcing universities to abolish the teaching of abortion techniques in the medical curriculum. This strategy has extended to the foreign policy of the United States, as these groups propose banning foreign economic aid to countries with active programs that permit abortion as a means to control population growth.

The issue of militant anti-abortionism illustrates the difficulties defining groups of this kind in the terrorist spectrum. By using the qualifier "militant" I mean to distinguish between those who oppose abortion on principle and those who are willing to commit violence against others in support of their opposition. That militants of this kind do not belong to the left goes without saying, but they cannot be simply counted among the right. One could list them among the religious fanatical sects, but this does not seem to be a satisfactory category either. The question of why they should be willing to engage in terrorism because of this specific issue remains.

To find an explanation for these and other single-issue militants, one should go back to the subjects of psychological types, of fanaticism, of violence, aggression, and hate. Being absolutely convinced of the rightness of his cause, the fanatic needs an enemy, and he is bound to have enemies since the majority will seldom agree with him. Hate plays a central role in his personality structure; paraphrasing Descartes, he can rightly say *Odio, ergo sum*—I hate, therefore I exist. The substance of his belief system may vary greatly according to history, culture, or the influence of charismatic leaders. But the burning passion is primary; ideological content is secondary.

Where does the fanaticism, the passion, originate? To what extent are biological factors involved, and to what degree social and cultural factors? Is there a biochemical trip wire that is set off by a childhood trauma? These issues have been widely but inconclusively discussed for many years. But it is not helpful to define radicals of this and similar persuasion as right wing or left wing, as is often done. The usual defining characteristics such as "reactionary" and "revolutionary" get mixed up in these mindsets. Some fanatics are simply nihilists, even though they will seldom admit it.

To argue that the Algerian terrorists, the Palestinian groups, or the Tamil Tigers are "left" or "right" means affixing a label that simply does not fit. Taken from early nineteenth-century Europe, these terms have little meaning in other times and parts of the world. The Third World groups to which we refer have subscribed to different ideological tenets at different periods, and it is as wrong to take Leninist slogans seriously as it is to subscribe to fascist rhetoric. The foundation of their movements is extreme nationalist orientation, frequently including religious motives in recent times. Such a religious-nationalist-populist movement can to Western eyes appear to be left wing one moment and right the next, as history has shown time and again.

Why should one even try to classify terrorist groups using categories that are no longer relevant? In some respects, using these constructs can point up certain differences in basic attitudes that distinguish them, at least in Europe and North America. While an element of paranoia can be found in most contemporary terrorist groups regardless of their ideology, this is more pronounced at the present time among the extreme right, where worldviews are frequently more removed from reality than even these of the left. For this reason terrorists of the extreme right are more likely to acquire and possibly use weapons of mass destruction in the future.

This proposition may appear doubtful in the light of historical experience. But in recent years there have been more attempts to obtain deadly substances for the production of terrorist weapons by extremist organizations of the so-called right than by other groups. In 1995, a "patriot" group in Minnesota was caught stockpiling ricin; a sympathizer of the Aryan Nations located in Idaho tried to obtain bubonic plague germs; and an Arkansas resident connected with another white supremacist survivalist group was accused of having smuggled ricin from Canada into the United States. These are only a few examples.

To begin to understand the mind-set of this new breed of terrorist, his cruelty and hate, the shedding of all moral restraints, the great rage about everything and nothing in particular, the joy generated by killing and destruction, one has to go, initially at least, over familiar ground: fanaticism and paranoia.

PSYCHIATRY AND TERRORISM

There have been heated debates in recent years over whether communism or fascism caused more deaths, and over the role of individual and group psychology in the development of fascism. It is not the intention of this book to rank the evils of fascism and communism, but to explore the mind-set of small extremist groups that may have had their stimulus in such political mass movements. In looking for the motives of postmodern terrorism, paranoia seems to play a more important role than the political philosophy of various great and not so great thinkers of the last two centuries. If one were to draw a map of the regions of the earth where paranoid suspicions have played a pronounced part in political life, the Mediterranean, the Arab world, and parts of the Far East would show a greater prominence than other places.

Very little is known about the etiology of mental diseases, including paranoia. It is known that paranoia seldom appears out of the blue, and the prodomal symptoms, or early indications, are that the person afflicted comes to believe that his or her failures are due to the machinations of others rather than his or her own shortcomings. There are various physiological theories that try to explain paranoia as due to elevated serotonin and dopamine levels, but it is not known at this time whether these are causal factors or appear as a consequence of paranoid states. In the cases of a few terrorists who were medically investigated, brain lesions were found; Ulrike Meinhof is one, and the Pakistani Mir Aimal Kansi, who shot several CIA employees in Langley, Virginia, another. Mention has been made of the fact that Russian terrorists of the early twentieth century made a surprisingly high number of suicide attempts before beginning a terrorist career. But since clinical examinations were made in only a few cases, there is not sufficient evidence to establish a link between physiological changes, mental illness, and terrorism. There is the shame-humiliation concept, and the projection of identification theory of Melanie Klein, two psychological theories that try to explain why some people have the propensity to hate and fear without provocation. Even if we knew much more than we do about the early childhood of political or religious figures who come to mind in a discussion on paranoia—such as Stalin and Saddam Hussein—it is not at all clear whether these insights would be relevant to terrorism. For instance, scientists maintain that it is pointless to argue whether childhood violence is more genetic than environmental, for the simple reason that the determinants of all behavior are an inextricable tangle. While there is frequently a close relationship between hate, rage, and paranoia, they are not the same conditions. Paranoia is a delusional disorder, and the person afflicted frequently suffers from hallucinations. Banal daily occurrences assume a hidden significance, and paranoiacs believe themselves persecuted by enemies in every shape and form. They live in a world of demons, their thinking is often altogether illogical, and the world around them is interpreted in terms of persecution and of enemies. Paranoiacs are unwilling and unable to explain why these alleged enemies should persecute them. They simply maintain that the world has no understanding of the threats and plots against them.

But such a description hardly fits Stalin or a Hitler, nor, for all we know, does it fit Pol Pot, Saddam Hussein, or Idi Amin. There is no reason to believe that Stalin or Hitler ever believed that they were persecuted or that they were in real danger from the enemies they set out to destroy. Stalin was calculating in his actions rather than impulsive; he despised the opposition but did not fear it. Hitler hated the Jews, the democrats, and other opponents, but he did not think for a single moment that they constituted a real danger to him. Hitler was not particularly distrustful, whereas Stalin certainly was, but not consistently. Stalin certainly lacked vigilance in important matters, such as in his relations with Nazi Germany, and he was taken by surprise by the invasion of Russia in 1941. There were paranoid streaks in these as in other political leaders, but megalomania—not humiliation—was the dominant psychological state. Anger, rage, and aggression appear in a great many mental disorders other than paranoia, and paranoia appears often as a component of other mental diseases, such as schizophrenia.

The imposition of psychiatric categories in order to understand the actions of political leaders, including those mentioned above, is dangerous and often misleading. There may be elements of mental illness in the behavior of these leaders, but within the dynamic of their group they may be considered perfectly normal. One needs the concept of evil to make sense of these individuals. And this is largely true with respect to the "terrorist personality," if there is such a thing in the first place.

Psychiatry of a bygone age had a category called *folie à deux*. This referred to a close relationship between two people in which one person who suffered from persecutory delusion infected the other, weaker partner. It was said at the time that only in rare cases *folie à trois* had been observed. But in principle there is no reason why group paranoia should not exist, affecting not only two individuals but many more. The phenomenon of the "disciple mass killer" is well known to criminologists. Charles Manson ordered Leslie van Houten, Lynette Fromme, Tex Watson, and Bobbie Beausoleil, members of his cult, to kill whoever happened to be home at 10050 Cielo Drive, and these previously harmless young people did so unquestioningly. They had fallen under the spell of Manson and needed his psychological approbation. Told to kill by him, they did not need to be given any other reason for doing so.

It is well known that individuals in a group will shed restraints and commit acts they would never commit alone. It could well be that the paranoia mechanism works like the contagion of the persecution mania. There is undoubtedly a sense of psychological importance imparted to a member of a group that claims to have come into possession of the whole truth and who, therefore, has been singled out and persecuted by the rest of society.

But when dealing, for instance, with the terrorists in Algeria and other like countries, paranoia is not an explanation of behavior, and there is no good reason to enlist the services of psychiatry. The explanation for their motives can be found, in all probability, on a much more fundamental level.

CONSPIRACY THEORIES

Conspiracy theories exist across the political spectrum. They were particularly evident in Russia before the revolution of 1917, and Bolshevism added a great deal of grist to the conspiracy mill. They have pervaded African-American radical thinking in the United States; they have been prevalent in Italian politics and among the Arabs. They have frequently arisen in revolutionary movements of the left—for example, world affairs were interpreted by the Communists as one giant conspiracy of monopoly capitalism, engineered by Wall Street. A great many best-sellers in the late Stalinist period, such as Nikolai Shpanov's *Podzhigatelei,* were extreme manifestations of this spirit. The book proposed that nothing in international politics happens by accident; everything is part of a huge plot that has been planned in advance, in great detail, and has emanated from one sinister control center.

While the belief in conspiracies persists in sects of the left, it no longer appears with the same vigor and consistency. Most of the huge conspiracy literature nowadays is extremely right wing in inspiration, as even a short visit to the Internet will show. It is not easy to say why this should be the case—it might be related to the crisis of left-wing ideology in general. It could also be related to the somewhat more optimistic outlook of the left than that of the right-wing lunatic fringe. The left believes, by and large, in revolution followed by a better future; the extreme right-wing sects believe they are surrounded by enemies, and victory seems distant if not impossible. Alienated from their own land and people, these patriots are fighting a desperate rearguard battle. The list of the enemies of the patriot sects in the United States is indeed formidable. The government—for some, two conspirators in one, as in the "Zionist occupation government"—is at the top of the list, followed by American culture, damaged beyond redemption by various commercial and decadent influences; the financial system; the police and the FBI; all ethnic minorities; universities and schools, which teach false values; the churches (having strayed from the right way); all foreign countries; and also most white compatriots, who have been successfully brainwashed by mendacious official propaganda.

In composite, the conspiracy theorist knows the truth about the assassination of John F. Kennedy and the accident in which Princess Diana lost her life. He knows that nothing in this world is what it appears to be; he knows the truth about the plots of the Elders of Zion and the Club of Rome, the Council of Foreign Relations, the Trilateral Commission, and about every international organization, including, and above all, the United Nations. He knows the true purposes of AIDS, of UFOs and other aliens, and of the hollow earth theory. He is firmly convinced that FEMA (the Federal Emergency Management Agency) is preparing concentration camps for patriots all over America, and that foreign armies have invaded America and that the CIA is controlling the minds of virtually all Americans. He knows for certain that Presidents Bush and Clinton and virtually all their predecessors were tools of the Antichrist and that the American economy will be ruined by the introduction of a cashless society. Some conspiracy theorists claim to have been ritually abused in satanic cults in their childhood and argue that the New World Order, with the help of black helicopters, black storm troopers, and the media will induce multiple personality disorders through psychological torture. The world of the conspiracy theorist is similar to the world of the horror movie, except that in the movies the enemy is usually an animal or a plant, whereas in the case of the conspiracy theorist it is always a human being or a group. Many of those who subscribe to these beliefs resign themselves to the coming horrors, because they cannot even imagine how to resist a conspiracy so powerful and comprehensive. But there are others willing to fight to the end, and it is among them that one has to look for some of the terrorists of the next century. Many in these circles believe that up to three quarters of the world's population may have to be killed to redeem mankind. Others prefer not to be too specific about figures, but also think in terms of an apocalyptic purge or bloodbath.

The Turner Diaries, the bible of certain extreme-right activists, with its mixture of paranoia and sadism, might again be quoted in this context. Killing is perceived not as a dire necessity but as a matter of satisfaction or even joy. The hero of the story relates how he grabbed a black man and hit him in the face as hard as he could. "As he went down I had the deep, primitive satisfaction of seeing four or five of his teeth come washing out of his shattered mouth on a copious flow of dark red blood. . . . I straddled him and directed three kicks at his groin with all my strength. He jerked convulsively and emitted a short, choking scream with the first kick and then he lay still." After killing several more men and women, the hero reflects: "Six months ago I could not imagine myself calmly butchering a teen-aged White girl, no matter what she had done. But I have become much more realistic about life recently." The members of the Organization subsequently advance from killing individuals by way of knives, guns, and explosives to the use of nuclear bombs that murder millions and annihilate whole countries, including large sections of their own.

Military psychologists have maintained that killing does not come easy to the professional soldier. A good deal of indoctrination and desensitizing is needed, as well as strict obedience to commanders. It would appear that terrorists of a certain kind are abnormal and in no need of such training. This applies not only to the fictional characters in *The Turner Diaries,* but also to the Islamic radicals in Algeria who slit the throats and abdomens of their victims—often women and babies—with relish, drink their blood, and dance on their corpses. The leaders of the militant group that killed fifty-eight foreign tourists in Luxor, Egypt, in November 1997 made it known that they were shocked by the mutilation of the dead. Clearly the terrorists under their command had gone too far. But why had they acted beyond orders? Because they and the heroes of *The Turner Diaries* are psychological brothers. It seems obvious that today's generations of terrorists have no compunction about whom they kill—male, female, children, enemies or innocent bystanders, members of another ethnic group or their own kind.

This, of course, was not always the case; the early Russian terrorists and some of the nineteenth-century anarchists were willing to sacrifice their own lives rather than harm innocents, especially members of the families of their intended victims. More recently, however, when terrorists have recanted there have been few expressions of regret over the murder of innocents, even in Europe and North America. If sexual excitement is increased for sadists by inflicting torture or killing a partner, the same seems to be true for some terrorists.

In the descriptions of the anarchists of the 1890s, who opted for revolutionary violence, one finds an emphasis on the love of freedom, a highly developed moral sensitiveness, and a profound sense of justice. Such praise came not only from sympathizers such as Emma Goldman but also from observers not in the least involved with anarchist terrorism. There are constant references to the unselfishness, the frugality, the high moral caliber of these "modern saints and martyrs." I quote from comments made by contemporaries. The praise was exaggerated—they may have wept when they killed, but they killed nonetheless. Yet what a world of difference exists between these men and women and the fictional heroes of *The Turner Diaries,* or, in real life, the Islamic terrorists in Algeria and elsewhere, all guilty of bestialities.

The value placed on human life varies from culture to culture, but there is still a revulsion against sadism in every part of the globe. From a terrorist's point of view it is easy to find a rationale for killing, but it is impossible to justify the sadism displayed in many countries in our age. Do terrorists need less training and indoctrination for committing murder than professional soldiers because they are motivated by hate? Proabably, but it is also likely that some terrorists have a predisposition toward violence and cruelty, and this is why they became terrorists in the first place.

Sadism plays a crucial role in the terrorism of the extreme right, more so in some cultures than in others. In all likelihood, very few of the 200,000 readers of *The Turner Diaries* have committed murder, and most probably have not visited violence on any human, much less an animal. It is significant, however, that this fantasy has attracted so many readers. Reading those pages must give them a satisfaction akin to that gotten from pornography. And for a few, there must be a strong urge to act out these fantasies in real life.

FREEMEN AND THE TWILIGHT OF THE GODS

How can a few patriots defend themselves against forces of evil so superior in number and, of course, in firepower? The answer seems obvious—only by using weapons of mass destruction that would reduce the odds against them. The future, as they see it, is grim: it involves hecatombs of victims, perhaps billions. At this point, the influence of certain millenarian sects on militants of the extreme right becomes obvious. The sectarians, needless to say, have no interest in secular politics, but their nightmares are as frightening as those of the nonreligious characters of *The Turner Diaries*.

Apocalyptics believe that not all of the victims of the final event will perish in forms of unrest such as race riots, civil wars, and others; many will lose their lives as the result of natural disasters such as earthquakes, volcanic eruptions, wildfires, global warming, nuclear winter, famine, asteroid strikes, epidemics, and so on. The believers in apocalypse predict the emergence of the Antichrist as the head of the New World Order, with his headquarters in Jerusalem. This will lead to genocide and chaos. But eventually, following the rapture and final destruction of the wicked, the righteous will be removed to heaven or a new planet and receive new bodies there, full of youth and health and, of course, a new spirituality.

The secular extreme right has a parallel belief in the ultimate victory of a racial elite that will destroy inferior people, criminals, and degenerates—in sum, the majority of mankind—and will create a new paradise on earth. Their apocalyptic visions are not Christian in character but can be traced to Nordic sources such as the Edda (Ragnarok) and the Nibelungen, and to the Goetterdämmerung, in which the heavens disappear and earth is swallowed up by the sea, and in which a battle takes place between the good and the bad gods and all perish, yet life somehow continues. This is the last scene of Wagner's *Twilight of the Gods*: Brunhilde thrusts her torch into a pile that rapidly kindles, two ravens fly up from the rocks and disappear, and bright flames completely envelop the abode of the gods. Then the curtain falls, according to Wagner's scenario.

In the past such visions were discussed in aesthetic terms; they are depicted in paintings of the Last Judgment by Hieronymus Bosch and Jakob Jordaens and their contemporaries. In the age of *The Turner Diaries* and weapons of mass destruction, these nightmares have acquired a more immediate and sinister significance.

RELIGION AND TOMORROW'S TERRORISM

What does the religious terrorism of the future hold? Zealots and fanatics can be found in most religions in history, and most have tried to impose their values and practices on their coreligionists and the rest of mankind. To what extent is a religious mission the mainspring in such cases and to what degree do psychological or political factors drive individual human beings and motivate groups? One cannot generalize—each case seems to be somewhat different—but frequently a mixture of religious and nationalist motives is involved, and the importance of specific religious motivations—with the obvious exception of the terrorist motivation in Iran—seems to have been exaggerated.

The Muslim Brotherhood, the spiritual font from which Hamas and Gama'a and the Algerian Islamists derived, rejected nationalism, including Arab nationalism, as a foreign, secular importation. But, in fact, these offshoots have put nationalist aims, such as the liberation of Palestine, on the top of their agenda. They have advocated pan-Arabism as well as pan-Islamism. While they are preaching the Islamization of the radical Arab national movements, some of the leading figures in the terrorist struggle and many of the militants have by no means been particularly devout people. This contradiction might, however, be more apparent than real, for in political practice Islam is considered to be an inherited part of the Arab way of life, unlike that of the non-Arab Turks, Iranians, or Pakistanis. Having been present at the creation of Islam, Arabs are thought in these circles to be the more authentic Muslims than some of the latecomers, even though some of these latecomers, such as the Afghan Taliban, presently occupy the most fanatical high ground.

When the Babri Masjid, the Ayodhya mosque, was destroyed by extremist Hindus in 1992, which led to widespread riots and many deaths, the motivation was not so much religious as nationalist, since the mosque was a symbol of Muslim rule in past centuries. When various militant Sikh organizations, such as the Dal Khalsa and Dash Mesh, came into being, their inspiration was as much nationalist and cultural as religious. Mention has been made of the fact that the number of religiously motivated suicide attacks has been exaggerated. There were a few in Lebanon in the 1980s. In Israel one occurred in 1993 (in the Jordan Valley), four in 1994 (in Afula, Hadera, and two in Tel Aviv), three in 1996, and three in 1997. If one adds to this perhaps an equal number of missions that failed, the number is still small in comparison with the suicide missions undertaken by Tamil Tigers, who were not religiously motivated. The assumption that suicide missions only or mainly occur among believers in a transcendental religion and an afterlife is not borne out by the known facts.

Throughout the history of religion can be found among zealots the urgent desire to proselytize or to destroy nonbelievers. However, the scope of ambitions even of *ecclesia militans* were of necessity limited: the Crusaders wanted merely to occupy the Holy Land, not the entire Eastern world; jihad extended to the whole world only on an abstract level. Today the aggressive, expansive urge has gone out of the mainstream of all the major world religions, but it still exists on its fringes, and is strongest in Islam, from the Taliban in Afghanistan to the Algerian terrorists.

The worst kind of religious violence is not necessarily visited on people of other religions. It should suffice to recall the massacres in Algeria, and Saddam Hussein's use of poison gas against the Muslim Iranians and the Kurds.

Religious or sectarian fanatics may well be attracted to the idea of using weapons capable of destroying millions of people. The main obstacles facing them are practical rather than theological. The scope of destructiveness of the weapons has to be controlled, and at the present stage of technological development that points to the use of nuclear and chemical weapons rather than biological. And control of chemical weapons, as we have seen, may not always be easy. The Islamists in Egypt may want to exterminate the Christian Copts, but the Copts live among millions of Muslims; the same is true of Israel, with its Arab citizens and neighbors, of the Sikhs, who live among the Hindus, of the Kurds, who live among Turks, and so on. How to destroy Jewish Jerusalem without also killing the third of the population that is Arab, not to mention destroying the Muslim holy sites? To try to exterminate the Jews, the Nazis first had to isolate and deport them. Such procedures are possible only in time of war.

States and political movements of a certain size will be deterred by rational considerations of this kind. But what if the hate of the unbeliever is so great that the attackers might be willing to accept the death of millions of their own if it leads to the extinction of the enemy? The smaller such a group, the more radical it is likely to be, and the less rational its actions.

This takes us to the most radical sects and the doomsday cults that believe that the end of the world is close. Sects and their rituals have a long history. They were described in antiquity, for instance, in writings of Titus Livius in which he deals with various orgies and bacchanalia. Quite frequently, sects were banned by authorities because they were considered asocial and anti-state. During the Middle Ages in Europe they were even more severely sanctioned as bands of heretics. (There are, of course, many nonapocalyptic and nonviolent sects and cults that pursue various forms of healing and psychic states or ecological and quasicultural concerns; they belong to New Age and other such movements.) An official French survey in 1995 counted approximately 170 sects, of which 46 were considered antisocial, as they constituted a threat to public order and practiced forms of mind control and mental destabilization on their members. And France is not a country that encourages sects; the number of sects in in the United States is much larger.

Apocalyptic sects figure most prominently in the public consciousness because of some well-publicized mass suicides: Jonestown, Guyana, in 1978 with 923 killed; Mindanao in 1985 with 65 suicides; Part Soon Ja in Korea in 1987 with 32 suicides; 88 suicides and deaths in Waco, Texas; 53 deaths in the Temple Solaire in 1994 in Switzerland and Canada; and, of course, the mass suicide of the Heaven's Gate cult in California in 1997.

There is an interesting class difference to be found among these apocalyptic sects. The victims at Waco were predominantly from the lower class, as was true of Jonestown. The Heaven's Gate believers, on the other hand, were on the whole from the middle class. The Temple Solaire consisted of members who, in the words of Ted Daniels, one would usually find in a country club. They were all united by the deep belief in supernatural forces, "bridge burning" and "forsaking all others," and a special apocalyptic itinerary.

SECTARIANS AND SCIENCE FICTION

It is believed that the revival of sects in recent years, especially the more extreme among them, is part of a general religious renaissance. This may be true, but only if one counts various bizarre supernatural manifestations, from magic to UFOs, as religious. The phenomenon probably is more intimately related to the influence of science fiction in modern society. One of the tenets of today's apocalyptics is a belief in their own survival despite the end of the world.

Science fiction offers a solution to survival after Apocalypse: space travel. The subject appeared long before the twentieth century in the fantasies of scientists, including Kepler, and later in the fictions of Edgar Allan Poe and Jules Verne. But the idea became truly popular following the appearance of a new genre of films, such as *The Invasion of the Body Snatchers* (1956), *When Worlds Collide* (1951) (wherein a spaceship along the lines of Noah's Ark takes a few lucky people to the planet Zyra), and perhaps above all the very popular TV series *Star Trek*, first aired in 1966 and still watched, along with a number of movie spin-offs. This tradition has continued in the 1990s with the immensely popular *X-Files, Millen-*

nium, and other series that contain all the ingredients of the paranoiac vision: giant conspiracies, UFO abductions, and so on. Paranoia has become an all-pervasive subject in movies and television, from the sophisticated films of Oliver Stone to the B-grade horror movie.

These movies and television shows have had a profound influence on a great many contemporaries. While it is doubtful that the apocalyptic sectarians read the Bible, even Revelation, the Heaven's Gate people were made to see *Cocoon* repeatedly. And the Branch Davidians viewed *Lawnmower Man.*

Cocoon (for which Don Ameche received an Oscar) deals with an elixir that gives eternal life to a group of seniors in a Florida home who prefer space travel to their condominium swimming pools. *Lawnmower Man,* an ideal film for the cyberspace generation, shows how Dr. Angelo, a clever scientist, transforms a half-witted lawnmower man into a highly intelligent, albeit megalomaniac, being. Few actually believe this farrago of nonsense, but some, like the Heaven's Gate cult, were perfectly willing to accept the idea that following their suicide a spaceship would collect them and take them to another planet. After all, they had watched similar scenes in the movies.

PREPARING FOR THE APOCALYPSE

The fantasies about Apocalypse can be projected outward as well as inward, and find an outlet in terrorism. Aum Shinri Kyo, as mentioned earlier, is the best-known example in recent times of a sect that exhibited this tendency. Aum started as a Buddhist sect that promised to bring happiness to the world, but at a certain stage, around 1990, its guru, Asahara, reached the conclusion that Armageddon was at hand. There were references in some Christian sects to collisions with Halley's Comet and the Comet Austin, but Asahara preached at first that the members of the sect could do nothing except think of ways to protect themselves, perhaps by looking for distant hideouts and underground shelters. It should be mentioned that in Japanese popular culture, spaceships play a considerable role, such as in *Yamato,* a cartoon show, and *Akira,* a comic book serial. It remains to be investigated to what extent science fiction rather than spiritual inspiration influenced the behavior of Aum.

What Armageddon would mean in practical terms was never quite made clear by Asahara. It was merely said that mankind was divided into the saving remnant, the Aum, which would be taken to heaven, and the rest, who would go to hell. However, at this stage another jump occurred in the thinking of the guru, who went from passively waiting for the cosmic disaster to actively precipitating it. Asahara persuaded himself that the United States was about to bomb Japan as part of a giant world conspiracy and the sect had to make an all-out effort to defend itself.

Hence the search for weapons of mass destruction by Asahara's followers, who were not only entirely under his spell but in all probability also under the influence of drugs. There is no logical explanation as to how a poison-gas attack in a Tokyo underground station would deter an American aerial attack. All that matters is that such a mental jump was made, and that a madman could cast his spell over a fairly sizable number of intelligent people with advanced technical training. Interestingly, the sect continued to attract followers even after the arrest and trial of its leading members. Asaharas can be found in most parts of the world in one form or another, and the idea of an Apocalypse is not even Japanese.

The Book of Revelation, which describes angels sounding their trumpets, hail and fire mixed with blood, oceans drying up and a third of the sea becoming blood, stars falling from heaven and burning like torches, and a third of the sun and the moon destroyed, reads more like contemporary science fiction and disaster films than religious writ. Of course, it is not only in the realm of fantasy and conjecture that such horrors appear. Among the many human and naturally caused disasters today are AIDS, global warming, acid rain, dying forests, desertification and other ecological crises, and killer viruses and bees. To the susceptible personality, it may seem as if the Antichrist is well on his way to imposing a New World Order.

Some of the believers of the Book of Revelation, of Daniel and similar writings, prepare themselves for the time of tribulation by repenting of their sins in the hope of being saved. But there is also another way to react to a belief in end time. It says in the Book of Revelation, "Then I heard a great voice out of the Temple saying to the seven angels, 'Go your ways and put out the bowls of the wrath of God upon the earth' "(16:1).

This passage can be interpreted in a variety of ways. According to the Book of Revelation and other such texts, the forces of Satan are strong and will not give in without a last, desperate battle. Perhaps the saving remnant should not passively await the outcome of the battle but join the fight against the forces of evil? Perhaps they should even hasten Armageddon because there might be forces at work trying to delay it and the coming of the kingdom of God? This idea, a sectarian strategy of provocation, seems to have occurred to some Israeli zealots in the 1970s, and it can be found among some Muslim sectarians, as well as in other religions. On the secular front, in the 1960s some adventurous Communists, including apparently Mao, played with the idea of using nuclear war on behalf of the Communist cause and criticized the Soviet leaders for their temerity. The Chinese were not at the time a nuclear power, but it was their idea of *la lutte finale*, especially if executed by another nation.

The jump from believing in the proximity of the Apocalypse to actively promoting its coming, to giving eschaton a little push, will be made by very few. But these few may now have the means to do so, and there is no reason to assume that the Aum example will not find imitators in one form or another.

TOMORROW'S STATE-SPONSORED TERRORISM

It is almost certain that state-sponsored terrorism will continue into the foreseeable future. Nation-states will not disappear and, despite globalization, their power will not diminish, at least not in the near future. Conflicts will persist and so will weapons proliferation, which actually may gather speed. It is difficult to envisage effective international control over weapons of mass destruction before some major disaster occurs, and even more than one disaster may be needed to drive home the necessity of such control. Not every country will have such weapons in its arsenal, but many will. These weapons may be acquired for deterrence or for political blackmail, rather than with the intention of using them. But once they exist, it is always possible that they will be used either in warfare or in surrogate warfare—that is to say, as a weapon of state-sponsored terrorism.

The issue of proliferation is a much broader one than the use of weapons of mass destruction by terrorist groups, but the two issues are connected. The states most likely to acquire weapons of mass destruction, other than the major powers that already have them, belong to a variety of categories. Some are relatively small and poor, countries with ambitions that transcend their capacity to achieve world power. Libya is an obvious example—a country with five million inhabitants that is quite poor but for its oil revenues, which at the present time give it no more than a billion dollars of excess revenue per year. Such a country would normally play a modest role in world affairs, but because of the wide ambitions of its ruler it has attempted to enhance its influence through the acquisition of weapons of mass destruction. Hence, the decision in the late 1970s to produce blister and nerve agents at the facilities at Rabta, and subsequently the construction of underground facilities at Tarhunah. Chemical agents were used by the Libyans fighting Chadian troops in 1987.

Alternatively, a state looking for weapons of mass destruction could be a regime driven by a mission, nationalist or religious or both, that can be promoted only by the threat or use of such weapons. Or it could be yet another poor country driven to expansion by traditional reasons: coveting the wealth of its richer neighbors, or forced by its inability to solve its internal economic and social problems to "escape" into territorial expansion. Such a campaign could also be used to mobilize the masses, and it might be justified ideologically as the struggle of the haves against the have nots, of proletarian against capitalist (imperialist) nations, as early fascism envisaged. Among those countries acquiring weapons of mass destruction will be some that feel threatened by the possible aggression of their not so peaceful neighbors.

The number of countries that belong to these various categories is considerable. The trend toward proliferation may slow, and the spread of weapons of mass destruction to all these nations may take twenty rather than five or ten years, but it is difficult to envision that it will not take place.

Ironically, the major factor retarding the use of gases and germs by states and terrorists is not revulsion or moral constraints but technical difficulties. "Ideal" conditions for an attack seldom if ever exist, and the possibility of things going wrong is almost unlimited: aerosols may not function, the wind may blow in the wrong direction, missiles carrying a deadly load may land in the wrong place or neutralize the germs on impact. In the course of time these technical difficulties may be overcome, but it is still very likely that roughly nine out of ten of the early attempts by terrorists to wage chemical or biological warfare will fail. But they will not pass unnoticed; the authorities and the public will be alerted, and the element of surprise lost. The search for the perpetrators may begin even before the first successful attack. And what has just been said with regard to terrorists may also be true with regard to state terrorism.

It is difficult to be more specific on this subject. The rogue states of today may not necessarily be the same as those ten or twenty years from now. Variable factors, such as the appearance or disappearance of an ambitious and aggressive leader, make prediction impossible. A country presenting a threat at present may implode for one reason or another, and disappear, at least for a time, as an active player in world politics. The most that can be done now is to point to the less stable parts of the world that, for a variety of reasons, now constitute a particular threat. But to repeat: countries that appear strong and stable may suddenly undergo a deep crisis and become much less powerful; for example, few predicted the downfall of the Soviet regime in 1989. No one thought in 1950 that Lebanon and Ceylon (now Sri Lanka), islands of peace, would turn into scenes of bitter civil wars and terrorist campaigns. In some cases, however, such a prediction was easier. To those familiar with Balkan affairs it was clear that Yugoslavia, ruled by Tito with an iron fist after the Second

World War, would face a crisis of survival, and that sometime after his death the unity of the country would be put into question.

The three examples just mentioned, Lebanon, Sri Lanka, and Yugoslavia, have one feature in common—ethnic conflict. They show that in the contemporary world such conflicts can recur after long periods of peace, and that, while not intractable per se, they are fought with particular bitterness. Civil war, guerrilla warfare, and terrorism are more likely in such countries than in countries with a homogeneous population.

THE MAIN DANGER ZONES

We have seen that ethnic conflicts are not the only sources of terrorism; religious and social tensions also lead to terrorist activities within a national community. Algerians are fighting Algerians, Egyptians killing fellow Egyptians.

Europe was to a great extent ethnically homogeneous up to the 1970s when millions of "guest workers" arrived from the West Indies, North Africa, Turkey, and other parts of the world. Despite the conflicts of the past two decades, there is reason for cautious optimism that they will be resolved in a nonviolent way. There are the well-known exceptions, such as Northern Ireland, where in 1998 a peace process was voted in, although terrorist acts have continued; and the former Yugoslavia, where violence has taken the form of a civil war rather than individual terrorism. However, violence by, within, or against the new immigrant communities in Western Europe cannot be ruled out. Parallel to the immigrant influx in the 1970s, some sociologists and political scientists detected "new social movements," to which they attributed considerable importance. That such movements exist is not seriously doubted; they found their political expression, for instance, in the Green parties. But the potential for violence, such as riots and even terrorism, exists in the newly arrived ethnic groups who have tensions with the native population, rather than in the new social movements.

In some Latin American countries, the grievances of the native Indian population, such as in Peru and Mexico, have provided the impetus for political violence. Tribalism in Africa has provoked widespread violence in recent years, and in the future this could affect South Africa, where ethnic conflicts coincide with social tensions. Despite this, neither Latin America nor Africa is the most likely site for the use of weapons of mass destruction. The main danger zone seems to be North Africa, where religious fanaticism is greater and where a higher level of education combines with unemployment, especially among the younger generation. Access to modern technology is greater, and among a generation of young technicians and scientists unable to find jobs commensurate with their training, there are skills to use that technology.

The regions of the globe most widely affected by ethnic conflicts are the Middle East—and the neighboring Caucasus—and Southeast and Central Asia. Strife on ethnic lines has been endemic there for many years and is unlikely to diminish in scale and intensity in the foreseeable future. The Kurds have no state of their own, the Palestinian Arabs have only a mini-state at present, and the situation inside Lebanon is quiet only because of a Syrian military presence. But Syria could collapse and disintegrate into a variety of small states just as Yugoslavia did. The conflict between Sunnis and Shiites in Iraq is no nearer to a solution than it was in the past; there is ferment between locals and foreign workers in the oil-rich Gulf mini-states; and the future of Saudi Arabia is quite uncertain, as is the future of Kuwait and Bahrain. Old enmities between Turkey and Greece, the unresolved conflict in Cyprus, and the countless disputes in the Caucasus will likely continue unresolved into the future.

Central Asia, particularly Afghanistan and Tadzhikistan, have been the scene of internal fighting that could spread to neighboring countries, and there is little hope that the conflicts will be permanently resolved. The Congress party that ruled India since independence has broken down, and India has entered an era of political uncertainty unseen since 1947. The linguistic conflicts and the struggle for autonomy, not only among the Sikh but within many Indian states, are fueling new conflicts. The old antagonism between Hindu and Muslim on one hand, and the tensions between castes on the other, continue. In brief, it can no longer be taken for granted that India will survive intact. Pakistan has little hope of benefiting from India's misfortunes, because its internal divisions are arguably even more acute.

The future of Indonesia is also uncertain, as is that of other Southeast Asian countries. Violence in the years to come could be directed against the Chinese, against other minorities, or against each other.

A complete list of potential violent conflicts would be exceedingly long, and not all latent conflicts may turn into armed struggle. In any case, our focus is on terrorism rather than other forms of violence, even though the lines separating them in the real world are seldom as clear as in the books. War seems unlikely in all but a few cases because it has become the luxury of the rich; only big and wealthy countries can afford sizable standing armies. Terrorism will probably occur in many places, but quite often it will be overshadowed by riots, civil war, and other manifestations of collective violence. Afghanistan offers an example, as do some of the Central African conflicts. Political leaders on the village level have been killed, as have higher-ranking officials in the cities, but the former seldom gets reported outside the country concerned. At a time when thousands are killed weekly, the murder of an insignificant official is barely noted. Even the cases of prominent military and political leaders killed in Afghanistan over the years were hardly noted in the outside world. The more conflicts there are, the less notice is paid to most of them, as the mass media can focus only on one or two conflicts at a time. Attention is paid by the Western press if violence takes place in countries that, for one reason or another, are strategically important, or if they concern a major player in world affairs, or if there is spillover into international terrorism, or if the violence affects the global economy or the international balance of power. A struggle for power, however bloody and protracted, in Africa or Central Asia, or in Laos or Cambodia, will not normally cause much excitement in the world capitals. But chaos in the Persian Gulf or on the Indian subcontinent is seen as a worldwide threat.

However, it would become a major problem if unconventional weapons were used in these lesser-noticed conflicts. In most cases, their use is unnecessary, so chances are slim that a state or a terrorist group would deploy them. Why use complicated and risky arms if traditional weapons can bring about the same result? Their use may be considered only if the intention is to destroy rather than just defeat the enemy, or if the power of the enemy is so great that there is no hope of victory with conventional arms. The use of weapons of mass destruction is unlikely, but the dangers involved are immense even in the remotest possibiity.

Of the two hundred–odd wars, civil wars, and other violent conflicts that have taken place since the end of the Second World War, all but twelve occurred in parts of the world that, until recently, were called the "Third World." This pattern probably will not change in the years to come. Some of these conflicts were brief and relatively bloodless, but others lasted for five or ten years, some even longer, and the number of victims, military and civilian, was very high. Afghanistan, Kurdistan, Algeria, and some of the Central African conflicts are obvious examples. Many of these violent conflicts originated in the process of decolonization and the emergence of new states, and this process is now over. But it is not yet certain whether all the new nations are viable, and there are conflicts between states as well as within. It is also not certain whether or not India, Indonesia, and Nigeria, the second, fourth, and tenth most populous countries in the world, will retain their present borders. These countries may be too big and diverse in population to be ruled from one center. India, for example, has two states, Uttar Pradesh and Bihar, that are more populous than any European country, and three more, West Bengal, Madha Pradesh, and Hyderabad, that each have as many inhabitants as Germany, Europe's most populous country. China relapsed into warlordism and anarchy in the 1920s, and while a recurrence of that development seems very unlikely at the present time, it is not impossible.

What are the trends that make the countries of Asia and Africa particularly vulnerable to armed conflict and terrorism? Ethnic conflict has been mentioned, but there are various other reasons. While the countries of Southeast Asia and the Pacific rim have shown as much or more economic growth as any country in the world, this upsurge has come to a halt. The Middle East has stagnated and many African countries have experienced negative growth.

Throughout modern history, poverty per se has not led to more conflicts between states, but poverty has social consequences that cause destabilization and tensions. One of these consequences is migration. Since the end of the Second World War there have been several enormous waves of migration, the biggest being the exodus of Muslims from India and of Hindus from Pakistan. This was caused, of course, by politics, as was the exodus of Russians from the republics of the Soviet Union, the Armenians from Azerbaijan, various minorities from the Central Asian republics, and the migration of Palestinian refugees. More recently, war has caused mass exoduses from Rwanda, Zaire, and the former Yugoslavia.

However, the most significant reasons for the more recent waves of migration have been economic and social; people have been moving in search of work and a higher living standard. This includes the migration from south to north that affects North America and Europe, migration from Pakistan and other parts of the Muslim world to the Persian Gulf, from Syria to Lebanon, from Egypt to Libya, and from the Philippines and Indonesia to other Asian countries. Some of these migrants intended to return after a few years; others chose to stay in their new country. In some instances, the absorption of the new immigrants proceeded smoothly, but elsewhere it has led to violence.

Much of the terrorism in France and Germany in recent years originated in North African, Turkish, and Kurdish quarters, and it is of two types: between various factions of these nationalities and against the host country. These tensions are not a passing phenomenon, because they are as marked in the second generation of immigrants as in the first. Terrorist acts by the local population have also occurred as a backlash against the new immigrants. This cycle of terrorist violence has not been limited to Europe; refugees have played a major role on the terrorist scene in host countries in the Arab world, in India, and in Pakistan, to mention a few examples. Much, if not most, of urban violence in metropolitan centers such as Mumbai (Bombay) and Karachi has been carried out by refugees from other parts of India, or from some other part of the Indian subcontinent, or against these refugees.

Given the political climate in the Arab world and North Africa and the high birth rate, to mention only two obvious factors, demographic pressure in Europe will be intense in the years to come, and there could be similar pressure in Eastern Europe, the former Soviet Union, and in the Balkans. This could lead to terrorist acts both by immigrant factions and by groups in the native population. In other cases, particularly Africa and the Middle East, host countries have permitted refugees to organize militarily and infiltrate their countries of origin. Iraq, Syria, Lebanon, many African countries, India, and Pakistan are examples.

POPULATION PRESSURE

Predictions of population growth are risky because of a number of variables. H. G. Wells, one of the most famous and accurate futurists of all times, was asked by a British journal in 1900 to predict the main social trends for the next century. He predicted, among many other things, that London would grow and eventually extend from Devon to the North Sea. But in actual fact, the population of the city of London has shrunk for several generations in a row. Similarly, the rate of population growth in many Latin American countries has decreased for two decades, even though few would have predicted this. However, a few trends can be predicted with confidence; one is the rapid urbanization of the Third World.

All over the world, hundreds of millions of people have left the countryside in search of a better life in the big cities. Thirteen cities in Asia, two in Africa—Cairo and Lagos—and four in Latin America—Mexico City, São Paulo, Rio de Janeiro, and Buenos Aires—count ten million or more inhabitants, and some conurbations will soon have close to twenty.

Forty years ago, some of these megacities did not even have half a million inhabitants, like Lagos and Dacca. Even if this trend slows in the future, its consequences are already irreversible. Rural poverty has been transferred to the big cities, and urban poverty, in the words of a World Bank report, has become the most significant and politically explosive problem in the world. Guerrilla warfare has dwindled, but urban terrorism is on the rise.

In the heyday of guerrilla theory and practice, the great majority of mankind, particularly in the Third World, lived in villages and worked in agriculture. But now the global urban population is 2.7 billion, of which

1.8 billion live in the Third World, home to the poorest countries. This means the end of Mao's theory of the "encirclement of the world city by the world village." But it has other implications, one being that the megacities cannot absorb this influx. According to estimates, 85 percent of the population of Cairo lives in slums—including about a million people living in caves in cemeteries. In Bombay, Calcutta, Karachi, and Lagos more than half of the population live in slums and almost half do in Rio de Janeiro and Mexico City.

These cities are inhabited by what was once known in Britain and France as the "dangerous classes." For graphic descriptions one can turn to Dickens's *Our Mutual Friend*, which depicts subproletarian fishermen on the Thames who collected corpses and the ever-present "stinking dust heaps" (a Victorian euphemism for shit), and to *Oliver Twist's* account of the criminal underclass of London. This class also shows up in the novels of Eugene Sue about the Paris poor. But London and Paris each counted less than a million inhabitants at the time, and the worst rioters could do was burn a few buildings.

MEGACITIES OUT OF CONTROL

Rapid urbanization and the emergence of slums has brought about many unfortunate consequences: insufficient social services, growing crime rates, including organized crime, and terrorism. In cities in Communist China, such as Beijing and Shanghai, and in those of a few of the so-called Tiger economies, such as Seoul and Singapore, some of these dire consequences have been attenuated either by rigid control from above or by growing prosperity. But elsewhere the megacities have become unmanageable; Lagos, Dacca, Cairo, Karachi, Bombay, and Calcutta are obvious examples.

The megacities of Asia, Africa, and Latin America are becoming the twenty-first century's breeding ground for terrorism and other forms of political violence. Polluted, crime ridden, administered by authorities frequently ineffective and corrupt, they are barely inhabitable in a time of economic boom; it is not hard to envisage what life will be like in these cities when the economy stagnates or declines. It is estimated that at present one billion human beings live in slums, favellas, bidonvilles, or barrios, and the only factor that might prevent a dramatic increase in the population of these areas is the shortage of water. Part of the urban population has prospered and will in the future, but this will only add to the prevailing tensions. The social-economic polarization is greater in many parts of the Third World than in Europe, and the difference in lifestyle between rich and poor is more glaring. When the majority of the population lived in the countryside, all people were equally poor, but in today's megacities, glittering shops and restaurants, hotels, and casinos exist side by side with the miserable slums.

These conditions may lead to blind rage and sporadic riots, destruction and looting—what Los Angeles and other American cities have witnessed, only on a far more massive scale. Organized crime and organized terror may sprout, looking for victims, not in the poor sections but where the rich live. While the majority of slum dwellers in these areas lack drive, education, and political or criminal ambition, there will always be among these teeming millions a few thousand, certainly a few hundred, who have the initiative to organize and challenge the establishment. And these developments will not be restricted to the twenty or so best-known megacities. The most rapid growth has been in cities the names of which are wholly unknown to the majority of the outside world. Who but a handful of observers outside India has ever heard of Vishakapatnan, Vadodara, or Kanpur? These are all cities with more than a million inhabitants—and Bangalore has five million.

In past decades there have been frequent references in the media and in scholarly studies to the "urban guerrilla." The term is an invention of an age in which most terrorists were left wing in inspiration, the term *terrorism* had bad connotations, and a more positive word was often used by sympathizers or the ignorant. The guerrilla in the traditional sense of a Mao or Castro could operate only in the countryside, as I have pointed out, and aimed at the gradual liberation of areas, the establishment of revolutionary social and political institutions, and eventually an army of liberation. All this was impossible in the cities and led Guevara and Debray to the conclusion that they were the graveyard of true revolutionaries. All this could well change in future. For the first time there might be "no-go zones"—where police and soldiers may not dare to trespass even in daytime—springing up in in the big cities. In these areas, terrorist gangs might be able to organize and train, and keep their arms depots without fear of detection and seizure. To a certain extent this has already taken place. It is far easier to mobilize people in the big cities for violent action than in the countryside. The great advantage in the countryside was the relative safety from the authorities. There was little danger that the police would know what occurred in the countryside, let alone intervene. As control is lost in the megacities, even intervention by the army, as happened in recent years in Rio de Janeiro, has frequently been ineffective, and well-armed gangs can hold the security forces at bay. When a guerrilla or terrorist action next appears it will not be in the mountains or villages, but probably in the rich urban quarters encircled by the slums and favelas.

If violence gets totally out of hand, there will be either a descent into chaos or the installation of an authoritarian government, supported by the military and the police. As far as the behavior of the security forces in some of the megacities is concerned, this stage may be at hand. The movie *Escape from New York* (1981) got its timetable wrong; it portrayed Manhattan as an island of criminal anarchy surrounded by security forces by 1997. Still, it is too early to say that this fiction is altogether unrealistic.

An authoritarian government could not, of course, stamp out crime altogether, but it might subdue the terrorists. One of the most persistent myths concerning terrorism is that arrests and executions cannot suppress it, that its social and political sources have to be confronted in order to put an end to it. But historical evidence has shown time and again that massive violence has usually prevailed over terrorism, because there is not an unlimited reservoir of people willing to replace those who are executed or imprisoned. There was no terrorism under fascism and communism. Even military dictatorships that were not completely totalitarian in character easily defeated terrorism. Spain is the classic example; there was no terrorism under the dictator, Franco, but there was under the democratic regime that succeeded him. These regimes may be worse than the terrorists whom they combat, but what matters in this context is the simple question as to whether or not severe punishment or physical repression can defeat terrorism as we know it. The historical evidence points to a clear answer. There might be a regime in too much disarray to adopt harsh measures; Iran under a sick Shah is an obvious example. Ironically, in this case, the rebels won and established a dictatorship that far more effectively suppressed all opposition, democratic and terrorist.

If these trends persist there will be political repercussions in the part of the world in which most of mankind lives. Even the most advanced countries might be under pressure to adopt stronger, possibly authoritarian, governments—partly because of a spillover of Third World unrest and partly because of the threat of weapons of mass destruction. Having to make a choice between chaos and a dictatorship, the great majority of people will opt for the latter. In some of these countries, it is not certain that even a totalitarian dictatorship—clerico-fascist, national-fascist or fascist-populist—could function because the process of disintegration may have gone too far. But since politics, like nature, dislikes a vacuum, sooner or later some kind of order will be imposed.

There is no certainty that our worst fears will come to pass. Blake's satanic mills and Dickens's factories and poorhouses of nineteenth-century England were replaced, after all, by factories and homes that, while not paradigms of beauty and kindness, are not remotely as horrible as they used to be. They were transformed owing to a second Industrial Revolution. But it is difficult at the present time to foresee a similar revolution that could transform the worst megacities into livable places. At best, it will be a protracted and painful process, in the course of which there will in all likelihood be a great deal of terrorist violence.

TERRORISM
of the Future

Weapons of mass destruction are a fact of life today. We have seen the nuclear arms race intensify in Asia, and elsewhere the production and use of biological and chemical weapons, as I have described earlier. It is entirely possible that the terrorist of the future—tomorrow, perhaps—will avail him or herself of one of these weapons. In addition, the electronic age has now made cyberterrorism possible. A onetime mainstay of science fiction, the doomsday machine, looms as a real danger. The conjunction of technology and terrorism make for an uncertain and frightening future.

NUCLEAR TERRORISM

Nuclear terrorism is a distinct threat, and will remain one far into the future. There is a great deal of enriched fissionable material unaccounted for, mainly from the former Soviet Union, that is now smuggled from country to country. The amount of such material needed to make a bomb is not large; fifteen pounds of enriched plutonium or thirty pounds of enriched uranium would be sufficient for the construction of a sizable nuclear weapon. To do this there would be no need to employ highly qualified nuclear engineers; it could be done by advanced students in the field on the basis of readily available information.

Had an equal amount of nuclear material rather than explosives been used in recent terrorist attacks, the damage would of course have been immensely greater. It has been estimated that if the van used by the terrorists who tried to blow up the World Trade Center in New York had been filled with nuclear material rather than by ANFO (ammonium nitrate), the blast probably would have been sufficient to destroy lower Manhattan.

In 1997, General Lebed, President Yeltsin's former security adviser, revealed that in the 1970s a considerable number of "luggage nukes," small nuclear devices built in the form of a suitcase and transportable by one person, had been produced by the Soviet military industry for the KGB. The plan had been to use these weapons for acts of sabotage in times of war. Lebed also claimed that a certain number of these singular weapons were unaccounted for, an allegation that was confirmed by some Russian experts and denied by others. But no one denied that some small nuclear device had indeed been produced not only in Russia but in some of the successor states, such as Ukraine, Belarus, and Kazakhstan.

The advantages of such a nuclear weapon to terrorists are its relatively small size; the fact that it would produce an enormous bang (and thus have an enormous psychological impact); and its potential to destroy an enemy's center of power yet at the same time be more focused territorially compared to unpredictable biological weapons, which could spread much farther than planned or not as far. Chemical weapons are subject to meteorological conditions, whereas a nuclear weapon will explode summer or winter, rain or shine. A terrorist might argue that a nuclear bomb is somehow "cleaner," making it psychologically more easily justifiable, merely a more powerful extension of traditional explosives, whereas chemical and biological weapons represent a new and more vicious kind of destruction.

While the Manhattan Project, the original endeavor to construct atomic weapons, was by necessity very costly, over the course of time the making of nuclear devices has become much cheaper. Judging from information on the South African nuclear program, it is thought that a bomb could be made for little more than $100 million, provided the terrorists have at their disposal a certain quantity of highly enriched uranium or plutonium. Such sums are not out of the reach of the international backers of some terrorist groups. As the membership of the club of nuclear powers grows, the cost of a bomb is bound to decrease sharply.

It may no longer be necessary to construct a nuclear device from scratch, and it is not total fantasy that someday do-it-yourself assembling kits may be for sale. The poorer members of the nuclear club, notwithstanding all the promises never to part with these weapons, may find themselves in a situation where economic necessity coupled with ideological affinity will induce them to pass on some of their inventory.

The drawbacks of a nuclear bomb are equally clear. If they are to be used for threats and blackmail only, the terrorists have to prove that they are in possession of one. But how to convince the enemy that this is the case? It can hardly be achieved on the basis of a series of diagrams and drawings. In all probability, the terrorists would have to explode such a device somewhere in order to demonstrate that the threat is real. But if nuclear were the choice of weapon to be used to devastate an enemy, just one would not be sufficient for a sustained terrorist campaign, unless there was reason to believe that the enemy would be so shocked by the consequences of the explosion, so incapacitated, that it would immediately surrender, as Japan did in 1945. This is unlikely; hence the need for not just one but a number of nuclear devices, a whole nuke arsenal. This would create major acquisition difficulties. Furthermore, the threatened or targeted country would be on the highest alert, and would be likely to retaliate in kind against those suspected of supplying these weapons or helping to construct and deliver them.

But how does one retaliate against a small anonymous group? Uranium and plutonium are easier to trace than chemical or biological weapons. The number of governments who have both the motivation and the capacity to produce and deliver these weapons through terrorist groups is limited, and a country that has been the victim of such an attack is unlikely to wait for juridical proof. It may act first and investigate afterward, which means that not only the guilty could be hit in a counterblow. There is no reason to assume that a rationally acting government, however radical, would pass on nuclear weapons to a terrorist group, because the consequences could be devastating for the suppliers. A nuclear device exploded in New York or Washington would not destroy America, and a bomb in Beijing or Moscow would certainly not destroy China or Russia. On the other hand, a nuclear attack against a smaller country could bring down the regime in power.

Democracies that have faced a terrorist challenge have tended toward underreaction, because the identity of the perpetrator may not have been clear, or because restraint and a response commensurate with the damage caused and the number of victims suffered was called for. But the reaction to the use of a weapon of mass destruction might be the opposite, one of overreaction. In such a case there is bound to be overwhelming pressure to retaliate on a bigger scale, both as an act of revenge and to forestall future attacks.

Despite the reasons one can marshal against the use of nuclear bombs by terrorists acting as substitutes for foreign countries, one can still think of a variety of scenarios in which this could happen, whether because a country with a nuclear capacity has descended into chaos, or a government has temporarily lost control, or any other circumstance in which those in power have ceased to act rationally.

What if a domestic terrorist group should produce one or more nuclear devices without any foreign help at all? It is difficult to think at the present time of an effective defense to prevent an attack in this case. Given the amount of fissionable material that is available, the voluminous literature on nuclear weaponry, and military and state budgets in which hundreds of millions of dollars is a paltry sum, the chance that a terrorist group will come into possession of a nuclear device is significant.

BIOLOGICAL AND CHEMICAL WEAPONS AND THEIR TARGETS

In the 1990s the belief that biological and chemical weapons were perhaps the greatest danger facing mankind, and were the most neglected, gained ground. There had been warning signs before. In 1972, a biological and toxic weapons treaty was signed, and many countries, including the United States and the Soviet Union, had solemnly declared that they would no longer manufacture such weapons and would destroy their arsenals. The discovery of enormous quantities of such weapons in Iraq after the Gulf War came as a shock, all the more so because there was reason to believe that only a portion of them had been found, and that, furthermore, Iraq, as well as other countries, including Iran, were continuing preparations for BC (biological/chemical) warfare and could successfully resist inspection. There had been suspicions even before the Gulf War, but the extent of the BC buildup had been hugely underestimated. In fact, there should have been no surprise, for Iraq had used chemical weapons against both the Iranians and the Kurds, killing many thousands. But the outside world had taken little notice, and consequently it came as a shock that at the Al Muthanna laboratories, also known as Samarra, according to the Iraqis' own admission, they had produced 2,850 tons of mustard gas, 790 tons of sarin, and 290 tons of tabun in 1995. When the Gulf War broke out, Iraq had fifty missile warheads with chemical agents. The total amount of poison gas produced was probably considerably larger than the quantities Saddam Hussein publicly admitted to. Iraq had also experimented with radiological weapons—unsuccessfully—but, most shocking, it had started to produce botulinum toxin in 1988, and anthrax, and other biological agents from 1989 on. It had filled aerial bombs and warheads with botulinum and anthrax. By 1991, 6,500 liters of anthrax and 10,000 liters of botulinum had been weaponized—a staggering quantity, of which people outside Iraq had been quite oblivious.

Even Russia, which had solemnly vowed to destroy its BC weapons, did not adhere to its promise, and prevented access by foreign inspectors after 1993. A further shock was the realization that it was exceedingly difficult to discover these weapons, even in ideal conditions. Except for the defection of an Iraqi and some Soviet scientists, Western governments would not have known where to look and for what.

Only after the dramatic March 1995 attack by Aum in the Tokyo subway station in which sarin was used did Japanese security forces realize the danger. Up to that time, it had been widely believed all over the world that the possibility of such attacks were greatly exaggerated, if not altogether baseless, the product of a Cold War fantasy. Fortunately, neither the Gulf War nor the Tokyo attack led to a major disaster, and at least the authorities finally realized that these weapons were a tremendous menace. This new awareness led to a great many studies of the weapons most likely to be used, how they could be used, by whom, and what, if anything, could be done against them.

In 1997 a special issue of *JAMA*, the *Journal of the American Medical Association*, published the first systematic survey of biological agents. There seemed to be general agreement that bacillus anthracis and botulinum probably presented the greatest danger because of their toxicity, the fact that they were highly infectious, and because both had been found in vast quantities in Iraq, where they had already been "weaponized." Other agents prominently mentioned in the *JAMA* survey and other authoritative publications have been mentioned earlier on in this study: brucellosis, the plague, tularemia, Q fever, smallpox, viral encephalitis, viral hemorrhagic fevers, and several others. Some toxic cultures, notably aflatoxin, have been found in the Iraqi arsenals, which surprised U.N. inspectors because, given their low toxicity, long incubation period, and lack of resistance to heat and other natural conditions, these cultures seemed unsuited for use as weapons.

There are vaccines that can neutralize most of the existing agents, and antibiotics that can be given both prophylactically and as a treatment. But this is not entirely reassuring, because there is always the possibility that those bent on launching biological warfare may use an agent that has undergone biological mutation and against which existing antibiotics and vaccines are ineffective. Also, vaccines can be used only if there is advance knowledge of an attack, and stocks of antidotes are likely not to be sufficient, leaving the civilian population at high risk.

At the end of this century only a very few countries will have the industrial capability to produce nuclear weapons on a mass basis, but almost any country with a chemical and pharmaceutical industry could engage in BC production. Therefore, the number of countries known or suspected to engage in these pursuits is considerably larger. It is believed that between thirty and forty countries have the capacity to manufacture chemical and biological weapons. The greatest concentration of existing weapons at the present time is in the Middle East, including not only Iraq and Iran, but Syria and Libya.

BC agents have been called, with some justification, the poor man's nuclear bomb. Their advantages are well known: they are difficult to trace, they can also be used for acts of sabotage against crops and livestock, and the epidemic caused may spread widely and last a long time. But there are also factors that could make them the second choice after nuclear weapons. Their ease of production means that if they are used in a war between states, there is the certainty of retaliation in kind, making them weapons of despair. This could be the reason why these weapons have been used only in isolated cases since the First World War. Furthermore, there are technical hazards, some of which have been mentioned earlier. Botulinum is the most deadly toxin available, 100,000 times more poisonous than sarin gas, and one gram of it is, in theory, sufficient to destroy all the inhabitants of a city like Stockholm. The ideal way of delivering botulinum is by way of an aerosol; it is estimated that eight kilograms of this agent would be sufficient in optimal weather conditions to kill all living beings within an area of one hundred square kilometers. But ideal conditions seldom prevail, and such an attack could fail and kill only a small number of people. If the gamble fails, the attacker would still bear the onus and suffer the consequences, and he might consider the stakes too high for even trying.

There is also the time factor. In the cases of anthrax and botulinum a day or two will pass before the deadly symptoms appear, and in the case of other viruses the incubation period is even longer. This may not be enough time to extend medical help to the general population, but it is enough to prepare a devastating counterblow against the attacker.

There are many questions regarding the effective use of chemical and biological weapons. Chemical substances and biological organisms have to be more than highly toxic; they also need the right atmospheric conditions. Success depends on a variety of factors, including the direction and strength of the wind, the temperature, and other climatic factors. A massive dispersal may have a very limited effect, or it may create enormous damage.

Recent research in biotechnology has made the construction of fusion toxins possible, and bacteria and viruses can now be made more danger-ous and resistant to antibiotics through genetic modification. But at the same time, biotechnology makes it possible to manufacture antisera and vaccines to protect a civilian population.

The factors mentioned earlier that make chemical and biological weap-ons a high-risk option apply to a much lesser degree to terrorist groups intent on using weapons of mass destruction. The risk of detection is high in an air attack that uses artillery shells, bombs and rockets, or spray units; for example, biological aerosols can be detected by lasers that are carried on helicopters. But the dispersion of germs or poisons through water reservoirs entails fewer risks and is more difficult to detect. This kind of approach is likely to be chosen by small groups of saboteurs or terrorists, who may also use aerosol generators hidden in small containers. This was the method used, in a primitive way, by the Aum terrorists in Tokyo.

Against whom, and by what kind of people, are these weapons likely to be applied? They are unlikely to be used in Northern Ireland, given the mixed population in Belfast and other cities, not to mention the psycho-logical and moral constraints, which are found in Europe to a somewhat higher degree than in Asia and Africa. It was reported in the late 1970s that the German RAF (Red Army–Baader Meinhof) was instructing Pa-lestinian camps in the use of bacteriological warfare, and that in a raid in Paris police had discovered a small laboratory with a culture of botulinum. According to another report, terrorists threatened to poison the water supplies of twenty German cities unless one of their demands—the de-fense of some of their imprisoned comrades by three radical lawyers— was met. There were suspicions that efforts were afoot to use potassium cyanide, and speculation that microbiologists had been enlisted by ter-rorists in several countries, including Italy and the Palestinians in Leba-non. But the only proven case of a political group—or, to be precise, religious sect—having engaged in an operation of this kind took place in The Dalles, Oregon, where 751 persons were poisoned by salmonella planted by followers of Bhagwan Shree Rajnee in two restaurants in that small town. The motive, as far as can be established, was not to kill but to frighten off local inhabitants so that the sect could establish their head-quarters unimpeded in the town.

Whether this kind of nonlethal terrorism will be used in the future in North Africa, the Middle East, and South and Southeast Asia is open to question. There is so much hate and fanaticism based on nationalist and religious-sectarian viewpoints that these emotions may supersede the realization that the weapons of ultraviolence are not the best way to achieve political aims. The Saddam Husseins of the world produce anthrax, not salmonella. It used to be said in the 1970s that terrorists do not want many corpses but merely a big bang. But this referred to the terrorists of the extreme left in Europe and Latin America, not the very different species in Asia and Africa, where a high number of corpses is also a desirable aim. If these new weapons are not used, or used only rarely, the reasons will certainly not be humanitarian in character, but pragmatic. However, it is quite possible that small, fanatical groups will opt for this approach against targets in North America and Europe, to "punish" the richer and more advanced nations for the crimes they are believed to have committed against the downtrodden of the world. Or it may be used because a group thinks that it is God's wish, or to achieve certain specific aims such as the release of prisoners, or to bring about a policy change, or to extort money.

The Jihad organization, which masterminded the bombing of the World Trade Center and the planned bombings of the Holland and Lincoln Tunnels, the Manhattan office of the FBI, and the United Nations, could well be regarded as the prototype of such a fanatic group. Its members could have come out of a novel by Joseph Conrad; they included a blind and half-crazy Egyptian sheikh with some charisma; a young chemical engineer with three or four different identities, who two years earlier had been neither a practicing Muslim nor politically engaged; an Iraqi agent who provided money and technical help; an Egyptian counteragent; a Sudanese diplomat; and a Saudi billionaire acting as paymaster from afar. Some in this group simply followed the one or two major figures in the plot because of family ties or friendship. It was by no means a monolithic group, and there was strong internal dissent, partly over the money funding the enterprise. One of the chief protagonists, Shalabi, was found killed in his apartment in Brooklyn, presumably by his fellow terrorists.

And yet this small motley crowd of grotesque characters almost succeeded, as Senator Sam Nunn put it, in committing the first act of terrorism on American soil in which weapons of mass destruction were used—for poison gas, cyanide, was in the arsenal of the plotters. The gas had been procured, but because of technical difficulties it had been impossible to pack the gas into a bomb and thus to deliver. This group had contacts with Muslim governments, or at any rate with the secret services of several of them. However, the contacts and the guidance seem to have been ineffective, and the technical execution of the plot remained amateurish. It is frightening to imagine the results of a more professional approach, with fewer people involved and greater technical know-how.

According to some estimates there could have been 25,000 to 50,000 victims, even using conventional explosives.

True, even professionals slip up. In almost all terrorist attacks committed by Libyan and Iranian agents in Europe, traces were left leading to Tripoli and Teheran, which in turn led to diplomatic and sometimes military retaliation. The reprisals were never very severe, but they would have been if weapons of mass destruction had been used. Still, there is always the risk that a terrorist group may delude itself that its planning is so foolproof that the risks of detection and retaliation are small or nonexistent.

CYBERTERRORISM AND THE FUTURE

Because of the rapidity of change in technology, it may be pointless to speculate about the role of the electronic revolution in the future of terrorism. It goes without saying that the wide use of these technologies will have far-reaching repercussions for conflict between states, for organized crime, and for terrorists. Some observers have discerned a trend of electronic power migrating to small but sprawling networks that will replace hierarchical organizations. The specter has been conjured up of hydra-headed networks that are not easily decapitated. But the examples adduced are usually old-fashioned. Just as smuggling cassettes into Iran played a key role in the Khomeini revolution, enemies of the Saudi regime, to give one example, are engaging in subversive action by way of fax and e-mail. But no amount of e-mail sent from the Baka Valley to Tel Aviv, from Kurdistan to Turkey, from the Jaffna peninsula to Colombo, or from India to Pakistan will have the slightest political effect. Nor can one envisage how in these conditions virtual power will translate into real power. The hackers for hire often do not share the fervency of the insurgents eager to seize power.

Sectarians may spread their message on the Internet, thus reaching a wider public than in an earlier age, but they will be exposed at the same time to far more criticism, skepticism, even ridicule, than in the past. Information about how to manufacture bombs and weapons of mass destruction is now a click away on the Internet, although this material is not much different in kind from the bomb manuals available in the last century.

In the future, terrorist action aimed at information technology will continue to be destructive, but on a primitive level. Society is becoming much more vulnerable, and the places of greatest vulnerability are well known. Guerrillas in deepest Mexico and Colombia have been destroying high-voltage transmission lines. Power stations in Bosnia and elsewhere have been frequent targets. The consequences are that society can be shut down for hours, sometimes for days. About 95 percent of U.S. military communication channels run through commercial lines; they include intelligence data that can be jammed without great difficulty. The same is true with regard to weapons systems and civil defense. However, such operations will not add to the popularity of a terrorist gang, nor will it translate into political power. But it may fit the program of the pan-destructionists.

Computers and the services depending on them are exceedingly vulnerable. They can be paralyzed through viruses, worms, logic bombs, and spy chips. They can be disabled by HERFS (high-energy radio frequencies) and electromagnetic pulses. The technical expertise to generate and distribute viruses and other weapons of the infowar is now widespread, and will be even more popular among terrorists or simply among hacker-anarchists eager to have fun and create the maximum amount of havoc. But mayhem can also be achieved through far more basic means. A few switches thrown in a strategic site, a few hammer blows, or a hand grenade could have an even more dramatic effect.

THE EARTHQUAKE MACHINE AND THE DEATH RAY

In their search for weapons of superviolence, the scientists of the Japanese cult Aum, discussed earlier, went well beyond biological and chemical arms. They sought an ultimate weapon powerful enough to destroy a continent, if not the whole world—a doomsday machine. They discovered the work of Nikola Tesla, born in Croatia in 1857, who had studied electricity at the universities of Prague and Budapest, emigrated to America, and played a leading role, second only to Edison, in the early history of the applications of electricity in the United States. Tesla worked with and for Westinghouse and had some seven hundred patents to his credit. He designed and produced, among many other things, motors for multiphase alternate currents, and most students of radio are familiar with the Tesla coil. But Tesla also invented, or claimed to have invented, many contraptions that belonged to the realm of science fiction, and he became the model of the "mad scientist" in early cartoon series. In the very first of the Superman cartoons (1941), Superman fights Tesla, the inventor of death rays, who has unleashed an army of robots over New York.

In an interview with the *New York Times*, Tesla had claimed to have invented a death beam, or a concentrated beam of particles, powerful enough to destroy 10,000 planes at a distance of 250 miles. Tesla said that he had discovered the so-called cosmic ray first in 1896, many years before anyone else took up the idea.

The concept of such a ray with almost unlimited power preoccupied early science fiction writers, including H. G. Wells, and in the 1930s became a central theme in science fiction and fantasy stories about a future war. Eventually, with the invention of the laser beam, an idea that had been derided at first by scientists, this concept acquired a new significance.

Tesla's other claim seemed even more fantastic. It concerned the invention of an earthquake machine that he said could split the world in half, just as one would split an apple. In an interview with the *New York Times,* he referred to his invention many years earlier of a mechanical oscillator, claiming it could cause a vibration so powerful that five pounds of air pressure would be sufficient to bring down the Empire State Building. This new science of vibrations, which he called Tele-Geo-Dynamics, was said to have many applications, including the transmission of power, geophysical surveying, communication, and radar, but its dark side was the production of earthquakes.

The Aum scientists went to Russia and Yugoslavia, where Tesla's papers are kept and where he still has admirers to this day. (The Soviet army command was at one time intrigued by the idea of a death ray, which also played a prominent role in Soviet science fiction.) Aum's desire to find the earthquake machine was undoubtedly reinforced by the Kobe earthquake in January 1995. For some reason, Aum decided instead to gas the Tokyo underground, an attack that took place a few months later, and its quest for the doomsday machine came to an end.

But it would be wrong to assume that the search will not be resumed elsewhere at some future date. What if the quakes of Lisbon (1755), Krakatoa (1883), or Kobe (1995) could be repeated on a more massive scale? The crust of the earth would have to be pierced by an "earthquake ray" or by constructing an artificial meteor with which to bombard the earth. What kind of people would want to find such a weapon, aiming at the destruction of earth, or at least of life on earth?

These neonihilists are different from the traditional terrorists of the last 150 years, and from most of the new breed of terrorists. To find comparable candidates one needs to go back either to the fictional supervillains of an earlier age, such as Fu Manchu, who wanted to dominate the world, or to the mad idealists who believe that there has to be gigantic destruction before the regeneration of mankind can take place. Or to the early stories of H. G. Wells or Robert Cromie's novel *The Crack of Doom* (1895).

In a world of real terrorist hazards, why even consider lunatics driven by apocalyptic fantasies? Perhaps because the psychological line between them and terrorists with an agenda is thin, and because now the technology of mass destruction exists. There may be very few individuals with both the motive and competence to act out these fantasies. But there is little doubt that such individuals exist and will exist in the future.

TYPES OF TERRORISTS

What kind of group or individual would want to use weapons of mass destruction? The first category consists of deranged individuals. It should be recalled that most U.S. presidents who were assassinated (Garfield, McKinley, and Kennedy) were killed by individuals rather than political or terrorist groups. John Schrank, who shot and injured Teddy Roosevelt in 1912, was mentally unbalanced, and so was Zangara, who tried to kill Franklin Roosevelt but instead assassinated Mayor Cermak of Chicago. (Zangara thought that Roosevelt was somehow responsible for the stomach complaint from which he, Zangara, had suffered as a boy.) John Hinckley, who shot President Ronald Reagan, was mentally ill, as were several other assassins of political leaders in the nineteenth and twentieth centuries.

In some of these cases, the killers were driven by hate against their victims or wanted to draw attention to themselves, but in many other instances the act involved symbolism. The man suspected of having killed Swedish prime minister Olof Palme hated Sweden and Swedish society, not the prime minister himself. The same was true with regard to the assassination in 1966 of Henrik Verwoerd, the South African prime minister. The assassins wanted to register a protest against the system rather than just eliminate a single person.

In one of its rare publications of statistics, the academy of the Russian security forces asserted in 1997, that of all attempted aircraft hijackings they had tracked, 52 percent had been committed by mentally unbalanced people.

Many terrorist acts are committed by individuals following in the footsteps of Herostrat, the citizen of Ephesus in ancient times who burned the local temple simply so that his name would be remembered forever.

The second category consists of apocalyptic religious or religious-nationalist groups who believe the end is near for a sinful world. Members of a small Jewish sect in the early 1980s believed that it was their duty to create a catastrophe to force the hand of the "Master of the Universe," who would then wage a great and terrible campaign on their behalf. This led to the conspiracy of a few fanatics to explode the Mosque on Temple Mount in Jerusalem to start the third and final world war.

Retaliation will not deter those who believe the end of the world is already at hand. For some sectarians and millenarians, the ultimate disaster is a joyful prospect rather than something to be dreaded. Rational calculations, such as the likelihood of doing damage to themselves, do not apply. Sheikhs acting as gurus for extreme Muslim or Arab groups, and who declare that they love death and welcome it with the joy of a bride at the arrival of the bridegroom, will not be deterred, nor will sectarians convinced that a saving remnant will survive. The fallen will be taken to heaven in a *markabah,* or by special messengers sent by Allah, or in a spaceship. A few deranged individuals can be found in many religions, and while in the past they may have engaged in group suicide, they could, if they had access to weapons of mass destruction, prefer a deed aimed at others.

Third, fanatical nationalist groups, consumed by hatred against another national group in their midst or in a neighboring country, could opt to use weapons of mass destruction. This is especially likely in non-Western countries, where human lives count for less and humanitarian considerations seldom apply. These groups might believe that such desperate actions could at long last achieve their aim, by destroying the hated enemy or at least decisively weakening him. But evidence also tends to show that Western terrorist groups, including the IRA and ETA, and various factions in the former Yugoslavia, have shown greater cruelty in their attacks than European terrorist groups did in an earlier age.

Fourth, weapons of mass destruction could be used by various terrorist groups engaged in a long struggle without evident success and without much hope for success in the future. They may ask themselves: Why should our fight have been all in vain? We made many sacrifices and many of our best comrades fell in the struggle. Is it not our sacred duty to avenge the martyrs by engaging in one last desperate effort before admitting defeat?

Fifth, weapons of mass destruction could be used by terrorists acting on behalf of a state or even criminal-terrorist groups, who may calculate that the damage caused and the number of victims would be devastating but still limited. This could involve the use, for instance, of small nuclear devices or chemical substances to be sprayed over a limited area. (Some of the most deadly biological-warfare agents mentioned earlier, such as anthrax, would kill but would not cause an epidemic.) The intention might be to use such weapons to inflict dramatic but limited damage for the purposes of, say, threat and blackmail. One might argue that there is only a quantitative difference between such a biological weapon and a powerful bomb. However, most would conclude that the use of such weapons would cross a hitherto uncrossed barrier, and would lead to a war in which weapons that cause epidemics may be used.

Last, weapons of mass destruction could be used by small groups of individuals who suffer from one delusion or another and have personal grievances rather than political ones. This category is similar but not identical to the first category, because more than one person would be involved. These could be homicidal characters, or paranoiacs who believe the whole world is conspiring against them, or mad geniuses with unlimited ambitions (the mad scientist and the master from the world of science fiction). Unfortunately, there is almost an unlimited variety of this type. In the past, the damage they could inflict on the rest of the world was of necessity limited, but in the future this may no longer be the case. A single fanatic might be able to infect others who are in search of a message and a leader with his brand of madness.

Even this brief summary shows that a considerable variety of types qualify as candidates for committing attacks with weapons of mass destruction. Psychiatry is of only limited use in this connection. The term "psychopath" is frequently used when violence on this scale is discussed, although some of the standard textbooks prefer the term ASPD (antisocial personality disorder). Psychiatry has shied away from dealing with this topic, partly because there are hardly any agreed-upon ways to measure this condition and partly because so little is known about the etiology of it. There is not even agreement as to whether it is a mental disease in the traditional sense, and there is no known cure in severe cases. Psychopathic traits have been described as apathy toward others, lack of remorse and conscience, disregard and violation of the rights of others, and the refusal to be bound by any rules of society. Early English psychiatry used the term "moral insanity," which has much to recommend it. Psychopaths have also been described as charming, deceitful, remorseless, possessing a great sense of self-entitlement, and as being devious, unemotional, and cold-blooded in their behavior and in their crimes. All that can be said with any degree of certainty is that more men than women belong to this category: according to some researchers, men outnumber women by three to one, and according to others, by five to one. Another observation is that with age these traits become less pronounced and intense. Psychopaths seem to mellow as they grow older.

However, more recently it has been claimed by some forensic experts that while most criminals belong to the ASPD category, they are by no means all psychopaths. In the present context the use of violence is the chief criterion, and not all psychopaths are violent; some will commit nonviolent crimes, and others, despite their condition, will not cross the legal line and will never see the inside of a prison.

Literature does not give us many insights into this personality. Dostoevsky is usually quoted in this connection, especially with reference to one of his characters, the murderer Raskolnikov. But Raskolnikov becomes a repentant sinner in the end. He hands himself over to the police, having been assured by his mother and girlfriend of their undying love; this is not typical psychopathic behavior. Some of the characters in *The Possessed,* especially Verkhovensky, are nearer the stereotype, as are some of Zola's villains, especially those in *L'Assomoir,* but they are alcoholics, genetically preprogrammed, and anything but master criminals. Fagin in *Oliver Twist* is not really violent; Bill Stines, the murderer, is violent, but he is more a brutal gang leader than a full-fledged psychopath. Mr. Hyde makes sense only in juxtaposition to Dr. Jekyll. The psychopathic criminal does appear in the detective novel; it is not entirely clear what motivates Dr. Moriarty, but neither he nor the villains of the James Bond stories are masterpieces of psychological characterization. Pinkie Brown, the juvenile gangster in Graham Greene's *Brighton Rock,* comes very near to being a psychopath, but the author puts the blame for his condition partly on bourgeois society. Even in the early days of science fiction the figure of the pathologic blackmailer threatening the world with extinction made an appearance. Some of the books written around the turn of the last century bear rereading, such as the *The Crack of Doom* by Robert Cromie, Fred T. Jane's *The Violet Flame* (1899), and S. Andrew Wood's *I'll Blackmail the World* (1935). The modern movie has come nearer to a convincing characterization, with Peter Lorre as a serial killer in *M,* James Woods' character in *The Onion Fields,* and above all the character of Alex in *A Clockwork Orange* (a Stanley Kubrick movie based on the novel by Anthony Burgess). These characters commit acts of violence because they like it, and Burgess's villain in particular has fascinated students of psychopaths in action.

Another interesting example of a terrorist psychopath is Carlos Ramirez Santos, a.k.a. the Jackal. His wealthy parents were active in left-wing Venezuelan politics, and young Carlos become a graduate of the Lumumba University in Moscow. He claims to have killed some eighty people in his subsequent career, which is probably an exaggeration. Originally a member of the extreme left, he moved far away from his original inspiration. He operated on behalf of Libya, Syria, Iraq, and other regimes that were anything but left wing or revolutionary in character. He acquired the reputation of a gun for hire, mainly in the business to finance his opulent lifestyle. There could have been other ways to earn money, such as smuggling drugs, to pay for his nightlife in the capitals of Eastern Europe and the Middle East, but that employment might not have satisfied his destructive needs.

Carlos certainly liked to kill people, and when he was brought to trial in Paris in 1997 after being extradited by Sudan in 1994, he showed no remorse whatsoever. Like most psychopaths, he was quite fearless and he never admitted that what he had done was wrong. While a prisoner in Paris he complained to the European Court of Justice in Strasbourg that he had been illegally kidnapped and taken in chains to France. This complaint was ironic, for he had made his career, after all, by kidnapping people such as the OPEC ministers in Vienna. When he complained about his own misfortune, it was not an expression of a sense of humor, a quality notably absent in his mental makeup, but of the genuine conviction that he had been wronged.

There are variations of psychopathology that are rooted in culture and religion. Carlos would not normally have killed women, for this did not fit the Latin American macho revolutionary ethos. But the Islamists of Algeria and Afghanistan seem to specialize in the murder of women, and this has mainly to do with the position of women in the Islamic world. It is also connected to the negative attitude of the Koran toward women, which resembles the antifeminist nature of much of medieval Christianity. The *Malleus Malleficarum*, the standard work on witches and how to hunt them, says that women are a necessary evil and it should never be forgotten that they are liars and deceivers by nature. This expressed in a grotesque way what Christian theology had been saying for over a thousand years; it should be recalled, too, that the Talmud would not be mistaken for a feminist text either.

A psychopath need not necessarily be a sadist. While serial murderers need the "personal touch"—proximity to their victims—to gain satisfaction, sexual or otherwise, the modern mass murderer does not necessarily witness the death of his victim. By the time the bomb explodes he may be many miles away, or he may even detonate it from a great distance. For the heroes of the Marquis de Sade, torture was the greatest pleasure; Minski, one of Sade's characters, constructed a machine that enabled him to watch from his bed while as many as sixteen people were tortured or killed at the same time. On the other hand, it is not known whether Stalin or Hitler ever witnessed a murder, and it is known that Himmler positively disliked extermination camps, which he never visited while they were in operation.

So far our emphasis has been on individuals or small groups of people because they are the most likely candidates to use weapons of superviolence—a Unabomber at a higher level of technological sophistication. Individuals, in contrast to groups, might be exceedingly difficult to detect, as in the case of the Unabomber, or in the case of Franz Fuchs, the Austrian letter bomber, who remained undetected for years. A combination of features need to come together—madness and fanaticism on the one hand, and scientific and technological sophistication on the other—minimizing the prospects of realizing our worst fears. But the percentage of violent psychopaths in society is still considerable; even if we projected only one in a thousand, it would amount to fifty thousand in a country of fifty million. The degree of technical knowledge necessary to make superweapons is becoming accessible to an ever-wider circle of people as time goes by, and the number of potential users of these weapons is growing exponentially.

The issue of weapons of mass destruction has been discussed so far in terms of individual psychopathology. But the new kind of terrorism could also be considered by some to be a rational strategy. Hitler, Stalin, Pol Pot, Idi Amin, Bokassa, and other reprehensible twentieth-century leaders fit the terrorist type, but that they were textbook psychopaths is doubtful. They had some of the specific features of the disorder but not others. The one common denominator was the use of terror as a political tool.

In the future, weapons of mass destruction will be considered as a rational means of achieving military and political aims under certain conditions. Had they been available in the past, their use almost certainly would have been seen as reasonable to a considerable number of Roman emperors and their antagonists, to Byzantium and its northern and eastern neighbors, to the Crusaders, and to Islamic armies. Their use would have been unfashionable in the age of chivalry and the eighteenth century, but one can be less certain about Napoleon and his enemies. In the First World War these weapons were actually used. They were not used in World War II; the reason was, as noted earlier, fear of retaliation, and the same is true today.

Cultural and moral context is of decisive importance in a discussion of weapons of mass destruction. It is unthinkable that such weapons will be used by one European or American country against another, but it is not at all unthinkable in Asia and Africa. And since the fear of retaliation will continue to exist, the temptation will be great to use proxies who may be difficult to trace. At this point the possibility, or indeed the likelihood, of terrorists operating with weapons of mass destruction has become part of the international agenda.

The use of weapons of mass destruction may proceed gradually rather than swiftly. This might involve the use of a small nuclear device, or biological or chemical weapons on a limited scale. The number of victims in such a contingency would be counted in the thousands rather than hundreds of thousands or millions. Retaliation in such a case would also be limited. But once such a border is crossed, the danger of escalation is very great.

Discussion of the weapons of superviolence and their use leads us, of course, well beyond the confines of the issue of terrorism. Traditional terrorism is bound to persist side by side with these new weapons, and the use of these weapons may not be limited to terrorists, since they can be used by states as well as by individuals. But there is little doubt that access to these weapons is likely to be the most striking new development in terrorism in the years and decades to come.

THE NATURAL HISTORY OF PANIC

One of the consequences of terrorism on a massive scale is seldom mentioned and has been infrequently studied. Yet it could cause as much damage as the terrorist act itself: panic—the chaotic and disruptive response on the part of the population that is likely to occur when weapons of mass destruction are used or the threat exists that they may be used.

This subject has not been more widely discussed because such a disaster has not occurred, and because the only precedent passed without panic. The meltdown at Chernobyl in 1985 and the panic that ensued was in essential respects untypical. To begin with, the facts were known to those in authority almost from the very beginning, even if the full implications were not clear to them. It happened in a dictatorship, and the media were kept under strict control, and later on allowed to publish only information that had been approved by the government. It happened in a society that was not affluent; the majority of people had no private cars, and thus they could not try to escape and, by doing so, cause giant traffic jams on the roads leading away from the site of the disaster, making any orderly evacuation impossible. It is easy to imagine what might happen if a biological weapon—the precise character of which remained uncertain for hours, perhaps for days—were used in a terrorist attack. Unless there were some control over the media, the consequences could be devastating, leaving people in a state of shock and confusion. If such an accident were to happen in the densely populated areas of Europe or America, the ensuing panic would make both evacuation and effective countermeasures exceedingly difficult.

One should not confuse panic with the condition called panic disorder. Students of psychiatry are familiar with panic disorder, which afflicts slightly more than one percent of the population in the United States and probably an equal percentage elsewhere. (Panic disorder appears frequently together with agoraphobia and somatic symptoms. It has been well studied, and its symptoms can often be controlled through medication.) Panic disorder is not triggered by major disasters; paradoxically, a disaster can have a curative effect inasmuch as it restores sanity to the sufferer by a form of shock therapy. Facing real danger, the imagined danger disappears, at least temporarily. True panic is contagious, a crowd phenomenon, not an individual one.

The consequences of a mass panic in both material and human terms can be huge; they can lead to a paralysis of normal life, epidemics, post-traumatic stress, and tremendous anxiety, especially if the nature and extent of the danger remains unknown. How is one to know in a case of radioactive contamination how widely the radiation has spread? How to know in the case of a biological attack who has been infected and who not? The immediate effect, to give one example, of spraying an infectious biological agent in the distribution vents of an airport would be limited, restricted to a few hundreds or thousands. But in the meantime an equal number of people, infected without knowing it, would have flown to other parts of the country or abroad, spreading the disease to faraway places. The economic consequences could be disastrous and the political consequences horrible. They may exceed the fantasies depicted in the most ghastly horror movies. All that can be said with any certainty is that the more developed a society, the more vulnerable it is to the consequences of panic.

No society is entirely defenseless against the most insidious act of terrorism: attack with biological agents. There is intelligence that can, at least in general terms, alert a victim country to possible dangers. And there are technical means, which will be improved no doubt in the future, that can detect at least some of the agents soon after the event.

In the case of an attack by nuclear or chemical weapons it should be able to know the extent of the area affected within a short time. A 1995 Presidential Decision Directive (number 39) outlined bureaucratic responsibility for dealing with such an emergency with regard to both the short term—crisis management—and the long term—consequence management. Present plans have the FBI as the lead agency for the short term, and FEMA in charge of dealing with the long-term consequences, with the Departments of Health, Energy, and others involved.

Such management has to be hierarchical, because there can be no confusion in an emergency about bureaucratic responsibilities and the chain of command. It is another question altogether whether the local authorities are prepared to cope with such emergencies—whether they have the know-how, the personnel, and the technical facilities. Few states have made contingency plans and set up the means to carry them out.

In other parts of the world these problems have not been approached on even a theoretical level, nor is it likely that such attention will have been given or resources allocated before a major disaster occurs. This contingency planning is not a priority in democracies, but dictatorships are not any more apt to be prepared, except by virtue of having the means to impose censorship, which might limit the spread of panic during the early stages.

Is a major terrorist attack always bound to lead to panic? There was little panic after Oklahoma City, the World Trade Center, and terrorist attacks in other parts of the world that involved great loss of life. In Algeria there was an exodus from the villages attacked by Islamic terrorists to the greater safety of the towns nearby. But these occurrences concerned traditional weapons, whereas in the case of weapons of mass destruction the reaction is likely to be infinitely more intense and on a wider scale. Reactions during the Iraqi inspection crisis in early 1998 showed that the magnitude of the danger with respect to these weapons had not widely registered. Despite countless articles on the weapons of mass destruction and their likely consequences, the full implications are not understood. Most countries believe that the threat is far from their borders, that it could not happen at home, and have exhibited the well-known tendency to repress menacing information. There is the hope that medical science will find an antidote against anthrax and sarin, and that diplomacy and international conventions against biological and chemical weapons will work, even if there is no effective inspection system and sanctions against violations. All this seems to make a dangerous panic more likely, for the deeper the illusions about the efficacy of international action, the greater the shock that will follow the use of such weapons on a massive scale.

"JUST TERRORISM" OR JUST BLOODLUST?

Much of the emphasis so far has been on the possibility of weapons of superviolence becoming accessible to terrorists. During the 1950s and '60s, a great many apocalyptic scenarios were created that in the end did not come about, even though some of the cleverest people of the time were among the experts constructing these scenarios.

But the state of affairs today is not comparable with the situation forty years ago. At that time nuclear weapons were in the hands of a small number of states, and there was mutually assured destruction, whether it was spelled out or not. Those who had access to these weapons were more or less responsible people, acting rationally, at least as far as their own survival was concerned. There was no laughing and dancing in the streets of America or later in the Soviet Union when atomic bombs were detonated, unlike the mood in the streets of New Delhi and Karachi in 1998. Those who originally constructed atomic bombs were not fanatics or religious warriors or rabid nationalists bent on world conquest or the destruction of large stretches of the globe. Today access to these weapons has become much wider, and there is no mutually assured destruction against terrorists, only deterrence or retaliation to a limited extent. There is no modern Clausewitz to draw up the rules of war for the atomic age, and there are no known strategic solutions in this new age of conflict.

For some governments in Asia and the Middle East weapons of mass destruction used by proxies may become the means for continuation of war that has become too costly by other means. There are more of these actors than states, and the convictions, mental states, and behaviors of the new players are unpredictable. Hence the need to think the unthinkable.

Traditional terrorism will certainly continue; for years to come it will remain the prevalent mode of conflict, sometimes in its "pure" form, at other times within the framework of civil wars or general lawlessness.

In the past, some observers assumed that terrorists were idealistic and courageous young people, patriots and social revolutionaries, driven by intolerable conditions, by oppression and tyranny, to undertake desperate actions. This assessment was not always incorrect: there was oppression then and there is now; there were and are social conflicts in which violence seems to be the only possible effective response. There are no doubt patriots and genuine revolutionaries among current terrorists.

But this is no longer the typical pattern of terrorism. Any survey of the world map of terrorism that looks at those parts of the world where the most people are killed and maimed will show other related features. The map will show growing fanaticism. It also will show the growth of indiscriminate murder and sheer aggression, with ideology or religious motivation, once believed to be all-important, often taking a secondary place.

With this in mind, we should reassess the role of ideology in terrorism. It should be clear that in every generation it was not the people most deeply convinced of the righteousness of their cause who were the activists, but the most aggressive and militant. Wordsworth once made a comment on a Shakespeare play about the "motive hunting of a motiveless malignity." This consideration has been ignored for too long.

Of course, some creed is usually needed—even blind rage has to find a focus—but how often could a terrorist of the extreme left, but for some biographical accident, say, the influence of a friend or some charismatic figure he encountered, have turned to the extreme right or some sectarian group, and vice versa? Carlos was a precursor of this breed, and so were the "Afghanis," and the guns for hire, who are now involved in much of the terrorism from Algeria and Bosnia to the Philippines. The six young Islamists who slaughtered foreign tourists at Luxor in 1997 belong to this breed. Far from being desperate and deeply religious, investigation established that they were neither, but rather misanthropic, aggressive students from middle-class families, eager to find an outlet for their anger.

An Egyptian Muslim thinker has aptly described the mainsprings of this activism: in a time of transition in which nothing remains constant, people become very insecure. "A young Arab, part of an oversized family, competing for scarce jobs, unable to marry because he is poor, perhaps a migrant to a rapidly expanding city feels like a man lost in a desert without signposts. One morning he picks up a copy of a book by Sayid Qutb [a radical Muslim Brotherhood thinker executed under Nasser] and he is born again on the spot. This is what he needed, instant certainty, a framework in which to interpret the landscape before him, to resolve the problems and tensions of life and, even more deliciously, a way of feeling superior and in control." But the initial enthusiasm, usually acquired in one's early twenties, "loses steam some seven to ten years later. Prison and torture, the frequent lot of the Islamic radical, may serve to prolong commitment but ultimately a majority of these born-again Muslims relapse, seemingly no better or worse than before." The writer calls it the "Salafi burnout," after a radical sect in the history of Islam.

This pattern describes very well the origins of one brand of the new terrorism. But there are others, and they do not fit the stereotypical assumptions of an earlier age according to which evil was banal, jihad was an Islamic synonym for something like a combination of introspection and the Salvation Army, and all criminals were sick people who needed to be treated in hospitals. Evil and malignancy were not terms widely used, and aggression was thought to be rooted in an unhappy, deprived childhood or other unfortunate social circumstances.

Extending understanding to the terrorist by advocating cultural and moral relativism is easy in the safety of Western universities, but the perspective of the victimized residents of Algerian and Afghan villages or the inhabitants of Rwanda is likely to be different.

More recently the conviction has gained ground that aggression is, at least in part, in our genes, that there are very few truly peaceful societies, and that primitive man often mutilated his victims. It is the story of Achilles at Troy not just killing Hector but dishonoring his corpse. It is Atreus in Greek mythology killing the sons of his brother Thyestes and serving them up at a banquet of reconciliation. Hate, revenge, and evil are a genetic problem, and civilization has faced an uphill struggle in its attempt to sublimate this murderous instinct and spread the gospel of peace.

But it is a genetic problem only in part, and education, culture, and the values of a society still play a paramount role. If the findings of the ethnologists and biologists are right, there is a general predisposition toward aggression, but in fact only a few people engage in systematic acts of violence.

St. Thomas Aquinas asked whether it is always sinful to wage war, and he reached the conclusion that given three preconditions it is permissible to do so: first, the blessing of the sovereign—for it was not the business of the private individual to declare war—second, a just cause, and third, a rightful intention, that is to say, the advancement of good or the avoidance of evil.

A just cause per se was not sufficient, and Augustine before Aquinas observed that the passion for inflicting harm, the cruel thirst for vengeance, an unpacific and relentless spirit, the fever of revolt, and the lust for power are all rightly condemned in the conduct of war. Four hundred years after Aquinas, Hugo Grotius noted in an often quoted statement that he saw in the whole Christian world a license for fighting at which even barbarous nations might blush: wars were begun on trifling pretexts or none at all, and carried on without any reverence for law, divine or human. A declaration of war seemed to let loose every crime.

Of course, all this is equally true with regard to terrorism. Terrorism so often is not the ultima ratio after all other means to reach agreement have failed, but the immediate response to any provocation. It certainly lets loose every imaginable crime. Most terrorists claim to conduct a just war and insist on being treated as soldiers. But they want to have it both ways, for at the same time they think they are entitled to ignore the norms anchored in international law that protect the rights of innocent noncombatants and require the humane treatment of hostages, to give but two examples. International law does not bind them; it is an invention of the imperialist West or of the exploiting classes; it does not apply to the treatment of infidels, or to those who belong to another class, or people, or religion.

Until a decade or two ago an unwritten law—or at least certain norms—ruled the behavior of terrorists. This law was not always observed, but only a few boasted of ignoring it. This has now changed, which raises the question of whether there can be any just terrorism, even if the cause is just and we ignore the issue of the weapons of mass destruction. Bayard, the war leader who was the epitome of chivalry, had all prisoners killed who were crossbowmen, on the grounds that the crossbow was a cowardly and treacherous weapon. One wonders what Bayard would have made of the terrorists of the late twentieth century, our contemporary crossbowmen, placing bombs in supermarkets and killing babies. But terrorism will go on, and indications are that the struggle will become more bitter.

Can one speculate about the frequency and intensity of terrorism in the years to come, about national conflicts and messianic expectations, about aggression, fanaticism, and paranoia? Much of the terrorism rampant at present has to do with national and ethnic conflict, and unfortunately there is no reason to expect that these conflicts will decrease in intensity in the years to come. William James once wrote that the only hope for peace is redirecting the passion for war into other channels. Paradoxically, the passion for war is redirected now into civil war and terrorism, because full-scale war has become so expensive.

There are regions of the world in which there is much less terrorism than in others, and there have been periods in modern history in which terrorism occurred very rarely. But these were usually times or places in which disasters, such as world wars, totalitarian rule, major economic crises, or natural calamity preoccupied the people. Terrorism existed long before the age of nationalism, and will continue beyond it. There is much terrorism today that has nothing to do with national liberation or ethnic conflict, and this includes some of the bloodiest varieties, such as that in Algeria.

Such conflicts do not go on forever, and after the bloodletting has reached a certain stage it often decreases or even vanishes. Traditionally, people have fought for gain and for glory, to become masters of others, as Hobbes and the realistic school put it, to which one should add food and, in the future, water. But these motivations are those of societies rather than individuals; terrorists by and large are not primarily interested in gain and glory, but instead want a state or a society in their own image, cleansed of their enemies.

THE MUSLIM QUESTION

Nationalist and religious fanatics have been active around the globe: the Aum were Buddhist, a Jew killed Prime Minister Rabin, a Hindu killed Mahatma Gandhi, a Sikh assassinated Indira Gandhi and a Tamil her son, Rajiv. Christianity had its jihad, the Crusades, seven hundred years ago. But to deny the specific virulence of Islamic terrorism in our time is self-deception, an exercise in political—or ecumenical—correctness. If we ignore for the moment the tribal violence in Africa, about 80 percent of war and violence occurs at the present time inside and between Muslim countries, and among the myriad factions within the Muslim world.

It is perfectly true that in the Middle Ages there was more tolerance in Muslim Spain than in Christian Europe, that Mehrez ibn Khalaf saved the Jews of Tunis in the tenth century, and Emir Abdelkader the Christians of Damascus in the twelfth. Once upon a time the Koranic message "La Ikraha fi'l dini" ("no coercion in matters of religion"), was enough to stop a pogrom. But Ibn Khalaf and Abdelkader have been dead for a long time, and nowadays it is the message of jihad in the literal sense rather than the tolerant one that is the most prominent feature of militant Islam. These terrorists may be a minority, but few dare to speak out against them.

Is a decline in Muslim violence at all likely? All one can say is maybe, in some countries but not in others. The miserable political, social, and economic situation in many of these countries are significant factors, and there is no sign of improvement on the horizon. Overpopulation and poverty generate new tensions, and the access to weapons of mass destruction refuels desires for power, aggression, and expansion. In principle, given oil riches and a united Arab front, a new revival along the lines of the golden age of Spain is not impossible, but today it seems only a distant dream.

RULES OF ENGAGEMENT?

Fanatical violence is found almost everywhere, among Hindus destroying an old mosque and slaughtering Muslims and Sikhs, among Israelis plotting to kill Arabs, and in Christian Europe and America. It may even increase in the future, as the result of the emergence of some new sects preaching their violent message or because of social or political upheavals. War has certainly become more brutal in many respects since the eighteenth century. Emmerich de Vattel, one of the fathers of international law, wrote in 1740: "Let us never forget that our enemies are men." We cannot count how often that has been forgotten in the twentieth century.

Restraint in warfare goes back to ancient days. When the Greeks sent emissaries to Troy, Homer notes that they were treated "in accordance to the laws which govern the intercourse between nations." The fighting between the two sides was to stop at nightfall, and the heroes would exchange presents, such as swords. (But it is also true that Diomedes and Odysseus on occasion did attack and kill sleeping enemies.) As for the civilian population, less humane standards prevailed; if they were lucky, they survived as slaves. In the age of chivalry, Orlando or Roland would never fight at night, and he and the Saracen nobleman with whom he had been engaged in a heroic duel would sleep peacefully side by side. There was no fighting during winter in those days, and there were other laws, written and unwritten, such as the obligation to help the shipwrecked, even of the enemy.

In 1139, the Second Lateran Council not only banned certain treacherous weapons such as the crossbow and siege machines but established the Treuga Dei, the Truce of God, according to which whole categories of people were protected: travelers, pilgrims, merchants, and peasants and their animals. Fighting, at least in theory, could take place only on certain days. These rules applied only to conflicts among Christians, and not to wars against infidels. The Saracens and the Turks behaved then, by and large, as the Christians did during the age of chivalry. Curiously, the IRA and some other terrorist groups retained something of this tradition in the age of terrorism by announcing truces over holiday periods. And longer truces were declared by the IRA, the ETA, and other terrorist groups while political negotiations went on with the authorities.

War in Europe in the Middle Ages, except for the wars of religion, were more of a game of kings; this was also true with regard to the Indian subcontinent. Then, during the seventeenth century, an international law of war developed, which was followed around the turn of the last century by various conventions that established rules for land and sea warfare. After the Second World War, the Geneva Conventions (1949) brought these rules up to date. In several subsequent international agreements, biological weapons were outlawed (London, 1972), as were the development, production, and stockpiling of chemical weapons (Paris, 1992). The use of nuclear and thermonuclear weapons was banned by resolutions of the General Assembly of the United Nations (1961–62).

Other conventions dealt specifically with terrorist attacks. One of these referred to crimes against diplomats, another to hostage taking, and a third to the hijacking of aircraft. These conventions were not universally welcomed. To justify the production and use of nonconventional weapons some radical Arab states, such as Iraq, argued that Europe and North America should not be allowed to keep at least some of their arsenal of unconventional weapons while Third World countries were forbidden to make and use them. The same spokesmen maintained that it was impossible to apply in the Middle East rules that had developed in Europe and America. For while war between two European countries was unthinkable except perhaps in the Balkans, the Middle East was far less stable and to defend themselves governments had to consider all kinds of weapons— or, in the case of Iraq, to use in an attack. Earlier, in 1973, a United Nations resolution had declared that the struggle of people under colonial or alien domination and racist regimes for their self-determination and independence was in full accordance with the principles of international law. This referred specifically to guerrilla warfare and terrorism, and, because "alien domination" and "racist regime" could be claimed by almost any ethnic minority in the world, this legitimized a great deal of terrorism all over the globe.

Some of the international conventions listed have been observed, but most of them have not. Why this is the case is of considerable interest but is of little relevance in a discussion of terrorism, because terrorists have not been bound by international law and conventions. Terrorists might argue with some degree of justification that to accept humanist rules would condemn them to impotence, for their only chance to succeed is precisely through breaking established norms. There was a code of behavior among European terrorists before World War I, such as not deliberately killing innocent people. But nationalist terrorists seldom observed this rule, for the victims were likely to belong to the enemy ethnic group and for this reason were unworthy of special consideration. Before the turn of the century, one anarchist terrorist proclaimed that there were no innocents, the first argument justifying the killing of uninvolved bystanders.

The idea of finding an acceptable code of behavior for contemporary terrorists is a contradiction in terms. To rule out the indiscriminate violence of terrorism is to emasculate it, to defang it. Terrorist groups may refrain from using weapons of mass destruction, but only for pragmatic reasons—that is to say, for the same reasons that chemical weapons were not used on the battlefields of World War II.

To what extent will the stigma attached to the use of biological and chemical weapons influence terrorist groups? Various reasons have already been given for the fact that many terrorist groups will probably refrain from using weapons of mass destruction. It is also possible that the more radical elements will be restrained by their own comrades. But it would be unrealistic to build on this hope at a time when many governments are undertaking major efforts to acquire such weapons. Governments have obviously more to fear from using such weapons or even merely threatening to do so than do small, sometimes anonymous groups.

Even if nationalist passions and religious fanaticism should abate, there is not much ground for optimism, because the idea of a holy war that is a sacred duty and permits the use of all weapons and unlimited bloodshed may be put in service of nonreligious interests. The baby killers of Algeria are not pious Muslims, for according to Islam, Muslim women and children should not be killed or mutilated, even in the course of a jihad. In fact, most historians believe that the Islamic wars of conquest in the past were motivated more by secular than religious reasons.

The sad truth is that the new terrorists may appear on the fringes of nearly any extremist movement. Even if radicals should become more moderate, there will be for the foreseeable future individuals firmly convinced that, in the words of Goethe's Mephisto, all that comes into being is worthy of destruction. Neither madness nor fanaticism will vanish from the world, even if the current terrorist frenzies give way to more sober trends. All that one can hope for is that the damage will be limited to one country or two and not cause a general conflagration, and that the punishment meted out to transgressors will be so devastating as to deter imitators. But the new terrorists do not seem to be skilled in balancing the liabilities and assets that accrue as consequences of their actions.

There has never been a "just terrorism" doctrine analogous to the idea of a "just war," but some of the terrorist campaigns of the past were fought for a just cause, with self-imposed rules of engagement, against oppressors and tyrants. But this notion belongs to a period in which terrorist acts were directed against individuals who were considered personally guilty for one reason or another. Since then terrorism has proceeded from limited to total and indiscriminate warfare, certainly as far as the targets are concerned, quite often the aim is simply to kill or maim as many people as possible. For some terrorist groups, the campaigns have become total with regard to not only the acts but also the objectives: the Islamic radicals active in Algeria or Egypt or elsewhere in the Middle East want not reform or a negotiated peace but the overthrow of the system, and those fighting against Israel want its annihilation. (There are exceptions: the objectives of other terrorist groups, such as the IRA and the ETA and the Tamil Tigers, have been more limited.)

Can there be a just terrorist campaign that is total in character and aims at the complete destruction of the enemy? The answer of the protagonists of holy war will be affirmative, but the philosophers of international law will hardly agree. Once the number of victims produced by a war that is trying to right a wrong becomes incommensurate, the carnage cannot be justified by any accepted moral standards. The terrorists, of course, do not accept this but the escalation of terrorism in the future will not occur without a response from the attacked. When terrorism becomes a real danger, those engaging in it will no longer be able to run and hide, but will be treated by those attacked as they see fit, as a *hostis*, an enemy of humankind, and thus outside the law. This will apply, *a fortiori*, if the weapons used are nonconventional. Such an escalation is now gradually under way in the Middle East, Africa, and Asia. Diderot once noted that the transition from fanaticism to barbarism is but one step, and if present trends continue there is every reason for grim forebodings. What we know about past ages of barbarism is frightening enough; the consequences of aggressive madness in the age of high technology and the era of weapons of mass destruction may well be beyond our imagination. Megaterrorism could well become what Florus, a Roman historian, wrote about a contemporary: *fax et turbo sequentis centuri*—the incendiary torch and the devastating storm of the coming century.

Bibliographical Essay

TERRORISM AND HISTORY

The most comprehensive handbook on terrorism is Alex P. Schmid, *Political Terrorism* (Amsterdam, 1988, 2nd edition). Since this is now partly out of date, the reader may find the first edition, published in 1984, more useful. Of the many chronologies and bibliographies, those edited by Edward F. Mickolus are probably the most detailed. The first was published by the CIA in 1976, subsequent ones in 1980, 1988, 1993, and 1997. Amos Lakos, *Terrorism 1980–1990* pub. date should also be mentioned. There exist valuable databases—above all the one at St. Andrew's University supervised by Bruce Hoffman, who is also the author of *Inside Terrorism*, London, 1998.

The two leading journals in the field are *Studies in Conflict and Terrorism*, published in the United States, and *Terrorism and Political Violence*, which is published in London. For a general survey readers are referred to W. Laqueur, *Guerrilla* (Boston, 1976; most recent edition, with a new introduction, New Brunswick, 1997) and *Terrorism* (Boston, 1977; a later edition appeared under the title *The Age of Terrorism*, Boston, 1985). I am also the editor of two resource books, *The Terrorism Reader* (New York, 1978 and 1987), and *The Guerrilla Reader* (New York, 1977).

Terrorism in Northern Ireland has been documented and analyzed more fully than any other such movement. For general surveys, see J. Bowyer Bell, *The Irish*

Troubles: A Generation of Violence, 1967–1992 (New York, 1993), and Tim Pat Cogan, *The IRA* (Glasgow, 1987). See also J. Bowyer Bell, *IRA Tactics and Targets* (Dublin, 1990); M. L. R. Smith, *Fighting for Ireland* (London, 1995); Patrick Bishop and Eamonn Malliem, *The Provisional IRA* (London, 1989); Andrew Boyd, *Holy War in Belfast* (Belfast, 1987); Steve Bruce, *The Red Hand: Protestant Paramilitaries in Northern Ireland* (Oxford, 1992); and the same author's *The Edge of the Union,* about the Ulster Loyalists (Oxford, 1994). For an earlier work on the Protestant paramilitary groups, see Sarah Nelson, *Ulster's Uncertain Defenders* (Appletree, 1984), and Kevin Kelley, *The Longest War* (London, 1990). Personal accounts include Shane O'Doherty, *The Volunteer* (London, 1993); Eamonn Collins, *Killing Rage* (London, 1997); Douglass McFerran, *The IRA Man* (Boulder, CO, 1997); and Colm Keena, *The Biography of Gerry Adams,* the head of Sinn Fein (Dublin, 1990). Current official pronouncements of the IRA can be found in the periodical *An Phoblacht/Republican News.*

The literature on ETA is much more sparse. For the historical background and a general survey, see Stanley Payne, *Basque Nationalism* (Reno, 1975); Robert P. Clark, *The Basque Insurgents, .ETA, 1952–1980* (Madison, WI, 1984); John Sullivan, *ETA and Basque Nationalism* (London, 1988); Jose M. Garmendia, *Historia de ETA* (San Sebastian, 1980–83); Luciano Rincon, *ETA (1974–1984)* (Barcelona, 1985); and Juan Linz, *Conflicto en Euskadi* (Madrid, 1986). On the activities of ETA in France, see James E. Jacob, *Hills of Conflict: Basque Nationalism in France* (Reno, 1994). For a more recent review based on a wide reading of the literature, see Goldie Shabad and Francisco Jose Llera Ramo, "Political Violence in a Democratic State: Basque Terrorism in Spain" in Martha Crenshaw (ed.), *Terrorism in Context* (University Park, PA, 1995).

The literature on West German terrorism has been surveyed elsewhere in this book. For the short-lived French ultraleft terrorism, see Michael Y. Dartnell, *Action Directe: Ultra Left Terrorism in France 1977–87* (London, 1995). Postmortems on Italian terrorism are D. Novelli and N. Tranfaglia, *Vite sospese. Le generazioni del terrorismo* (Milan, 1988); Leonard Weinberg and W. L. Eubank, *The Rise and Fall of Italian Terrorism* (Boulder, CO, 1987); and H. Hess et al. (ed.), *Angriff auf das Herz des Staates* (Frankfurt, 1988).

Almost all the literature on terrorism has focused until recently on left-wing and ethnic terrorism. Peter Waldmann, *Beruf Terrorist* (Munich, 1993), a study of individuals who became terrorists, does not include a single right-wing terrorist. The massive survey edited by Martha Crenshaw, *Terrorism in Context* (1995, mentioned elsewhere), does not contain a single contribution on right-wing or religious terrorism. This is understandable, since left-wing terrorism was far more prominent until the 1980s, and academic studies, as a rule, do not deal with events that happened a mere few years ago. On the other hand, a perspective was created that did not quite correspond with events in the real world, and this could lead to generalizations based on the assumption that terrorism was mainly (or solely) a left-wing phenomenon. More recently, to redress this balance, a great number of monographs and articles in professional journals have been published focusing on right-wing and religious terrorism, sometimes to the detriment of the study of the terrorism of the extreme left, which, after all, has not altogether disappeared from the world.

WEAPONS OF MASS DESTRUCTION

Among the indispensable sources in this field is first and foremost Ron Purver, "Chemical and Biological Terrorism: The Threat According to the Open Literature," published in June 1995. The author, a member of the Canadian Security Intelligence Service, has provided a very detailed review of the significant publications in the field. The first major technical study on which most of the subsequent works have drawn was B. J. Berkowitz, *Superviolence: The Civil Threat of Mass Destruction Weapons.* It was published in 1972 on behalf of the ADCON Corporation. Among the many subsequent publications were Robert Kupperman and *Darrell Trent* (1979); *Kupperman and David Smith* (1993); Brad Roberts (ed.) *Biological Weapons* (Washington, 1993); and Brad Roberts, *Terrorism with Chemical and Biological Weapons* (Alexandria, VA, 1997). The OTA (U.S. Government Office of Technology Assessment) study, *Technology against Terrorism* (Washington, January 1992 and September 1991), should also be mentioned, as well as the various congressional hearings, such as *The Global Proliferation of the Weapons of Mass Destruction*, Committee on Governmental Affairs (March 1996), and earlier reports (1993); *Countering the Biological and Chemical Weapons Threat*, House Committee on Armed Services; and *The Biological Weapons Anti-Terrorism Act*, Senate Committee on the Judiciary (1990). The earlier Senate Committee on Foreign Relations Hearings (1989) work, *Chemical and Biological Weapons Threat: The Urgent Need for Response*, is still of interest.

The most up to date and authoritative source on biological warfare as of this writing is the special issue of *JAMA*, the *Journal of the American Medical Association*, August 6, 1997, which also includes many bibliographical references. Among the books on the Aum attack in March 1995 the following should be singled out: D. W. Brackett, *Holy Terror: Armageddon in Tokyo* (New York, 1996), and also David E. Kaplan and Andrew Marshall, *The Cult at the End of the World* (New York, 1996). Another invaluable source of material from the general literature is a privately published quarterly digest by members of the BETAC Corporation, *Quarterly Clippings Information on Chemical and Biological Terrorism* (1995/1996). Two important works on the early history of chemical welfare are Donald Richter, *Chemical Soldiers* (University of Kansas, 1992), and L. F. Haber, *The Poisonous Cloud* (Oxford, 1986). Also M. Szölösi-Janze, *Fritz Haber* (Munich, 1998).

The literature on nuclear terrorism, or, to be precise, the potential of nuclear terrorism, is extensive, but most of it is dispersed over a great many congressional hearings, papers published by the Departments of Defense and Energy, publications of the International Institute of Strategic Studies in London and SIPRI in Stockholm, and hundreds of position papers published over the years by a variety of think tanks.

Among earlier collections of essays are the following: A. R. Norton and M. H. Greenberg (eds.); *Studies in Nuclear Terrorism* (Boston, 1979) and P. Leventhal and Y. Alexander (eds.), *Preventing Nuclear Terrorism: The Report and Papers of the International Task Force on Prevention of Nuclear Terrorism* (Lexington, 1987). See also Peter de Leon and others, *The Threat of Nuclear Terrorism* (The Rand Corporation, Santa Monica, 1988). Among other Rand papers, Brian Jenkins, *The Likelihood of Nuclear Terrorism* (1985), and B. Jenkins, *Will Terrorists Go Nuclear* (1976), should be mentioned, as should Bruce Hoffman, *The Potential Threat to Nuclear Commercial Facilities* (1985). Various articles on the subject as well as reports on conferences dealing with these topics have appeared in *Terrorism, An International Journal* and in *International Security*—for instance, Thomas Schelling, "Thinking about Nuclear Terrorism" (Summer 1982).

The literature about proliferation, especially after the disintegration of the Soviet Union, has been equally extensive. A few examples should suffice: Graham T. Allison et al., *Avoiding Nuclear Anarchy* (Cambridge, MA, 1996); a recent Senate report (Committee on Governmental Affairs) titled *Global Proliferation of Weapons of Mass Destruction* (Washington, March 1996); *Proliferation: Threat and Response*, published by the Office of the Secretary of Defense (April 1996; new edition October 1997); *The Threat of Nuclear Diversion*, a statement by the then director of the CIA, John Deutch, also published in March 1996; and *The Nuclear Black Force*, a CSIS Task Force Project that appeared in 1996. Mr. Deutch's statement includes a day-by-day chronology of nuclear smuggling incidents that occurred during 1994–96. Other reports and chronologies concerning nuclear smuggling can be found in *Trends in Organized Crime* and *Transnational Organized Crime, 1995–1998*.

The literature on information warfare and cyberterrorism is of very recent date; much of the information can be found on the Internet and in articles in the professional literature, such as the *Journal of Electronic Defense*. By necessity much is speculative, and in view of rapidly changing technology it is quickly overtaken by new developments. Two useful bibliographies should be mentioned: *Information Warfare* by Diana Simpson, issued by Air University Library in August 1997, and the more comprehensive *Information Warfare* by Tomma Pastorett, also issued by the Air University Library, December 1996.

Among recent publications and extended position papers are the following: *Critical Foundations. Protecting America's Infrastructures*, the report by the President's Commission on Critical Infrastructure Protection (Washington, October 1997), and a collection of essays published by the Rand Corporation, edited by John Arquilla and David Rondfeldt, *In Athena's Camp* (Santa Monica, 1997). Among earlier works are Martin Libicki, *Defending Cyberspace* (New York, 1996), and the same author's *What Is Information Warfare* (1995). See also Lawrence T. Greenberg et al., *Information Warfare and International Law* (1997); Alan D. Campen et al. (eds.), *Cyberwar* (1996); Gary D. Wheatley et al., *Information Warfare and Deterrence* (1996); Science Applications, *Information Warfare* (1995); and another collection of essays published by the National Defense University, *Information Warfare*, 1995.

TERRORIST MOTIVES

The professional literature on violence and aggression is enormous. Articles on the subject can be found in periodicals such as *Advances in the Study of Aggression,* vol. 1 (1984 et seq.), *Violence and Victims, Journal of Preventive Psychiatry, Deviant Behavior,* and *Advances in Criminological Theory.* On fanaticism and extreme behavior, see Maxwell Taylor, *The Fanatics* (London, 1991), and Josef Rudin, *Fanaticism, A Psychological Analysis* (Notre Dame, 1969). A good overview covering attempts to explain fanaticism is Guenter Hole, *Fanatismus* (Freiburg, 1995). A psychoanalytical approach is presented in A. Haynal, M. Molnar, and G. de Puymege, *Le fanatisme* (Paris, 1980). Other works of interest in this context are U. Aeschbacher, *Faschismus und Begeisterung* (Essen, 1992), and St. Pfuertner, *Fundamentalismus, die Flucht ins Radikale* (Freiberg, 1991). Details on assassinations and multiple homicide can be found in new editions of standard forensic texts such as John Gunn and P. J. Taylor, *Forensic Psychiatry* (Oxford, 1993). A history of political assassinations is Franklin L. Ford, *Political Murder* (Cambridge, MA, 1985).

On the psychological roots of terrorism and on the limits of psychological inquiry into this subject there have been relatively few articles, but see Walter Reich and Jerrold M. Post in Walter Reich (ed.), *Origins of Terrorism,* (Cambridge, 1990), as well as articles by Franco Ferracutti and David C. Rapoport. A recent contribution to this field of study is Robert S. Robins and Jerrold M. Post, *Political Paranoia, the Psychopolitics of Hatred* (New Haven, 1997). Relevant articles by H. H. A. Cooper, David G. Hubbard, W. Rasch, and R. R. Corrado can be found in the professional literature. On suicide, H. L. P. Resnik (ed.), *Suicidal Behaviors* (Northvale, NJ, 1994), is a good introductory work written by many hands; U. Singer, *Massenselbstmord* (Stuttgart, 1980) deals specifically with the phenomenon of mass suicide.

If the literature on the psychology of terrorism (and violence in general) is enormous, the literature on violent religious sects is truly boundless. It includes works on the most recent manifestations, such as Stuart A. Wright (ed.), *Armageddon in Waco* (Chicago, 1995), and the U.S. Department of Justice official report on the events at Waco (Washington, D.C., October 8, 1993), as well as general works dealing with millenarian prophecies in America, such as Paul Boyer, *When Time Shall Be No More* (Cambridge, MA, 1992), and Klaus Vondung, *Die Apokalpsye in Deutschland* (Munich, 1988).

The classic books about apocalyptic movements in the Middle Ages are for the early Middle Ages: Steven Runciman, *The Medieval Manichee* (Cambridge, England), and Norman Cohn, *The Pursuit of the Millennium.* Essential handbooks for the contemporary scene in the United States are J. Gordon Melton, *Encyclopedic Handbook of Cults in America* (New York, 1986), and George A. Mather and Larry A. Nichols, *Dictionary of Cults, Sects, Religions, and the Occult* (Grand Rapids, 1993), which has a detailed bibliography, as well as Ronald Enroth, *Youth Brainwashing and the Extremist Cults* (Grand Rapids, 1977).

On Satanism, see specifically the novel by Stanislaw Przybyszewski, *Satan's Kinder*, first published in Berlin in 1897, to which reference has been made in the text. See also M. Wesolowski, "Szatan w tworczosci. Przybyszewskiego" in *Revue de litterature comparée* vol. 3 (1979). Among the basic writings of this cult are the books of Alisteir Crowley, as well as the authorized biography of Anton LaVey, by Blanche Barton, *The Secret Life of a Satanist* (Los Angeles, 1990). LaVey is the author of *The Satanic Bible* (New York, 1969). There are biographies of Alisteir Crowley by Ralph Tegtmeyer in German (1989) and by John Symonds in English. Thomas Schweer, *Stichwort Satanismus* (Munich, 1997) is a good, albeit very brief, introduction.

TERROR AND THE FAR RIGHT

A good general introduction is Tore Bjorgo (ed.), *Terror from the Extreme Right* (London, 1995). For the terrorist right in the United States, see *The Turner Diaries* by Andrew Macdonald (pseud.), first published in Hillsboro, West Virginia, in 1978 and, by the same author, *Hunter* (Hillsboro, 1989). Among the basic how-to-do manuals, *Maccaba—The Road Back* (Torrance, CA, 1973) is perhaps the most detailed. But there is also the *State Security Handbook* by the Florida Militia and the *Free Militia Field Manual* (n.p., n.d.), as well as a *U.S. Militia Handbook*, an anonymous *Militia Manual, Information Manual* of the Militia of Montana, and several others. The Militia of Montana (MOM) has its own pages on the Internet, one among many, and regularly publishes reports and statements.

Among the other writers on the American extreme right, Louis Beam, *Leaderless Resistance* (n.p., n.d.), should be mentioned. Also Ben Klassen, *Nature's Eternal Religion* and *The White Man's Bible* (Otto, NC, 1981). There is a radio station, WWCR, in Nashville, Tennessee, as well as a stream of periodical publications. Most of them are short and not easy to obtain. Among the leading ones at the time of this writing are the *New World Order Intelligence Update*, a monthly newsletter, The Citizen's Forum, the Sovereign Citizen Resource Center, and Asset Protection specializing in the dissemination of position papers. Details can be obtained from an Internet site named American Patriot Network. Other such publications are *The Seditionist, WAR*, and the *Jubilee*, to name but a few. The material collected by the ADL is invaluable; it ranges from the indispensable *Extremism on the Right, A Handbook* (New York, 1988) to publications throughout the nineties such as *Paranoia as Patriotism: Far Right Influences on the Militia Movement* (1996) and *Armed and Dangerous* (New York, 1994), and it includes detailed studies and collections concerning the militias, the Klan, and various other hate groups, professional Holocaust deniers, Skinheads, neo-Nazis, neo-Nazi rock music, and virtually all other relevant topics. Other works by close observers of this scene include Morris Dees, *Gathering Storm* (New York, 1996); James Corcoran, *Bitter Harvest* (New York, 1995); James W. Gibson, *Warrior Dreams* (New York, 1994); and Bill Stanton, *Klanwatch* (New York, 1991).

Among academic studies the following should be mentioned. The most authoritative source on German right-wing violence is the annual *Verfassungsschutzbericht*, published by the Ministry of Internal Affairs, as well as the regional reports published each year by the Laender (for instance, Bavaria, Nordrhein Westfalen, etc.). In addition, the Ministry of the Interior publishes position papers such as *Rechtsextremismus in der Bundesrepublik Deutschland* (March 1997) and similar reports on the *Anti-Castor Campaign* (Ruhleben, November 1996), on militant "Autonome" (November 1996), *Islamist Extremism*, the *Kurdish PKK* (February 1997), and other topics.

The history of right-wing violence in Germany has not attracted nearly as many students of history, sociology, or psychology as the story of the terror of the left, but there is still a considerable literature. Only a few works of which use has been made can be mentioned: Bernhard Rabert, *Links und Rechts. Terrorismus in der Bundesrepublik Deutschland von 1970 bis Heute* (Bonn, 1995); Julian Belicki, *Der Rechtsextreme Gewalttaeter* (Hamburg, 1993); Christoph Butterwegge and Horst Isola, *Rechtsextremismus im vereinten Deutschland* (Bremen, 1991); Klaus Farin and Eberhard Seidel Pielen, *Skinheads* (Munich, 1993); Armin Pfahl Traugber, *Rechtsextremismus* (Bonn, 1993); Joachim Schwagerl, *Rechtsextremes Denken* (Frankfurt, 1993); Hans Uwe Otto and Roland Merten (eds.), *Rechtsradikale Gewalt im vereinigten Deutschland* (Bonn, 1993); Helmut Willems, *Fremdenfeindliche Gewalt* (Opladen, 1993); and Rainer Erb and Werner Bergmann (eds.), *Neonazismus und rechte Subkultur* (Berlin, 1993).

On Italy, see Richard Drake, *The Revolutionary Mystique and Terrorism in Contemporary Italy* (Bloomington, Indiana, 1989); Leonard Weinberg and Tore Bjorgo, *Terror from the Extreme Right*; Franco Ferraresi, *La destra radicale* (Milan, 1984). On Evola, see W. Laqueur, *Fascism* (New York, 1996), and Anna Jelamo in Ferraresi, op. cit. Also a University of California, Berkeley, dissertation by Jeffrey McKernzie Bale, *The Black Terror International. Neo-fascist Paramilitary Networks and the "Strategy of Tension"* (Berkeley, 1994).

There are many studies of radicalism and neofascism worldwide and in individual countries, but few specifically on right-wing violence. See, however, Tore Bjorgo and Robb Witte, *Racist Violence in Europe* (New York, 1993), as well as contributions in journals such as *Terrorism and Political Violence* and *Studies in Conflict and Terrorism*. Lastly a basic work, Michael Barkun, *Religion and the Racist Right* (Chapel Hill, 1994), and the studies by Jeffrey Kaplan in Tore Bjorgo (see above) and elsewhere.

RELIGION AND TERRORISM

The general literature on radical religion and politics is great and growing. Among the most comprehensive and influential are the five volumes edited by Martin E. Marty and R. Scott Appleby, including *Fundamentalisms Observed* (Chicago, 1991), *Fundamentalisms and Society* (Chicago, 1993), *Fundamentalisms and the State* (Chicago, 1993), *Accounting for Fundamentalisms* (Chicago, 1994), and

Fundamentalisms Comprehended (Chicago, 1995). Also to be mentioned in this context are Bruce B. Lawrence, *Defenders of God* (San Francisco, 1989); Lawrence Kaplan (ed.), *Fundamentalism in Comparative Perspective* (Amherst, MA, 1992); and Emmanuel Sivan and Menahem Friedman (ed.), *Religious Radicalism and Politics in the Middle East* (Albany, NY, 1990). Of considerable interest are B. Tibi, *Die fundamentalistische Herausforderung* (Munich, 1992) and other books by the same author, and M. Juergenmeyer, *The New Cold War* (Berkeley, 1993). Specifically on Islam, consult F. Halliday, *Islam and the Myth of Confrontation* (London, 1996); Olivier Roy, *The Failure of Political Islam* (Cambridge, MA, 1994); and Siegfried Kohlhammer, *Die Feinde und die Freunde des Islam* (Goettingen, 1996).

Valuable biographies of radical religious leaders directly or indirectly connected with extremist movements or terrorist organizations can be found in R. Scott Appleby (ed.), *Spokesmen for the Despised* (Chicago, 1997). Of specific interest with regard to Shiite politics is Juan R. I. Cole and Nikki R. Keddie, *Shi'ism and Social Protest* (New Haven, 1986). See also A. Abrahamian, *Khomeinism* (Berkeley, 1993).

Many books have been published about terrorism in Algeria in the 1990s. Among recent publications are M. Ahnaf et al., *L'Algerie par ses islamistes* (Paris, 1991); Mohammed Harbi, *L'Algerie et son destin* (Paris, 1992); Pierre Devoluy et al., *La poudrière algerienne* (Paris, 1994); Werner Herzog, *Algerien* (Munich, 1995); O. Roy, *L'echec de l'Islam politique* (Paris, 1992); Abed Charef, *Algerie le grand dérapage* (Paris, 1994), *Reporters sans frontieres: Le drama algerien* (Paris, 1994); Aissa Khelladi, *Les islamistes algeriens* (Algiers, 1992) and her subsequent books; and R. Leveau, *Le sabre et le tourban* (Paris, 1993). Of recent foreign language works, Michael Willis, *The Islamist Challenge in Algeria* (New York, 1996), should be mentioned.

The most detailed and authoritative writings on Hizbullah are those by Martin Kramer, beginning with *The Moral Logic of Hizbullah* (Washington, 1987) and *Hezbollah's Vision of the West* (Washington, 1989). There are some journalistic accounts of Hizbullah, and the articles and speeches of Sheikh Fadlalla are available on audiocassettes, CDs, and a number of collections in Arabic, such as *Al harakat al islamiya fi Lubnan* (Beirut, 1984). Only a digest of a few of these have been translated.

Of the literature on religious extremism in Egypt and other Arab countries, the following should be singled out: T. Meyer, *Fundamentalismus* (Hamburg, 1989); G. Kepel, *Muslim Extremism in Egypt* (Berkeley, 1993); and other studies by the same author. On the PKK and other Kurdish militant organizations, Robert Olson (ed.), *The Kurdish Nationalist Movement in the 1990s* (Lexington, KY, 1996); Jonathan Rugman et al., *Ataturk's Children: Turkey and the Kurds* (London, 1996); and G. Ismet, *The PKK: A Report on Separatist Violence in Turkey, 1973–1992* (Ankara, 1992).

On Jewish terrorism in Israel see, above all, Ehud Sprinzak, *The Ascendance of Israel's Radical Right* (New York, 1991) and *Brother against Brother* (New York, 1999).

An interesting study on the extreme right in India is T. Basu et al., *Khaki*

Shorts, Saffron Flags (Hyderabad, 1993). Specifically on terrorism, see S. C. Tiwari (ed.), *Terrorism in India* (1990); S. H. Subha Rao, *Terrorism and Crimes in India* (Bangalore, 1992); Ian Mulgrew, *Unholy Terror, the Sikh, and International Terrorism* (Toronto, 1993); R. C. Dikshit and Giriray Shah, *Narco Terrorism* (New Delhi, 1996); and Misa Khan Jalalzi, *Sectarianism and Politico-Religious Terrorism in Pakistan* (Lahore, 1993).

STATE TERRORISM

On Khadafi and Libyan terrorism, see Bryan L. Davis, *Quaddafi, Terrorism, and the Origins of the U.S. Attack on Libya* (New York, 1990), and Henry W. Prunckun Jr. and Philip B. Mohr, "Military Deterrence of International Terrorism: An Evaluation of Operation El Dorado Canyon" in *Studies in Conflict and Terrorism* (July–September 1997). On the Libyan bombing of the French airliner, see Jean Marie Pontaut, *L'attentat: Le juge Bruguière accuse Kadhafi* (Paris, 1992). For general background, see David Blundy and Andrew Lycett, *Qaddafi and the Libyan Revolution* (London 1987), as well as Benjamin Kyle, *Muammar el Qaddafi* (New York, 1987).

The literature on Iranian involvement in international terrorism is considerably richer and more detailed. See, among others, Kenneth Katzman, *Hizballah* (Washington, October 1993); Bruce Hoffman, *Recent Trends and Future Prospects of Iranian Sponsored International Terrorism* (Santa Monica, March 1990), as well as other studies by the same author; Michael Eisenstadt, *Iranian Military Power* (Washington, 1996); Edgar O'Ballance, *Islamic Fundamentalist Terrorism, 1979–1995: The Iranian Connection* (New York, 1997); Mohammad Mohadessin, *Islamic Fundamentalism* (Washington, 1993); and Kenneth Katzman, *Warriors of Islam* (Boulder, CO, 1993). For the earlier period of Iranian terrorism, see Amir Taheri, *Holy Terror* (London, 1987), as well as Hooshang Amirahmadi, *Iran and the Arab World* (London, 1993), and Roy Mottahadeh, *The Mantle of the Prophet* (New York, 1985). There is an official biography of Ayatollah Khomeini published by the Teheran Ministry of Islamic Guidance in 1982. Also covering the early period is Shaul Bakhash, *The Reign of the Ayatollahs* (New York, 1984). The surveys on Iran in the annual *Middle East Contemporary Survey* written by David Menashri are of great value, and so is Daniel Brumberg, "Khomeini's Legacy," in H. Scott Appleby (ed.), *Spokesmen for the Despised* (Chicago, 1997). A list of the Iranian émigrés assassinated by the regime is in E. Avebury and R. Wilkinson, *Iran, State of Terror* (London, 1996).

On Soviet involvement in international terrorism there are, not surprisingly, only a very few sources except for the earlier period—namely, Roberta Goren, *The Soviet Union and Terrorism* (London, 1984), a few references in Christopher Andrew and Oleg Gordievsky, *KGB, the Inside Story* (New York, 1990), as well as sporadic articles in the Russian and Western press, mainly based on personal recollections.

Far more sources are available with regard to East Germany, above all the official report of the government inquiry committee (the Gauck Behoerde), *An-*

atomie der Staatssicherheit. MfS Handbuch, Die Hauptabteilung XXII: Terrorab-wehr (Berlin, 1995). If there were similar authoritative works on other East European countries, the definitive study on the subject could be written, but unfortunately these do not exist. The following also deal with the involvement of the Stasi (East German State Security) with foreign terrorists: Butz Peters, *RAF, Terrorismus in Deutschland* (Stuttgart, 1991); Andreas Mueller and Michael Kanonenberg, *Die RAF–Stasi Connection* (Berlin, 1992); and Peter Siebenmorgen, *"Staatssicherheit" der DDR* (Bonn, 1993). The memoirs of Markus Wolff, former chief of DDR foreign intelligence, *Man Without a Face* (New York, 1997), are an essential source but should be read with caution because the author tends to put the best possible gloss on the connections between the Stasi and the foreign terrorists. Earlier authors on Baader Meinhof and other terrorist groups were not fully aware of the connection with the Stasi, or if they surmised it, could not document it.

The most important general source on international terrorism as far as figures and the chronology is concerned is the *Annual Pattern of Global Terrorism*, which has been published by the U.S. Department of State since 1983. There was a considerable literature on international terrorism in the 1970s, but there were few hard facts available at the time and the interpretations attributed exaggerated importance to international terrorism in general and to the Soviet Union in particular. On the other extreme, there was the denial that there was anything like international terrorism in the first place, that the very concept was imperialist propaganda.

Among the books and shorter studies published during that period were J. B. Bell, *Transnational Terrorism* (Washington, 1976); D. Carlton and C. Shaarf (ed.), *International Terrorism and World Security* (London, 1975); R. Cline and Y. Alexander, *State Sponsored Terrorism* (Washington, 1985); G. Guillaume and G. Levasseur, *Terrorisme International* (Paris, 1977); U. Ra'anan et al., *Hydra of Carnage* (Lexington, MA, 1985); Claire Sterling, *The Time of the Assassins* (New York, 1984); and Paul Wilkinson, *Terrorism, International Dimensions* (London, 1979).

The literature about the most colorful figures in this field was in inverse proportion to their intrinsic importance. The Library of Congress has nineteen books in English on Carlos the "Jackal" (Ilich Ramirez Santos) on its shelves, not to mention the books published in other languages, the TV program, etc. They include several thrillers that became best-sellers, such as Robert Ludlum's *The Bourne Identity, The Bourne Supremacy,* and *The Bourne Ultimatum,* published between 1980 and 1990, and which must have made a small fortune for the author, though most likely not for the hero of the story. Even before, in 1979, *The Carlos Contract,* by David Atlee Philips, had appeared. Among the Carlos biographies, the following should be mentioned: David Eisenberg and Eli Landau (1976), Christopher Dobson and Ronald Payne (1977), Colin Smith (1977), and David Yallop (1993).

Abu Nidal, as far as is known, attracted only two biographers: Yossi Melman, *The Master Terrorist* (New York, 1986), and Patrick Seale, *Abu Nidal, a Gun for*

Hire (London, 1992). Those interested in the minor figures of international terrorism will find such information in George Rosie, *The Directory of International Terrorism* (Edinburgh, 1986).

There are many accounts of the Gulf War and Saddam Hussein, but few dealing specifically with the Iraqi participation in international terrorism. For the early period, see Fuad Matter, *Saddam Hussein* (New York, 1981). For the later years, Efraim Karsh and Inari Rautsi, *Saddam Hussein: A Political Biography* (London, 1991). For general background with regard to the character of the Ba'ath regime, see Samir el Khalil, *Republic of Fear* (New York, 1990), and Amatzia Baram, *History and Ideology in the Formation of Ba'thist Iraq, 1968–89* (London, 1991). For the postwar period, see Fran Hazelton, *Iraq Since the Gulf War* (London, 1994). On Syrian involvement with international terrorism, see the two biographies of President Asad by Patrick Seale, *Asad of Syria: The Struggle for the Middle East* (London, 1988), and Moshe Maoz, *Asad: The Sphinx of Damascus* (London, 1988). On Cuban activities in this field, see the Congressional Hearings of 1982, *The Role of Cuba in International Terrorism and Subversion*, Committee on the Judiciary, U.S. Senate 97th Congress (Washington, 1982).

EXOTIC TERRORISM

About the early history of Sendero Luminoso, see Lewis Taylor, *Maoism in the Andes* (Liverpool, 1983), and Carlos Degregori, *Sendero Luminoso* (Lima, 1986), as well as the same author's study of Ayacucho in the 1970s, titled *Ayacucho 1969–79* (Lima, 1990). A comprehensive history is Gustavo Gorriti, *Sendero, historia de la guerra milenario en el Peru*, vol. 1 (Lima, 1990). Gabriela Terrazona Sevillano, *Sendero Luminoso and the Threat of Narco Terrorism* (New York, 1990), is an account by a Peruvian judge with firsthand experience.

For the later period, there is a voluminous literature by American Latin American specialists such as David Scott Palmer (ed.), *Shining Path of Peru* (2nd edition, New York, 1994), and Cynthia McClintock, "Sendero Luminoso" in *Problems of Communism* (September/October 1983), and the same author's "Why Peasants Rebel: The Case of Peru's Sendero Luminoso," *World Politics* (October 1984), and her essay in Susan Eckstein (ed.), *Power and Popular Protest* (Berkeley, 1989). See also Rojas Samanez, *Sendero de Violencia* (Lima, 1990), and James D. Rudolph, *Politics in Peru* (Stanford, CA, 1992). The manifestos and pronouncements of Sendero have appeared in the Peru underground but also in the legal newspaper *El Diario* and have been distributed by well-wishers in North America and Western Europe.

The literature on the Tamil Tigers is much more limited, but the organization has quickly adapted to the Internet and publishes daily news reports as well as polemics against the Colombo government. An essential work is M. R. Nayaranswami, *Tigers from Lanka: From Boys to Guerrillas* (New Delhi, 1994). *A Broken Palmyra*, Rajan Hoole (ed.), is the collective work of five Sri Lankan authors (Madras, 1993). A. S. Balasingham, *Liberation Tigers and Tamil Eelam Freedom*

Struggle (1983) is an early account by the then chief ideologist of the movement. S. C. Sardeshpande, *Assignment Jaffne* (New Delhi, 1991), is the account of an Indian who was one of the commanders of the Indian expeditionary corps. The commander of this corps, General Depinder Singh, *IPKF in Sri Lanka* (New Delhi, 1990), has also provided an account of this failure of a mission.

The Tamil Tigers have published many brief statements, such as *Towards Combat* (1983), *Towards Liberation* (1984), and *Diary of Combat, 1975–1984* (1984). Events in Sri Lanka have been analyzed in far greater detail in Indian newspapers and periodicals than in the United States or in Europe. An excellent summary of the terrorist campaign is Manoj Joshi, "On the Razor's Edge: The Liberation Tigers of Tamil Eelam," *Studies in Conflict and Terrorism* (January–March 1996). Most recently a German study, Jakob Rosel, *Der Bürgerkrieg auf Sri Lanka* (Baden Baden, 1997).

The literature about the Ugandan civil war and the warring groups is sparse. Most of the information can be found in East African newspapers. For background information, see A. B. K. Kasozi, *The Social Origins of Violence in Uganda* (Toronto, 1994); Kenneth Ingham, *Making of Modern Uganda* (Greenwood, 1983); Godfrey Amaza, *Museveni's Long March* (London, 1997); Michael Hodd (ed.), *East Africa Handbook 1998* (London, 1997); and Rita M. Byrnes, *Uganda: A Country Study* (online text, Library of Congress, 1996).

The literature about the militant wing of the ecological movement is very extensive. A good survey from a left-wing point of view is given in Carolyn Merchant, *Radical Ecology* (New York, 1992). The best history of Earth First published so far is Martha F. Lee, *Earth First* (Syracuse, NY, 1995). The following specifically deal with ecoterrorism: Ron Arnold, *EcoTerror* (Washington, 1997), and Sean P. Egan, "From Spikes to Bombs," *Studies in Conflict and Terrorism*, 19 (1996). Among the early cult books of the movement were Edward Abbey, *The Monkey Wrench Gang* (Philadelphia, 1979), and David Foreman (ed.), *Ecodefense* (Tucson, 1973). There is a more recent revised edition dated 1985. See also David Foreman, *Confessions of an Ecowarrior* (New York, 1991). Christopher Manes, *Green Rage* (Boston 1990), is the best-reasoned manifesto of the ecoradicals.

Other important studies include Andre Rowell, *Green Backlash* (1996), and Susan Zakins, *Coyotes and Town Dogs* (New York, 1995). See also John Davis (ed.), *Earth First Reader* (Salt Lake City, 1991). Ric Scarce, *Ecowarriors* (Chicago, 1990), was widely discussed in these circles, and Judith Plant (ed.), *Healing the Wounds* (Philadelphia, 1989), provides an ecofeminist perspective. Much current material can be found in the periodicals of the movements, such as *Earth First*, the *Wild Earth Journal*, and the *Green Anarchist*, published in London, England.

One of the earliest works on animal liberation was Peter Singer, *Animal Liberation* (New York, 1975). Later developments are described in David Henshaw, *Animal Liberation* (London, 1989); Ingrid Newkirk, *Free the Animals* (Chicago, 1992); James Jasper and Dorothy Nelkin, *The Animal Rights Crusade* (New York, 1992); and David T. Hardy, *America's New Extremists* (Washington, 1990).

The activities and ultimate arrest of the Unabomber generated a literature of varying value and interest. A good chronology and the salient documents are contained in John Douglas and Mark Olshaker, *Unabomber* (New York, 1996).

TERRORISM AND ORGANIZED CRIME

The most widely used textbooks on organized crime are Howard Abadinski, *Organized Crime* (Chicago, 1994, 3rd edition), and Michael D. Lyman and Gary W. Potter, *Organized Crime* (New York, 1997). On the theory of organized crime, G. Vold and T. Bernard, *Theoretical Criminology* (New York, 1986, 3rd edition), and D. Cressy, *Theft of the Nation* (New York, 1969).

The literature on the history of organized crime is huge on the academic and even more on the popular level. On the Italian mafia, see above all the writings of Pino Arlacchi, such as *La mafia imprenditrice* (Florence, 1983). The author later became head of the U.N. drug control agency. Raimondo Catanzaro's social history of the mafia *Il delito come impresa* (Padua, 1988) is essential reading, as is his more recent essay in Giovani Fiandaca et al. (ed.), *La mafia, le mafie* (Roma-Bari, 1994). Alexander Stille's *Excellent Cadavers*, which covers events in the 1980s and '90s, has also appeared in English. Henner Hess, *Mafia. Zentrale Herrschaft und lokale Gegenmacht* (Tuebingen, 1988, 3rd edition) is a noteworthy German contribution, and the books of Nicola Tranfaglia, such as *Mafia, politica e affari, 1943–1991* (Bari, 1992) should also be singled out. An English-language study is Judith Chubb, *The Mafia and Politics* (Ithaca, 1989). On Yakuza, see David Kaplan and Alex Dubro, *Yakuza* (New York, 1986). The relationship between terrorism and organized crime has been discussed in various contributions to the following two periodicals: *Transnational Organized Crime* and *Trends in Organized Crime*.

The links between transnational organized crime and terrorist crimes is discussed in *Transnational Crime* (Winter, 1996). The books by Rachel Ehrenfeld, *Narcoterrorism* (New York, 1990), and above all by Claire Sterling, such as *Thieves World* (New York, 1994) and *Octopus* (New York, 1990), have been attacked by critics from the left but also by some academic writers and government sources because of their overemphasis on the element of conspiracy and failure to distinguish clearly between terrorism and organized crime. For such critiques, see, for instance, Abraham H. Miller and Nicholas A. Damask, "The Dual Myths of Narcoterrorism" in *Terrorism and Political Violence* (Spring 1996), and R. T. Naylor, "From Cold War to Crime War" in *Transnational Organized Terrorism* (Winter 1995). The Sterling books were dismissed as simplistic, but subsequent events make it appear that they were to some extent close to the truth.

Colombia is the state in which the narcobusiness and cooperation and conflict between growers, cartels, and guerrillas can be studied most profitably. On the history of modern Colombia, see David Bushnell, *The Making of Modern Colombia* (Berkeley, 1993). On the Palace of Justice tragedy, see Ramon Jimenos, *Noche de Lobos* (Bogotá, 1988), and Ana Carrigan, *The Place of Justice: A Colombian Tragedy* (New York, 1993). Two important studies on political and economic repercussions of the drug business in Colombia are Camilo Granada and Leonardo Rojas, *Los Costos Economicos del Conflicto Armado en Colombia, 1990–1994* (Bogotá, n.d., printed as a manuscript), and Ciro Krauthausen, *Moderne Gewalten, Organisierte Kriminalitaet in Kolumbien und Italien* (Frankfurt, 1997). Both studies include extensive bibliographies. See also Malcolm Deas and Gaitan Daza, *Dos ensayos especulativos sobre la violencia en Colombia* (Bogotá, 1995).

On Sendero Luminoso and the drug traffic, see the book by Gabriela Tarazona Sevillano quoted above in the section on Peru, as well as Manuel Jesus Granados, *El PCP Sendero Luminoso y su Ideologia* (Lima, 1992). Also Edmund Morales, *White Gold Rush in Peru* (Tuscon, 1989).

Of the countless studies on the drug trade, the following should be given special mention: Renssellaer Lee III, *The White Labyrinth: Cocaine and Political Power* (New Brunswick, 1989), and Francisco Thoumi, *Political Power and Illegal Drugs in Colombia* (Boulder, 1995). Two French studies are noteworthy, namely *Observatoire Geopolitique des Drogues, Etat des Drogues, Drogues des Etats* (Paris, 1994), and Alain Labrousse and Alain Wallon, *La Planete des Drogues* (Paris, 1993), which is especially enlightening on the issue of money laundering. The annual reports of the DEA (Drug Enforcement Agency) and the Bureau for International Narcotics and Law Enforcement Affairs at the Department of State are essential sources.

Among the earlier studies of organized crime in Russia were A. Dolgova and S. Dyakov (ed.), *Organizovannaya prestupnost* (Moscow, 1989); Konstantin Simis, *USSR: Secrets of a Corrupt Society* (London, 1982); Aleksandr Furov, *Krasnaya Mafia* (Moscow, 1990); Arkady Vaksberg, *The Soviet Mafia* (London, 1991); Stephen Handelsman, *Comrade Criminal* (New York, 1994); Claire Sterling, *Thieves World* (New York, 1994); and Lydia S. Rosner, *The Soviet Way of Crime* (South Hadley, 1986).

A great deal of material has been published inside Russia after 1989, but the books are on the whole disappointing, not so much in view of the absence of footnotes but because the writers clearly felt inhibited to put on paper all they knew. At the same time, some of these books include much of interest; see, for instance, Nikolai Modestov, *Moskva Banditskaya* (Moscow, 1995), for a review of the major criminal groupings and some of their leaders.

Translations from the current Russian press can be found in the periodical *Organized Crime Digest.* The special issue of *Transnational Organized Crime* (Summer/Autumn 1996) should be mentioned, as well as the CSIS Task Force Report, *Organized Crime* (Washington, 1997).

TERRORISM TODAY AND TOMORROW AND TERRORISM OF THE FUTURE

Not much work has been done so far on the psychological sources of terrorism, with the exception of essays by Jerrold M. Post and Franco Ferracuti. Most terrorism experts have regarded it as a political phenomenon. Some believe that attempts to interpret terrorism in psychological (let alone psychiatric) terms is an attempt to denigrate these movements. Psychiatrists, on the other hand, usually lack both interest and expertise to deal with terrorism; some think, not without justice, that given the difficulties analyzing the psychodynamics of a single individual, how much more difficult (and risky) is an attempt to analyze groups. In addition to the studies listed earlier in this book, the following should be singled out: W. W. Meissner, *The Paranoid Process* (New York, 1978); W. Baeyer-Kaette and D. Classens, *Analysen zum Terrorismus*, part 3, *Gruppenprozesse* (Darmstadt, 1982); W. Bonime, *Paranoid Psychodynamics in Contemporary Psychoanalysis*, 15, 3 (1979); K. Dewhurst and J. Todd, "The Psychosis of Association: Folie à deux," *Journal of Nervous and Mental Disorders* (1956), p. 451 et seq.; N. Cameron, "The Paranoid Conditions and Paranoia," in S. Arieli, *American Handbook of Psychiatry*, vol. 1 (New York, 1959). A recent study is Joseph H. Berke (ed.), *Even Paranoids Have Enemies* (New York, 1998). Some articles of relevance in the present context have appeared in the *Journal of Paranoia*.

On paranoia in politics, Richard Hofstadter's famous essay, "The Paranoid Style in American Politics," in the book of the same title (New York, 1967), has unfortunately not been seminal in generating many other studies, but see Robert S. Robins and Jerrold M. Post, *Political Paranoia* (New Haven, 1997), and Daniel Pipes, *Conspiracy: How the Paranoid Style Flourishes* (New York, 1997).

The impact of science fiction stories and, above all, of movies and television serials on sectarian thinking is considerable but has not been studied as yet in any detail. This refers to issues such as weapons of mass destruction, space travel, UFOs, and the invasion of aliens, survival, etc. John Clute and Peter Nichols, *The Encyclopedia of Science Fiction* (New York, 1995), is an indispensable work of reference. With regard to the cinema, the following should be mentioned: Walt Lee, *Reference Guide to Fantastic Films* (Los Angeles, 1972 et seq.), and Donald C. Willis, *Horror and Science Fiction Films* (Metuchen, NJ, 1972 et seq.). Also Ronald M. Hohn and Volker Jansen, *Lexikon des Science Fiction Films*, 2 vols., (7th edition, Munich, 1997); Phil Hardy, *The Aurum Film Encyclopedia: Science Fiction* (London, 1995); Frank Allan, *The Science Fiction and Fantasy Handbook* (London, 1982); William K. Everson, *Classics of the Horror Film* (Secaucus, NJ, 1974); F. Jung et al. (ed.), *Der Horror Film*, 2 vols. (Munich, 1977); Harris M. Lentz, *Science Fiction, Horror Fantasy Film and TV Credits*, 2 vols.; Frederik Pohl et al., *Science Fiction Studies in Film* (New York, 1981).

There is also recent literature on television series such as *Millennium* and the *X Files*. The *X Files* has been exceptionally popular, and it is very much in the conspiratorial tradition. At the time of this writing, there is an *X Files* official magazine as well as scores of companions, authorized and unauthorized, and guidebooks by N. E. Genge, Phil Farrand, Frank Lovece, Hal Schuster, Mark Shapiro, Ted Edwards, and countless others. Pauline Kael in her film reviews has been dealing with horror and science fiction films and Susan Sontag's essays are frequent quoted (*Against Interpretation*, New York, 1988).

There is an immense literature on the demographic, social, and political problems of the Third World, but only certain aspects are of relevance here. For ethnic conflicts, see Donald L. Horowitz, *Ethnic Groups in Conflict* (Berkeley, 1995). For wars and other conflicts in the Third World, see Klaus Juergen Gantzel (ed.), *Die Kriege von 1945 bis 1992* (Hamburg, 1992). On migration, the SOPEMI annual reports, *Trends in International Migration,* OECD (Paris, 1992 et seq.), as well as a number of specialized periodicals such as *International Migration, International Migration Review* (New York), *Journal of Refugee Studies,* and *Refugee Survey Quarterly* (Geneva). For urbanization in the Third World, see H. Birg, *World Population: Projections for the 21st Century* (New York, 1995), as well as the publications of the United Nations, such as *Long Range Population Projection* (1992), *World Population Prospects* (1996), and *World Population Monitoring.* About urbanization, see Jorge Hardoy et al., *Environmental Problems in Third World Cities* (London, 1992); Nigel Harris (ed.), *Cities in the 1990s* (London, 1992); and a U.N. publication, *The Challenge of Urbanization: The World's Large Cities* (New York, 1992).

Some of the standard work on the weapons of mass destruction, their history and character, have been mentioned earlier on. At the time of this writing, the most authoritative general survey is the Office of the Secretary of Defense, *Proliferation, Threat and Response* (Washington, November 1997). Another general review published by the Swedish government is *FOA: A Briefing Book on Biological Weapons* (Stockholm, 1997, revised edition). There is a similar such book by the Swedish government on chemical weapons. The most detailed technical survey of biological warfare is the special issue of *JAMA, The Journal of the American Medical Association,* August 6, 1997.

Various reports have been issued by the Security Council of the United Nations on the inspection teams in Iraq and their findings. Hearings on the spread of weapons of superviolence were held by the U.S. Senate (Permanent Subcommittee on Investigations, Washington 1995–96). The 1993 reports by OTA (Office of Technology Assessment) have been mentioned earlier on.

Two early papers on the likelihood of the use of these weapons are Brian Jenkins, *The Likelihood of Nuclear Terrorism* (Rand, Santa Monica, 1985) and Jeffrey D. Simon, *Terrorists and the Likely Use of Biological Weapons* (Rand, Santa Monica, 1989). More recent studies are Brad Roberts (ed.), *Terrorism with Chemical and Biological Weapons* (Alexandria, VA, 1997). Two unpublished studies should be mentioned: John K. Campbell, *Weapons of Mass Destruction and Terrorism* (Monterey, December 1996) and W. Seth Carus, *Bioterrorism, Biocrimes, and Bioassassination* (National Defense University, September 1997).

For information on psychopaths and antisocial personality disorder, one should consult *DSM IV* (mentioned above) and, more specifically, Bridget Dolan and Jeremy Coit, *Psychopathic and Anti Social Personality Disorders* (London, 1993); H. M. Cleckley, *The Mask of Sanity* (St. Louis, 1976), a standard work, originally published twenty years earlier; and R. D. Hare, *Without Conscience* (New York, 1993). In addition, there have been contributions to the periodical *Aggression and Violent Behavior* that are of relevance in this context. There has been, to the best of my knowledge, no study as yet on aggression and violence with respect to terrorism.

Panic is a subject that has yet to be investigated in depth. Among the studies of relevance are J. S. Smith, Jr., "Three Mile Island: The Silent Disaster," in *JAMA*, 245, 16, (1981); Robert E. Ebel (ed.), *Chernobyl and Its Aftermath* (CSIS, Washington, 1994); T. J. Singer, "An Introduction to Disaster," *Aviation Space and Environment Medicine*, 53, 3, (1982); and C. Doutheau, "Prevention and reduction of Panic in the Military Milieu" in *Ann Med Psychol* (Paris), 142 (2), 1984. The full text of the U.S. official guidelines, including the presidential directive, remains classified; the same is true of the FBI Nuclear Incident Contingency Plan and the FBI Chemical/Biological Incident Plan. See, however, FEMA, *Federal Response Plan, Notice of Change* (Washington, February 1997), and the Senate Hearings on the *Global Proliferation of Weapons of Mass Destruction* (March 1996).

The debate on just war and restraints in warfare has been going on since the early Middle Ages (and even earlier). For a brief survey, see J. T. Johnson, *Just War Tradition and the Restraint of War* (Princeton, 1981), and for the more recent period, Geoffrey Best, *Humanity in Warfare* (New York, 1980). With specific reference to terrorism, see R. G. Frey and Christopher Morris (ed.), *Violence, Terrorism, and Justice* (New York, 1991), and Rosalyn Higgins and Maurice Flory (ed.), *Terrorism and International Law* (London, 1997).

On holy war and jihad, see Rudolf Peters, *Islam and Colonialism* (The Hague, 1979); H. M. T. Ahmad, *Murder in the Name of Allah* (Cambridge, 1990); John Kelsay and J. T. Johnson (ed.), *Just War and Islam* (Westport, CT, 1991); and J. T. Johnson, *The Holy War Idea* (University Park, PA, 1997).

Index